THE LUCKY ONES

DORIS MORTMAN

☆ —————————— ☆

THE LUCKY ONES

Zebra Books
Kensington Publishing Corp.

http://www.zebrabooks.com

ZEBRA BOOKS are published by

Kensington Publishing Corp.
850 Third Avenue
New York, NY 10022

First Kensington Hardcover Printing: July, 1997
First Zebra Paperback Printing: July, 1998
10 9 8 7 6 5 4 3 2 1

Printed in the United States of America

For my daughter, Lisa,
who believes that even one person can make a difference.
And she does.

Writing—like politics—is a process that can exhilarate and exasperate, often at the same time. I am grateful to those who helped smooth the rough patches by contributing information or offering support and counsel when necessary. I'm also indebted to those who provided the inspiration to delve into this intriguing world.

Special thanks to Jeff Eller, Kathleen Brown, Mel French, Mary Ann Peters, Sarah Searls, Ambassador Clay Constantinou, and the New Jersey group known as Clay's Crew, who not only introduced me to the hard work of grassroots politics, but also embraced me as their friend, especially: Jane Halligan, Jane and Jim Moore, Betty Hutcheon, Edith Payne, Ken Pentony, Tom Byrne, Georgie Evans, and Rick Lerner.

As always, my deep appreciation to Peter Lampack. And my love to David and Alex—for their unwavering support, their unflagging confidence, and for making me smile, no matter what.

Prologue

☆ JUNE 1977 ☆

It was Zoë's idea of the perfect wedding: a gorgeous summer day. An exquisite ceremony on the grounds of a magnificent estate. A string quartet playing Bach. Urns overflowing with orchids, orange blossoms, and pale peach roses. The air redolent with the scent of tuberoses and mint. An elegantly clad assemblage of friends and family. And the man she loved waiting at the altar.

Unfortunately, Zoë Vaughn was not the bride; she was simply one of the guests.

When it was the maid of honor's turn to walk down the aisle, Celia Porter paused, milking the moment. A stunning blonde, Celia was used to standing in the spotlight. She was equally accustomed to standing in her cousin Felicia's shadow. While their looks may have rivaled each other, Felicia possessed the cultivated polish and carriage that only money could buy.

To her credit, there was not a single sign of defensiveness or intimidation in Celia's demeanor. Her head, covered with a pale peach wide-brimmed hat, was held high. Her shoulders, bared by a gracefully swooping neckline, were back and upright. As she strolled the length of the aisle, her look-but-don't-touch expression drew the eyes of the crowd and held them in her thrall.

She had just reached the altar when the organ struck the familiar notes of Lohengrin's wedding march. Suddenly, an audible gasp rippled through the audience. The bride had appeared. Celia turned to look at the perfection that was Felicia and sighed. Her moment was over.

Georgie Hughes had no one to blame but herself for her current state of heightened anxiety. For six months she had told her boyfriend, Lyle Mercer, that she was the youngest of four children, her family lived in Dallas, her father ran a family business, and her mother was a housewife.

The truth was, Georgie's father, Roy Hughes, had been an immensely popular two-term governor of Texas and was still considered one of the Lone Star State's power brokers. Her grandfather had founded Hughes Oil & Gas, one of the nation's largest suppliers of crude. Her mother's family owned one of Texas's largest cattle ranches and practically ran San Antonio.

When the invitation arrived for Ben and Felicia's wedding, Georgie knew her charade was over. Ben, a close friend whom she had met when he was at Harvard also, knew who her family was. Felicia's parents, Oliver and Avis Coburn, and most of their guests knew. And since the Coburns and her parents were longtime friends, she knew that Governor and Mrs. Roy Hughes would be at the wedding.

"Why wouldn't you tell me your father was the famous Governor Roy?" Lyle asked, incredulous.

Georgie owed him an honest answer. "Because I wanted you to love me for me, not for him."

"I do love you for you," Lyle said, reassuring her with

a kiss. "Roy Hughes is an awesome man, I grant you that, but he doesn't make a difference to us. Understand?"

She nodded, but in her heart she knew better. Having Roy Hughes as a father mattered.

Other than Zoë Vaughn and Celia Porter, the only other unattached female at the wedding was Kate Wolff, one of Ben's classmates from Yale Law School. She and Zoë had met—and bonded—two evenings before at the Coburns' dinner for out-of-town guests. Perhaps, as Zoë pointed out the next day when the two of them spent the day sightseeing, it was because in this crowd of high-salaried, high-visibility, already-accomplished people, they were completely out of their element.

Zoë was from Boston, the youngest child of an Irish tavern owner and his Italian-born wife. Kate came from an upper-class suburb in New Jersey, the only child of Jewish parents who had invested all their hopes and dreams in their daughter's intellect. While both young women were academic achievers with high hopes for the future, their expectations and ambition held no currency with those who could claim status in the real world of money and power and prestige.

"Where are you going to practice?" Zoë asked Kate.

"I'm starting as an associate in a big, wildly prestigious New York law firm."

"Lucky you." Zoë was impressed.

"They're paying me a ridiculously high salary for what is an extremely low-profile position. But," Kate said with a grin, "this was one case I decided not to argue."

"Smart move."

"And you?" Kate asked. "How are you cashing in on your Harvard degree?"

It was Zoë's turn to chuckle. "I haven't the foggiest. I wasn't sure what I wanted to do, so I applied to graduate schools with an eeny-meeny-miny-moe approach: one offers a degree in languages, two in political science, and two in international studies," she explained. "My theory was that since I need a hefty scholarship, I'll take whichever program comes through with the best offer."

"So who have you heard from?"

"All of them except Johns Hopkins."

"When do you have to decide?"

Zoë laughed. "Yesterday."

If Zoë had thought watching Ben pledge himself to another woman was difficult, the reception, with its incessant toasting, proved even harder. There were good wishes from senators, congressmen, several ambassadors—both current and former—a few governors, an ex-president and a former First Lady who predicted that one day Felicia Knight would hold that very same title.

When it came time for Ben's best man, Clay Chandler, to make his toast, Zoë wanted to leave, but found herself being talked into a photograph. Clay gathered Ben, Felicia, Georgie, Celia, Kate, and Zoë, arranged them behind him in a horseshoe, and called for a drumroll. Once the photographers were ready, he lifted his crystal champagne flute. As flashbulbs popped, he addressed the assemblage.

"This day marks the beginning of Ben and Felicia's journey toward the future," he intoned. "Those of us who surround them with our friendship and good wishes hope their future includes enormous success, reasonable popularity, unbelievable prosperity, and modest fertility."

He waited for the applause to subside.

"Most of us don't know where we'll be in twenty years." He paused. "Some of us don't have a clue as to where we're going tomorrow."

The crowd tittered. Clay became misty.

"Having known the groom all my life, I have to believe that wherever he is twenty years from now, we're all going to want to be with him as we are now, repeating this wonderful moment of celebration. The lucky ones will be."

Clay tipped his glass toward Ben, who bowed graciously, and then faced his audience again.

"As for the rest of you?" He shrugged dramatically. "We can't all be winners!"

By late afternoon, when one of the Coburns' butlers summoned her to the phone, Zoë was tipsy from too much champagne. The call was from one of her brothers: the dean of Johns Hopkins's School of Advanced International Studies had called and wanted to speak to her as soon as possible.

"I'm sorry to disturb you," the dean from Hopkins said when Zoë returned his call. "I've been trying to reach you for days."

She explained that she had been away. Then, eager to get the call over with, Zoë asked if there had been a problem with her application.

"Yes and no," he said. "For months, we'd been told funding for this particular program was going to be drastically cut and that we would be able to award only partial scholarships. Your application was so outstanding, I held on to it with the hope that something might happen. I'm delighted to say that at the last moment, it has.

"We've been granted a reallocation. Thanks to the miracle of creative accounting, I've been authorized to offer you a full scholarship to SAIS, including all your expenses during the first year in Bologna, Italy. I know this offer comes very late and I apologize. I only hope you haven't accepted another program."

"All my expenses? Bologna?"

He laughed. "Is that a yes?"

Zoë's head was reeling. "May I call you right back?"

"Of course."

She put down the phone, sat in the nearest chair, and held her head in her hands until she felt more in control. Was this really what she wanted? Was foreign service the right career for her? Despite her grandiose talk about wanting to wander the earth, she had never left Boston. She had never lived anywhere but in her parents' house.

She stood and began to pace, hoping the exercise would sweep away her mental cobwebs and present her with some desperately needed clarity. As she passed the large bay window that overlooked Mrs. Coburn's cutting garden, she spotted Ben and Felicia beneath one of the giant oak trees that had given the estate its name. She felt foolish watching them from behind a curtain, yet she couldn't help staring. When they came together in a passionate embrace, she experienced her moment of clarity.

Quickly, as if they could see the tears welling in her eyes, she turned her back on the man who had been her past and dialed the number of the man who had offered her a future.

He had barely said hello when Zoë said, "When do I leave?"

THE
ANNOUNCEMENT

☆

☆ APRIL ☆

The images were horrifying. Nurses, their white uniforms sullied with dirt and their own blood, being dragged out of an American hospital in Kuwait. The kidnappers, their faces hidden behind carefully wrapped black-checkered kaffiyehs, held guns to the heads of their terrified captives as they shoved them into unmarked trucks.

Zoë Vaughn's sage green eyes narrowed as she watched the scene play on the studio monitor. Her lips tightened. She had warned them something like this would happen.

Doug Wetson, delivering the background piece for *Newsline,* reminded the audience that this was the second hijacking of Americans abroad.

Another piece of tape rolled, this one showing twenty American soldiers who had been kidnapped from their base near the demilitarized zone in South Korea.

A red light blinked. As she faced the camera, Zoë instinctively realigned her features until her expression was one of complete inscrutability. Scott Alexander, the host of *Newsline,* introduced her by reciting the facts of her résumé: former Deputy Chief of Mission at the American Embassy in Moscow, career diplomat with postings in Turkey, Jordan, Italy, and Israel, currently a director at the Hightower Institute, a well-regarded think tank for American foreign policy, and frequent television commentator on matters concerning international emergencies.

Also on the program was Lamar Basalt, head of the powerful Senate Foreign Relations Committee. Outspoken and cantankerous, often accused of treating the committee as his own private fiefdom and pursuing a personal agenda under the guise of senatorial advise and consent, Basalt had held a press conference that afternoon to demand immediate action from the White House. After delivering a fiery speech and enduring a question and answer session he derided as "headline hunting," he accused Yuri Borofsky, the president of Russia, of orchestrating these kidnappings as a way of humiliating the United States.

Scott Alexander began the interview by reiterating the senator's charge. "It's my understanding, Senator, that Red Rage, the group which has claimed responsibility for the kidnappings, has no known association with Borofsky. To the contrary, they are reputed to be in favor of the forceful overthrow of the Russian president."

Basalt flushed with anger. He hated being patronized by TV talkmeisters, as he called all network anchors.

"I don't care who claims responsibility! These dastardly acts have Borofsky's fingerprints all over them," he insisted, his round, white face screaming irritation. "Am I the only one who remembers that before he was elected president of that floundering democracy he was a director of Soviet Covert Operations?"

"Kidnappings in broad daylight can hardly be called covert," Zoë said, breaking in. "These are the very obvious actions of well-organized terrorists."

Basalt shook his head, dismissing Zoë with the twitch of an eyebrow. "Perhaps you're simply too young to be able to see the parallels between Borofsky's KGB activities and these current-day gangsters."

Zoë's expression hardened. "If that was meant as a compliment, I thank you, Senator, but I am neither a neophyte to the ways of Soviet politics, nor am I unaware of the daily roster of horrors that had been perpetuated on the Soviet citizenry in the name of the Republic. Notwithstanding his past, or his present political predicament, I don't believe Borofsky is the mastermind behind these outrageous criminal acts."

Again, Basalt twitched an eyebrow. His expression was one of arrogant assurance, the familiar Beltway face of a man who'd been in a position of power for so long, he believed he was impervious to challenge and could speak with impunity.

"I'm sure that when you were posted in Moscow, Ms. Vaughn, you informed yourself about everything pertinent to the disposition of your responsibilities."

He paused, like a trial lawyer hesitating before hammering home a point to the jury.

"But it's been a while since you were relieved of your duties," he said, deliberately emphasizing the word *relieved.* "Being out of the loop as you are, perhaps your antennae have rusted. Perhaps you've underestimated the level of anger among the Russian people and the effect that anger has on its leadership."

On the surface Zoë appeared unfazed; inside, she recoiled. Officially, she had left the State Department at her own choosing. In truth, she had been forced out, which was why Basalt felt free to assail her credibility.

When Zoë didn't rebut his charges, Basalt faced the camera with the smug authority born of triumph.

"Ever since the breakup of the Soviet Union, Russia has gone from being a world-class power to a giant welfare state. We give. They take. And just as those who fill America's welfare rolls hate the hand that feeds them, so do the Russians!"

Believing the segment to be out of time, Basalt sat back, certain his word would be the last.

"And therefore . . . ?" Zoë said, stomping all over his sound bite.

"Borofsky has a problem," Basalt sputtered, suddenly

more tenuous. "He has an infuriated populace and an inept government. He needs our money to support his so-called reforms, but at the same time, he needs his people's respect or he'll be tossed out before you can say coup d'état!"

"With all due respect, Senator," Alexander said, "operations as brazen as this normally are done either to gain a political advantage in some anticipated international negotiation or to make a political point to a local constituency. There is no upcoming election and no summit scheduled for the near future. So, if indeed Borofsky is, as you claim, the culprit behind these crimes, what's the point?"

"I didn't say this was a brilliant move, Scott. Alas, this is the work of a politically desperate, morally spineless man."

Basalt screwed his face into a blend of pity and disdain. He let it linger for a moment before allowing a glint of mastery to sneak into his eyes.

"Perhaps now, my esteemed Senate colleagues will listen when I entreat them not to give American dollars to those who have no respect for American citizens."

"I would probably agree with the Senator that the intended goal of both actions was the international humiliation of the United States," Zoë said. Basalt nodded. His eyes remained suspicious. "But he is wrong on several other key issues. The architect of that humiliation is not Yuri Borofsky. And the underlying reason for these terrorist acts is far more complicated than international one-upsmanship. And far more dangerous."

The red light clicked off. They had gone to commercial. An assistant producer powdered Zoë's face, handed her a glass of water, and adjusted the small microphone attached to the lapel of her suit jacket. Zoë proffered a quick smile of thanks, but she was clearly preoccupied. Lamar Basalt's attack on her character had stung her deeply, and she was having difficulty shaking it off.

A red light blinked. Scott Alexander's voice came

through her earphone, intruding on her ruminations. Zoë forced herself to attention.

"Before the break, Ms. Vaughn, you intimated that this situation is even more perilous than we've imagined. Would you care to enlighten us?"

"In both cases," Zoë said with the confidence of one who has not only done her homework, but extra credit assignments as well, "there was a ransom note signed by Red Rage. The head of this radical organization is believed to be Borofsky's longtime nemesis, Yegor Durgunov."

"Many call Durgunov a madman," Alexander stated.

"That may be," she said with the customary caution of a trained diplomat, "but in Russia, many think he's a hero."

While Zoë had a dossier on Durgunov that would have herniated a horse, what she could reveal on air wouldn't have bent the spine of a flea.

"Yegor Durgunov is an ultranationalist elected to the Russian Parliament by a constituency still smarting over the sharp decline in their country's influence. By making the world—and in particular, the United States—tremble once again at the growl of the Great Bear, he gets them to forget how hungry that Bear is."

"Precisely what I said," Basalt asserted.

"About Borofksy," Zoë pointedly reminded him, "who is trying to move Russia forward. Durgunov's mantra is that democracy doesn't work. His goal is to overturn the present government and reconstitute the Union."

"Oh, please," Basalt exclaimed. "You're portraying him as an intelligent man with a carefully plotted game plan. I say, he's a buffoon! Aside from demanding that we return Alaska to Russia and pay reparations for all the fish we've taken from the Bering Sea, he recently bounded onstage at the Folies Bergère in Paris and fondled several of the dancers." Basalt's nostrils flared with barely contained contempt. "How can anyone take this man seriously?"

"If he's foraging Americans, sir," Alexander said, "I'm

afraid we have to take him seriously. Do you agree, Ms. Vaughn?''

"Absolutely.'' By looking at the split screen on the monitor, Zoë noted with satisfaction that her calm was in stark contrast to Basalt's obvious agitation. "If you need further proof of his intentions, simply look at those with whom he's aligned himself. They're all aggrieved political factions with little in common except an unabiding hatred for the United States.''

"Like . . .'' Alexander probed.

"The Serbs, militant Muslims from former Soviet states, Palestinians of Hamas, and several radical fundamentalist groups with known loyalty to Iran.''

"And how exactly are these international hoodlums going to wrest power from the United States?'' Basalt's voice boomed with exaggerated incredulousness. The spotlight had shifted off him onto a young woman without comparable credentials, and he didn't like it.

"By purchasing nuclear materials from the Russian Mafia,'' Zoë said. "Hence, the ransom.''

Basalt was stunned. He had never thought of that. Worse, there was a terrifying logic to it. Alexander, clearly as rattled as Basalt, asked Zoë if there was any evidence to support her contention.

"At this point it's mostly circumstantial,'' she admitted, "but there's enough to make it too powerful to dismiss.'' Zoë leaned into the camera, as if underlining the importance of her words. "After the Soviet Union fell, there were enormous discrepancies in the inventories of several major nuclear facilities. Materials listed as stockpiled were missing. Intelligence sources reported that one of the kingpins within the Russian Mafia had boasted about the thefts.

"The *rafia*, as the Russian Mafia is sometimes called, is more violent and more mercenary than any of their counterparts,'' she said grimly. "Not only wouldn't they care who bought this potential devastation, but they wouldn't care what was done with it.''

"You've been accused of being a fearmonger before,

Ms. Vaughn,'' Basalt blustered. "I would think you'd have learned the folly of spreading unfounded rumors that arouse unwarranted fear.''

Zoë paused, as if weighing the wisdom of continuing. Almost to herself, she nodded. *Forewarned is forearmed* had always been one of her credos. It may not have served her well in the past, but she hadn't stopped believing in its inherent truth.

"The folly, Senator, would be to wait until the agents of some rogue nation smuggle a small nuclear device onto American soil and threaten to explode it.''

"Are you suggesting that such an incident is imminent?'' Alexander asked, his voice evidencing concern.

"There are terrorists throughout the world who have the will to destroy the United States. There are also groups within our own borders who believe that the annihilation of the federal government is a desirable end. The *rafia* can provide the means capable of that destruction. If we ignore the signals, sit back and allow them to combine forces,'' Zoë said with chilling intensity, "the tragedy in Oklahoma City will seem small by comparison.''

☆　　☆　　☆

Elton Haynes turned his back on the office he had spent most of his life seeking and stared out at the Rose Garden. He was a tall man with a physique that once would have been described as strapping. Over the years, however, mental exertion had replaced physical workouts. His face, which was usually defined by his supporters as kindly, this morning showed his age.

"Mr. President. Your National Security team is assembled and waiting.''

His secretary's voice was soft, apologetic. Loyal to a fault, she kept hoping he would figure a way out of this crisis and get on with the business of writing his chapter for history.

Reluctantly, he left the Oval Office, headed down the hall and down the stairs to the Situation Room. He tried to summon a positive attitude, but it was difficult. In his hand, he held a report from Hal Kingsley, his pollster. According to Hal's numbers—and he was rarely off by more than a percentage point—just as the future of those hostages hung in the balance, so did Elton Haynes's presidency.

A marvel of technology, the guts of the Situation Room contained a bank of computers set up to monitor different areas of the globe and were manned by special assistants to the National Security Council. Messages were received and sent, all carefully crypted and secure. There was a computer to send messages to Air Force One, another to patch secure phone conversations from the White House to anywhere in the world. Scattered throughout the room were burn bags, large paper garbage bags with red stripes down the middle. Several times a day, the military took these bags and whatever refuse was contained within, and burned them.

As Elton Haynes entered this electronic maze, fax machines whirred. Computers clicked. Telephones rang. The director of the Situation Room rose to greet him. The cadre of technicians also turned from their work. Their faces registered shock, and then alarm. Normally the president held meetings in the Cabinet Room, the Map Room, or the Roosevelt Room. If he was meeting down here, the situation was truly grave.

Elton smiled at the director and nodded to the crew, quickly turned left, and entered the soundproof, bugproof conference room. A large wooden table anchored the space, surrounded by plush leather chairs. He took his place at the head and instantly took attendance.

Awaiting him was an elite assemblage of diplomats and policy experts: the secretaries of State and Defense, the National Security Advisor and one of his deputies, the chairman of the Joint Chiefs, Senators Lamar Basalt and Benjamin Knight from the Foreign Relations Committee, the chair and ranking member of the House Foreign Affairs Committee, the majority and minority leaders of both houses, Chip Thompson, the president's chief of staff, the head of the CIA's antiterrorism unit, a professor of Strategic Studies at the Johns Hopkins University School of Advanced International Studies, and former minister-counselor, Zoë Vaughn, one of the school's most accomplished graduates.

"Gentlemen," Haynes said, perusing the group, then nodding to the lone woman at the table. "Ms. Vaughn. Thank you for coming."

At the mention of her name, Senator Benjamin Knight's attention was drawn to the blonde in the sober navy suit.

The president reviewed the situation and opened the floor to a discussion of options. The head of the CIA proposed a covert operation. Several people offered possible diplomatic avenues, others leaned toward a military solution. Lamar Basalt, though normally a hawk, advocated draconian economic sanctions.

Haynes shook his head. "Economic sanctions take too long."

The secretary of state preferred a high-level diplomatic mission as a first step. No ransom. No negotiations. The only thing extended would be a face-saving opportunity in exchange for the release of the prisoners.

Benjamin Knight favored an all-out rescue operation. "You can't compromise with terrorists," he said.

The secretary of defense agreed. "We have the weapons systems for a quick strike offensive. I say we make them fight it out."

"The public is wary of armed intervention," warned a congressman known for his reliance on public-opinion polls.

Several others afflicted with the habit of taking their political temperature on a daily basis concurred.

"With all due respect, sir," Zoë said, addressing the congressman, "it's dangerous to conduct foreign policy based on polls."

Lamar Basalt seemed to agree. "There are three basic rules of foreign policy: Don't negotiate with terrorists. Don't send money to people you don't trust. And don't ask the public what they think." He turned to the president. "Sanctions!" he insisted, as if his advice was above questioning.

Zoë challenged the codger with implacable confidence. "Economic sanctions starve innocent people. They don't prevent power-hungry despots from feeding their egos."

Ben silently applauded her nerve. Few took Basalt on. She had done it twice in a month and had won both times.

"What about a diplomatic mission?" the Senate majority leader asked. "Like the secretary said. No negotiations, just a chance to save face and get our guys out."

The question sparked a debate between those who were willing to do whatever was necessary to achieve resolution and those who wanted to maintain current policy.

"It should be noted that Red Rage is not your ordinary terrorist cell," Zoë informed. "They're not a homogeneous group driven by a single ideology. They're a conglomerate of malcontents being exploited by a savvy politician eager to make a power grab. While dispatching a high-ranking diplomat might result in the release of the hostages, it legitimizes Durgunov and increases his viablity as an alternative to Borofsky."

The director of the Federal Bureau of Investigation had been listening quietly, but intently. "The last thing we want to do is burnish the image of someone like Durgunov," he said, injecting himself into the meeting. "We have enough problems dealing with the rising tide of antigovernment militias as it is."

"What's the connection?" a congressman asked.

"Home-grown extremists are prone to identifying with the grievances of ultranational movements like Red Rage. Please! Let's not give them a new poster boy to worship."

Breaking the uncomfortable silence that followed, Zoë turned to the head of the table. "While you're deciding the best course to take, Mr. President, we might consider

THE LUCKY ONES 25

using Durgunov's favorite weapon, the media, against him."

Haynes was fascinated. So were most of the others. Zoë was encouraged to explain.

"Durgunov took American hostages because he knew it would be covered by the international press. He wants to be a superhero, and he's counting on CNN to stamp the S on his chest. What we should do is mount a communications blitz that makes him appear to be a thug, a heartless bully who would use women and children to line his pockets with ransom money. The Russians are a compassionate people. They're not going to find that heroic."

Elton Haynes agreed and, after presiding over one more go-around-the-table, adjourned the meeting. After three sometimes contentious hours, an unspoken accord had been reached.

After the president had left the room and others were saying good-bye, Ben walked over to Zoë and said hello.

"It's been a long time," he said, shaking her hand.

"Good to see you, Senator," she said, offering him a soft smile.

Her Boston accent had faded, but not completely, he was pleased to note. He had always found it charming. Or "chahming" as she might have said. "I didn't expect to run into you here."

"It's not my usual venue, but neither is it my first time," she said, displaying diplomatic prowess with her modest brag.

"Do you have time for a cup of coffee at the Grill?" he asked, referring to Ebbet's Grill around the corner from the White House.

"Thanks, but I'm meeting Caleb Lind down the hall in the Mess. Some other time, perhaps."

They said good-bye at the door to the dark, wood-paneled room with the leather pub chairs and nautical paintings that served as a private eatery for some of those who worked in the West Wing. Ben watched as Zoë made her way toward the president's National Security Advisor. At every table, an entitled someone stopped her. She might have been forced out of the State Department by the previous regime, but clearly in this administration, she was not out of favor. Probably because Zoë was one of the few to whom the big picture was still more important than a personal portrait.

While she chatted with several Cabinet officers, Ben reluctantly turned and headed out of the West Wing to where his car waited. As his driver turned onto Pennsylvania Avenue, Ben smiled and mused about how brightly his first flame shone.

☆ SEPTEMBER ☆

The elegantly paneled den of Scottie Edwards's Georgetown house was filled with cronies accumulated over a
lifetime of politics. Sliding in between puffs of expensive
cigar smoke, a butler quietly refreshed drinks and poured
coffee. Most of the men were debating which teams would
survive the playoffs and make it to the World Series. Several
stood huddled in a corner, enmeshed in an analysis of the
effect the hostage crisis was having on the stock market.
Still others stared into the glass case housing their host's
collection of antique guns.

Prescott Edwards moved from one group to another
with the ease of one who knew he was the hive around
which others buzzed. As he slapped backs and exchanged
ribaldries, he congratulated himself on having amassed
such an impressive cadre. Milling about this room was a
corporate alphabet of power and wealth—the CEOs,
CFOs, and COOs of many of America's largest companies,
all of them present for one reason: they liked being
attached to Scottie Edwards's star.

At precisely nine o'clock, Eastern Standard Time, the
women came in from the living room and joined their

husbands. Emily Edwards, a slim woman with short-cropped salt-and-pepper hair, wove her way through the throng to take her place at Scottie's side. The butler pressed a button, and a large television screen descended from the ceiling. The room stilled as the camera zoomed in on Elton Haynes.

"My fellow Americans, I come to you this evening with a heavy heart. After a great deal of soul searching, I have decided not to seek a second term as your president. As much as I would like to continue in service to my country and finish what we've started in so many other areas vital to our growth as a nation, I feel my efforts are better spent finding a way to free those brave Americans being held hostage.

"Mounting a presidential campaign would simply be too distracting," he said.

"In other words, his polls say he doesn't stand a chance," Colonel Arlo Reid, Edwards's former aide-de-camp and constant shadow, said dryly.

Scottie could have joined in the ensuing laughter, but he kept his cobalt eyes trained on Elton Haynes as the president finished delivering his political epitaph. When the networks returned to their anchors, everyone looked expectantly toward their host.

"The field is wide-open," a longtime supporter said. "You are going to run, aren't you?"

"No one else has your unique qualifications, General," a communications titan advised. "And whoever runs from Haynes's party will be walking a terrible tightrope. He has to campaign on the same issue that's brought Haynes down, without appearing to slam his leader." The man snickered. "You gotta love it!"

While others laughed, Edwards's mien became serious. "I've always believed that life serves up moments of opportunity," he said. "You either grab them by the throat or stand on the sidelines and watch someone else bask in the glory."

Emily, recognizing that this was the highlight of the

evening, stepped to the side, allowing her husband the full gleam of the spotlight.

"I committed myself to that philosophy as a young man, and I've never wavered from its path. As a general, it meant having the courage to wait for that perfect moment to strike and then going in without hesitation. As secretary of state, it meant having the patience to stand back while factions scuffled, holding out until the toll in lives and money was so great any compromise was preferable to certain defeat. And as ambassador to the Soviet Union, it meant having the nerve to plot a course and stick with it, no matter what."

While his words were rewarded with generous applause, to Scottie, the real reward was the belief that in exchange for a lifetime of service, he was being offered the ultimate opportunity.

Raising his brandy glass, he stared covetously at the Oval Office, where Elton Haynes was being questioned about the crisis that had bedeviled him. Scottie's arm slid around Emily's waist. She looked up at him with a practiced smile of love and adoration.

"History is like a galloping horse," he said, addressing his fans, his tone a careful balance of humility and self-possession. "If you don't mount it and ride it, it will gallop on and leave you standing in the dust."

He paused and glanced down at his wife as if he was asking for her approval. Both of them knew that little she said could influence a decision he had already made. Then he let his eyes roam around the room with dramatic deliberateness, allowing his stare to linger, as if eye contact constituted a pledge of support. When he had completed his review and was assured that his troops were in line, he continued.

"Yes," he said, speaking to the man who had asked, "I am going to run for president."

Throughout the room, there was spontaneous applause and cheering. He accepted it with a solemn nod.

"Yes," he said, allowing his voice to tremble with conviction, "I am going to mount the horse called history."

And, thought Emily, still gazing up at him, a smile iced on her lips, *he's going to ride that nag straight to the White House, no matter what it takes.*

It was nine o'clock in the morning. At The American School in Ankara, classrooms were filled with youngsters hard at work. The halls were empty. The teachers' lounge was quiet. The small cafeteria which fed the children of the Armed Forces personnel based in Turkey was busy setting up for the day's lunch.

Silently, ten men in full attack gear entered the building, proceeding to the second-grade classroom nearest the exit. Brandishing machine guns, they slid into the room, terrified its occupants into mute attention, and herded them out the door into a waiting truck. Fifteen eight-year-olds and their twenty-five-year-old teacher: the latest hostages in the war between Yegor Durgunov and the rest of the world.

Benjamin Knight, his mother, and two children were glued to the morning news. Normally, watching television during meals was forbidden, but everyone was anxious about the escalating crisis. The most difficult part for Ben was trying to explain to his son, Ryan, and his daughter, Keeley, why someone would want to take children from their school and hold them prisoner for months in some unknown place.

"What if the bad guys decide to come to the United States?" Ryan said.

Loretta, who had been standing near Ryan's chair, bent down and hugged her grandson. "Nothing's going to happen to you, sweetheart. You're perfectly safe."

"Those other kids were in schools on army bases, with American soldiers all around, and they were kidnapped,"

Ryan said, his young eyes filled with fear. "If it could happen to them, Grandma, it could happen to us."

Ben felt as if someone had knocked the wind out of him. Ryan had just voiced the stultifying dread afflicting every child and every parent in America. Ben looked from Ryan to Keeley. She, too, seemed moved and highly disturbed by the continuing hostage saga. Loretta, rarely at a loss for words, suddenly could find none with which to soothe.

Without further comment, Ben went into his den and made a telephone call that would change his life, and theirs.

Ben's startling announcement—"I'm thinking of entering the race for president"—was greeted with a thick silence by his four closest advisors.

"I'm against it," Sam Trout said at last, relieving the others assembled in Ben's Senate office of having to express an opinion.

Sam had been Ben's friend and advisor for fifteen years. Now, he was chief of staff. His words carried weight.

"Why?" Ben folded his arms across his chest and waited for the onslaught.

"Because presidential campaigns take years to organize," Sam exclaimed, looking at Ben as if commitment to a mental institution was not out of the question. "Because you need to have a war chest that's full to overflowing. Because you need an advance staff, schedulers, media advisors, pollsters, and strategies. Because you need fund-raisers set up in every state and thousands and thousands of bright-eyed volunteers to ring doorbells, hand out flyers, and get petitions signed. That's why!"

Ben had no reaction to the tirade. After so many years, it had been expected.

"That may be true for an ordinary cycle," he said. "But this is hardly an ordinary cycle." There were mumblings of agreement. "And besides, this is not the first time we've talked about making a run at the White House."

Several heads nodded, but only as an acknowledgment of what Ben had said. No one was ready to issue an endorsement; too much was at stake. As professionals, everyone in that room knew that in the business of politics, winning was the bottom line; there was no such thing as an honorable defeat. Presidential campaigns were grueling, and no one of sound mind committed himself to a race of that magnitude unless he believed he had a chance.

While there had been rumors circulating about several challenges to Haynes's nomination before his announcement, none had formally declared. Tradition cautioned against running against an incumbent in your own party; usually, it proved self-destructive. Immediately after Haynes's announcement, however, the scurrying had begun. Four men had declared themselves candidates. Three were well-known, older statesmen with national profiles. The fourth, Mack Kenton, was Ben's age, had served four terms in the House, his last few as ranking member of the Judiciary Committee and a powerful voice on the International Relations subcommittee on human rights. Kenton was good-looking, came from quality Iowa stock, and was married with three extremely telegenic children.

"Don't you want to get your two cents' worth in?" Ben asked Phil Halpern, his political advisor.

"It's not your time," Phil said. "Thanks to Haynes's blundering, I don't think anyone from the party stands a chance. My advice is to let Kenton take the loss."

"Who says he's going to lose?"

Sam rolled his eyes at Ben, picked himself up off the couch, and marched to a chair at the far end of the room, distancing himself from the insanity. Phil responded.

"Scottie Edwards's record in foreign affairs is rock solid. My guess is he's going to mow down every one of his primary opponents and march into the convention like Caesar entering Rome."

Adam Schwartz, Ben's administrative assistant, corroborated Phil's assessment. "The man's been putting an organization together for years. It's up and more than ready to roll."

"Besides," Sam said, unable to stay quiet for long, "the guy's a retired one-star general, a onetime ambassador to the Soviet Union and a former secretary of state. We're in the middle of an international crisis. Edwards has *savior* tatooed on his damn forehead!"

"You're young, Ben," Phil said. "You can afford to wait this one out."

Ben lowered his eyes and stared at his shoes. These men only wanted the best for him; he knew that. They were also extremely savvy about politics. They were giving him intelligent reasons not to subject himself to the rigors of a campaign they clearly believed was lost before it was even begun. The problem was that Ben couldn't forget the look on Ryan's face or how he had felt when he saw it.

"Listen, Ben," Sam said, dropping the guise of political advisor and speaking as a friend. "I know you well enough to know that you are well-intentioned, and that you wouldn't even be considering this if your heart and your conscience weren't prodding you to do so."

"But?" Ben said, his eyes still fixed on the floor.

"One, I don't think you stand a chance. And two, whoever wins this election has a humongous problem. He will have been elected on what is really a solemn promise to do one thing—free those hostages. If he does, great! He becomes a saint and is assured a second term. If he doesn't, he's out on his ass no matter what else he does."

"And Kenton becomes the front runner," Ben said, surprised at the competitiveness he heard in his voice.

"Not after Edwards gets finished with him," Adam said. "He wants to win more than he wants to breathe, which is why you can bet he's going to run a scorched-earth campaign."

Phil agreed. "His opposition-research team will dig into every little nook and cranny of that guy's past, looking for something that even smells slightly off. Believe me, whoever Edwards's opponent is, he's in for the beating of his life.''

Sid Guest, who had remained relatively quiet until now, chimed in. "They're right, Ben. By the time Edwards gets finished with Kenton, or whomever, he'll be lucky if his family wants anything to do with him, let alone the voters.''

Ben walked behind his desk and stood at the windows, looking out onto Constitution Avenue.

Sam watched and worried. Though Ben appeared to be listening, Sam didn't think he was absorbing what was being said.

"I think you'd make a great president, Ben." There was no doubting the respect and admiration in Sam's voice. "I'd rather see you run when your chances are better. That's all.''

Ben nodded, but remained at the window, staring at the dome of the Capitol, where he felt privileged to work. Why would he want, or need, any more power than he already had? What made him think he was any better qualified or more sincerely motivated than those who had already announced?

His gut. That's what was telling him to run. That's what was telling him he could do the job and do it well. *His gut.* Years of studying the system—the way it worked, why sometimes it didn't. Years of analyzing problems, devising policy, and fighting to see it enacted. Years of observing and examining and appraising what he had done, or not done, and what those in power had done, or not done. Years of building toward an anonymous something that suddenly had a name—the presidency.

He had tiptoed around it before. Sam had brought it up several years ago, but Ben had dismissed it. Then, his gut had said no, not now, not yet, not me. It felt different this time. Suddenly, the notion didn't strike him as absurd or unthinkable. But was it ego that was telling him the presidency of the United States might actually be within his grasp? Arrogance? That tiny portion of the human brain so far removed from rationality its only output were the seeds of insanity? Or was it that other segment of the cerebellum, known as intuition, that seemed immediately to understand a set of facts without reasoning?

For the next half hour, Ben's advisors threw arguments at him and each other. He listened. They listened. He agreed on some things, disagreed about others. When, finally, he thought they had exhausted every possible position, he held up his hands. "Enough," he said.

Throughout, he had been pacing the room. Now, however, he walked in front of his desk and stood there, facing his friends. They stared back at him, expectantly. For a few moments, he remained pensive and absorbed. When he had gathered himself and felt ready, he took a deep breath and began.

"All I ever wanted to do was to make things better, to take what was wrong with America and make it right. Granted, the distinction about what was right and what was wrong was made according to my definitions and the guiding vision was colored by my particular experiences. But since I've been in the Senate, I've authored a number of meaningful bills that actually have changed the lives of millions of Americans for the better." His voice was soft, as if he needed to make his case first to himself and then, to them. "I think I've served my state and my country well, but, somehow, I feel as if these times are demanding more of me."

Again he paused. So many thoughts were careening through his head, it was difficult to isolate those that were significant from those that were not.

"We're in the midst of a crisis that's much larger than the kidnappings. It's a crisis about where our center is. Who we are as a nation. What we stand for. And what we stand against."

He sat on the edge of his desk—his favorite perch— looked at his advisors and shrugged. He didn't know any other way to express the sense that *something* had tapped him on the shoulder, *something* had injected him with the conviction that not only *could* he be president of the United States, but that he *should* be.

"So," he said to Sam, who seemed to be struggling almost as much as he was, "what do you think?"

"It's a big risk, Ben. It's not like your other races." Sam rested his arms on his knees and leaned forward. "This is the major leagues, my friend. On a good day, it's vicious and often humiliating. On a bad day, it's brutal and hurtful and stressful beyond anything you've ever experienced."

"I know." Ben's face registered anxiety, exhilaration, fear, and, oddly, confidence. "Believe me, I'm not contemplating this because I'm bored or I need an ego boost." Again, he looked at them, one by one. "I wouldn't do that to you. I wouldn't do that to me. And I sure as hell wouldn't do that to my family."

"We know that," Phil said somberly, as the others nodded.

"Then you're with me?"

Four pairs of eyes took sideways glances. A faint smile illuminated Phil's face. Adam laughed outright. Suddenly, they were all laughing—albeit nervously—sharing in the knowledge that they had just committed themselves to a wild yet perilous adventure that would either bring them the biggest prize imaginable or take from them those few precious things they had prized for themselves: dignity, privacy, and reputation.

☆ OCTOBER ☆

Vaughn's, a popular bar in Boston's South End, was filled to overflowing with family, friends, pub regulars, and a few freeloaders eager to scarf down a cold draft and a fistful of hors d'oeuvres. That afternoon, Paul Vaughn had been sworn in to the Boston Police Force. Naturally, his grandfather, Paddy Vaughn, had invited everyone in the neighborhood to a celebratory party.

Zoë stood off to the side, watching her large, raucous family revel in the joy of their tradition. The youngest of seven, Zoë always had been different from the other Vaughns. Although her brothers and sisters were intelligent, they tended to limit the spheres of their curiosity. Zoë hated limits, almost as much as she reviled the notion that she couldn't—or shouldn't—do something simply because no one in her family or the neighborhood had done it before. She dreamed of learning a dozen foreign languages and traveling to faraway places. She was fascinated by cultures the rest of her family deemed exotic, entranced by the notion that children in other countries read different books than she did, or didn't have television or didn't know what football was or rode camels instead of buses and lived in huts instead of houses.

As she watched them now, so easy with one another, part of her envied their obvious harmony. The other half was resigned to the fact, that hard as she tried, she would always be off-key.

Feeling somewhat like an outsider, she shifted her attention to the television that hung over the bar. The sound had been muted, but as always, a telecast of one of Boston's teams was playing for the masochistic pleasure of Paddy's customers. This evening, it was the Red Sox. No one was watching. It was one of those years when being a fan was an act of faith.

Suddenly, the network cut away for a news update. Fearing something had happened to the hostages, everyone fell silent. Paddy raised the sound. The anchorwoman's image disappeared and Benjamin Knight filled the screen. Standing in front of his son's elementary school, surrounded by his family, a group of teachers, nurses and children, the senior senator from Pennsylvania announced his candidacy for president of the United States.

As people crowded around, Zoë studied the man she once had known so intimately. Graying slightly, his softly planed face sharpened by a few extra lines, Ben remained a striking man. Recalling his contributions during the meeting of the National Security Council, Zoë knew he was also a plain-speaking, clear-thinking senator.

While he explained why he'd decided to make the run for the White House—to keep America's children safe— Zoë looked behind him to his children and recalled the day she had read about Felicia Knight's fatal car crash. It had come over the wire to the embassy in Moscow, offering little more than the cold facts: Felicia Coburn Knight had been killed in a head-on collision with a drunk driver on a highway just outside Washington. Her son, thrown from the car and critically injured, was barely clinging to life.

Zoë had spent hours studying the photos of Ben's face at Felicia's funeral. She had cried for him and his children, for their shock and their grief. She had written to Ben to convey her sympathy and while he thanked her for her condolences, she feared her note had sounded perfunctory. She had wanted to convey the depth of her commiseration, but to do that, she would have had to tell him *why* she understood how he felt.

And she couldn't do that.

Body parts. Uneaten food strewn about on a cold floor. Bloodstained nurses. Frightened children being dragged into trucks. The incessant rat-a-tat-tat of machine guns spraying bullets into an unsuspecting crowd. Devastating bombs exploding like Fourth of July firecrackers. Black-checkered kaffiyehs. White surgical coats. Black woolen ski masks. Red blood. A woman dead in a car wreck. Another woman nearly dead on an operating table. A severely injured boy. A dead baby. A man grieving. A woman screaming.

When Nona came to awaken Zoë, she found her daughter in a deep sleep, but bathed in sweat. It wasn't the first time.

"Zoë," Nona said, shaking her gently. "Wake up, darling." Zoë's eyes opened. They were red and puffy and lined. "Are you all right?"

Zoë nodded, but she remained groggy.

"There's a call for you." Nona placed a steaming cup of black coffee on the nightstand and tucked an extra pillow behind Zoë's back. When Zoë had taken a sip or two of the coffee and Nona was certain she was conscious and functioning, she handed her the telephone and left the room.

The caller identified himself as Sam Trout, Senator Knight's chief of staff. Zoë forced herself to attention. To say that her curiosity was piqued was an understatement. After several minutes of polite preamble during which he lauded her accomplishments and reminded her that she and the senator had been college classmates, he came to the point.

"Do you think you might be available to meet with the senator?" he asked. "He has a proposal for you."

Zoë smiled at the odd choice of words. "I'll be in New York on Monday and back in Washington Wednesday morning," she said. "We can set up an appointment in either place. Whatever is convenient for the senator."

"He'll be in Boston tomorrow, Miss Vaughn."

"No. I'm sorry, but I'm here on a personal visit. I prefer to conduct business at my office."

"I appreciate that," Sam Trout said, impatience slipping into his voice, "but the senator has said that his meeting with you is of the highest priority. I believe you just said you would allow us an appointment at the senator's convenience. That would be sometime tomorrow, somewhere in Boston."

Unable to parry with another reasonable excuse, Zoë relented, but uneasily. She would have preferred keeping her dealings with Benjamin Knight strictly professional.

"Okay," she said. "What's his schedule?"

She could hear Sam Trout rifling through a notebook. "He's flying from Philadelphia to New Hampshire for two town meetings and then, late tonight, will head to Boston. Tomorrow morning, he has breakfast with the Sons of Ireland, lunch with the Daughters of Italy, and, at two o'clock, he's addressing the Greater Boston B'nai Brith. He'll be free at about five."

"And at six?" she asked.

Trout laughed. "Actually, Miss Vaughn, the staff is banking on you to get us a brief respite in what is shaping up to be a backbreaking month."

"I beg your pardon?"

"Senator Knight has blocked out the entire evening for you. If you agree to meet with him, we get the night off."

"Far be it for me to ruin everyone's evening."

She had to admire Sam Trout's style. Zoë hated being pushed into a corner, but he had managed it with such grace, it deserved to be rewarded. She arranged time and place, put the phone down, and fervently hoped she had not made a terrible mistake.

"What was that all about?" It seemed as if at the precise instant the phone was back in its cradle, Nona was back in Zoë's room.

"Benjamin Knight will be stopping by the house tomorrow." Zoë paused, affording her punch line the optimum effect. "He has a proposal for me."

Nona stared at her daughter for a second, then threw back her head and laughed.

"Well, it's about time," she said, grateful that for now, at least, the ghosts had gone.

They met when she was a freshman at Harvard, he a senior. Benajmin Knight was then, as she supposed he would always be, a man in a hurry. Everything he did was at breakneck speed, including, as he had told her on their second date, falling in love.

They had been strolling along the Charles in companionable silence when suddenly he stopped, held her arms, and turned her to face him.

"I think I'm crazy in love with you." He had said it quickly, almost desperately, as if he were afraid that if he didn't get it out, the feeling would disappear. "I know it sounds like a line, Zoë, but I'm not a line kind of guy."

He studied her face, watching for a reaction, but she was too stunned to do or say anything.

"What are you thinking? Do you want to slap me? Call the police? Run for your life?"

He feinted to the right, held up one hand, as if expecting a right jab to the chin. Though inside she was grinning, her face remained expressionless.

"Okay," he said, retreating slightly. "Do you want to forget I said anything and just see what happens? Or is there a remote possibility that you might want to kiss me and tell me I haven't made a total jackass out of myself?"

"The kiss is a possibility," she said, delighting in the

grin that suddenly enlivened his face. "As for the jackass part? The jury is still out on that."

She had tried very hard to rein in her feelings, but it was easy to love Ben. He was smart and quick and handsome and charming. He made her laugh the way no one else had, and when they were in bed, he made her feel the way no one else did.

Zoë had never experienced anything as joyous as this, or as mystifying. While she had come to the relationship a virgin, it wasn't the newness of the sexual experience that had her so enthralled. *Ben* was the excitement. His mind stimulated her as much as his hands. His thoughts lingered as long as his scent. And his soul fulfilled her as surely and deeply as his body did.

When they met, Ben was older than his fellow classmates, having served two years in Vietnam before entering Harvard. While he had certainly had his fair share of liaisons, most of them had been purely sexual, inspiring little or no emotional commitment. He thought it was because he was so singularly focused and, therefore, impervious to love.

Zoë Vaughn hit him with the force of a bullet. Tall, lean, with this rippling curtain of honey blond curls and large eyes the color of celadon, she exuded an aura of delicacy. It was later that he discovered this look of fragility was but an illusive veil covering a steely resolve. Zoë didn't avoid intellectual debate the way some women did. Rather, she seemed to relish it, challenging statements with which she took issue, demanding that he either back up his positions or back down. Yet as tough as she could be, that was how soft she could be. As determined and concentrated as she was about her studies, that was how adventurous and playful she was about life. She made him laugh, she made him think, she made him lustful, and, most important of all, she made him happy.

For a while they were inseparable, which was how they thought they'd be for the rest of their lives. Then, Ben started Yale Law School, Zoë returned to Harvard, and reality intruded on the idyll. With slow yet steady insistence, a lack of money and time began to nibble at their romance. She went to New Haven a few times; he visited her in Boston as often as he could afford.

The next summer, Zoë was offered the chance to assist one of Harvard's most highly esteemed history professors research a book on the Third Reich. Ben landed a job in Washington, D.C., working for a Federal Circuit Court judge. They spoke as often as they could and sneaked an occasional visit, but it was a lonely couple of months. Zoë filled her spare time by adding German to her bank of languages. Ben had only a few off hours, but during one of them he met Felicia Coburn.

The second weekend in September, Zoë decided to surprise Ben. When the taxi turned onto Willard Street and stopped at the three-story redbrick building where Ben lived, she was too excited to notice the limousine that had pulled up right behind her. Zoë jumped from the cab, set her suitcase down in the small foyer, and buzzed Ben's apartment.

"I'll be right down!"

Zoë grinned. He must have seen her arrival from his window. Within seconds, he came bounding down the stairs. The fact that he was wearing a tuxedo didn't register. The expression on his face when he saw her did. He was stunned.

"Zoë!" He opened the door, swept her into his arms, and held her close, but he was sputtering. "What? When? How?"

"I thought we deserved a reward for all our hard work this summer," she said. "So, here I am!"

A car horn honked impatiently. When Ben leaned around her and waved, she turned. It was then that she noticed the limousine and, looking back at Ben, his tuxedo.

"Either Judge Westheimer has some strange ideas about

proper office attire, or you're on your way to a fancy-dress ball.''

He laughed uneasily. "Actually, I'm on my way to a dinner party at Senator Reston's.''

John Reston was the Senate majority leader. Zoë was impressed.

"It's some kind of birthday thing. The vice president is going to be there.'' He seemed astounded at his good fortune. "Can you imagine that?''

"No,'' she replied honestly. "I can't. So who invited you? Westheimer?''

He hesitated, his eyes moved past her. She followed his gaze out to the street. The rear window of the limousine was open, framing an incredibly beautiful blonde.

"Felicia Coburn,'' Ben explained quickly. "Celia's cousin? The one from Atlanta? You know.''

Zoë knew very well. Celia Porter was one of her best friends.

As Ben ushered Zoë to the curb and introduced the two women, Zoë understood why Celia always referred to Felicia as the "peachtree princess.''

"I'm delighted to meet you.'' Felicia offered a gloved hand and a smile that was as cool and artificial as the air that surrounded her. "Ben's spoken of you. And, of course, Celia simply adores you.''

The way she said it made Zoë feel like Celia's pet spaniel.

"I wish we had time to get to know each other,'' Felicia purred, "but I'm afraid we're running terribly late. Ben, darling . . .''

"Give me a minute,'' he said.

Back in the entry of his building, Ben caressed Zoë's cheek. "It'll be an early night. These things never go past ten.''

"How many of *these things* have you been to?'' she asked, suddenly remembering the growing infrequency of Ben's phone calls, the one-sided conversations.

He laughed and shook his head. "More than I ever would have imagined. Felicia's been really generous about introducing me around. I've met people you read about in newspapers. I've talked to them. About the law. Issues. Government policy." A look of wonder passed over his face. "And you know what? They've listened!"

"That's great, Ben." Zoë trembled from the chilling realization that there was no way to compete with a woman like Felicia. She was using power to seduce Ben. And he was falling for it.

He looked at his watch, then out to the car, then at Zoë. "Wait for me upstairs, will you? I won't be late." He fished around in his pocket, found his keys, and handed them to her. It was probably the first time he had really looked into her eyes. "I feel terrible leaving you here. If you had called, I could have . . ."

"No problem," Zoë said, forcing her lips to curl. "Just go. After all, you can't keep the vice president waiting."

If he caught her sarcasm, he didn't react. Instead, he kissed her and ran to the car. Zoë left his keys under the mat outside his apartment and caught the next plane back to Boston.

"I thought something terrible had happened to you," he said when he called her the next day. "Why'd you leave?"

Because you didn't stay. "I shouldn't have come without calling first."

"It was a great surprise. It's just . . ."

"You had places to go and people to see," she snapped.

"You're making more out of this than it is," Ben protested.

"Okay, then tell me what *it* is."

He paused. She could almost see him gathering his thoughts.

"It's a chance to hook up with some very powerful people who just might be helpful to me in the future."

I thought I was your future, Zoë thought.

"I guess I didn't see it that way," she said, begging her emotions to hold on just a little longer, "but you're right. I shouldn't have asked for an accounting, especially since it seems clear that whatever we had has run its course. It's time for both of us to move on."

"But I love you, Zoë! I don't want to *move on.*"

Zoë struggled to maintain her dignity as she said quietly, "You already have, Ben."

Zoë was annoyed that when she opened the door and saw Ben standing there, her pulse quickened.

"Thanks for seeing me," he said, his lopsided grin a confession that he was as wary and unsure as she.

Over his shoulder, Zoë spotted the convoy that had accompanied him: Secret Service agents, numerous aides, press vans, cameramen, dozens of reporters streaming toward the house.

"It's not every day I receive a request to meet with a presidential candidate," she said, quickly closing the door.

She took his coat and led him inside, where Paddy and Nona waited. Paddy looked stiff and rather formal, Zoë thought. Perhaps it was the suit and tie.

"Good afternoon, Senator," he said, grasping Ben's hand and shaking it firmly.

Ben returned the older man's greeting and tried to make conversation. Paddy kept his responses short and almost curt. Zoë was bothered by his behavior until she realized what was going on.

When she had first brought Ben home to meet her father, Paddy dismissed the young man from Philadelphia as an unlikely suitor for his youngest daughter. He wasn't Catholic, he wasn't finished with school, he didn't come from a large family, and he hated whiskey. The only thing in Ben's favor was that he rooted for his home teams— even those perennially losing Phillies—and had served with honor in the armed forces.

Over time, Ben had worn Paddy down: stopping by the bar, hanging out like one of the guys, debating everything from baseball to Watergate. The clincher, of course, came when the Celtics won the NBA title and Ben showed up at the bar with a Celtics shirt, a Celtics hat with a big #1 on it, and his face painted green as a shamrock. After that, Benjamin Knight could do no wrong.

Thinking back, Zoë recalled that when she told her parents the relationship was over, Paddy left the room and never spoke of Ben again. She hadn't seen it then, but when Ben chose someone else over Zoë, Paddy felt he, too, had been rejected.

Nona, on the other hand, opened her arms and wrapped Ben in a warm embrace, clucking over him just as she had so many years before. She ushered him to a chair, offered him a giant antipasto, and bombarded him with questions, most of them personal.

"I hate to interrupt," Zoë said, cutting her mother short. "Mr. Trout said you had some matters you wanted to discuss with me, Ben. I know you've had a busy day, and it's getting late."

Ben quickly adjusted to the change in room temperature. "Okay, I'll get straight to the point. I'd like you to join my campaign as foreign policy advisor. The resolution of this hostage crisis and the political consequences of that resolution are clearly the overriding issues in this election. And no one knows more about that area of the world than you."

Zoë's eyes narrowed. His offer wasn't a complete surprise. It didn't take a genius to deduce that after announcing one's candidacy for the presidency, one didn't reacquaint oneself with an old girlfriend for old times' sake; unless, of course, the woman in question could contribute something worthwhile to the cause.

"In case I didn't tell you, not only were you impressive at the White House, but you were dazzling on *Newsline*." Ben chuckled at the memory. "I don't think Basalt's recovered from the pasting you gave him—either time."

"The man didn't show her the proper respect." Paddy sounded pointedly indignant.

Ben stared at Paddy. Slowly and quite deliberately he said, "I couldn't agree more. Your daughter is an exceptional woman, which is why I'm here. I need her expertise on my campaign. I can't win without her," he said flatly.

"Yes, but if she signs on with you and goes the distance," Paddy countered, relishing the uniqueness of being able to challenge a man seeking the presidency, "what does she get out of it?"

"That's it!" Zoë rose from the couch, her obvious pique silencing both men. "We're leaving!"

Zoë went to the foyer, retrieved Ben's coat, tossed it at him, and slipped into hers.

She was halfway to the back door when Paddy took Ben's arm.

"You never answered my question. What does Zoë get out of all this?"

Ben looked Paddy squarely in the eye. "Who knows? If we win, she could be secretary of state!"

They took Paddy's '89 Chevy from the alley behind the Vaughns' house and drove away without anyone noticing them.

"That was easy," Ben said, heading north on Tremont Avenue.

"It proves a point," Zoë said. "I've always believed that if you have someone you want to protect, you don't put him in a motorcade with a dozen limousines, a brigade of motorcycle cops, and snipers posted on every bridge. That's like painting a target on the car, and saying, 'shoot me!'

"Instead, you put your important dignitaries in cars like this. No one's going to look twice at a Nova. And there would be fewer traffic tie-ups."

Ben chuckled. "Brilliant! Is that what you do at Hightower?"

"Exactly! My job is to think brilliant thoughts," Zoë said, finally beginning to feel at ease. "And so I do."

"Do you have any brilliant ideas about where to go?"

"Nope. I'll leave that to you. After all, you're running

for president. You need all the practice you can get making on-the-spot decisions.''

''Funny,'' he said, shaking his head and laughing. ''Very funny.''

Ben maneuvered through the city toward the harbor. He turned onto Hanover Street, the North End's main thoroughfare, and took a quick right onto Richmond, stopping in front of a small mom-and-pop Italian bistro where a valet offered to park their car. As the owner proceeded to lead Ben and Zoë inside, there were several astonished looks, a few waves, and three autograph seekers. One man stood and gave Ben his theory on how to rescue the hostages. Another blamed Saddam Hussein for the crisis. A few people simply wished him luck.

Over a bottle of Chianti, they talked about the situation overseas and its impact on the race.

''It is *the* single most important issue,'' Ben said, ''and not only because there are lives at stake. This crisis has become symbolic of all that's at the root of America's discontent: women and children at risk, and a government the people can't trust to protect them.''

''Can one person solve such an enormous problem?'' Zoë asked, already fairly certain of his answer.

''Obviously not.'' He thought for a moment before continuing. His eyes darkened; the lines at the outer corners deepened. ''Most politicians think it's heresy to say so, but I think Americans want someone who's willing to tell them the truth even if it's not pleasant. What's good politics is often bad leadership. And frankly, I think the country's sick of it!''

Zoë nodded. The public had been screaming ''foul'' for a long time. It was nice to know someone had listened.

''How do you get the public to believe you when they've been disappointed so many times?'' she asked.

Ben leaned across the table. His gaze was intense.

''By telling them the truth! We create a policy we think is sound, craft a platform we think has the best interests of most Americans at heart, make a pledge to do the best we can, and then," he said, "we stick to it!"

If Zoë hadn't had a history with this man, she still would have been moved by the sincerity underlining his words. But she did have a history with him, and the last thing she wanted was for their past to color a decision she might make about her future.

Ben sensed she was conflicted about casting her lot with him and rushed to convince her of his worthiness.

"That's why I need you so badly, Zoë. You know how to translate the harsh realities of foreign policy into relatively intelligible campaignspeak."

Zoë laughed. "Intelligible campaignspeak is an oxymoron."

Ben's mouth curled in a smile. "It may be, but for the next several months, it's going to be the language of the land."

Zoë sat back in her chair, twirled a lock of hair around her finger, and pursed her lips. "Who else is working the campaign?"

Ben knew she was stalling, that there were still some questions that remained unresolved for her, but he could only answer those she asked. And so, he listed those who had signed on to the "Knight for President" campaign.

Zoë knew some personally, others by reputation. Most, like Jed Oakes, Ben's chief political strategist, were the best and the brightest. Still, Zoë wondered how it would be working side by side with Benjamin Knight. She wasn't in love with him. That had faded years before. Nor was she angry. That, too, had diminished with time. She bore faint scars of a romance ended long ago, but in fairness, she had received and recovered from wounds far deeper and more devastating than any blows Benjamin Knight had delivered.

"Well?" he asked as the waiter set down their entrees.

"I'm not sure I'm the right person for this job," Zoë blurted.

"Why? Because we were once involved?"

Zoë's expression was one of mild amazement. "That was ages ago and, with all due respect, is incidental to the central issue."

Ben winced in spite of himself. While he hadn't envisioned a woman carrying a torch, neither had he expected their romance to be dismissed so offhandedly.

"Okay," he said, regrouping. "Is it because you're a woman and conventional wisdom prefers men at the foreign policy helm?"

She smirked, amused by his bluntness.

"It is certainly true that most men have a difficult time accepting the notion of women being anywhere on board the ship of state, let alone guiding it. But, no. My concern is not my gender. Madeleine Albright and Jeane Kirkpatrick already poked holes in that barrier. It's my past and how it might affect my usefulness to your campaign."

"I don't see how one determines the other."

"When Basalt came at me about my departure from the State Department, I realized how badly my credibility has been damaged. You can't afford to have someone on staff whose integrity is open to question."

"Why don't you lay it out for me and let me decide whether or not you have the credentials I'm looking for."

"Fair enough." Zoë's aspect sobered. "As minister-counselor for political affairs and second to the ambassador, I was charged with providing him and the State Department thorough background information on what the thinking was and who the players were in Moscow. My reports were expected to contain sufficient data for those in charge to formulate a successful American policy within the region.

"When Borofsky ran for president he was challenged by another reformer, Vladimir Baburin. My sources felt Baburin was the better choice. He was a gradualist. Borofsky insisted shock therapy was the only way successfully to move Russia from communism to a market economy.

"Also, my sources were concerned about Borofsky's lack of character."

Zoë kneaded her forehead. Ben refilled her wineglass. The strain of this tale had paled her face.

"Frankly, he was considered a political prostitute who would climb into bed with whomever offered the most rubles."

"Who were your sources?" Ben asked.

"I had many. Aside from the embassy staff, I sought the advice of our intelligence agents in the field."

Ben nodded. It was well known that the CIA often sent operatives into a country under diplomatic cover.

"Also, during my years in Moscow, I had befriended many people who sometimes provided me with valuable information."

A shadow eclipsed her eyes, but just as quickly as the darkness came, it passed.

"One friend told me he suspected Borofsky had worked deals with several of the hard-liners, Yegor Durgunov included."

"Is there any proof of that?"

Frustration veiled Zoë's face. "None that I know of."

"Was your source credible?"

"Extremely, but I couldn't—and wouldn't—reveal his name."

The fierceness of her tone intrigued Ben, but he filed it away for another time. "So who'd you tell and what did you say?"

"I informed Ambassador Petrie and the assistant secretary of state of my concerns. Specifically, my fear that Durgunov's influence on Borofsky could prove detrimental to America's long-term goals in the region. Ambassador Petrie told me that President Rumson's administration felt otherwise. They believed Baburin didn't have enough backing to make him viable. Borofsky was their man. Durgunov was a bit player who would quickly fade from the scene."

"So much for the wisdom of their conclusions," Ben said.

Unresolved anger tightened Zoë's mouth. "When I persisted, they bumped the matter up to the secretary of state, the honorable Prescott Edwards.'' Her voice dripped with sarcasm. ''I was called back to Washington to explain to him personally why I insisted on questioning American policy. I told him I didn't question our basic policy, simply our choice of Borofsky as the Russian president. I presented a lengthy defense of Baburin, augmented by economic analyses done by our Treasury Department as to whose economic policies would best serve the Russian public and make the best use of American aid. I also presented Edwards with a lengthy investigation of Borofsky's shady dealings.''

''Did the embassy staff support those conclusions?''

''Initially. My people not only did the research, but traveled to Washington with me to make our case.''

Ben was certain he heard disappointment in her voice. ''What about the others? What happened when push came to shove?''

Zoë arched an eyebrow and smiled. ''Their support waned,'' she said dryly.

Ben was upset. Foreign policy was about the successful conduct of nations, not the preservation of personal image.

Ben leaned forward and rested his arms on the table. ''Did Edwards or Rumson hear anything you said?''

''They had already invested too much political capital in Borofsky to back off.''

''Did you back off?''

''Not at first.''

Ben felt ill. Pointing out an obvious mistake was rarely welcome. Telling the president of the United States and his secretary of state they were wrong was career suicide.

''They stripped me of my title and my diplomatic passport, issued a press release announcing my change of status, and brought me back to Washington so that I could be properly harassed.'' Her mouth was so tight, her jaw was grinding. ''Since they didn't want to fire me outright and risk a lawsuit, they buried me in the Bureau of African Affairs.'' Ben looked quizzical. ''It's State's Siberia. I stuck it out for six months. When I decided I had been banished long enough, I went to Edwards and asked to be reassigned."

"He said no, and you quit."

"In a word, yes."

Ben didn't need to wonder about the humiliation Zoë had suffered, or the agony she had felt at being dealt such a devastating blow to her reputation, or the waves of self-doubt that must have threatened to drown her then, and threatened her still. It was written all over her face.

For a while, they sat quietly. Zoë appeared drained. Ben was absorbed in his own thoughts.

"I'm truly sorry about what happened," he said at last, his tone serious, yet gentle, "but I don't see how that affects the question on the table. Edwards's and Rumson's bad judgment doesn't alter my view of your qualifications or my desire to have you as my advisor. Recent events more than validate your competence in assessing and judging potentially volatile situations."

"Funny," Zoë said, looking anything but amused, "it's those very events that have caused me to question my ability and reexamine my decisions."

"Why?"

"When the first hostages were taken, I wondered if there was any connection, so I tried to contact my colleagues in Moscow to see what they knew." Her brow furrowed. "I discovered that my two closest aides, Dixon Collins and Maura Silver, had left the service rather abruptly. Three others who had helped research the findings had been transferred to remote postings. And the four remaining refused to take my call."

She studied her fingernails for a minute or two.

"You'd make a fine president, Ben. The last thing I want to do is to hurt your chances."

He reached across the table and took her hand in his. His eyes fixed on hers. They were sure and steady.

"Then don't turn me down."

For years, Zoë had been scratching her way back. Now,

a man she believed in was running for president. By asking her to contribute her expertise to his campaign, Ben had presented her with the best chance she might ever have to resurrect her reputation and, finally, take back her life.

"So," Ben asked, hopefully, "have I convinced you to hop on the 'Knight for President' bandwagon?"

Zoë wrestled a minute longer, calculating risks, evaluating possibilities, weighing possible gain versus the certainty of loss.

"It would be an honor, Senator Knight," she answered, raising her wineglass in a toast. "Here's hoping the ride is . . . relatively smooth."

He touched his goblet to hers, his mouth wreathed in a satisfied smile, his eyes filled with thanks. "Nice thought, Vaughn, but you know as well as I do, in politics there's no such thing as a free lunch or a smooth ride."

Or, Zoë thought, knowing she was gambling on far more than a presidential race, *a sure thing.*

☆ NOVEMBER ☆

"Congresswoman Hughes. What are your thoughts on the growing field of presidential candidates?"

A gaggle of reporters ringed Georgie Hughes as she left Longworth, one of the House office buildings.

"I think it's wonderful that even in the most trying of times, there are people willing to put themselves on the line and serve the public."

"Anyone you find particularly interesting?"

"Everyone who runs for president is interesting," she said, sliding quickly into the front seat of her car.

"Ben Knight was a classmate of yours at Harvard," one of the more aggressive reporters shouted, trying to prevent her from closing the door. "Does that make him more interesting than the others?"

"No," she said, firmly extricating the door from the man's grip and closing it. "It makes him my friend. Happy turkey, guys!"

With that, her driver took off.

"You must have been counting the days until this Thanksgiving recess," her young aide said, constantly amazed at the way the press followed his boss around.

Her staff referred to her as Queen Bee because she was always in the midst of a swarm, with people buzzing around her, waiting for one of her now-famous Texasisms.

"Just think," he said. "Ten days of peace and quiet."

"Peace and quiet?" Georgie threw her head back and laughed. "In my family? Compared to a holiday with the Hughes clan, Congress is a piece of cake!"

Georgie made the plane with only minutes to spare. She settled into her seat and piled her newspapers on her lap. The *Washington Post*, the *Washington Times*, the *Dallas Morning News*, the *New York Times*, the *Wall Street Journal*. Left in her briefcase for a quick perusal before she went to sleep, the *Chicago Sun-Times*, the *Houston Chronicle*, and the *LA Times*. And, because she liked to know what was going on elsewhere in the country, one other newspaper picked at random each day by her staff. Today, it was the *Philadelphia Inquirer*.

After skimming the national news—more or less the same in all papers—she scouted the political news. Naturally, the majority of stories centered around the names now floating in the campaign pool. Most didn't stand a chance. Either they had no national name recognition or they were single issue candidates whose issue was not the most pressing of the day. They weren't running to win; they were out to make an impression on the national consciousness and to reconfirm their political strength in the minds of their constituents—as well as the lobbyists who paid big bucks for those credited with legislative influence.

If Georgie were to handicap the races right now, she would hand the Republican nomination to Scottie Edwards and tell the others to just go home. The Democratic nomination, on the other hand, was far more interesting. In conventional terms, each of the announced candidates—Representative Tom Ujvagi from Ohio, Governor Harrison Wilcox of Wyoming, Representative Mack Kenton from Iowa, and the senior senator from Pennsylvania, Benjamin Knight—was viable in that they were currently in public office and had voting records that could be maximized by their friends and challenged by their enemies.

The Republican strategy was simple and neat: beat up on Elton Haynes. The Democrats had a more difficult task; they had to find a way to pat Haynes on the back and punch him in the stomach at the same time. Georgie, a Republican, was sympathizing with the political strategists on the Democratic side when she saw on page twelve of the *Inquirer* that Ben Knight had hired Jed Oakes as his campaign guru.

Georgie smiled. Ben Knight's chances of securing his party's nomination had just zoomed from possible to probable. And the odds of an Edwards landslide had just decreased. Jed Oakes was that good.

Throughout their nearly fifty-year marriage, Roy and Bunny Hughes had an arrangement: he ran the state, she ran the house. Even when his third term as governor had come to an end, and they decided to renovate their house in Dallas, Roy was not allowed to voice any opinions about the decor. He was to keep his mouth shut and his wallet open.

Bunny, who had been through more than her fair share of design incarnations, had decided that she and the governor should spend their golden years immersed in the splendor of the English Regency style. Out went the heavy woods, leather couches, and other Southwestern touches that had distinguished the mansion when her husband was the preeminent politician in the state and it was important that he display a loyalty to Texas tradition. In came velvet chairs, floral chintz sofas, gilded mirrors, and chinoiserie screens. The master suite was filled with so many rosebud prints and vases of fresh flowers, Roy could often be heard grousing that he felt as if he had been laid to rest in a florist's shop.

The dining room, which had been enlarged to accommodate all the children and grandchildren, had Chinese red-lacquered walls, a silver tea-paper ceiling, a working fireplace, a crystal chandelier fit for a palace, and an eighteenth-century table that seated twenty-four with ease.

Thanksgiving day saw the entire family gathered around the lavishly set table. In addition to Roy and Bunny, there was their son, Wade—a United States senator—his wife, Charlotte, and their three children. Their daughter, Bobbie (née Roberta), her husband, Branston Davis—the current leader of the Texas State Assembly—and their four children. Georgie, her husband, Lyle Mercer—CEO of Hughes Oil & Gas—and their twins, Olivia and Hunt.

As expected, the conversation centered around the field of candidates vying for the presidency. After dissecting them all—and finding each wanting—Roy raised the issue of Wade tossing in his hat. For several minutes, intense excitement filled the room. In this house, the thought of a Hughes as president was more stimulating than a drug.

If Wade were elected, Roy would automatically become an elder statesman. His grateful son would grant him whatever he wished, probably ambassador to the Court of St. James. Charlotte would become First Lady and could finally move out of her mother-in-law's shadow. Lyle could anticipate a major appointment. Wade's Senate seat would open up. And Branston could graduate from local pol to national politician.

When Georgie interrupted their collective web-spinning by saying, "Wade's not ready for a run at the White House," a flabbergasted hush swept the room.

"What the hell are you saying!" Roy reacted as if she had found an errant chromosome in the family DNA.

"I'm saying that this is not the time for Wade."

Georgie kept her voice even, her tone matter-of-fact. She wanted them to listen first. Then, if they wished—and she knew they would—they could debate her premise from now until Christmas.

"He's built his career on domestic issues. The country's in the midst of an international crisis. With Scottie

Edwards's résumé, he'll blow everyone, including you, my darling brother, out of the water.''

"That's why God invented advisors," Lyle said. "Wade's a natural-born leader, darling. Everyone knows that. All he has to do is assemble a topflight foreign policy team that will show the American public he's got the matter under control."

"The smarter move," Georgie said, unruffled, "is to lobby Edwards to put Wade on the ticket as his vice president. Edwards is weak on the domestic side. We may be stuck in a global gluepot right now, but the country isn't going to shut down until this problem is solved. To balance his ticket, Edwards is going to need someone to mind the store, someone with a nationally recognized name and reputation."

The Hugheses waited for Roy to react before expressing their own opinions. Georgie often wondered if anyone other than she, her father, and Lyle, even had personal convictions.

A sly smile took posession of Roy's mouth, as his eyebrows arched. "That's very clever, Georgie. In fact, it's positively inspired!"

He laughed, filling the room with a basso tone that sounded as if it had started at his shoes. Georgie was still reacting to her husband's irritating condescension and her father's tone of complete surprise. It grated on her that both of them continued to view her through such a narrow scope. While outwardly, those in her inner circle expressed pride in her drive and her intellect, she knew it was lip service, that neither her father, her husband, her brother, nor even her mother fully supported her ambition. To a man, every Hughes believed her place was in the home, not the House.

"Vice President Hughes," Roy bellowed. "It has a nice ring, don't you think, son?"

Wade grinned and raised his wineglass, tilting it toward his father, as if to accept the gauntlet he believed had just been passed on to him. "It does indeed!"

Though exultant at the prospect of national office, Wade's pleasure was diluted by a sudden shift in the family dynamic. Over the years, Wade had learned to tolerate Roy's glorification of Lyle as some kind of financial genius. But seeing the sparkle of respect in Roy's eyes for Georgie's political acumen was worrisome. In the past, it had been easy to dismiss Roy's soft spot for his youngest. It was an emotional thing, nothing that would ever challenge Wade's place in the hierarchy. After all, when Georgie had announced that she wanted to run for office, his father's disapproval was quick and loud. When she lost, Roy's response was, "I told you so." When she defied him and declared she was running again, Roy laughed at her. But she won. And won again. Roy wasn't laughing now.

"I appreciate that expression of confidence, Georgie." Wade gave a quick bow of his head and kept his tone affable. "Your political insights are surprisingly shrewd."

"How nice of you to say so." Georgie's smile was as false as his generosity of spirit.

"And, I suppose, if this ingenious plan of yours should happen to work, and Wade is placed on the ballot, *you* would run for Wade's seat."

Georgie shifted her attention to her older sister. Seated directly across from Georgie, Bobbie was Roy's clone: round-faced, brown-eyed, blessed with beautiful skin and great legs, cursed with thin hair and a body that was permanently engaged in the battle of the bulge. She was addicted to labels, Chanel in particular, and was always so perfectly coordinated, she looked as if she had been put together by computer. Tonight, she was awash in red bouclé and pearls.

"Now, I didn't say word one about that, did I?" Georgie, whose extraordinary features had clearly come from her mother's gene pool, long ago had given up trying to be her sister's friend. Blood might be thicker than water, but in this case, Georgie believed envy was thicker than blood. "You know, Roberta Lynn, if you keep fretting over nonsense like that, you're going to ruin that pretty new face-lift of yours."

Bobbie bristled at the accompanying laughter. Georgie's gaze remained fixed.

"You can sling as many arrows as you wish." Bobbie's voice reverberated with anger. "And you can try to convince everyone here that your suggestion was altruistic and well-intended, but I'm not buying it." She drew herself up, tossing her highly teased, frosted blond coif in a gesture of hauteur. "I think it's self-serving and designed simply to further your own agenda."

Georgie's silver blue eyes narrowed. A mocking smile tilted her lips. "And what exactly do you think is number one on that agenda, Bobbie dear?"

"The United States Senate sounds about right."

"That's not a bad idea," Georgie said, granting her sister a condescending nod, "but Daddy's Law of Succession is very clear on that point. Since *you're* older, Branston gets first dibs at the Senate.

"As for me," she said sweetly, turning away and addressing the entire table, "I guess I'll just have to cool my heels in the House until it's my turn . . . to run for president."

"You really shouldn't taunt Bobbie like that," Roy said when dinner was over and the family had dispersed to various rooms in the house. The grandchildren and most of the men had gone to the media room to watch college football. The women had congregated in the living room. Roy and Georgie had headed for the library.

"She's not as sharp as you, Georgina. You took advantage."

"I did no such thing." Georgie sat on the footstool in front of the fireplace and waited for her father to take his customary seat in a nearby armchair. "I made an intelligent suggestion. She challenged my integrity. I don't take that lightly, Daddy."

"Nor should you," Roy agreed.

Georgie turned and warmed her hands, comforted both by the heat of the fire and the security that came from repeated family customs. She and Roy had been having fireside chats ever since she was a little girl. Even on the hottest summer day, if she had a problem, it was discussed, debated, and, usually, solved hearthside.

"You have to give her points for standing up for Branston," Roy said, watching his favorite child carefully. "She's a loyal wife. I like that."

"Yeh. She's a regular Tammy Wynette."

Roy chuckled, reached into a thin wooden box on the table next to him, and stuck a big cigar in his mouth. It had been ten years since he had smoked anything; now and then, he satisfied his craving for tobacco by chewing on a stogie. Without saying a word, Georgie took it out of his mouth and tossed it into the fire. Roy leaned back in his chair and pouted.

"You could learn a thing or two from your sister."

"I already know how to shop."

Roy stifled a laugh. "I just think somewhere along the line you got your priorities mixed up."

"Meaning?"

"Well, if you had been home more, maybe Hunt wouldn't have had his ... uh ... problem. And Lyle wouldn't seem so, well, so discontented."

Georgie made no effort to curb her anger. "You don't know what you're talking about! Hunt's problem, as you so delicately put it, is under control now, thanks to me. Not thanks to you or Lyle. Thanks to me! As for Lyle ..."

"He's a good man, Georgie. Smart as a whip and handsome as a movie star. I see the way the ladies look at him. And I know how lonely he is with you up there in Washington."

"I'm sure he cries himself to sleep every night." *In someone else's bed.*

Georgie's contempt was so swift and so complete, it set

off an alarm in Roy's brain. "Have I missed something? Are you two having problems?" he asked.

Georgie lowered her head, averted her eyes, and laced her fingers together, struggling to suppress her emotions and avoid further confrontation. When, at last, she turned toward her father, her face was as expressionless as a mask. "You don't have to worry about Lyle and me, Daddy. Everything's fine."

"I'm glad to hear that." Roy stroked her arm as if she were a cherished pet. Her muscles were tense, reaffirming his suspicion that something was not right. More than once over the years, Georgie had accused him of preferring Lyle over her. He had denied it, of course, but now he wondered if because she believed that, she was keeping things from him. Things he should know. "If ever there is a problem, I'm here for you."

"I know." She leaned over and kissed his cheek. "I've got to go now." She rose and started for the door.

"I love you, Georgie," Roy said calling after her, hoping she would come back so they could talk some more.

When she didn't, he retreated to his chair by the fire and ran his hand across the top of the footstool. She hadn't been gone more than two minutes and already, he missed her. It had always been like that. Wade was a good son: ambitious and eminently capable. Bobbie was darling in her own way and had made Roy proud by following Bunny's lead and making her way in Dallas society. But Georgie was the one with the spark. She was the unqualified joy of his life.

But, he realized, frowning, she seemed void of joyousness. Thinking back, he realized that sometime when he hadn't been paying attention, a veil of sadness had dulled her gorgeous blue eyes. He had thought it was stress, that she was working too hard and trying to accomplish too much, but tonight, he sensed it went deeper than that. Much deeper.

* * *

Georgie's head was pounding. She and Lyle had been arguing nonstop. Thankfully, the children had opted to stay at their grandparents'.

"I am not going to stand on the floor of the House and humiliate myself by demanding additional tax benefits for your oil-baron buddies."

"I promised that you would."

"That's your problem. You shouldn't have promised anything."

"Why not? You don't have to get it passed, you just have to get your face on C-Span so Jock sees you made the effort. In exchange for a few minutes of bullshit, something you and your colleagues throw around all day long, I'll be able to make an extremely profitable deal for Hughes Oil & Gas."

"I don't care about your deals. I've told you a hundred times, Lyle, don't use me like that. I'm not your mouthpiece."

Lyle glared at her. His lips flattened against his teeth. "Let's see, we rarely have sex, so you're no good as a wife. You're rarely home, so you're no good as a mother. We can't stand each other's company, so you're no good as a confidante. And you don't give a damn about the business that puts food on your table and fancy clothes on your back, so you're no good as an advisor." His face was only inches from hers. She could feel his enmity. "So exactly what the hell are you good for?"

Georgie could pinpoint the precise moment when she had fallen in love with her husband—at Ben and Felicia Knight's wedding when she told him for the first time who her family was and he told her it didn't matter, that he had fallen in love with her, not her family name. She could recall with the same vividness, the precise moment when she had fallen out of love with him—the night she had lost her race for the state legislature and, after giving her concession speech alone on the podium, had found Lyle in their hotel suite putting the make on one of her campaign aides.

"We were consoling each other," he had said unashamedly when she demanded to know what he was doing. "It's disheartening to lose."

"I'm the one who lost," she said. "I'm the one you should be consoling."

"You have a hundred relatives to bolster your shattered ego and put a good face on a wasted effort," he said, coldly.

She had been so crazy about him for so long, that when the bottom fell out of their relationship, it stunned her. Yet while she clung to the belief that seeing him in that hotel room had precipitated her marriage's crash, in truth, it had been sliding downhill since they said "I do."

They had been different from the start. Georgie was open and gregarious and generous of spirit. Lyle always seemed to be holding something back. Georgie gave of herself without a marker. Lyle was a debit and credit man who gauged people by their utility. The one thing they shared had been a need for acceptance: Georgie as an individual separate and apart from her family; Lyle as a peer within the very group Georgie took for granted.

For years, Georgie had closed her eyes to Lyle's flirtations, just as she had learned to close her ears to his abuse. At first, she had told herself it wasn't his fault, that the Hughes family was a formidable bunch—rowdy, outspoken, and highly competitive. Unfortunately, to Lyle, his main competition was his wife.

After he ran for the city council and won, things improved. He finally felt as if he were truly one of them, as if the Hughes political magic had rubbed off on him. Then he decided to run for the state legislature. He lost—badly.

Several years later, Georgie decided to take her chances in the election lottery. Knowing how temperamental he was, she asked Lyle to manage her campaign. *They* lost, but his ego demanded he blame it all on her.

Then she ran for treasurer and won. She wanted to leave him then, but she didn't see how. Politics was the family focus, but Hughes Oil & Gas paid the bills. To those who benefited from his financial skills, Lyle was a very important man. Roy doted on him. Bunny fussed over him. The rest of the family pandered to him. Also, she had been raised on political isms, one of which convinced her that by winning her election she had lost the opportunity to extricate herself from a bad marriage. In politics, the saying went, there was no such thing as a quiet divorce.

Recently, however, Lyle's amorous adventures had grown more frequent and flagrant, and his abuse had become more vicious. Tonight's nasty exchange had pushed her over the top.

"I want a divorce," she said.

"Why would I agree to something as stupid as that?"

"As you just pointed out, we can't stand each other. How's that for a start?"

"Not bad, but quite irrelevant," he said with annoying calm. "I'm very happy with my life in the Big D. I've got a great house, great kids, more money than I can spend in a lifetime, and dozens of good-looking women who'll do anything I ask, anytime I want."

"I'll file without your consent."

Lyle shook his head, appearing far too cocky for Georgie's taste. "I don't think so."

"And why not?"

"Because, my precious, a long time ago, you told me some things you shouldn't have." His eyes hardened. "Don't push me, Georgie. If you do, you'll all be sorry."

Long after he left the room, Georgie trembled from rage and self-recrimination. More than anything else, she wanted to be rid of him. But in the war that was their marriage, she had made the fatal mistake of letting down her guard. She had handed him a weapon that could destroy her.

And, damn him! He had turned it around and aimed it right between her eyes.

☆ DECEMBER ☆

Titus Mitchell, the president of the news division for the National Television Network, took his place at the head of the large conference table. He had gathered his forces from both the Washington and New York bureaus to discuss assignments for the primary cycle. Among the thirty assembled was Dean Walsh, anchor of NTN's highly regarded nightly news show, Clark Aiken, senior political correspondent, Anthea Ogden, who reported on Congress, and Celia Porter, who had been covering the State Department and handling special assignments for NTN ever since she joined them three years before.

Titus opened the meeting. "The good news is we have a clear and unmuddied issue driving this election. The bad news is the public is singularly focused on finding a solution to the hostage crisis. The only way they're going to tune in to presidential politics is if this thing drags on long enough for it to become crucial as to who replaces Haynes.

"Now," he said, surveying his troops, "let's discuss the candidates. As I see it, there are only three men who count: Scottie Edwards on the Republican side, Mack Kenton and Ben Knight for the Democrats."

Clark Aiken shook his head. "I disagree. This crisis is too volatile for the ordinary rules of politics to prevail. The voters are looking for a messiah. Any one of the declared could strike a chord. And if they don't, you can be certain there's someone on the sidelines waiting to jump in."

Anthea Ogden rarely sided with Aiken. This time, she voiced her support. "Ujvagi's well-known in the Rust Belt and has a good rep in the House for common-man issues."

"He'll never get to the show," Dean Walsh said. "I wouldn't even put anyone on him."

Walsh was the nation's number one news anchor. Waspishly handsome, a vision of sartorial elegance, a man capable of conveying insight and intelligence without ever seeming to patronize, he was one of the shrewdest politicians this side of Capitol Hill. In the news business, talent was nothing without opportunity; Walsh had mastered the art of being in the right place at the right time.

"Should we be ignoring Lincoln Sheffield?" Celia Porter asked. "He's been making noises lately about his visions of the presidency."

A unanimous chuckle greeted her comments. Lincoln Sheffield was a former California congressman who had run for the state house in the last gubernatorial elections, spent nearly twenty million dollars of his own money, and lost. He was, in the vernacular, an empty suit: a man with no clearly defined position on any issue. Worse, it was believed that he was in the thrall of his wife, who was an acknowledged member of a strange, New Age cult.

"Well," said Walsh, rolling his eyes, "it's nearly Christmas. Soon he'll be having visions of sugarplum fairies."

Opinions were offered about the other candidates challenging Edwards, but within five minutes, they, too, were dismissed.

Clark Aiken decided to end the discussion. "If I had to place a bet right now, I'd smack my dollar down on *former* secretary of state, *former* ambassador, *forever* the general, Edwards. He is the man! Everyone else is the field."

Suddenly, the room sounded like a sports bar just before

the start of the Super Bowl: odds were given, the strengths and weaknesses of each team were assessed, gut reactions were verbalized, bets were placed. Titus indulged his staff for a bit, then refocused the meeting on the subject at hand: who would cover whom. When Dean Walsh suggested that Celia Porter cover Scottie Edwards, the room went silent as a tomb.

"With all due respect," Clark Aiken said, nodding briefly to Celia, "since it appears as if our private straw poll has declared Edwards the most-likely-to-be-inaugurated, he warrants the most highly regarded reporter on our staff. Anything less could be construed as an insult."

"Also, there are Celia's various . . . connections," Anthea Ogden said, with a disingenuous smile. "Ben Knight is Celia's relative. Zoë Vaughn is a close friend. There are rumors that Wade Hughes is interested in getting on the ticket. His sister, Georgie Hughes, is another bosom buddy." Anthea turned to Celia. "Every closet has its skeletons. Do you really believe you can report on people close to you with an unbiased eye?"

Celia clenched her fists, but her visage remained calm. "I will track any legitimate story to its honest conclusion, whether it's about Ben or Georgie's brother or Zoë Vaughn or anyone else. If it's newsworthy, and it's the truth, I'll go after it no matter where it leads. If it's nothing but gratuitous sleaze, I won't waste my time, the network's money, or the public's patience."

Anthea felt the mood in the room shift. She had misjudged Celia. "You've blown this way out of proportion," she said with what she hoped sounded like honest contrition. "I wasn't questioning your integrity, Celia."

"That's precisely what you were doing, Anthea."

"Look," Titus said, holding up his hands to silence them. "We've been playing in the same sandbox with these guys for so many years, it's impossible for any of us to maintain a true professional distance."

"And really," Walsh enjoined, "what are expense accounts for, if not to court cronyism?" He waited for the laughter to still before continuing. Then, with an expression he usually reserved for human tragedies or issues that went to the core of the nation's soul, he said, "I think we ought to thank Celia for so eloquently reminding us what it is we're supposed to be doing here. She's one hundred percent right. We're journalists reporting the news. If a story's true and relevant, we should tell it. If it's not, we should leave it in the trash heap where it belongs."

Celia cringed and glared at Walsh. This last endorsement was so cloying, it stripped away all cover and revealed Walsh's motives. Edwards was high-visibility. Covering his campaign would provide nightly, on-air auditions for Walsh's job. Aiken and Ogden were seasoned reporters with status and seniority. If they performed well, one or the other might slide into a co-anchor seat. In Walsh's mind, Celia could be on every night without any realistic chance of being elevated to the co-anchor chair. When Titus accommodated his ratings star and awarded Celia the slot, she felt as used and as phony as a carnival shill.

Titus quickly moved on to the posting of reporters to the various Democratic camps. After much discussion, it was decided that because Ben Knight was the only single male running, a man should be assigned

"The last thing we need," Titus said, "is to have one of our women accused of being biased because she was smitten with the candidate or being vengeful because he wasn't smitten with her."

"You're semirelated to Knight, aren't you, Celia?" Walsh asked, still glowing from his triumph.

"His late wife was my cousin."

Walsh nodded. "Is he seeing anyone now?"

"Not that I know of."

"Any female skeletons rattling around in his closet that we should know about?" Titus asked.

"None that I know of," Celia said calmly. *Other than me.*

Their affair had been a long time ago, shortly after Felicia had died, and very brief. Celia had come around frequently to care for the children and to help Ben through his mourning. It seemed quite natural for them to form an attachment, to sublimate their grief in a burst of passion. Celia squirmed in her chair. Even now, she could feel the heat that had passed between them. But the timing had been off. Ben wasn't ready to fall in love, particularly with another member of the Coburn clan.

"What about Mack Kenton?"

Titus surveyed the room, counting angry faces, hoping this campaign would be enough of a horse race to salve their egos and resharpen their edges.

"Over the years, I've heard rumors about trouble in his marriage. In fact, I think he and his wife were separated for a while, but they're together now, so who knows. For all intents and purposes, he seems relatively clean," Anthea Ogden said.

Not exactly, Celia thought, squirming yet again.

"You think he's going to get the donkey's nod?" Titus asked Walsh, who nodded.

"He's viewed as a tough guy with a strong set of principles and a solid reputation in foreign affairs."

"He punted on Vietnam." Aiken's statement came without emotion or judgment.

Celia wasn't certain about the latter, so she set the record straight. "He didn't punt. He was a conscientious objector."

"In lots of households, that's a punt," Aiken said.

Celia shook her head in disagreement. "Kenton's a religious man who had publicly sworn that he could not take another man's life. He brought his case to the proper authorities and was given a pass. Quite frankly, I think that strength of conviction will play very well with the voters."

Anthea Ogden debated whether to join Celia or Aiken. Clear thinking won out. "Celia's right. The public isn't screaming for blood. They just want the hostages set free."

"You interested in reporting his campaign, Anthea?" Titus said.

"Sure. Why not? A conscientious objector with a rumored history of philandering? It beats the hell out of the soaps!'' Her mouth curled upward. ''Besides, we all know there's no such thing as a saint on Capitol Hill.''

''I don't think the identity of Kenton's mistresses past or present will matter,'' Titus said in a tone designed to end debate. ''I'm picking Knight to nab his party's nomination. Clark, how 'bout it?''

''I would have preferred Edwards,'' Aiken said, stating the obvious. ''But I must admit, Knight's campaign sounds interesting. Aside from grabbing Jed Oakes, he's enlisted the services of Zoë Vaughn. Not only does she have an IQ that fries eggs, but the woman is a babe!''

Everyone laughed, except Celia. *Ben and Zoë Vaughn.* Hearing their names together took her back to a time when she had thought they were perfect for each other. She had been as wrong about them as she had been about her own failed romances. Ben had married Felicia. Zoë had devoted herself to a career. As far as Celia knew, they hadn't seen each other in twenty years.

Celia was still ruminating about that when the meeting ended. As she headed for her office, she was stopped by Dean Walsh.

''I have the distinct impression that you're annoyed with me. If I've offended you in any way, I'd like to apologize.''

His eyes fixed on her face. It was the first time he had ever allowed himself to gaze at her without censure. When Celia had first joined the news department, Dean had been so thunderstruck by her beauty that he had gone out of his way to avoid her. Tall, lithe, blond, with soft brown eyes and a smile that warmed rather than sizzled, she telegraphed sensuality with the slightest gesture. It would have been so easy to become involved with her, but office romances tended to be messy, especially when the office was a newsroom.

''You did everything but demand that I cover Scottie Edwards. Why?''

''He's the front-runner,'' he said, his shoulders set in the prideful stance of the misunderstood. ''I thought you'd be grateful.''

"So grateful that I'd be blinded to the real reason behind your generosity."

"Which is?"

"Everyone knows Clark and Anthea are after your job. But instead of allowing them a legitimate crack at an anchor chair, you shoved me in their faces. You think I'm a lightweight in a short skirt and that I can't possibly hurt you."

Dean's expression was one of respectful amusement. "And you think?"

"You'd better watch your ass!"

☆   ☆   ☆

Ethan Siegel sat in the den of his New Jersey home, his eyes glued to Public Broadcasting's *Evening News Report*. A notebook rested on the arm of the couch, a pencil poised and ready in his hand. Tonight's social studies assignment was to watch the segment on the upcoming presidential primaries. Ethan was to choose a candidate and be prepared to defend his choice.

Scottie Edwards's interview was predictable: touting his war record and his tenure as ambassador to the Soviet Union and secretary of state in the previous administration, he implied that no matter what any of the others—from either party—claimed, he alone had the credentials to be president at this critical juncture in America's history. Underlining that point, he had been introduced as—and insisted upon being called—*General* Edwards.

A hard-edged, yet handsome man who wore whatever facial lines he had gained over sixty years as marks of character, he spoke directly into the camera. With his silvered hair, cobalt eyes, and crisp, no-nonsense way of speaking, he exuded an air of authority and decisiveness. Ethan thought he came across well and found his résumé quite compelling. His mother, Kate, agreed that he was extremely well qualified, but she cautioned Ethan to hear everyone out before he settled on a candidate.

She would have liked to tell her son about the way General Prescott Edwards had mistreated her friend, Zoë Vaughn, and how irresponsibly he'd acted, but venting his mother's anger and frustration was not part of his homework assignment.

Mack Kenton's appearance was almost jarring in comparison to the General's. Younger, his dark hair sparingly flecked with gray, he had onyx eyes which seemed almost too focused and a reluctant smile that never spread wide enough to show any teeth. He also came across as tough, but there was an edge to him that made Ethan uncomfortable.

Kenton listed his legislative accomplishments and committee posts in the House, embellished them as much as he dared, and then, despite the fact that they were from opposing parties and wouldn't be facing each other in the primaries, he went to great lengths to remind the voters that unlike Edwards, he had a constituency. He understood what the public wanted because he was their servant and accountable to them, not an appointee who served at the pleasure of the president.

As Kate explained, Kenton's strategy was to show the public that he should win the Democratic primaries because he was the one who could beat Scottie Edwards in the election.

Congressman Tom Ujvagi from Ohio and Governor Harrison Wilcox of Wyoming were next. Each cited his history as a public servant and reiterated his desire to find a solution to the terrible hostage crisis that had crippled Elton Haynes. Both presented themselves well, but Ethan didn't think either had said anything that would convince him to sign on to their campaigns.

Suddenly, Ben Knight's image filled the TV screen.

"Your announcement took many of your colleagues by surprise, Senator. Many of those we spoke to had been unaware that you harbored presidential ambitions."

Ben's pose was relaxed, but his eyes telegraphed an inner tension that had nothing to do with nerves and everything to do with passion.

"My decision to run for the presidency is not a matter of ambition. It's a matter of conscience. My children's mother was taken from them in a brutal act of vehicular violence. When I was eight years old, my father and brother were victims of a senseless, random act of violence."

Ben's brow furrowed as old memories surfaced. "I know what it is to have a loved one stolen from your life," he said, his voice rumbling. "I know what it is to live with a dark hole in your heart that can never heal. I know what it is to want justice."

Without taking his eyes from the screen, Ethan's hand found Kate's. Silently, they held on to each other.

"These recent kidnappings are not random acts. They were well planned and carefully executed by a group of terrorists who wanted to extract as much pain and anguish as possible. I don't care what their grudge is, what their cause is, or what their ultimate goal is. Innocent people have been taken hostage. It's not only unjust, it's unforgivable!"

"United States policy dictates that we don't negotiate with terrorists," the moderator said.

Ben's jaw tightened. "I know what our country's policy is, but it was framed with the belief that even terrorists abide by certain rules of war. By savagely plucking children and nurses from schools and hospitals, Red Rage has changed the rules."

"Are you saying that the United States should formulate a new policy?"

"What I'm saying is that we certainly should consider trying ways other than negotiation to deal with these matters."

"That sounds like rather harsh criticism of President Haynes."

Ben's answer was sharp. "The president is doing the best he can given the circumstances."

"Do you think his best is good enough to bring about a successful resolution?"

"That's a question no one should be asked at the present

time. We don't know what's going on behind the scenes. To insinuate oneself into the process would be selfish and extremely dangerous. At this point, all anyone can do is pray that President Haynes's efforts are successful."

Kate's eyes were glassy with restrained tears, but she nodded in fierce agreement.

"If I was old enough to vote, he'd be my choice," Ethan said quietly.

"Smart boy," Kate said, forcing herself to shake her dark clouds away.

"You should get involved in his campaign," he said to his mother, his eyes bright with the excitement of a brainstorm.

"I would love to, honey, but I can't."

"Why not? Senator Ben's been a good friend."

Kate nodded. "I know, but we have legislation pending, and we need people from both parties to vote for it. If it looks as if we're on his side, the other side might not vote the way we want."

"That's not fair," Ethan said. "Our bill has nothing to do with this election."

Kate ruffled her son's hair and smiled. At twelve, he was still young enough to be called cute, but all the signs pointed to his becoming a heartbreakingly handsome man. He had his father's dark hair, hooded brown eyes, and trim physique. The full mouth, oval face, and straight, narrow nose were clearly Kate's.

Appearances aside, Ethan was his father's son: creative, enlivened by a quick sense of humor and a quirky logic. With Mira, his older sister, the opposite had been true. She had looked like Rick, but her personality had marked her as her mother's clone.

"When it comes to politics," Kate said, refusing to give in to the sudden wave of grief that threatened to drown her, "everything has something to do with everything else."

Ethan scribbled in his notebook. His face described an internal debate. "If Senator Ben's campaign is based on the idea of keeping children safe," he said, his voice strained, making Kate think he was fighting the same wave, "then maybe he should also talk about the bad things that happen to children here in the United States."

At first, Kate felt as if she had been punched in the heart. Not only couldn't she breathe, but the pain that gripped her was sharp and fierce. It abated, but in its place was the fizz of an exciting notion.

"You know," she said, "that's a pretty good idea."

"Actually," Ethan said, slyly, "I thought it leaned on the brilliant side."

"Okay." Kate laughed. "A brilliant idea."

"Much better."

Kate marveled at how kind and compassionate he was, and how surprisingly healthy, considering what they had lived through.

"Besides," Ethan said, looking at her as if he couldn't believe he had to be telling her this, "you went to law school with a guy who's about to run for president of the United States. How can you not help him out?"

She took her son's grinning face in her hands and kissed him.

"How can I not, indeed," she said.

Kate Wolff had met Ben Knight her first day at Yale. They were seated next to each other at an orientation lecture. While waiting for it to begin, they chatted about where they were from, where they had gone to college, and what kind of law they wanted to practice. When Kate said she had graduated from the University of Pennsylvania, Ben's response was instantaneous.

"Philadelphia's the best!" he boasted.

"It's nice," Kate conceded, "but compared to New York, I'd say it's a seven."

"You live in New Jersey," Ben grumbled. "You have no say."

"Teaneck is *maybe* thirty minutes from midtown and the

last time I looked, Manayunk wasn't exactly around the corner from Rittenhouse Square!"

Ben surrendered, but for the next three years, the two of them debated everything from the potential health dangers inherent in a Philadelphia cheesesteak to Supreme Court rulings. They even debated nonsense like whose mother was more overbearing and whether it was harder to be an only daughter or an only son.

By the time graduation night rolled around, however, there was little debate about how they felt about each other.

"I want us to stay in touch," Ben said as the two friends embraced.

"We will," Kate assured him.

"Good, because odds are you're going to do some really incredible things. I simply want to be assured that I'll be invited to share in each of those magnificent moments."

Kate nodded and smiled. "Only if you promise to do the same for me."

Ben held up two fingers, Boy Scout style. "On my honor."

Over the years they did share many moments in each other's lives, but not all of them were magnificent.

Kate was in Atlanta when Ben buried his wife. And Ben was in New Jersey when Kate buried her daughter.

The nightmare began when Mira was eleven. It was a warm Saturday in October, the kind of Indian summer afternoon poets like to rhapsodize about. Kate had taken Ethan shopping. Mira and several of her friends were playing in the backyard. Rick was in the den, working on a script for another television show he hoped to pitch.

Rick Siegel was an award-winning advertising copywriter. He was a partner in one of the more successful agencies on Madison Avenue and had won his share of awards, but for Rick, it wasn't enough. Those who envied his success didn't understand his frustration. His admirers claimed he simply overflowed with talent. Kate felt it was more to the point to say that the problem was his cup wasn't large enough. Rick's dream had always been to write for television. Over the years, with Kate's encouragement, he had penned several pilots, all of which had been rejected. But neither Kate nor Rick was the kind who gave up easily.

That afternoon, before Kate left, she cautioned Rick to keep an eye on Mira. She had been born with a heart defect, and while surgery had repaired the problem several years before, Kate couldn't break her habit of worrying. For a while, Rick kept half an eye on Mira and her friends. Eventually, his concentration shifted to his project so completely that when the telephone rang, he practically jumped out of his chair. It was Mel Dobson, his agent, calling to say that NBC had optioned the sitcom they had submitted.

"Are you serious?"

"No," Mel said. "I make these calls because I'm a sadistic bastard who likes to get a rise out of my clients. Of course I'm serious!"

"Do we have a commitment to air? Who's going to produce? Do I have to go to L.A.?"

Rick was trying to listen to what Mel was saying, but the window was open and the high-pitched laughter of preadolescent girls at play was creating too much background buzz. He had been able to tune it out before, but for some reason, he couldn't manage it now. Maybe it was the excitement or his sudden case of nerves. Rick was about to close the window when the laughter stopped. It was so immediate and so definite that the silence sounded louder than the noise had been.

Rick looked out the window. One of Mira's friends was racing toward the house. She looked terrified. He dropped the phone and ran outside.

"Someone took Mira," she yelled to him as he bounded onto the deck. "A man. He just came out of nowhere and grabbed her and pulled her into the woods."

Rick's heart stopped. His eyes searched the wooded area

that bordered his property. As Mira's friends shouted their versions of what had happened, Rick took off, plunging into the thickly treed copse.

"Call 911!" he yelled as he headed farther into the woods.

An hour and a half later, he was back in the house, being interviewed by the police. They had caught up with him and, after assuring him that search parties were canvassing the area, brought him home. An APB had been ordered. Police stations in surrounding towns had been alerted. Dogs and helicopters were out. At the house, two female officers were taking the statements of Mira's friends and trying to allay their fears.

The police had located Kate and Ethan and brought them home. When they walked into the den, they found Rick sitting in a chair, holding one of Mira's sneakers. His eyes were dead.

"She's gone," he whispered.

It took six months to find Mira's body, two months more to find her killer: a parolee, previously convicted on several counts of child molestation. Three days before he kidnapped, raped, and murdered Kate and Rick Siegel's eleven-year-old daughter, he had been let out of prison for good behavior.

Throughout the long hunt, Kate buried her grief beneath a wall of rage which she channeled into a rush of activity designed to find her daughter. She organized search groups, sent out flyers with Mira's picture, and badgered the press daily to cover the story.

Outwardly, Rick was by her side. He trained searchers, used his sources to print flyers and tack up posters with Mira's picture, visited radio stations and press rooms, produced a televised appeal, even marched outside government offices trying to attract attention to their plight. Inwardly, however, he was swimming alone, sinking deeper into a pit of depression born of unremitting guilt. He had been home. If he had been looking out the window, if he hadn't been on the phone, if he had listened harder, if he had paid closer attention, if . . . if . . . if . . .

When the trial was over and the judge imposed sentence—life in prison with no parole—Kate's rage became uncontrollable. For a long time, emotion continued to spill out of her, always intense, always furious, always incapable of resolution. How did one resolve the fact that her daughter had been stolen from her, violated, and then murdered?

Rick retreated even farther into his own purgatory. At work, he became a body, a nonfunctioning physical presence, unable to create or advise or administer. At home, he was impenetrable. He spoke, but said little. He listened, but was rarely engaged. He spent time with his wife and his son, but remained distant and detached.

Months went by. Letters began to arrive at the house from other mothers whose children had been hurt by men let out of prison too soon, men who had been allowed to settle in ordinary neighborhoods, like ordinary citizens. At first, Kate refused to look at the letters. Then, she took them to the therapist who was helping her deal with her grief. The therapist suggested that Kate read a few of them.

"You're not alone, Kate. You need to know that. You need to share your pain with people who truly understand. And only those who've walked in your shoes can do that."

Slowly, cautiously, she began to dip into the dark communal pool of parental grief.

Indeed, there were other cases like Mira's, other parents whose hearts had been rent from their chests by someone who had been granted parole only to molest or kidnap or murder again, other people whose mates or siblings or parents had been harmed by those let go too soon.

On the day the family gathered at the cemetery to unveil Mira's tombstone, Kate decided to channel her negative energy into something positive. With that in mind, she founded a grassroots network of women like herself—NOMORE!—the National Organization of Mothers against Offenders being Released Early.

Rick was supportive and enthusiastic. He created ads—a large hand reaching through jail bars to grab a child, with a red X and the words, NOMORE! PAROLE—and lobbied his industry to donate free advertising space to the cause. He arranged to have ads on subway trains and at bus stops in major cities throughout the country. He printed up thousands of buttons and designed a white ribbon—symbolizing the innocence of the victims—with a red teardrop—symbolizing both the blood of the victims and the tears of the survivors—to be worn by sympathizers. He joined Kate on the podium at fund-raising dinners and spoke eloquently about the need for a public outcry on this issue. At home, he remained sullen and aloof.

Kate, on the other hand, was completely energized by the process. She spoke to her friend Celia Porter about covering the story for NTN. Celia's response was an incredibly moving series on crimes committed by parolees, particularly against children.

Then, Kate went to her friend, Senator Benjamin Knight, and asked him to propose legislation that would eliminate parole for those who committed crimes against children. Unwilling to leave anything to chance, she cornered her other friend, Congresswoman Georgie Hughes, and convinced her to raise the issue in the House of Representatives. Then she began her crusade to get each state to pass its own laws prohibiting parole for sexual offenders.

It had been four years since Mira's murder. Three years since the NOMORE! PAROLE bill had been proposed in Congress. Two years since New Jersey had passed the first NOMORE! PAROLE bill in the nation. And two years since Rick had moved to California.

When he told Kate he was leaving, she let him go. But she didn't let him off.

Ronnie Kramer was Kate's best friend. She also happened to be Rick's older sister. When they first met, Kate had heard so many horror tales about rivalries erupting between girlfriends and sisters that she had feared the worst. But Ronnie wasn't one of those women who had trouble sharing her brother's affection. To her, it was simple: if Rick loved you, she loved you.

Ronnie was with Kate during the search for Mira, the subsequent trial, and at every one of Kate's speaking engagements for NOMORE! After Rick left, she was on the phone and at Kate's house almost continuously. Which was why when Ronnie called and asked Kate to attend a meeting of the New Jersey "Knight for President" group, Kate had a hard time turning her down.

"I can't be affiliated with a particular candidate, Ronnie. As much as I'd like to help Ben, federal passage of Mira's law comes first."

"With me, too," Ronnie said, quietly.

"I'm sorry. I wasn't questioning that."

"I know." Ronnie took a moment to gather her thoughts. This was a difficult argument to frame. "Kate, I would never ask you to compromise your position. This legislation means a lot to all of us. I want every state in this country to pass our law. I want Ben Knight elected president and so do you. This is a way to accomplish both."

"Let me think about it," Kate said.

Kate had intended to drive to the meeting with Ronnie, but just as she was about to leave, the doorbell rang. She looked through the peephole and smiled. Only one person had hair like that.

"Zoë!" she said as she flung open the door and hugged her friend. "What are you doing here?"

"I had some meetings in New York and decided to bunk here overnight so we could catch up. Is that okay?"

"Okay? That's fabulous!" Kate and Zoë didn't get to see each other as often as they'd like, so they grabbed any chance they had to spend time together. "Have you eaten? I've got some stew left over from dinner I could heat up. Or some pasta."

Zoë laughed. "Do not Jewish mother me. I swear. I've eaten." She crossed her heart. "Besides, I don't want to be late for the 'Knight for President' meeting," Zoë said slyly.

Kate narrowed her eyes and turned slowly. Ethan was grinning at her. She looked back at Zoë, who shrugged innocently.

"I sense a conspiracy," Kate said to her son.

"Aunt Zoë called this afternoon and, well, we got to talking, she said she was going to be in New York and so . . ."

"I don't see that I have much choice."

Zoë and Ethan gave each other high fives. "You don't!"

It broke Zoë's heart to watch Kate's pre-exit routine: setting various security devices, notifying the police that she was leaving the house, checking the batteries on her beeper, going over various phone numbers with the young cadet from the police academy who served as Ethan's baby-sitter. In the car, they talked about the need for such precautions and how Ethan felt about being guarded.

"He hates it. I hate it. But it is what it is."

They talked about Rick. Kate told Zoë about his various sitcom successes.

"Have you given any thought to getting back into law?" Zoë asked.

Kate's senior year in law school, she had been recruited by every one of New York's legal giants. When she joined Cooper, Lang, Wilson & Rose, she was looked on as a comer. By the time she married Rick, her feet were firmly planted on the fast track within the litigation department. But when Mira was born with a heart defect, Kate quit her job to stay home and take care of her. Having discussed this before, Zoë knew Kate never regretted a moment spent with her children. Still, she had to believe that every now and then, Kate experienced a rush of might-have-beens.

"Maybe when this legislative process is over."

"You've done an incredible job with NOMORE!" Zoë said, noting the emotion on Kate's face.

"Rick thinks it's a grief-substitute. He believes I allowed

it to take over my life so completely that I left no room for anything else. Including him."

"Does he have a point?"

Kate took a deep breath. It was minutes before she answered. "Maybe."

When Kate and Zoë pushed open the door and stepped inside the large conference room, heads turned. Conversation halted. Kate felt as if she had stepped into the beam of a gigantic spotlight. Ronnie greeted Zoë, who suddenly disappeared into the crowd, kissed Kate, and squeezed her hand. From the far end of a large wooden table, a stocky man with thick eyebrows and black eyes smiled.

"Our special guests have arrived," he said, his voice colored with a Mediterranean accent. "Welcome."

Ronnie had told Kate all about him. His name was Milo Kyriakos and he was head of fund-raising in New Jersey for the Knight campaign. The child of Greek immigrants who owned a diner in Newark, he was a partner in a prestigious law firm, a Democratic loyalist, and a passionate patriot.

Milo motioned for Kate to take the seat that had been saved for her between him and Ronnie. Zoë was already seated on his left.

"Everyone. This," he said, smiling at Zoë, "is Zoë Vaughn, an acknowledged expert on the former Soviet Union and Senator Knight's foreign policy advisor. This," he said, turning to his other side, "is Kate Siegel, the founder and president of NOMORE!, the group that's fighting to eliminate parole for those who commit crimes against children. Also, she has the double distinction of being Ronnie Kramer's sister-in-law and a law school classmate of Ben Knight. Let's welcome Zoë and Kate with a round of applause."

Kate smiled, feeling like a kindergarten student who had just recited the Pledge of Allegiance without a mistake.

"I consider it a special privilege to have Ms. Vaughn

here this evening," Milo said. "She's graciously agreed to brief us on the hostage crisis and what part it plays in the campaign."

Kate watched as Zoë rose and effortlessly explained who Yegor Durgunov was, what Red Rage was all about, why she believed they had taken hostages, and what it all meant for the security of the United States. The depth of Zoë's knowledge and her ability to disseminate it in easy-to-understand terms was impressive. When Zoë finished, Kate joined in the applause. When it stopped and Milo turned to her, she was caught completely off guard.

"Why don't you tell us why you've joined us here tonight, Kate."

Kate flushed. Ronnie nudged her to her feet. At first, she was flustered. A quick perusal of the group, however, showed them to be friendly and interested. A nod from Zoë and she began.

"Four years ago, my eleven-year-old daughter was kidnapped, sexually molested, and murdered. Losing a child to such heinous crimes has determined the way I conduct my life. It selects the charities I contribute to or raise money for. It decides how I spend my time and with whom. And it defines my politics.

"Though it may take a different turn between now and November, this election seems to be about crisis. Who is best equipped to deal with it. Who might be able to resolve it. And whom we should trust in the future with other crises that might affect the lives of our children.

"Benjamin Knight has been my friend for over twenty years. When my daughter was killed, he was there for me and my family. When I asked him to help me try and change the laws to protect other little girls like my Mira, he authored legislation now making its way through Congress and has promised me he won't stop working on it until it's passed.

"Sadly, the way our political system works, I'm not in a position to endorse any candidate. If I do, I risk compromising the credibility of my organization. What I can do is suggest that when New Jersey hosts an event for Senator Knight they remind him that this state has passed a bill prohibiting parole for those who endanger the lives of children. I can suggest that when Senator Knight voices his anger about the children who have been taken hostage overseas, he voice his outrage about the dangers facing children here at home.

"There are chapters of NOMORE! in almost every state. Senator Knight won't find a more receptive group for his message. Nor will he find a greater source of inspiration. I suggest he talk to these families, hear what they have to say and what they think we should do. And then, I would urge him to use his oratorical skills to raise the nation's consciousness about the consequences of carelessness and complacency.

"Keeping our children safe should not be a political issue, but owing to the actions of a heartless band of terrorists, it is. All I ask, is that while we pray for the release of those who are in prisons abroad, we don't forget about those we've lost at home."

The applause was spontaneous and thunderous. Several people shouted at her, begging her to chair a fund-raiser, to join their committee, to somehow lend her name to their efforts.

Kate hated to quell their enthusiasm, but she had her priorities.

"Over the next several months, I'm expected to appear before the Congressional committee reviewing this bill. I can't be accused of having any political bias. I hope you understand."

Kate took her seat, and the room went still. Beneath the table, Ronnie reached for Kate's hand. When Milo spoke, he was uncharacteristically muted.

"Of course we understand. Not only are we grateful that you came here tonight, but also that you had the courage to found an organization like NOMORE! You're a credit to all of us. You're a great American, Kate Siegel," he said.

Later, in the parking lot, Kate put the key in the ignition and then froze. Zoë's hand covered Kate's.

"I know how tough this was for you," Zoë said. "But you did a good thing."

Kate shook her head, her eyes glossy and fixed on the windshield. "I feel like a fraud. It didn't take courage to found NOMORE! It was an organization born of desperation and fear and uncontrollable rage. I'm not a hero. I'm not a great American. I'm just a woman . . ."

". . . looking to fill a void."

Kate's breath caught in her throat as Zoë so astutely completed her thought.

"I know," Zoë whispered. "Because I've been there."

THE
PRIMARIES

☆

☆ JANUARY ☆

It was early, but already New Hampshire was having a rough winter. It had snowed every two days since Christmas, making travel difficult. Nonetheless, politicians crisscrossed the state, barnstorming from Keene to Concord, Nashua to Lancaster, Ossipee to Hanover. The first major primary of the election cycle was only a month away.

Zoë waited for Jed Oakes in a corner of the small airfield at Laconia, sipping a cup of hot coffee, going over her notes and reviewing their schedule, which was bruising. It had been only two months since she had agreed to join Ben's campaign. It felt like two years.

Once Zoë had come on board, the campaign team was complete. Jed and Ben had already filled the other top slots. Hal Kingsley had decided to leave the president and do the polling. Ernie Dibbs took charge of setting up field operations in all fifty states. Chad Jaffy was going to head the press detail, Tom Hall fund-raising, and Sarah Jenks scheduling. Zoë's contribution, other than organizing the foreign policy squad, was to set up a national recruiting network that would sign on every able-bodied college student willing to go door-to-door or man telephone banks or set up campaign posts or arrange rallies or do the tedious grunt work involved in grassroots politics. She had it up and working in two weeks, which was a good thing, because as she had suspected, when she told her superiors at Hightower that she was consulting with the Knight campaign, they had screamed CONFLICT and let her go. Ben's campaign suddenly had become her only job. And her only hope.

While each of the candidates and their staffs had been to New Hampshire many times over the past several months—some had been "testing the waters" for more than a year—this was Zoë's first official trip. Though she didn't have to be here, these first few weeks were vital. The primaries, which used to be spaced over a span of time stretching from February to June, had been compressed. According to the new schedule, it was possible for candidates from both parties to be determined by April. Which was why a win here was so important. Not only would it validate Ben's candidacy, but it could set up some valuable momentum that might bring more money into the coffers. Unfortunately, the polls favored Mack Kenton.

"And who do we have here?"

Zoë looked up and into the piercing blue eyes of Scottie Edwards. He was standing over her with his arms crossed, his posture at-attention straight. Accompanied by the ubiquitous Arlo Reid and surrounded by a fawning entourage, he looked every bit the general he still believed he was.

"Why it's Ben Knight's foreign policy advisor," he said to anyone who cared to listen. "Zoë Vaughn. How good to see you again."

He proffered his hand and smiled. Zoë, cynically searching for the cameraman she assumed was recording this meeting, acknowledged him with a benign nod, but neglected to put down her notes or her coffee cup so that she might accept his handshake. Edwards reacted to the obvious snub with an instant change of expression. Gone was the political smile; replacing it was a scowl of annoyance.

"You still haven't learned," he said, his voice lowered so that only she could hear. "In government work, chronic insubordination is unacceptable."

"In case you've forgotten," she said, rising to meet his steely gaze, "I no longer work for the government."

"And the nation sleeps better at night because of it."

"As for unacceptable behavior in government officials," she continued, ignoring his snipe, "I'd say ego-driven intractability is the worst."

"That kind of talk is irresponsible."

"It may be impertinent," Zoë corrected, refusing to back off, "but I am not now and was not then, irresponsible. You were."

"You're in no position to judge me," Edwards snapped, sorry he had engaged her in the first place.

"I wasn't judging you then. I was performing the function of my office which meant advising you of a potentially serious situation. Unfortunately, my advice didn't coincide with your personal agenda, so you chose to disregard it."

He glowered at her, his expression one of barely controlled aggression. Had they been alone, Zoë truly believed he might have slapped her.

"Now let me give you some advice," he snarled. "Go home to Boston, find yourself some nice young man, and settle down. Get out of politics."

"And why would I want to do that?"

"Because you don't have the instincts for the game or the stomach for the fight."

A malevolent smirk licked his lips. Zoë's eyebrow arched, but she resisted his invitation to step inside his ring.

"You surrounded yourself with a misguided, ineffectual staff in Moscow. You aligned yourself with the wrong people at Hightower. And now you've hitched your badly tarnished star to a losing campaign."

Zoë was thunderstruck. In a display of astounding audacity, he had looked her in the eye and crowed about his hand in the destruction of her embassy staff and her firing from Hightower. It took all Zoë's restraint not to exhibit so much as a hint of anger.

"Once again, General," she said, with casual condescension, "we seem to have a difference of opinion. The Senator's campaign is a winner and do you know why? Because the more the people get to know him, the better they're going to like him. I doubt the same will hold true for you."

"I'm confident of a victory in New Hampshire," he brayed, letting his voice rise, hoping the group behind them would think this discussion had been about the primary rather than the past.

"Oh, you'll win the race here," Zoë said. "And I'm sure you'll carry your party's nomination. But I wonder how the voters will feel in November after the press and the opposition have had a go at you and the rank and file discover that you refused to heed well-grounded warnings about how weak Borofsky was and how dangerous Yegor Durgunov was. How will they feel when it becomes obvious that if your judgment hadn't been blinded by your ambition, there might not have been any hostage takings?"

He leaned forward, his jaw tight, his eyes blazing with unmistakable menace. "Don't do anything you'll regret, Miss Vaughn."

"I don't have any regrets," Zoë said pointedly. "Do you?"

Instead of answering, Edwards turned on his heel and, with Arlo Reid at his side, strode toward the door leading to the tarmac where his chartered plane was waiting to take him to a rally in Keene. As his aides and the press corps trailed after him, Zoë wrestled with her rage.

She was speeding down a dead-end path of ill wishes and petty vengeances when she was sidetracked by a familiar face. "Celia!"

The instant she heard Zoë's voice, Celia's face broke into a grin. "Hey! Fancy meeting you here!" She returned Zoë's embrace, but only briefly.

"It's a small world," Zoë said.

"Is there anyplace *smaller* than New Hampshire during a

presidential campaign?'' Celia chuckled, but she appeared distracted.

Zoë waved her hand in front of Celia's face, commanding her attention. "Did you get contact lenses since the last time I saw you or are your eyes twitching for some other reason?"

"I know I'm acting like a jerk," Celia said, finally looking straight at Zoë, "but if His Lordship sees me conspiring with the enemy, he won't grant me an interview until well into his second term."

"God forbid," Zoë mumbled, her utter loathing of the General more than obvious. "Actually, I find it hard to believe you're not Edwards's campaign poster girl. With your looks, I would've expected him to have you glued to his side."

"Hardly." Celia rolled her eyes with exasperation. "I'm so far down in the pecking order, I'm not even within viewing distance of the fringe."

Zoë's glance wandered out onto the tarmac, where Scottie Edwards was boarding his plane. It bothered her that so much of a candidate's personality could be hidden from the public, but campaigning was more staging than anything else. What the public saw was what the strategists wanted them to see—a handcrafted, poll-dictated visual reality that didn't necessarily have anything to do with truth.

"Are you the only woman on his press detail?" Zoë asked.

"The one and," Celia said. "There are loads of women on the trail, but they must have had more juice with their brass than I did. They're covering candidates who want news coverage and are willing to cooperate. I've nabbed a guy who thinks he's entitled to the front page, yet treats me as if PMS is catching!"

Zoë laughed, but there was an acrid overtone to it. She knew exactly what Celia was talking about. She had been there.

"His problem is not with women who act like *women* and

fawn all over him," she said. "It's with women who present themselves as *professionals* and have the nerve to expect an appropriate level of respect."

Celia scrunched her nose in distaste. "Where was he when everyone else's consciousness was being raised?"

"Earning his star in Vietnam."

"Ah, yes. Forgive me," Celia said, bowing her head in mock reverence. "How could I have forgotten that while we were at home burning our bras, he was slogging through rice paddies and guerilla-infested jungles singlehandedly saving us from the Yellow Peril?"

She licked the tip of her index finger and mimed flipping through a book. "Page twenty-six of General Prescott Edwards's gripping biography, *A Grateful Nation.*"

Zoë smiled. To her, Edwards's self-aggrandizing bio had read like a six-hundred-page pat on the back. When it didn't make the best-seller list she secretly congratulated the American public.

"Ah, yes. According to that memorable tome, if the Pentagon had let him have his way, we would have won that war. Still," Zoë said, her face becoming a portrait of solemnity, "he did a hell of a job."

Celia, aping Zoë's serious mien, nodded in accord. "It was a truly remarkable effort . . ."

". . . for a man who rarely left his desk," Zoë said, finishing the thought.

The two women laughed, enjoying their moment of conspiracy. Suddenly Celia looked uncomfortable.

"I wish I were covering Ben's campaign," she said. "Then maybe you and I could have spent some time together. It's been a while."

"That it has," Zoë said, mindful of the ups and downs of their friendship.

"Besides, I don't like feeling as if we're in opposite camps." She paused, gauging Zoë's reaction. "I never have."

Zoë sighed, amazed at how some situations never really

resolved themselves. "It's been years, Celia. I've forgiven you for introducing Ben to Felicia. Honest, I have."

Celia smiled, yet her unease remained visible. "You may have forgiven me, but you don't trust me. Not completely."

Before Zoë could answer, they were interrupted by someone yelling for Celia. "The bird's about to fly!"

Celia looked torn. Zoë squeezed her arm.

"I love you, Celia. I always have. And I probably always will."

"I'm not sure I deserve you."

Zoë pondered that for a second. "You don't, but I've applied for sainthood, and you're my eternal good deed."

"Bless you." Celia laughed and gave Zoë a quick hug.

As Zoë watched Celia run to the plane, she marveled at her. Even in layers of sweaters, a bulky coat, clunky boots, and a woolen newsboy cap, the woman was breathtakingly beautiful. How ironic, Zoë thought. Celia had spent half her life trading off her looks and the next half fighting them.

As she watched the plane lift off, Zoë's thoughts remained grounded and heavy. While her surprise meeting with Celia had poked at a few unpleasant memories, her run-in with Edwards had proved positively unnerving. She tried to restore her normal pluck, but it was hard being brave and resilient when just moments before, the man wearing the boot that had crushed her had made his intentions quite clear: instead of allowing her to crawl out from under his heel, he intended to grind her deeper and deeper into the dirt.

☆   ☆   ☆

The airplane had barely leveled off when Edwards's press secretary wandered into the rear of the cabin hoping to get their opinions on how his man had done at the last stop and, in case they had missed it, to reiterate the message of the day. When he came to Celia's row, he stood over her like a disapproving parent, and in a voice certain to attract attention, proceeded to dress her down.

"In the future, it would be appreciated, Miss Porter, if you could make more of an effort to stick to the schedule. This is a presidential campaign, after all, not a kaffeeklatch."

For a very long minute, Celia said nothing, but his insinuation that taking two minutes to talk with an old friend was in some way unprofessional truly grated. Although every nerve cell in her body longed to scratch his eyes out, she refused to give him more grist for his mill. Instead, she leaned back in her seat, folded her arms across her chest, and looked at him quizzically.

"And what makes you think I didn't know that?" she asked.

"Everyone had boarded, and you were still dallying in the lounge."

"If I was dallying," Celia said, oozing innocence, "what was Quinn doing?" She pointed to a reporter from a rival network who had been talking to Jed Oakes while she was chatting with Zoë and had boarded well after her. "Dillying?"

"And a good job of it I did," Sean Quinn said in his best faux-Irish brogue, bounding out of his seat, leaning on the back of the one in front of him and clearly enjoying the moment. "Nothing I like better than a good dilly before plane time."

"You should try it some time," said the man from NPR to the suddenly beleagured aide.

Raucous laughter erupted all around, prompting the red-faced man to make an immediate retreat. Celia stood and blew kisses to her supporters. "Thanks, guys. I owe you."

"Awright!" someone shouted.

"When can we collect?" someone else said with a leer.

Celia rolled her eyes. "It was only a figure of speech."

A loud groan resounded throughout the cabin. When Celia took her seat, Quinn sat down beside her.

"I'll tell you my scoop, if you tell me yours," he said, leaning toward her with a lascivious grin on his face.

"Rocky road," she said, without looking at him.

He chose to ignore her dismissal—precisely because she had been ignoring him ever since they had taken off on this trip.

"I take it from the icy tone you're still mad at me."

Celia took out her *New York Times* and opened it as wide as she could, creating a barrier.

"I just saved you from a spanking. Don't I win a few points for that?"

Celia made a project out of turning a page, rustling the paper, snapping it in his face, and reestablishing the barrier, behind which Quinn was grinning. Celia was not.

"Okay, I stepped on your toes. I'm sorry, but hey! It's the business, Celia."

Celia crushed the paper in her lap and glared at Quinn. "The *business* is to gather information, verify it, and then, if it's accurate, print it with a modicum of integrity. It is not to *steal* information someone else has gathered and print it without regard to consequences."

He started to protest. Celia held up her hand.

"State wasn't ready to reveal those murders in Kabul, Quinn. They needed time to make sure the covers of the victims were solid. I had given my word that I would wait. You tricked me into giving you the story and ran with it. Not only did you make my name mud at the department, but you put people's lives in danger. Is *that* the business we're in?"

Honest chagrin defined Quinn's face. "I was being flip before, and I shouldn't have. What I did was totally irresponsible."

"To say the least!"

"I was too eager for the grab."

Celia responded with an emphatic, slightly imperious nod. He knew she was right and he was wrong, and he was more than willing to grant Celia a grovel, but no one was a virgin when it came to headline grabbing.

"I said I was sorry."

"Fine! Now will you please leave me alone?"

"Well," he said, chuckling, "since you put it so nicely . . ."

After Quinn returned to his seat, Celia tried to work, but she found herself hopelessly distracted. What was it about him that nettled her so? she wondered. He was certainly talented. He had done several incredible series, including one on poverty in America as seen through the eyes of children. She recalled that several of those reports had made her weep. She couldn't fault him for lack of courage, either. He didn't have to volunteer to go to the Gulf or to Sarajevo, yet he had, and his pieces had been brilliant. And while she couldn't excuse his lack of ethics, nor ignore the occasional rumors about him usurping sources, there wasn't anyone in the business, including Celia, who didn't know how difficult it was to balance one's conscience with one's ambition.

Celia watched as he stood in the aisle and exchanged quips with others in the corps. Quinn was an intriguing jumble of humor, intellect, compassion, and ego bundled into an immensely appealing package. But Celia already had more than her share of unpleasant experiences at the hands of men who talked the talk, and then walked away.

She was not going to get burned again.

☆   ☆   ☆

Ben Knight rested his elbows on his knees, his body pitched forward so he could hear what Ethel Crookshank was saying. The gray-haired, bespectacled septuagenarian looked particularly frail in her worn cardigan sweater and a tweed skirt that had seen her through many a winter. She was trying to maintain her composure, but it was difficult. Ben had come to speak to Ethel and Rob about their grandaughter Molly, one of the children who had been taken from her classroom in Ankara and was being held by the terrorists.

"My son, Rob Junior, is a pilot," Ethel said, her pride evident. "A captain in the United States Air Force."

Ben nodded. The television camera drew back, taking both Ben and Ethel into the frame. A video camera owned by the Knight campaign also captured the scene for possible use in future commercials.

"He and his family lived at the base, there in Turkey. They didn't mind being so far from home because they were together. The three of them. Robby and Cathy and my precious little Molly." Ethel bit her lower lip. From behind her, Rob senior squeezed his wife's shoulder. "She's my youngest grandchild. Only eight years old."

She shook her head. Ben reached over and patted her hand. Slowly, as if it had been scripted, Ethel raised her head and looked directly into Ben's eyes.

"This kind of thing shouldn't happen," she said, her voice quaking. "Not to children."

She shrugged. The effort it took to hold back her tears showed in her face.

"My Robbie is a professional soldier. I'd hate it if he was taken, but he's well trained. It's his job. Molly's just a baby."

Back in the hotel room that served as their makeshift headquarters, Zoë watched as Ben comforted Ethel and Rob senior with words she would hear a thousand times more before the campaign was done: "If children can't feel safe, we, their parents, should feel ashamed."

"It works," she said, nodding, her eyes narrowed in concentration. "It's short, strong, and quotable."

"Heads up, loyalists," alerted one of the volunteers manning another channel. "It's the competition."

Mack Kenton had spent the afternoon at an elementary school, talking with teachers about what had happened in Ankara. After a cathartic discussion of what these teachers thought their colleagues must be feeling, Kenton went to great lengths to assure them that according to his sources, all the hostages were being well treated.

"I'm in constant touch with the State Department," he said, in a way meant to convey power and privilege, "and I assure you, I shall maintain my vigil until every last one of our citizens is home, safe and sound."

"I don't care how well treated they are," one of the teachers said. "Bottom line: they're prisoners."

Anthea Ogden took that as her launching pad and proceeded to interrogate Kenton as to what he thought should be done, "other than maintaining a vigil, of course."

Kenton sidestepped the question by claiming he felt the situation was "too precarious at the present time" for him to be publicly offering suggestions that might contradict the president.

"He's fumfering!" the young Knight volunteer reported gleefully.

"He is, after all, still in charge," Kenton said with a touch of exasperation. "If, Heaven forbid, this situation isn't resolved soon, however, I will feel compelled to speak out. Right now, I think the worst thing we can do is send mixed messages to the terrorists. The best thing we can do is pray."

"That setup with the Crookshanks was brilliant, Zoë," Ben said as he and his key staffers reviewed their progress. "It's played on every major news report, and according to scouts, most of the locals as well."

Zoë simply nodded. Successful campaigns needed a thousand brilliant strokes. This was one and that was yesterday. The question was what were they going to pull out of the hat today and then, tomorrow.

Tom Hall, national fund-raising chairman, had other concerns. "Major fund-raising events are on the calender for this month in New Jersey, New York, Texas, and Florida. The problem is that you, Senator Knight, are the main attraction and the last time I checked, you can't be in two places at the same time."

"Maybe not," Ben said, "but we have to give it our best shot."

"We could do New York and New Jersey in the same night if the sites are close and the organizers are flexible," Hall ruminated, poring over a map.

"Milo Kyriakos wants us the day after the primary," Sarah Jenks, the campaign's scheduler said. "He thinks a victory in New Hampshire will add punch to his event."

"I hope we can accommodate him." Ben's expression showed how worried he was. His figures had remained steady, which was another word for static. Suddenly, Ben had an idea. "If we're going to New Jersey, why not have Kate Siegel speak for us?"

"Is Kate Siegel the one who started NOMORE!?" Jed asked. When Zoë said yes, he practically hooted. "She's a one-woman grassroots phenom. Getting her to pimp for us would be terrific!"

Zoë winced. At any other time, she was certain Jed would have been sickened by what had happened to Mira. Now, however, Jed was functioning in that narrow mode peculiar to those involved in creating successful presidential candidacies. He saw Kate's loss only in terms of her national profile and what it could do for the campaign.

"Kate has congressional hearings coming up," Zoë said. "She can't be listed on any fund-raising committees, and she can't formally endorse Ben." She turned away from Jed and faced Ben. "When I visited her recently, she suggested that you work the efforts of NOMORE! into your overriding theme of securing safety for children. I think it's a very strong angle."

"Will she travel for us?" Jed pressed.

Ben, noting Zoë's discomfort, answered. "Kate's a good friend. She'll do whatever she can."

"Has anyone figured out how we send Ben to Texas and Florida without giving up any time campaigning here?" Tom Hall asked, somewhat impatiently.

Zoë suggested setting up a series of small town meetings in New Hampshire. "Using a satellite feed and local cable hookups, we could connect the larger town meetings Ben's scheduled to do in Texas and Florida to the smaller ones here."

Tom looked at Ben, whose eyebrows lifted in surprise.

"We could also arrange house parties that you would

connect with via phone calls from airplanes or airports or stops between events," Zoë continued. "It's dead time for Ben, but it means the world to those who've gathered in a neighbor's house for coffee and cake to get a call from the candidate."

Ben shook his head in amazement. "Where did you learn all this stuff?"

"I helped Bill Rutledge when he ran for the Senate. California's a huge state. We needed some novel ideas."

"That was a big win," Ben said, mentally retrieving details of the campaign that put the former ambassador to Israel into the Senate.

"It was a good win," Zoë said. "Bill is a terrific senator."

"You were part of his embassy staff."

Ben wasn't asking a question; he was verbalizing a sudden recollection. One of the few times he and Zoë had seen each other between the day of his wedding and the day he came to her father's house in Boston two months ago, had been in Israel. He hadn't known Zoë was attached to the embassy until he ran into her at a dinner arranged by the ambassador in honor of the visiting congressional delegation.

Tom Hall pounded the table, demanding everyone's attention.

"Can we leave this charming little romp down memory lane and get back to the matter at hand, which, in case you have forgotten, is M-O-N-E-Y! Without it there's no gas for the car, no funds for the troops, no tickets for the plane, no campaign!"

The conversation returned to the matter of campaign financing. Tom read off the names of the fund-raising chairman in each state. A discussion ensued as to who could do what and how soon. Some were old hands who understand how to negotiate the briar patch of political fund-raising. Others were newcomers who had come to this race because of a sudden sense of civil urgency. Zoë remained quiet until Jed mentioned a familiar name.

"I'd love to get to Amalia Trilling. She controls a group that's overflowing with funds."

"I might be able to arrange a meeting between Ben and Amalia," Zoë said.

Jed's eyes boggled at the possibility. "May I assume from your comment that you are on a first-name basis with the estimable Madame Trilling?"

"I've known Amalia for years. It's an easy call for me to make."

"Then, please," Ben said, again looking at Zoë with a touch of astonishment, "make the call."

The meeting ended late. Zoë, like the rest of them, dragged her body out of her seat, thankful they were staying in a small inn. She didn't think she could have negotiated the long hallways of a large hotel. Her energy was sapped. All she wanted was to fall onto her bed, but just as she reached her room and put her key in the door, Ben stopped her.

"I can't tell you how much I appreciate all you're doing for the campaign," he said.

"I'm just doing my job, Senator."

She tried to smile, but fatigue dragged at her mouth. Ben barely noticed. He was too caught up in his own good fortune.

"This contact with Amalia Trilling could be major." His eyes were glistening at the prospect. "She could turn the tide, Zoë."

Zoë nodded, but she had had enough politics for one evening.

"I can't promise anything," she said.

"I understand."

Zoë didn't think he did. His face showed that he clearly believed her call would result in nothing less than a commitment of funds and support from Amalia Trilling.

"All I can do is make the call," she said, trying to make a point before she collapsed on the rug. "Which I will do first thing in the morning." She turned and unlocked the door to the room. "Good night, Ben."

He took hold of her wrist. "Have I told you how incredible you are?" he said. "I don't know what I'd do without you!"

She didn't know whether it was a side effect of her fatigue or the way he said what he had, but suddenly, she was beseiged by flashbacks. She hadn't suffered from them in years. When she had, they had been mostly memories of another man and another time. Although even then, an occasional memory of Ben had insinuated itself into that agony. But, as her doctor had told her, the pain of one loss often reasserted itself at the time of another loss, heightening the sense of emptiness and compounding the pain.

She hadn't realized that she had swooned, but she had. Ben caught her in his arms and held her until she regained her equilibrium. He looked worried.

"Are you all right?"

"I'm fine."

Embarrassed and slightly unnerved, she pulled free of him and again attempted to enter her room. Again, he held her wrist.

"Are you sure?" She nodded. He smiled, but his eyes remained locked on her and filled with concern. "I hope so, because I meant what I said before. I don't know what I'd do without you, Zoë."

The only two men she had ever loved had told her that. Suddenly, unbidden memories collided and phrases merged, *"I don't know what I'd do without you"* converged with *"he's gone"* and *"you have to get over it."*

"I'll tell you what you'd do without me," she snapped, too tired to suppress the bitterness bubbling up within her. "The same as you've done for the last twenty-two years. You'd do just fine!"

☆　☆　☆

Scottie Edwards stood behind the pulpit of a quaint New England church. Behind him, an enormous window of stained glass depicted Christ carrying the cross to Calvary,

His crucifixion and His resurrection. The advance team had done a masterful job. The image was strong and unmistakable: Edwards was the Lord's messenger. He was to be listened to, and believed.

"As it says in the Bible, 'Be strong and of good courage.'" His voice thundered throughout the church, filling it with the force of his being. "Be not afraid, my friends. Be not dismayed. The Lord, thy God is with you."

He reminded the congregation—and the television audience—that he was a father and a grandfather and that he would be devastated if any of his kin "ever were made pawns in a despot's game." And then he unleashed the heart of his sermon: a blistering assault on the qualifications of his political opponents.

"These are terrible times," he said, adopting the omniscient tone of a former commander. "There are evil forces loose in this world who are not bound to the laws of God or the ethical standards of a civilized society."

He gripped the sides of the lectern and leaned out over the podium. His voice roared through the church.

"But do not be misled by the excuses being offered by those with no answers. They say there are no solutions. I say there are!"

The audience was alert. Their silence practically crackled with anticipation.

"One simply has to be experienced enough to know what those solutions are and be brave enough to implement them."

Edwards wasn't being subtle. Nor was he being specific. This was intimidation by innuendo, elimination by implication. And, if his assessment of the congregation was correct, it had worked. He had tapped into their fear and exploited it. They *thought* they wanted a plan. In truth, all they wanted was hope. And that was all he gave them. The applause was deafening.

Assured that this fabulous moment had been properly recorded by the media, Edwards's campaign staff hustled him out the side door. They had refused to allow questions by the press inside the church—it would have been disturbing to the parishioners. Instead, they scheduled the follow-up to coincide with a walk through town. Not only did the delay assure that Edwards's carefully orchestrated performance would hit the early-evening news unfiltered and unchallenged, but it forced the press corps out into the elements, where they had to shout their questions at Edwards as he shook hands with townsfolk. The press looked pushy and abrasive. He looked sensitive and sympathetic.

Most of the questions centered around the hostage crisis, each reporter trying to trick Edwards into detailing some kind of plan. He was too skilled. They were getting nothing but platitudes.

Celia Porter decided the only way to get a story was to shift gears. "I respect your decision not to voice a specific plan for fear of further jeopardizing our hostages overseas, but what about those Americans who are being held hostage in this country by racism, poverty, and crime? How do you propose we rescue them?"

Edwards bristled. He preferred sticking to issues where he was the clear authority. Domestic problems were not his best suit. His answer was a jumble of hackneyed bromides about big business unregulated by government, unfettered by health care, and boosted by a cut in the capital gains tax.

Celia's follow-up question dug the knife deeper: "Could you explain how a cut in the capital gains tax will impact those currently subsisting on unemployment or government assistance?"

Later, when Edwards and his team viewed the video on the late edition of the local news, he looked disingenuous, out of synch, and dangerously out of touch. He was talking in grand terms about the virtues of large corporations while walking down a street in Smalltown USA, shaking the hands of mom and pop shopkeepers. Worse, the piece ran the following evening on the national nightly news, embellished with a narrative by the network's reporter on the scene: Celia Porter. Not only had she made him look bad in New Hampshire, she had embarrassed him coast to coast.

☆　☆　☆

The Sheraton Tara Wayfarer in Manchester was filled with politicos of all persuasions. The primary was only days away and both sides were frantically filling every remaining second with hard campaigning. While the candidates continued barnstorming the state, their aides held impromptu strategy meetings in the lobby and arranged private clutch sessions with possible contributors in suites throughout the hotel. As it had for years, the Wayfarer bar served as unofficial press headquarters for the New Hampshire primary. This night, however, the bar was empty; the press was covering the main event, a fund-raiser/rally for Scottie Edwards.

The ballroom overflowed with party faithful waiting to catch a glimpse of their messiah. A rainbow of enormous red, white, and blue balloons floated from one end of the stage to the other. Bouquets of smaller balloons and miniature American flags decorated each table, along with baskets overflowing with THE GENERAL FOR COMMANDER IN CHIEF buttons and bumper stickers. A local band played their entire repertoire of patriotic music. And offstage, a high-school choir warmed up for their go at the national anthem.

The room was packed, but as at most political functions, no one was at his table; everyone was working the room, shaking hands, exchanging business cards, making certain they were seen by whoever they believed would do them the most good. Networking was the name of the game, especially during presidential cycles, and whether it was with an eye to doing business with the government or gaining access to power, everyone wanted to be a player.

This evening, there was a great deal of buzz about the guest speaker; Georgie Hughes was scheduled to introduce the General. While there were those who had never heard of the congresswoman from Texas, there were many who had, and they couldn't wait to see her in person.

Outside the ballroom, Georgie was hurrying down the hall to her room, unceremoniously dragging a suitcase behind her. Coming from the other direction and racing toward the elevator was a familiar face, but she didn't see it until they collided.

"Late again, eh?" Jed Oakes steadied her and grinned. "The woman's got everything working except her clock."

Georgie laughed, but inside, she remained unnerved. He was the last person she had expected to see. "Are you coming or going. Or, as usual, aren't you sure?"

"All you have to do is say the word, darlin', and I could be talked into staying."

"Uh-uh! I have places to go and voters to meet and a speech to give." She tried to sound offhanded and impersonal, but his presence was making her heart pound.

"And after you wow the folk? How about wowing me?" Jed's leer was deliberately comedic, but his eyes asked the question in a different, more serious tone.

Georgie sighed. Her mood sobered. "Nothing's changed, Jed. I still have a husband at home."

"You're not home. And he's a poor excuse for a husband."

"You're right on both counts, but . . ."

"I know. I know. It's complicated." He stepped back and studied the carpet, still and silent. When he looked at her again, his eyes looked pained. "You know, Georgie, to me, it's always been real simple."

"It's never been simple," she said, wistful for what might have been.

Without warning, Jed slid his arm around her and drew her close. Before she could stop him, he kissed her. The moment his mouth touched hers, an avalanche of feeling overwhelmed her, smothering all reason. It had been like this from the first—heated, almost primitive. Jed Oakes seemed to be the sole possessor of the key to the place where Georgie hid her deepest emotions.

She withdrew, completely breathless. "We can't do this," she mumbled.

He caressed her cheek with the back of his hand and shook his head. "We can't not."

Georgie was so torn, words failed her. When he offered his hand she accepted and leaned against him, needing to feel his body next to hers, even if only for a moment. As his lips grazed her hair, her eyes pooled with the folly of her own decision. When she had ended their affair, she had been certain it was the right thing to do. Now she couldn't imagine anything more wrong than letting him go.

"I'm late," she said, her voice scratching against the lump in her throat.

"Right! Me too." He dropped her hand and tugged at the knot on his tie. His gaze never left her face. "Ben's doing a first-time voters gig at the high school."

Georgie nodded, but her eyes were blank. He might have said the Chinese were invading Manchester and gotten the same reaction.

Jed checked his watch and the number on her room key.

"Go," he said, nudging her toward her room before heading for the elevator. "Do your thing, babe. I'll see you later."

She started to protest. But now he wasn't listening.

Jed Oakes had swept into Georgie Hughes's life like a tornado, in 1986, when she had decided to run for state treasurer. Having lost one election, she scouted the field for a top-notch political strategist to manage her campaign, someone with an instinctive feel for politics, a belief in the process, experience on all levels, a creative approach, and an open mind. What she didn't want was someone whose initial responses to new suggestions were: "We tried that once", "That won't work", "No", and especially, "What would your father think?'' Jed Oakes's name came up with amazing frequency.

While she would have preferred keeping their initial meeting private, Roy got wind of it and invited himself, Lyle, Wade, and Branston. After Georgie finished with the introductions, she outlined her campaign for the state legislature. When she finished, Lyle, followed by her father and Wade, presented their analyses. Branston wisely remained silent. The consensus seemed to be that she had been defeated because of her gender. Jed Oakes thought that was claptrap and said so.

Lyle's reaction was immediate. ''We were up against a strong incumbent who had held that office for a long time.''

''I don't care if he was born in the damn job,'' Oakes said. ''I checked his record. As far as I can see, the man didn't do anything more exciting than show up. He could've been beaten.''

''Obviously the voters didn't agree with you,'' Wade said.

''That's because no one gave them a reason to vote otherwise.'' He nodded his head to the left, pointing at Georgie, who was sitting on the couch alongside him. ''This fine-looking woman was tossed out on the stump with a message no one was gonna listen to.''

''The message,'' Lyle said, straining, ''was one of fiscal fairness. In Dallas County, we pay some of the highest taxes in the state. Why shouldn't we have a greater say about how that money is spent?''

''Because, my friend, in these United States, it's one man, one vote. Not, I get my way because I've got a million bucks in the bank and you don't.''

Jed saw the fire in Lyle's eyes, but he had no regrets. The man had a serious attitude problem.

''If you want to get right down to it,'' he said, ignoring Lyle, looking at Georgie, ''you lost because you ran as Georgie Mercer.''

''I beg your pardon?'' Lyle had disliked this man instantly.

"Who the hell is gonna care about Georgie *Mercer?* No one!" Jed said, throwing his hands up in a display of utter exasperation. "Georgie *Hughes* could've won that election in a walk."

Lyle seethed. He had argued against Georgie's running for state treasurer—it seemed an unnecessary exercise in humiliation—but when she defied him, he had assumed he would be in charge of the campaign. Not only did he resent her bringing Oakes here without any consultation, but having his previous efforts judged by some self-styled political guru from Oklahoma's dust bowl seemed beyond the pale.

"Her name," Lyle snapped peevishly, "in case no one thought to tell you, *is* Georgie Mercer, and, with all due modesty, I am not unknown in Dallas."

"Lyle is head of the Texas Energy Congress. He's a former city councilman and a leader in the business community." Roy sounded as if he was reading off a cue card.

Not to be outdone, Wade and Branston offered their own kudos. Georgie wanted to scream. This meeting was turning into a testimonial dinner.

Oakes simply rolled his eyes. "I'm sure you're a real VIP, Mr. Mercer, but in this state *Hughes* has the juice. Not Mercer."

"I'll have you know . . ." Lyle started to say.

"If I may." Georgie's interruption was so unexpected and so sharp it silenced him and put the others on alert. When she turned to the man sitting at the other end of the couch, her tone vibrated with annoyance. "Mr. Oakes, we need to get a few things straight."

Jed afforded her his full attention.

"First," Georgie said, *"I* am the candidate. I have my own beliefs, my own vision, and my own ideas about governance. Two, I will not be discussed as if I am neither present nor relevant, particularly since I am the one who brought you here. And three, the people of Dallas are not morons. They're not going to rush to the polls to vote for me just because my maiden name is Hughes.

"If that's all you think it takes to win this election, and if that's the only reason you came here today, you're not as good as your résumé, nor are you the right man for this job."

"Well," Jed said, a lazy smile moseying across his lips, "I believe I was just given a world-class what-for!"

The smile faded. His gaze remained focused on Georgie. "You are hardly irrelevant," he said. "You're very much present, a formidable candidate and a woman whose vision is probably incredibly clear. As for me: I'm better than my résumé and most definitely the man for the job. However, as long as we're getting things straight . . ." He leaned in her direction, his body language explicitly excluding the others from this dialogue. "You can go with your former campaign manager and call yourself whatever the hell you please. But if you really want to win this thing, you'll throw in with me."

"And?" Georgie said.

"And," he said, his slow smile returning, "you'll leave Mrs. Mercer at home where she belongs. Either Georgie *Hughes* runs for office, or Jed Oakes hits the road. It's your choice."

Despite Lyle's strenuous objections, Roy's grumblings, and the inevitable toll she knew it would take on her marriage, Georgie chose Jed Oakes to manage her campaign. After the first few weeks, during which they debated both message and strategy, they became a team. And they won.

When he ran her campaign two years later for the House of Representatives, they became lovers.

The chairman of the evening's event was finding it almost impossible to capture the attention of the crowd. The incessant buzz of the side conversations had grown so loud it had drowned out the previous speakers. He had tried to demand silence. He had signaled the band to give a drumroll. It was only when he mentioned the name of

Georgie Hughes that the audience even looked at the stage.

"And now," he said, "it is with great pleasure that I introduce the loveliest rose Texas has ever produced, Congresswoman Georgie Hughes!"

Georgie stepped onto the stage to generous, curious, but not uproarious applause. She wasn't exactly a household name in the provinces. Acknowledging that, as well as how stark regional differences could be, Georgie had dressed quite carefully. Hurdle number one for women in politics was to try and make what they *said* more newsworthy than what they *wore*. Tonight there were no boots, no bolos, no fringe, no big Dallas-dos. Her chin-length, thick black hair was softly brushed, forming a natural frame for her face. Subtle, gently smudged pencil and a dollop of mascara drew attention to her pale, almost translucent blue eyes.

Her dress—almost the same shade as her cherry red lipstick—was simple, attractive, and stylish, but not so *Vogue* that it made a Fashion Statement. A narrow belt enhanced her figure while a just-above-the-knee hemline revealed long, slender legs. There was nothing about it that said TEXAS, except for the small enameled bluebonnet pin she wore on the collar. Texas's state flower, Jed had given it to her when she won the treasurer's race. She had worn it for luck ever since.

"Good evening, ladies and gentlemen, and thank you for giving an out-of-town gal such a warm welcome."

She smiled and paused, giving the audience a chance to applaud their own hospitality.

"On my way up here, I was listening to a couple of newscasts that said this is one of the worst winters in the history of the New Hampshire primary. Now, I don't claim to be an expert on this sort of thing, but I think they've got it wrong. It seems to me, y'all have the most patriotic weather I've ever encountered. The snow is white. My nose is red. And my toes have turned a wonderful shade of blue!"

A friendly titter rippled throughout the hall.

"Personally," she continued, "I think it's right and fitting that the first presidential challenge takes place here.
Hell! If you can survive a winter like this, you can survive
anything!"

The room exploded. From every corner, they shouted
their approval, hooting and cheering as if Georgie had
just promised each and every one of them a free snow-
blower. She ingratiated herself further by telling a few
amusing stories about herself and what it was like to go
from Texas to Washington. She moved on to a thoughtful
discussion of the hostage crisis and then seamlessly segued
into her pitch for Scottie Edwards.

"Earlier, we had a good laugh at the notion of surviving
difficult weather. But I think we all know that real, life-or-
death survival is no joke. Tonight, while we sit here safe
and sound, enjoying our freedom, dozens of Americans
are being held against their will." She paused. Her face
was stern. "That makes me angry."

Many in the audience muttered in agreement.

"They've been taken prisoner by a group of thugs who
think they can get what they want by shoving America's
back up against the wall."

The muttering was becoming an angry undercurrent.

"I don't know about you, but I don't like the idea of
anyone thinking they can kidnap our children, demand a
ransom, and get away with it!"

Again, the audience responded. There were so many
"right ons," it was beginning to sound like a revival
meeting.

"And while I know there are those who think vengeance
is the answer, that's not the American way. Revenge is not
what this election should be about. It should be about
justice and security and finding solutions to unthinkable
problems like the ones facing us tonight. To do that, we
need a president with a cool head, a strong fist, and a
warm heart. A president who's marched on the field of
battle and walked the delicate line of diplomacy. What we

need is a president who speaks from experience. Ladies and gentlemen, we need General Scottie Edwards!"

Three hundred people clambered to their feet. The band struck up "The Stars and Stripes Forever," and Prescott Edwards strode out onto the stage with a triumphant strut. When he reached the podium, he pumped Georgie's hand.

"Great job!" he said, honest respect written all over his face.

When Roy Hughes had first suggested having Georgie introduce him, Scottie had agreed, but with trepidation. He was concerned about having a woman introduce a soldier. He was afraid the images might conflict, that she was too female to rouse a mostly male crowd. He needn't have worried. They were positively frenzied.

After Georgie had exited the stage, he stepped up to the podium and turned to face the crowd, but instead of an orderly, attentive group, many were out of their seats mobbing Georgie as she tried to make her way to her table. He strained to look patient while she politely, but firmly promised to greet each and every one of them later. When finally the atmosphere had calmed and he felt they were ready to receive him, he began his speech.

It was a rousing oration, striking many of the themes he had laid out in other speeches throughout the state: "You don't hire a private to do a general's job," "There're no substitutes for experience"; and his personal favorite: "You can't stand tall if you won't stand tough." He had been interrupted several times with applause and had received a standing ovation. He should have been euphoric, but just as he took his seat, the band struck up "The Yellow Rose of Texas," and the audience began to chant Georgie's name.

Georgie glanced at Edwards, who, recognizing he had no other choice, stood up, motioned for her to go back onstage, and led the clapping that accompanied her walk to the microphone.

"I had no idea y'all were such country music fans,"

Georgie teased, taking the mike from its stand and walking away from the podium. "But if you insist . . ."

She smiled at the loud response and nodded to the band leader. After delighting them with "Mama, Don't Let Your Babies Grow Up to Be Cowboys" and "Lookin' for Love," she told the audience her last song was a message from her to them about the upcoming election. Blowing a kiss to Scottie Edwards and pinning one of his campaign buttons to her dress, she brought them to their feet with "Stand by Your Man."

When the dinner was over, the autographs had been signed, hands had been shaken and all the press interviews had been given, Scottie Edwards thanked Georgie again.

"You were something else, Congresswoman Hughes," he said, tipping an imaginary hat. "I'm impressed."

Georgie smiled appreciatively. "I hope you didn't mind my singing."

Edwards laughed. "What kind of politician would I be if I didn't accede to popular demand?"

A faint blush rouged Georgie's cheeks. "It's sort of gotten to be my signature," she explained. "But this was your night, General. I didn't mean to steal any thunder."

Edwards studied her carefully. She was a fine-looking woman, smart and wildly appealing. Interestingly, women as well as men had cheered her. He would have thought someone that exceptional would be threatening to women. Then again, Emily was always telling him he knew nothing about the female psyche.

"You created the thunder. You had every right to swipe some of it." He smiled, but his eyes were calculating. "This is going to be a tough campaign, and frankly, I'm going to need all the help I can get. I would be quite appreciative if you could join me in several other key states."

Georgie's mind was racing. She had accepted this engagement with the hope of gaining the inside track with Edwards so that when it was appropriate, she—or Roy— could suggest that Wade be the General's V.P. selection. Texas was an important state. And it was Hughes territory.

What better time to make that pitch than after a hugely successful fund-raiser?

"I'd be happy to do whatever I can, General," Georgie said. "Including, if you'd like, asking my father to chair an event in Dallas."

He nodded approvingly. She had picked up on his cue and responded correctly. For that, he awarded her points. "Yes," he said, offering her a quick, perfunctory smile. "That would be wonderful." He turned so sharply, Georgie found herself listening for the click of his heels. "My staff will be in touch."

Georgie almost responded with an obedient, "Yes, sir!" but even if she had, he wouldn't have heard her. She had been dismissed.

It was well past three when Jed Oakes slipped into Georgie's room and into her bed. He lay there quietly for a few minutes, watching her sleep, breathing in the scent of her delicate floral perfume. She was turned away from him, but there wasn't an angle at which he didn't find her beautiful. Her dark hair, her ivory skin, the seductive shimmer of her silk nightgown, the gentle curve of her body.

He wondered if perhaps he shouldn't be there, if he was being selfish and making trouble where he didn't have to. He thought about leaving as quietly as he had come, but then, she turned over and looked at him. He could tell that she had been awake for several minutes. She must have felt him come into the bed and had been debating what to do.

"I told you I'd see you later," he whispered, trying to read her decision in her eyes. "I'll leave if you want me to."

Wordlessly, she slithered out of her nightgown and opened her arms. He wanted to ravage her, but at the same time, he needed to savor her; he didn't know if or when they'd ever be together again. He pulled the sheet away from her body and indulged himself in the sight of her. He knew she'd disagree, but he thought she was Venus incarnate. Round, soft, curvaceous, lean, she represented all that was perfection in the female form. His hand trembled as he reached out and brushed the velvety softness of her skin. He moved nearer. Her lips parted and she drew his face toward hers. He groaned as they kissed and their bodies touched for the first time.

Gently, he lifted her on top of him, shivering as she lowered herself onto him. He had forgotten how well they fit together. Her hips began to undulate, radiating a heat that ignited a blaze deep within him. His fingers raked her hair. His mouth sucked at her flesh like a starving man. He devoured her lips, her tongue, her neck, the supple mounds that were her breasts, but still, it wasn't enough. His hands rushed to explore elsewhere, to seek the dark, fiery font of her womanhood.

As he pleasured her, she set about gratifying him. Rising slightly, so she could watch his face as her hands traveled over his physical landscape, she stroked him until he thought he'd burst. How many nights had he dreamed of her touching him like this? Exciting him like this? Loving him as passionately as this?

With an urgency neither one could deny, they came together, he demanding that she give what he needed so badly to take, she desperate for a physical union so intimate it defied what was possible. Hungrily, he found her mouth, biting her, tasting her, drinking in the very air she breathed. Greedily, she took him in, surrendering so completely to the overpowering thrall of passion that there was no thought, no reflection, no consideration of consequence. There was only feeling, only an exquisite, pulsating rush of emotion that grew so intense, it erupted with a force that left their bodies shuddering long after the quake had stilled.

Spent but satisfied, they lay next to each other in silent communion. Jed cradled her in his arms and stroked her hair. As she nuzzled closer to him, she knew there was no way she could convey how extraordinary she felt. He drew her closer and somehow, that made her sad. Perhaps because she had only made love to two men in her life, and in all the years they had been married, Lyle had never made her feel like this.

"I don't see how you can deny feelings as strong as these," Jed said, as if he had intuited her thoughts.

"I don't deny them."

"Oh, really? You could have fooled me." He straightened up and leaned against the headboard. "We haven't been together like this for years and not because I wasn't ready, willing, and able."

"It's not your fault." Georgie propped herself up against the pillow. Suddenly she felt the need to cover herself with the sheet. "It's mine."

He gritted his teeth and stared at the opposite wall. When, finally, he looked at her, his face showed his exasperation.

"Why the hell do you stay with that lout? You don't love him. He doesn't love you. Your kids are grown."

"What do you want me to do?" She sounded confused. Anguished would have been closer to the truth.

"You're a smart girl. What do you think I want you to do? Get rid of the damn dog!"

"And after I divorce Lyle, then what?" Georgie said. "Do I marry you? You're a cowboy. You like being footloose and unencumbered."

Jed blushed. He couldn't contradict her. There was a lot of truth to that. His expression turned serious. His tone was gentle, almost shy. "You're the only woman who's ever made me think about hitching my horse to a post."

Georgie kissed him lightly. "That's sweet, but thinking is not a synonym for commitment."

Jed shook his head. "Whew! The C word. You play rough, girl."

"Divorcing a husband and upsetting a family is rough."

"Granted, but so is staying in a situation where you're gonna be miserable for the rest of your life."

As she had every time he raised this subject, Georgie

countered with her standard explanation about sticking with Lyle because of the children and because an affair would bring shame to her family and jeopardize her career. Jed shot down everything she said.

"Number one, your children are already hip to the fact that you and Lyle were never Ozzie and Harriet. Number two, I'd bet that Daddy Hughes suspects you and I passed platonic a long time ago. Number three, if divorce was a reason not to elect someone, Congress would be one empty dance hall. And number four, I make your socks roll up and down!"

She laughed. "That part is definitely true."

"So is everything else I just said." Jed pulled her to him. His gaze was so intense he almost frightened her. "I love you. And you're just as nuts about me."

"That I am."

"Then leave him. Start over with me."

It wasn't that she hadn't thought about doing just that. In the months and years since they had parted, not a day had gone by that she didn't ache for him.

"If you can't cut the cord right now," Jed said, preferring compromise to rejection, "I can deal with that. But, please, at least give us a chance."

Thoughts swirled around in her head. Roy would be concerned about the future of Hughes Oil & Gas. There was the deal with Edwards to consider. If indeed, Wade was added to the ticket—and her gut said it was more than possible—Lyle's leverage increased. He knew things that could sweep the entire family up in a maelstrom of controversy. Then again, power and prestige were the two things Lyle held dearest. Perhaps she could convince him that the success of the Edwards/Hughes ticket would greatly benefit him. If he believed Edwards's election would result in a plum appointment, he might cooperate. But Lyle was nasty and vindictive. It wouldn't be out of character for him to sabotage the ticket and somehow blame it on her.

"I need time," she said, mentally going over details and adjusting her plan. "It could be months."

"Thanks to you, I've become the world's most patient man."

If Georgie had needed another reminder about why she loved this man, there it was. She had given him an ambiguous response, yet he hadn't pressed her to be more specific. He hadn't asked any questions, nor had he made any demands. He trusted her, which was more than she could say for her husband.

"Certain things have to fall into place."

A hopeful smile began to tilt Jed's lips. "And while we're waiting for that miracle to happen?"

Georgie rubbed her temples. *Miracle* was the word, all right.

"We can't be seen together," she said. "I can't give him anything to hold over my head."

"Anything more than what he already has, you mean."

Georgie nodded, glumly.

"Are you ever going to tell me what it is?"

Georgie had been waiting for that. It would have been unreasonable to think he would never ask the obvious.

"One of these days," she said, clearly begging him to stretch his trust a little further.

"It'll kill me, but I won't push."

She thanked him with a kiss.

"This is going to be a very long couple of months."

"For me, too."

They stared at each other, as if memorizing features and feelings. "You're going to be really busy with Ben's campaign," Georgie said, as if work would displace his loneliness. "With this new, cramped primary season, you'll be going night and day."

"True, but . . ."

"I have my own reelection campaign, work for the party, and another session of Congress to get through."

Jed was beginning to find this scheduling report extremely amusing. First, he thought he knew where it was leading, and, second, it was being given by an exceedingly delectable, totally naked woman.

"The press is going to be busy chasing the White House hopefuls," she continued, quite aware of the effect she was having. "Lyle is going to be busy chasing whatever skirt he thinks will have him. And my father is going to be busy making sure my brother is the second man on the ticket."

Jed slid next to her and took her in his arms, planting delicate kisses behind her ear. "It sounds as if everyone's going to be too busy to pay us any mind."

"It does seem that way," she said, wishing she could silence the small voice in her head that was screaming at her not to throw caution to the wind.

Jed's mouth journeyed down the curve of her neck.

"You know," she said, unable to stifle her need for him, "it's possible that we could wind up in the same city at the same time."

He threw off the sheet and covered her body with his own. "If that happens," he said, in a voice laced with equal amounts of desire and determination, "we're going to wind up in the same bed or my name isn't Jedediah Tertius Oakes!"

Georgie knew she should dissuade him. She knew she should tell him they had to wait, that there was simply too much at stake to risk being discovered. She could hear her father denouncing her recklessness. She could hear her husband threatening to expose her. She could hear constituents and colleagues expressing shock and dismay. She could even hear the voice of reason, urging her to go slow.

But her heart said to ignore every voice but Jed's.

When Georgie came downstairs for breakfast, the maître d' informed her that someone was waiting for her. Georgie flushed, assuming it was Jed. Instead, she found Zoë Vaughn, her head buried in a newspaper, her hand clutching a cup of steaming black coffee.

"What a wonderful surprise," Georgie said, grinning as

she took a seat. She grabbed Zoë's hands, gave a squeeze and did a quick once-over. She noted dark circles beneath the pale celadon eyes and clucked her tongue. "If you feel as bad as you look, girlfriend, I'd suggest you double up on that caffeine."

"Well, thank you for that beauty tip, Congresswoman. Any more hints for the helpless?"

"Bear grease," Georgie advised. "It's the only thing that'll save your delicate, parchment-like skin from this *un-be-lieve-able* cold."

Zoë chuckled. "Is that a Hughes family recipe?"

"Absolutely! Handed down from one gorgeous generation to the next." Georgie laughed. "Not that any female Hughes other than yours truly has ever been to New Hampshire in February."

"I heard you knocked 'em dead last night," Zoë said with obvious pride.

Georgie nodded shyly. "It went okay."

The waiter took their breakfast order and poured fresh coffee. Zoë sipped hers. Georgie held her cup in both hands, warming them.

"I saw a clip of Ben and the first-timers on the morning news," Georgie said. "I'm not a pollster, but I'd bet every kid in that auditorium signed onto the Knight crusade after that performance. The man knows how to talk to young'uns."

Zoë agreed. "He knows not to talk down to them."

"I saw your fine hand in his answers about Russia, the Middle East, and Eastern Europe. Crisp. Concise. Full of context."

"Just doin' my job," Zoë said with a slight bow of her head.

The waiter laid out their food, heated up their coffee, and disappeared. Zoë sprinkled cinnamon on her oatmeal. Georgie dived into her scrambled eggs.

"Is this awkward?" she asked, after a bit.

"What?"

"Me stumping for Edwards. You advising Ben."

"Different strokes," Zoë said casually.

"How is it working with Ben after all these years?"

"It's been a bit odd," Zoë confessed.

Georgie appeared wistful and a little awestruck. "Isn't it wild to think that someone we hung out with in college, someone we drank with and goofed around with—hell, someone you slept with—is running for president?"

"What's even wilder," Zoë said pointedly, "is that despite you giving your considerable all for the opposition, Ben's going to win!"

Georgie offered a conciliatory smile, but it lacked conviction. "I know how you feel about the General. And you know how I feel about Ben, but . . ."

"You're a party loyalist, and Edwards is your guy."

"He's a good candidate, Zoë. This hostage thing is an international crisis that has to be solved the right way. If it's not, the consequences could be disastrous. Scottie has the experience and the credentials to get the job done."

Zoë avoided Georgie's gaze. Scottie Edwards didn't deserve that kind of respect from someone of Georgie's stature.

"By the way, I ran into Celia the other day," Georgie said. "You'll be pleased to know she shares your negative view of Prescott Edwards."

"I always said Celia was incisive."

"I wonder if she based her conclusion on his policies and previous performance or," she tiptoed, "because of what he did to you."

"What he did to me is emblematic of how he formulates his policies. If something doesn't fit his preferred scenario, the message and the messenger are trashed. Wait until someone brings him the results of an unfavorable focus group or a negative poll. You'll see: Scottie Edwards doesn't permit the facts to interfere with his opinion."

Georgie tried another route, continuing to step lightly. "I admit I don't know the whole story, but what if you don't either? What if there were other issues at risk? Other matters of security that you knew nothing about?"

Zoë had heard similar rationales from others. Listening to Georgie justify Edwards's ruthless behavior hurt.

"Granted, he was awful to you," Georgie continued, trying in vain to explain her position.

"But you don't think I should let my personal life interfere with something so much larger, something that's for the greater good?" Zoë's sarcasm was biting.

"I might not phrase it just that way, but yes. This is about the presidency and the hostages and where the country is going," Georgie asserted. "Ben would make a wonderful president. His vision is clear and well intentioned, but he's not equipped to do battle with the likes of Red Rage and Durgunov."

Zoë forced a smile. "I love you. But you're wrong."

"As long as you love me," Georgie said.

After a beat, Zoë leaned across the table, her voice so low it was almost a whisper. "I don't think I'm the only one."

"What?"

"Before coming down here for breakfast, I stopped by your room. I saw Jed Oakes leave, and, even through my bloodshot eyes, I could see that was no handshake."

"Whew!" Georgie sighed and slumped back in her chair. "You don't miss much, do you?"

"I try not to. Especially when my best friend is involved. And," she said with an arched eyebrow, "you and Jed are most definitely involved."

Georgie indulged a sudden urge to examine her coffee.

"That embrace looked mighty intense," Zoë prodded.

"Intense barely begins to describe it," Georgie said at last, blushing from a rush of memory from the night before.

"And this is going . . . where?"

Georgie shrugged her shoulders. "He wants me to divorce Lyle and marry him."

"Sounds like a plan." Zoë smiled and patted Georgie's hand. Her feelings about Jed were so raw and profound, it was almost painful to witness.

"It's what I want, too, but . . ."

Zoë groaned. "But it's a presidential year and your family and your party have burdened you with a pile of expectations you believe you have to fulfill because if you don't, you'll forever be labeled a naughty girl who failed those who count on you." Zoë shook her head in sympathy. "If you have a chance to be happy, Georgie, take it. I know I would."

"Would you?"

"In a heartbeat."

Georgie ruminated a bit, then offered Zoë a wry smile. "I don't get it. We're two fabulous-looking, shockingly intelligent females with personality to spare. We should be rolling in happiness. Instead, our wheels seem to be stuck in the muck."

Zoë laughed, but her face sobered quickly. "I hate to bring this up, but have you considered how sticky it can get mixing politics and romance? Might I remind you that Jed Oakes is Ben's campaign coach and you've signed with the opposing team?"

"You're worried about a possible slip of the lip."

"It did cross my mind." Zoë's discomfort was evident. "I trust you, you know that. And I think I know Jed well enough to trust his professionalism. But Georgie, let's be real. Insider knowledge is seductive stuff. Especially when the stakes are this high. Jed could say something he shouldn't. You could let something slip that you shouldn't. Scottie could gain an advantage that he shouldn't."

"And Ben could lose."

"When he shouldn't." Zoë waited a second before adding, "And Jed would be completely discredited. To say nothing of what this would do to your reputation."

Georgie sighed. "Why can't life be easy?"

"You're asking the wrong person," Zoë said, ruefully. "*Easy* doesn't seem to be in my vocabulary."

"We're not planning on parading our relationship in public," Georgie said. "We know how to be discreet. And believe me, we know what's at stake."

Zoë twirled a lock of hair around her finger. She looked extremely uncomfortable.

It suddenly dawned on Georgie that Zoë had more than just civic concern invested in this campaign.

"A light's beginning to blink," she said, tapping her finger against the side of her head, eyeing Zoë carefully. "I can't believe I didn't tune into this before. You've pinned your reputation on this election. If Ben wins, your opinions and judgments are validated, and you can come in from the cold."

"In a manner of speaking, yes!" It was Zoë's turn to be defensive.

"Do you see this as some kind of pissing contest?"

Zoë thought before answering. "In a way."

Georgie smiled; Zoë was honest to a fault. "Okay. I can buy that. Edwards savaged you. It would be only natural to make his defeat a priority."

Zoë nodded, glad that Georgie was beginning to get the point.

"Which is why you wouldn't take kindly to your campaign strategist aiding and abetting the enemy, even inadvertently."

Zoë nodded again.

"I'd never do anything to hurt you," Georgie said, softly.

"I know, and I'm sorry if it sounds like I'm accusing you of something before the fact, but for me, there's a lot on the line—both professionally and personally."

She paused, measuring her words, wanting them to be clear, yet without unnecessary menace.

"Jed's a terrific guy. He obviously makes you deliriously happy and for that I'm glad." Zoë's smile was genuine. "As for your political choice, you've made it, and you shouldn't have to defend it—no matter how misguided I think it is." Zoë tried to smile again, but her lips refused. "It's early. Kenton's numbers are strong. Ben might not make it to the general. If he doesn't, this whole conversation is moot."

"You may not believe this, but part of me wants Ben to

make it," Georgie said thoughtfully. "I'd like to see him take his shot. The other part of me says this isn't his issue. This isn't his time." Her eyes grew sad. "If he runs against Scottie, I'm afraid he'll lose. And if he does, so will you."

"It's a gamble we're both willing to take."

"You could back out after the primary," Georgie said gently. "It's not unusual for advisors to change their minds."

Zoë shook her head. "I'm committed to Ben for the long haul. If you're committed to Scottie, so be it."

Georgie took Zoë's hand and held it. "What happens if Ben does make it to the general? What happens with us?"

"We agree to disagree."

"And if the race heats up?"

"We abide by Paddy Vaughn's Pub Rules: No hair pulling. No poking at each other's eyes. No hitting below the belt. And," she said, looking Georgie squarely in the eye, "no pillow talk."

☆ FEBRUARY ☆

The day after the Iowa caucuses, all hell broke loose in the Knight campaign. It had nothing to do with Mack Kenton's win; he was a native son, and it was expected. Also as expected, Mack Kenton was making the rounds of the morning shows touting his victory and claiming momentum. Zoë didn't care about that; he was entitled to his horn-blowing. What disturbed her was a story that had first seen the light of day in 1992. Headlining every newspaper and leading every morning news report, it linked Ben Knight and Fabia Guevera romantically and reiterated old charges of influence peddling by an agent of a foreign government.

Fabia Guevera was a fiery and well-educated woman who had fled her native land in a handmade boat. An ideologically and biologically distant cousin of the famed Cuban guerilla, she had become the symbolic leader of a large group who felt Castro had betrayed the revolution. When her relationship with Ben became public, those in Congress who opposed her tough stance wondered aloud why their esteemed colleague chose to speak out on the floor of the Senate so many times about the need to tighten the embargo on Cuba. Was it something he felt deeply? Or, they suggested via innuendo and nuance, something he had been paid to say?

Kenton had decided to pick up the chant. Over and over, he said that while he "didn't have any proof that Knight had taken money in exchange for lobbying the Senate on behalf of the side that wanted sanctions on Cuba stiffened," it was well-known that "Senator Knight and Señorita Guevera had been involved in a long-term relationship." The implication that intimacy and influence peddling went hand in hand was extremely damaging, especially because, in several interviews, it went unchallenged. In politics, the more outrageous the falsehood, the more often it is repeated, the greater the chance that, sooner or later, it will be believed. The last thing Zoë wanted was for this story to become New Hampshire's Big Lie.

She canceled whatever meetings were on her schedule and grabbed the first flight out of Washington's National Airport back to New Hampshire. En route, she informed herself by reading the various accounts of Ben's relationship with the peppery Cuban exile. Each one ended with the unsupported allegation that he had received money in exchange for championing anti-Castro concerns on the floor of the Senate.

As Zoë tried to analyze the situation and digest enough facts so that she could respond intelligently to any questions thrown at her by the press, she discovered she had a problem. As much as she wanted to be able to denounce the story unequivocally, she couldn't spring to Ben's defense with total confidence. It was what she had told Georgie: the Benajmin Knight she had once known so intimately was no more. The man he was now was a stranger.

She arrived at Knight headquarters amid a swirl of explanations, efforts at damage control by the Knight campaign staff, and outbursts of temper by Ben himself. Over the next two days, tension mounted as the story's legs got stronger despite denials of wrongdoing by Knight and counterattacks against Kenton claiming that not only was this story old and used, but that it had been brought up as a way of making Knight's single status seem somehow immoral.

"I am not a bachelor," Ben said during an interview, affecting the perfect blend of anger and personal pain. "I'm a widower."

Many on the Knight staff had tried to unearth the name of the person who had dredged up that old saw. Concentrating primarily on the Kenton camp, they had come up empty. It wasn't until CNN asked Scottie Edwards's campaign manager for a comment that Ben knew from whence the scandal had sprung.

"Clay Chandler." He didn't say the name as much as he spit it from his lips. "I should have known!"

If Zoë needed confirmation of how little she knew this man, Ben provided it when he spoke of Clay Chandler with such obvious venom.

"Why would Clay do anything to hurt you?" she asked. "He was your best friend, the best man at your wedding."

Ben nodded, his expression grim. "And now he's my worst enemy."

It was 1979. After graduating from Yale Law School, Ben had been accepted into the Honors Program at the Justice Department. Clay Chandler, his boyhood friend, had graduated from the University of Virginia Law School, spent a year clerking for a judge in the Second Circuit of Virginia, and had just been awarded the chance to clerk for a justice in the Supreme Court.

Ben had been at Justice for a year when the department received a tip that several justices were abusing their perks and initiated an investigation. Several months went by. When the facts began to paint a troublesome picture of misappropriation, a preliminary report was sent to the man in charge. Ben was that man's assistant.

The evidence was circumstantial, but reading between the lines, Ben recognized that his superiors feared revealing such a breach of ethics. It would create a scandal that could drag on indefinitely, crippling the administration. The implication was that perhaps the public would be better served if someone less visible took the fall. The two considered as possibilities for that ignoble distinction were the clerks of the justices in question: Huxley Thornton and Clay Chandler.

Ben wrestled with his conscience, weighing the impropriety of alerting Clay against the consequences of keeping quiet and perhaps allowing a friend to become an unwitting victim. When his superior elected to continue the investigation, Ben convinced himself that the process would work and, in the end, the truth would win out.

When several months went by without any resolution, Ben grew nervous. Frightened for himself, yet compelled by loyalty, he breached the department's rules of confidence and made a date to meet Clay at a local chophouse.

They ordered dinner and exchanged news from home over a drink.

"Now that we've shaken down every leaf on our family trees," Clay said in his clipped, quasi-British tone, "why don't you tell me why you're plying me with viands and beer."

Ben told Clay about the investigation.

"It's absolutely not true! Why would I falsify vouchers for something as petty as a limousine or lunch at the Jockey Club? What would I have to gain?"

Ben couldn't disagree. "When I first heard about this, I thought they'd simply bury the whole thing. If they want to preserve the image of the Court, that certainly would be the best course of action. By bringing it up, they're putting it out there where it doesn't belong."

Clay's head was bobbing slightly. Ben guessed he was tapping his foot; he always did that when he was upset.

"How long have you known about this?" Clay's voice was chilly.

"For a while," Ben admitted.

"Why didn't you tell me earlier?"

"I didn't think it would go anywhere."

Clay's silence was deafening. Ben squirmed.

"Did you think I was guilty?" Clay asked.

"Never," Ben lied.

"Then why didn't you give me a chance to do something about this?"

"What would you have done?"

"I don't know!" Clay exploded with frustration and fear. "I might have spoken to Justice Rodale."

"And said what? 'Justice Rodale, you're being investigated by the FBI for being a greedy little bugger, but they're going to blame it on me, so please, Your Honor, won't you confess to your sins and help me save my ass?' That would've gone over real well!"

"It would have been worth a try," Clay said, his voice so low it was rumbling. "Especially now that I know I can't count on you."

Ben was stung. "That's not fair."

"It's the way I see it."

Ben leaned across the table so that they were nose to nose. "I put my job on the line by telling you this."

Clay nodded. He knew the rules. Ben had broken them. "I'm sorry."

Ben patted Clay's hand and sat back. "Me too."

Ben ordered another round of drinks. For a few minutes, neither man spoke. Clay broke the silence.

"You're my best friend," he implored. "You can't let them do this to me, Ben. All I've ever wanted is to be a Supreme Court justice. If they pin this phony rap on me, I'm finished before I ever get started."

Clay's father was a judge on the Pennsylvania Superior Court and a nationally recognized jurist. His grandfather had been a judge, as well as the dean of the University of Virginia Law School. For as long as Ben had known him, it had been Clay's dream to surpass his predecessors and bring the Chandler name to the highest court in the land.

"I don't think there's anything I can do."

Clay fixed his eyes on Ben's, locking them there. The muscles of his face were tense and tight.

"You could alter the reports."

Ben's brows pinched into a frown. While he understood the desperation behind the request, he couldn't believe what was being asked of him.

"No, Clay," he said, "I couldn't."

Several months later, the story broke with Clay's name in the headlines. Ben, who had been following the investigation, felt sick. He had believed they were zeroing in on Thornton. When he nosed around he found out that Thornton had indeed been the target—until someone intervened on his behalf.

Clay, tainted with the veil of scandal, knew he would never be a justice on the Court, nor a federal judge. It was also entirely possible that he might never be named partner at a major law firm. The only thing that remained certain was that he would never forget how he had been disgraced. And by whom.

It was late. Zoë was in bed, thumbing through the *Washington Post,* while at the same time, trying to sort out what Ben had told her about the rift between him and Clay Chandler.

As Zoë knew, when Ben's father and brother were murdered, it was Clay's father who presided over the trial of their killers. When the trial was over, Judge Chandler befriended the Knights. He mentored Ben, wrote his recommendations to Harvard and Yale Law School, guiding and advising Ben the way a father would. Zoë recalled that Ben had told her many times how much he owed Judge Chandler. "He gave me my future," he used to say.

She was still mulling the vicissitudes of life when her eye caught a name in the obituary column: Dixon Collins. Dixon had been her assistant in Moscow.

According to the brief notice, Dixon Collins of Silver

Spring, Maryland, had died in his home. Formerly of the State Department, currently employed as a librarian, he was thirty-four years old. His body had been discovered by a friend. Cause of death was not revealed.

The next morning, Zoë made a dozen phone calls until she tracked down Dixon's longtime lover, Jack Brynner, a prosecutor with the Justice Department. They talked for a long while until Zoë finally built up enough nerve to ask how Dixon died.

"He hanged himself."

After a period of stunned silence, Zoë said, "Why?"

"He was afraid."

"Of what?"

"Of having his life distorted by the press into something disgusting and evil."

Zoë's stomach knotted. "Why would you think something like that would happen?"

"A couple of months after you left the embassy, Dixon received a packet of photographs. They were of Dixon and several lower-echelon Russian diplomats at an embassy reception. Dixon had his arm innocently draped around one man's shoulder. The accompanying note was a jumble of words cut out from newspapers and pasted on a card."

"What did the note say?"

"THE GAY CHARGE."

Zoë could do nothing but groan.

"Dixon left the foreign service in disgrace. We moved to Maryland, and, for a long time, he did nothing except look over his shoulder. I finally convinced him to see a shrink. It took a while, but his mood improved, especially after he took a job at the library. I thought he was doing okay."

Zoë was certain she heard Jack stifle a sob.

"What happened?" she prompted softly.

"A few weeks ago, we received more photographs, this time of Dixon and me, taken six months ago when we were on vacation in Mexico."

Zoë closed her eyes and rubbed them with her fingers. Her head was pounding with dread. "And the note?"

"WOULD YOU TRUST THESE MEN WITH STATE SECRETS?"

"Why do you think these pictures were being sent to Dixon?"

"To make sure he kept his mouth shut."

"About what?"

There was a click and the line went dead. For a long time, Zoë stared at the telephone. She wanted to call Jack and tell him no one would have published those pictures. It had been an empty threat. But, she realized, her advice would be too little, too late. Whoever had mailed those pictures already had accomplished his goal: He had scared Dixon Collins to death.

☆   ☆   ☆

"Ben Knight has won New Hampshire." Scottie Edwards leaned back in his seat, sipped a double Glenlivit, and studied his campaign strategist. "What happened?"

"Kenton blew it," Chandler said, completely unruffled. "We leaked information that should have put a major hole in Knight's flank. Instead, Kenton used it to shoot himself in the foot. If he'd played up the foreign-agent angle, instead of dangling sex before the voters, he would have won hands down."

"Funny," Edwards said, "I would've thought the more prurient side would have been the most damaging. Especially in puritan New England."

Chandler shook his head. "We're in the midst of a hostage crisis. People are frightened. They want to know if Ben Knight's someone they can trust with their lives, not their virginity."

Edwards considered that for a moment. "How damaged is Kenton?"

Chandler gulped his Jack Daniel's, chased it with a swig of water, and waited for it to glide down his throat. "They're both wounded. Knight's no longer a lily-white

Lancelot. And Kenton, who's usually exceedingly cool under fire, panicked over the poll numbers and pushed the wrong buttons."

"Who'd be the best one to run against?"

"Six of one, half a dozen of the other."

He poured himself a refill, swirled the bourbon around in his glass, and watched its ebb and flow as if it were prophetic. His large, bulging eyes continued to stare at the amber liquid as his lips tightened into a frosty smile.

"Kenton's got a good record and a nice-guy image, but I've got our research team digging into areas that should uncover the soft spots beneath his armor."

He downed the bourbon in a single gulp. The smile disappeared along with the liquor.

"As for Knight, he has the widowed, single-father sympathy thing, but he's been far from celibate, and, if need be, we'll publish every name in his little black book."

"He's well respected in the Senate," Edwards said, pushing a button of his own. "It might be hard to trash his record."

"You don't have to trash it," Chandler said with unflappable sangfroid. "You just have to twist it."

Edwards smirked. This was why he had hired Chandler—the man was a veritable campaign commando. He had a razor-sharp mind, a backbone of steel, the charm of a schoolyard bully, and a take-no-prisoners approach that his supporters liked to call, "laserlike focus." His critics labeled him reckless.

When Scottie announced he was bringing Chandler in to head his campaign, many advised against it, particularly his wife, Emily, who pointed out that Clay's ferocious single-mindedness was trouble waiting to happen. Scottie argued that in politics the bottom line was the win, and Clay Chandler won more often than he lost. Since no one could debate that wisdom, everyone went along.

In fact, Scottie and Clay had discussed the wisdom of Scottie making a presidential run when they first met back in '84. Clay believed Scottie would make a formidable candidate and urged him to start planning immediately. Together, they made lists of possible fund-raisers and supporters, targeted issues on which Scottie should speak out, and met whenever Scottie was faced with a crossroad and wanted directional advice. By the time Scottie formally announced his candidacy, he and Clay believed they had planted the seeds of a winning campaign and that nothing could stop them. Neither one had envisioned the taking of hostages. Or the entrance of Benjamin Knight into the arena.

Scottie never told Clay he knew about his feud with Ben. First, he liked knowing another man's secrets; one never knew when one would need an edge. Too, why check the fallout from a long-term vendetta if it worked to his benefit. If and when Clay's gnawing hatred ceased to be helpful, Scottie would deal with it. For now, that enmity worked to Scottie's advantage.

When Clay spoke of Mack Kenton and the other Democratic hopefuls, he discussed each of them with the detached clarity of a professional political engineer. He saw their positives and how to play them down, as well as their negatives and how to play them up. Mention Benjamin Knight, though, and Clay's efficient detachment changed to intense involvement. When it came to damaging Knight's reputation, Clay defined the strategy, charted the tactics, and ordered the moves. He wasn't simply plotting a win, he was going for the kill.

Which was perfect since Scottie was counting on Clay killing two birds with one stone: Benjamin Knight and his advisor, Zoë Vaughn.

☆   ☆   ☆

Ben Knight used to take pride in describing himself as a politician. It upset him that these days there were so many negatives attached to the word politician. When he was young, politics was a noble profession of people who used the democratic process to improve society's lot. Public servants did what the name implied and were lauded for their efforts. But then the system ran amok. Corruption and greed proliferated, campaigns became vicious, and government officials became rascals to be thrown out of office. Fewer and fewer citizens voted, and, when they did, it was *against* more often than *for*. Cynicism exploded, and a highly suspicious, increasingly fearful population began to splinter into the tight-knit, homogeneous, xenophobic clans they had once fought so hard to get out of. Suddenly, the whole of America was being divided into its parts.

To Ben, who still believed "in union there is strength," this renunciation of diversity was worrisome. Division led to weakness, which led to vulnerability, which led to a certainty of attack—both from without and within.

"Push aside the extraneous layers my opponents have drawn around this election and see the issues clearly," Ben beseeched his audience. "Is your family prospering? Do your friends have jobs? Are your children safe?"

He looked out into the crowd, making eye contact with the women whose faces had pinched at his last question.

"Are your children safe?" he asked again, this time in a voice that was barely above a whisper. "Molly Crookshank wasn't safe. She was doing her lessons in school, now she's a prisoner somewhere in Europe." His voice grew louder. "Polly Klaas wasn't safe. She was at a slumber party in her own home. Sara Anne Wood wasn't safe. Neither was Megan Kanka."

His eyes found one particular woman standing in the front row.

"Mira Siegel lived in a nice house on a quiet street just like the ones you live on. She was eleven years old, playing in her backyard with her friends. But she wasn't safe."

His voice rumbled, filling the eerily silent room with the thunder of incomprehensible tragedy. He turned away from Kate. He didn't have the courage to see the pain in her eyes as he talked about her daughter.

"We don't know what's happened to Molly Crookshank. But Polly, Sara, Megan, and Mira are dead."

He paused. Women dabbed their eyes. Several men

cleared their throats. Tension rippled through the crowd as they anticipated his next words.

"Are *your* children safe? Are mine? Not when six-year-olds are being raped and murdered! Not when eleven-year-olds are kidnapped from their homes! Not when eight-year-olds are being held in foreign prisons!"

His eyes flamed with outrage.

"Ladies and gentlemen, our children's lives are on the line, and until each and every one of them is safe, we have no right to go about our business as usual. We have no right to do anything until every six-year-old and every eight-year-old and every eleven-year-old in this country feels free to go to school or out to play or to sleep in their own beds without fear!"

After the frenetic applause died down, Ben worked his way through the crowd slowly, as was his style, stopping to answer questions, shake hands, listen to advice or accept complaints. Human contact energized him, and it showed as the fatigue from the battle in New Hampshire faded from his countenance. Every so often Ben looked to his side, checking that his buddy, Ethan Siegel, hadn't gotten lost in the crush.

Before Ben's entrance into the main room, the event chairs and several large contributors met with their presidential hopeful in a private suite called, in campaign parlance, a holding room. Kate had been invited to join them. She had brought Ethan.

Though many knew of Kate's past association with Senator Knight, they were surprised nonetheless to see the warm, exuberant greeting given to her son. Ben walked into the room, spotted Ethan and went straight for him. The man and the boy hugged each other, using the privacy of the embrace to exchange some serious words. Ethan presented Ben with a Giants cap, accompanied by a few disparaging comments about the Senator's beloved Eagles.

Now, his speech delivered and his fans assuaged, Ben was being led out of the main hall. Flanked by Kate, Ethan, and his Secret Service agents, he headed for the back door, where his limousine was waiting. Aides were pressing him about the time. He ignored them.

"Zoë arranged a dinner with Amalia Trilling and the fat cats," he said, hugging Kate, reluctant to leave her.

"It sounds like a rock group," she said, affectionately kissing his cheek.

"So it does," he laughed. His expression sobered. "This evening was truly fabulous, Kate. I know Ronnie was listed as the chair, but she told me how much work you put into this."

"Did you hear my idea about hooking up with the NOMORE! groups across the country?" Ethan asked, beaming with pride.

Ben smiled at the boy. "Zoë Vaughn told me all about it. You are one clever fellow, Ethan Siegel."

"It's in the genes," he said, grinning up at his mom.

"Well, you and your mother have been a big help, and I appreciate it."

Kate smiled and narrowed her eyes. "Stuff the compliments, Mr. Big Shot. I have a lot of points coming to me for packing the house tonight."

"Agreed."

Ben bent down, covered his mouth with his hand, and in a stage whisper, said to Ethan, "I sense an ulterior motive behind this show of goodwill."

"Probably," Ethan said, nodding to his coconspirator.

"Okay, what is on your mind?"

"I've always wanted to have dinner at the White House and sleep in Lincoln's bed," she said, as if ticking off a holiday gift list. "Your being elected president is the only chance I've got, so you'd better not blow it, Knight!"

He nodded as he embraced her and kissed her cheek. "I'll try not to," he said, crossing his heart.

After saying their good-byes, Kate and Ethan went to find Ronnie, who was standing just outside the ballroom instructing four women on how to tally the receipts. When she finished and joined the other two, she heard Ethan tell Kate he was going to call his father.

"Do you want me to tell Dad anything, Mom?"

Kate forced a smile. "Just say 'hi.'"

"Aunt Ronnie?"

"Same."

Kate's smile remained in place until Ethan was out of sight. Then, it faded.

"Anything new on the home front?" Ronnie asked.

"Same old, same old," Kate said. "Rick's there. We're here."

Ronnie shrugged. "His loss."

Kate gave her sister-in-law a quick kiss. "You're the best."

Ronnie nodded. "True."

"What a great success this evening was!" Milo Kyriakos threw an arm around the shoulders of each woman. "And you two deserve all the credit."

Ronnie turned to Kate. "If you think he's complimenting you on what you did for tonight, he's not. He's buttering you up for the next event."

"I wouldn't be unhappy if Kate helped us again," he admitted.

"And how do you propose she do that?" Ronnie asked.

Milo looked at Kate. It was clear that he had a very definite agenda. "You are obviously quite close with Senator Knight."

"I am," Kate said, keeping her eye on the pitch.

"With the primaries as compressed as they are, each state is going to be competing for his time."

"And you'd like me to put in a good word for New Jersey."

Milo smiled, but his eyes remained fixed. "New Jersey is a small state," he explained. "We have to produce twice as much as the bigger states to make an impact, but if we do the job and Senator Knight becomes President Knight, we won't be forgotten."

"I'll do what I can," Kate said. She knew Milo would have preferred a firmer commitment, but she had given what she could. Thankfully, someone called him away, eliminating his opportunity to press her further.

Seconds later, Ronnie's presence was requested. Kate guessed a couple of committee chairs were hoping that an added push by Milo or Ronnie would boost the size of an anticipated contribution.

Kate must have been lost in her own thoughts, because she was startled when Stan Jeffries handed her a plate of food and asked if she had eaten.

"I forgot all about it," she said, suddenly realizing she was hungry. She followed him to a small table and sat down. "Thanks, I think I will."

Stan was tall and pleasant-looking, with an easy smile and an extremely quick mind. He was a partner in one of New Jersey's largest law firms and, as it happened, another Yale Law School grad. She had spoken to him at several NOMORE! meetings, but couldn't remember ever exchanging more than a few words. She was about to ask about his wife when she caught herself. Several years before, his wife had been raped and murdered by a man who had raped several times before and had been freed from prison. Another memory surfaced: at a televised town meeting with the governor, Stan had spoken quite eloquently about the need to reconsider sentencing policies for sex crimes. After quoting the alarmingly high rate of recidivism among sexual deviates, he raised the notion of chemical castration for repeat offenders.

". . . I think he has a chance," Stan was saying.

It took Kate a second to realize he had been talking about Ben.

"I hope so," she said. "He's good people."

Stan nodded, then spent several minutes playing with the food on his plate. Kate sensed he was debating something.

"I'm heading up a Yale Law School graduates' fund-raising group," he said. "I'd ask you to cochair it with me, but . . ."

"Much as I'd like to . . ."

"You could help me organize the effort, though." His voice sounded oddly hopeful.

"I guess I . . ."

Encouraged, Stan said, "Maybe we could talk about it over dinner."

It amused Kate to note that this dynamic man, suddenly, appeared shy. She was flattered she had that effect on him. She was also nervous. This conversation had taken a giant leap. She wasn't certain she was ready for a date. *He had asked her for a date, hadn't he?* she asked herself, unsure, unwilling to make a fool of herself. *Over dinner,* he had said. Of course it was a date! But how could she go out on a date? Even if it felt like little more than a technicality, she was still married.

Then again, Rick was in Los Angeles, doing who knew what with whomever. When she had seen him on TV, he hadn't looked like he was sitting home pining away for her. She was the one sitting home. And she had been doing it for three years. This man wanted to take her out. *Why not* she said to herself.

"Why not?" she said to Stan.

Rick Siegel sipped a vodka and tonic and watched the sun set over Los Angeles. From the terrace of his rented hilltop home, the valley seemed to fade to gray, then silently explode with lights. In the background, Respighi's *Pines of Rome* accompanied the cessation of day with a tender melodic air. It was a mild night, balmy and clear, one of those rare treasures that Angelenos stored away as a memory to retrieve during times of oppressive smog, torrential rains or earthquake aftershocks. Sometimes, Rick wondered if swarms of locust would be next.

Ethan's call had both excited and disturbed him. He was excited by Ethan's elation about seeing Ben Knight again, and his utter glee when Rick mentioned that he had spoken to the Senator several days before and had agreed to be the creative advisor for the campaign.

"Wow! If you're going to do the slogans and the ads, Senator Ben can't lose!"

Rick smiled at his son's complete confidence in his ability

to influence public thinking. Unfortunately, selling a soda or a sitcom was a lot different from selling a candidate.

What had disturbed him was a little thing Ethan had said: he "would have called Kate to the phone, but this really nice guy had brought her some food and now, they're off in a corner yukking it up."

Whenever he thought about Kate—and he thought about her more than she might have imagined—it was never as a woman involved with another man. It was always as Ethan's mother or the wife she had been before Mira's death or, sometimes, the incredible girl he had met and fallen in love with.

He sipped his vodka slowly, lingering over it as if it were a balm for unpleasant thoughts. When a wavy, almost holographic image superimposed itself over the dark canvas of the new night, he blinked. Suddenly, he was back on that beach in Puerto Rico where they first met—arguing about football, making love on the sand, laughing at the moon.

Rick asked himself: *What happened to that man and that woman?* His only answer was the searing pain lodged in his heart.

☆   ☆   ☆

Amalia Trilling's New York apartment was a magnificent Fifth Avenue penthouse overlooking Central Park. It was a sophisticated apartment, one that was far more comfortable after sundown, when soft lighting and the scent of fragrant candles set the mood. From the moment one stepped through the gleaming mahogany doors, it became clear that sunlight was not welcome here.

Sinfully spacious, irrefutably grand, and decidedly *haute,* it was an elegant reflection of its owner. Replete with classic architectural detail, priceless rugs and fine French furniture, it housed only part of Madame Trilling's vast collection of art. Her Georgetown town house, equally regal but lighter in feel, provided a backdrop more esthetically receptive to an Impressionist medley. Her Tuscan palazzo, on the other hand, seemed better suited to the generously sized, majestically themed paintings of the Italian Renaissance. This dwelling, being in the heart of New York City, demanded art with an edge.

The chatelaine of this splendid abode was rumored to be in her sixties; good skin and a skillful plastic surgeon helped belie that number. Tall, reed slim, and perenially best-dressed, she had handsome features, but it was her eyes that dominated. The rich, deep blue of the finest Siamese sapphires, they were blunt and uncompromising one minute, sexy and flirtatious the next, glinting with the implication that hidden within was a multitude of secrets gained in the course of a fascinating life and the clear insinuation that they had seen things no one should ever see.

By the time Ben arrived, the gallery and the living room were swarming with guests, and the cocktail hour was nearly over. Amalia, exquisite in a long fall of pleated chiffon the color of cognac, greeted him warmly. She was gracious about forgiving his tardiness, but quick to introduce him around.

The guests were all bold-type names who controlled vast sums of personal wealth; more than that, their influence was legion. Among the prizes was a man who headed a publishing empire, another, a computer company. There were two Wall Street CEOs, a titan whose flagship was a cosmetics company with an international name, a radio personality with a cultish following, a pharmaceutical giant. Many of their wives were personages as well: lawyers, investment bankers, physicians, owners of thriving businesses. There was even a best-selling author and an op-ed columnist from the *New York Times*.

Ben was impressed with the breadth of Amalia's network, but he knew that personal influence only stretched so far. These people hadn't come simply because Amalia's chef was renowned or because they owed her a favor. Each had a specific interest. Each had an enormous ego. Each wanted to be a kingmaker.

Ben moved from one to the other, memorizing names, exchanging opinions and answering questions. The atmosphere was charged with expectation—his and theirs. He had only begun this race, so sometimes he forgot that the presidency was more than a title and an office, albeit the highest in the land. It was a mighty intoxicant, an overwhelming flame around which everyone wished to dance.

Since announcing his candidacy, he had noticed that while he thought of himself as a hands-on kind of guy, suddenly he found himself at arm's length. People who had achieved remarkable success were suddenly deferential. Shaking his hand was *a thrill.* Spending time with him was *an honor.* People seemed more curious, yet hesitant about getting too close. Whether it was fascination or intimidation, they stepped back and held back, leaving him oddly isolated. He wasn't certain he liked it.

As he was ushered into the living room, he saw her standing in a corner, deep in conversation with a man whose back was to Ben. Actually, he saw her hair first, that unmistakable tangle of long, honey-colored curls. Encased in a close-fitting black jersey top that slithered past her hips over a chiffon skirt that fell softly around her legs, she was a vision of restrained sensuality and elegance. She laughed, and her head tilted back, allowing a glimpse of her face: clear ivory skin with only a whisper of dusty pink on her cheeks and lips, celadon eyes enlivened more by personality than cosmetics. She looked ravishing, but as always her beauty astonished because of its complete lack of artifice.

Ben was overwhelmed by the sight of her, and that rattled him. After all, he had known she was going to be here. And, had he thought about it, he would have expected her to look lovely. Yet instead of viewing her rationally, he felt like a teenager having a hormone explosion.

As he and Amalia approached the duo, Ben eyed Zoë's companion like a gladiator assessing his competition. Within seconds after their introduction, he felt bested. Gianni Viabella was the nephew of one of the world's richest men, Silvio Viabella, head of the international clothing company Via Bella. Worth several billions of dollars, the Viabella empire was one of the few that had seen the accelerated growth of the eighties continue into the nineties. It was difficult to walk the streets of any major city anywhere in the world without seeing young men and women streaming in and out of a Via Bella boutique.

"When I studied in Bologna, Gianni was my guide to Italy," Zoë said, explaining their closeness.

Ben's teeth practically grated at the delight in her voice and the sight of her arm linked through Gianni's.

"He made certain I saw every inch of that country."

"Ah, but she returned the favor many times over." Gianni tipped his head graciously, then returned his attention to Ben. "Wherever Zoë was posted, I visited. Then it was her turn to show me around. Thank goodness she was never sent to some godforsaken jungle. I don't do well in primitive surroundings."

Zoë and Amalia laughed. Ben smiled and nodded politely.

"Zoë has told me a great deal about you," Gianni said. "All quite flattering, I might add."

Ben looked at Zoë. Her eyes appeared very green and very warm. Her mouth spread into a gentle smile.

"That's nice to know."

"Because of my family's vast investment in the United States, I'm very interested in American politics. Zoë tells me you're the man to back."

"I would hope that after we have a chance to talk and get to know each other better, you'll come to that conclusion on your own," Ben said.

"I look forward to that opportunity."

"Well, darlings," Amalia said, taking Ben's arm. "If you don't mind, you'll have to continue this conversation at dinner. My chef is extremely temperamental."

The dining room was large and long with eight nineteenth-century French tapestries set inside individual frames of specially designed walnut paneling and a subtly patterned Chinese rug that echoed the soft ochers, pale greens, and muted persimmons found in the tapestries. Four large tables greeted the guests as they entered the room. Dozens of candles suffused a golden glow. Lush bouquets of delicately blushed tulips and tangerine-tinted roses bloomed atop copper moiré cloths. And at each place, wrapped in cellophane and tied in red, white, and blue ribbon was a gold lapel pin: a plumed, visored helmet associated with knights of the Round Table, which would thereafter become the symbol of Ben's campaign.

As was Amalia's custom, husbands and wives were seated separately. For this evening, Ben was to have one course at each table, allowing everyone time to confer with him. At each venue, he was seated between men Amalia referred to as the "carrots": they led and others followed. Several times, Ben's patience was tested by picayune questions about issues he deemed secondary, but overall, the discussions were lively, to the point, and infused with an exhilarating display of intelligence.

Too often, politics meant dealing with those Jed Oakes called "headliners": folks who read only the headlines in their local newspapers. It was a rare treat to speak to people who read the small print.

At Zoë's table, which was to be his last stop, Tobias Kohl—a wealthy South African diamond merchant and Amalia's longtime companion—was to Ben's left, Gianni Viabella to his right. Terrorism seemed an odd topic to discuss over coffee and sorbet-filled *tuiles*, but it was on everyone's mind and, therefore, everyone's lips.

"We have to hold the governments who sponsor this kind of violence responsible," Tobias said.

"I agree." Viabella was grave and emphatic. His dark eyes were fierce, his square jaw firmly set. In the mid-seventies, in a case that garnered worldwide attention, his uncle had been kidnapped and murdered by the Italian terrorist mob, the Red Brigade. "Why isn't Elton Haynes bombing the hell out of Afghanistan or the Sudan or wherever Red Rage has its headquarters?"

"Because no one knows precisely where their headquarters are. More to the point, we're not sure where the hostages are housed," Ben replied. He understood everyone's anger. He also understood Haynes's dilemma. Storming unconfirmed targets and taking innocent lives was something the bad guys did.

"Unfortunately, the administration has no choice but to pursue a less volatile course. Diplomatic channels may not be the fastest route to resolution, but at this point, it's probably the safest."

"With whom are we negotiating?" asked one of the women. "Durgunov? Is he the head of Red Rage?"

"We believe so," Zoë said. "But since he hadn't openly declared himself their leader, we have to negotiate with surrogates." Her forehead furrowed in a rare display of frustration. "Durgunov may be holding the cards, but someone else is playing the hand."

"So that *he* can escape responsibility," the woman said, clearly upset.

"For now." Zoë glanced at Ben. He responded with a nearly imperceptible shrug. It was a no-win conversation, he seemed to say.

"That's precisely my point," Tobias said. "Even if Durgunov is behind these kidnappings, he's not solely responsible. The governments backing him are equally to blame." His tone was calm, but his face was flushed.

"Are you suggesting we declare war on the world?" another woman asked, slightly horrified.

The rest of the room had grown silent. Everyone had tuned in to this discussion. Amalia now stood behind Tobias's chair.

He looked exasperated. "It's not a matter of bombs and guns. The most effective weapon we have is money. What the United States has to do is form an alliance with the world's other economic powers and punish those who would wreak havoc on civilization.

"If Syria and Libya continue being havens for these criminals—isolate them! If Iran and Iraq insist upon financing these gangs—enforce sanctions. If Pakistan won't shut down that university that trains terrorists, cut off their foreign aid!''

Again, Viabella agreed. "Toby's right. Think about the car bombings in Israel and Lebanon. The World Trade Center. Pan Am 103. The Munich Olympics. The *Achille Lauro*. Murders and kidnappings by Black September, the Red Brigade, Hamas, Hezbollah. And now, Red Rage. *Something* has to be done!'' he exhorted, unable to quell his anger or his revulsion.

His eyes scanned the room and rested on Ben. His expression was doleful, almost plaintive. When he spoke, there was an undertone of intense urgency to his words.

"It has to stop, Senator.'' His eyes grew sad. "We simply can't afford to let them get away with these crimes.''

The two men looked at each other. Ben's expression was tight. He was still fighting his own hollow rage over a long-ago act of violence.

"No,'' Ben said, "we can't. There are far too many victims as it is.''

"And some of them are right here in this room.''

Gianni pointed to himself, Amalia—whose parents had been among the Italian Jews sent to Birkenau—Tobias, who had relatives in Israel killed in suicide bombings, several people at other tables, and Zoë, who quite abruptly rose from her chair and left the room. It had happened so quickly, Ben didn't know if Gianni had meant to single out Zoë or the man next to her. He got his answer when seconds later, Gianni excused himself as well.

The discussion continued briefly, but then everyone fell into a worried silence. Though Amalia adroitly filled the void by urging her guests to pin on their golden helmets, raise their champagne glasses and wish Ben well in the New York primary and beyond, Ben's eyes remained fixed on the gallery where Gianni was comforting a clearly distressed Zoë. He saw Amalia's butler appear with Zoë's coat. Viabella helped her into it, keeping an arm wrapped tightly around her shoulders. As he watched her leave he remembered a time when he had her confidence, when they had discussed anything and everything, when they had trusted each other with their innermost thoughts.

Clearly, that time had passed.

☆   ☆   ☆

Thomas Mackenzie Kenton was born in Otho, Iowa, a small farming town west of the Des Moines river. His father, Eustus, raised corn and, on Sunday mornings, pastored a congregation of the Nazarene Church. His mother, Bess, ran the Kenton home, helped manage the farm, tended three children, and taught Bible classes. They were plain-spoken, plain-living people whose lives revolved around the whims of Mother Nature and the steadfastness of their religion.

Secular entertainment had no place in their lives. Neither did tobacco or alcohol or movies or dancing or any type of personal adornment. Though outsiders shied from the creed bound austerity of the Nazarenes, Bess reveled in the sense of triumph it provided.

"Perfection is hard work," she told her children almost daily, "but if you prove yourself worthy, the Lord's love will more than reward your struggle."

Given that kind of transcendent goal, it wasn't surprising that Mack's most vivid childhood memories were of struggling and falling short. He fought hard to be worthy of God's love—and his parents' respect—striving for perfection in everything he did, from schoolwork to farming chores to combing his hair. Though he frequently achieved excellence, flawlessness eluded him. There was always some tiny glitch, some defect, some misstep that prevented perfection. He was an A student, but too introverted to be socially popular. He worked in his father's fields, but was too small to be more than mildly effective. He was devout and sincere in his worship, but couldn't seem to find the track that would lead him to the unquestioned conviction of his parents.

As he got older, the reach toward perfection seemed to

stretch even further. While he managed to control his physical cravings—most of the time—there was no way he could rein in the urges of his intellect. He asked when others accepted. He argued where others complied. He found solutions to things others didn't find problematic. Anything that limited his ability to know was anathema. He rationalized this incessant questing by reminding himself that the mission of the Nazarenes was to make things better and to change the world. While prayer was certainly an avenue of change, knowledge seemed the firmer footpath. Ideas were power. And Mack Kenton simply overflowed with ideas.

It was at Pilot Point College in a small, northeast Texas town just outside of Denton where the Church of the Nazarene was formed, that Mack Kenton discovered the two forces that would define his adulthood: politics and sex. The people who introduced him to those life-altering influences were Martin Luther King, Jr., Bobby Kennedy, and Maribel Talmadge.

Maribel was a pretty girl, although it was hard to tell beneath the restrictive modesty imposed by the college dress code. Her most disarming feature, her soft, doelike eyes, exuded an honest assumption of goodness.

While Mack liked to believe that it was the purity of Maribel's soul and the keenness of her mind that had attracted him to her, the prestige attached to her name and the size of her breasts would have been closer to the truth.

The Talmadge family was well-known in Nazarene circles. Maribel's grandparents had been traveling evangelists, holding revival meetings throughout the Bible Belt. Her father had carried on the tradition of winning souls for Jesus under big tents in small towns until his family grew too large to travel. Then he founded a Talmadge College in northern Oklahoma, a school exceedingly strict in its social codes and thoroughly grounded in Nazarene philosophy.

Mack had come to Pilot Point an unwilling virgin. While he had convinced himself he had maintained his chastity out of respect for his parents, in reality, he hadn't had much choice. There weren't exactly scores of eager young girls breaking down his door. At his high school, where jocks were king, Mack Kenton was worse than a commoner. He was a nerd. A brilliant student, a nice guy, but a nerd, nonetheless.

At Pilot Point, his rank improved. With no jocks as competition, no long-haired hippies blasting Jefferson Airplane and the Doors from their stereos, and no flower children embarrassing him with flagrant displays of their free-love philosophy, he didn't appear so odd or out of step. At home, his intelligence had set him apart and made him seem strange. Here, all the young men were serious and observant, and girls found that attractive. When it was learned that Mack had received the highest score on the entrance exam and had been handpicked by the head of the Philosophy Department to be one of his honored acolytes, he became the most sought-after bachelor at Pilot Point.

Adding to his sudden cachet were his looks. At eighteen, Mack appeared to have left his gawkiness behind. He had fleshed out handsomely, filling in the spaces between his strong Mackenzie bones. To some, good looks would have been a plus. To Mack, they presented another obstacle. Not only had his face caught up with his features, but his horomones were in agonizing sync with his physiology. Suddenly, like most other college students living away from home for the first time, the desire to explore his sexuality became too strong to ignore. Especially around Maribel.

She loomed like a divine test of his commitment to abstinence. There was no dress thick enough to disguise the rounded pleasures that lay beneath or long enough to hide those long sinuous legs. Despite rigorous attempts to block out her charms, he once again found himself the victim of his own weakness. Quite simply, he looked at her and lusted.

Sophomore year Mack returned to school with a car. Almost every weekend from then on, he and Maribel would climb into his blue '62 Ford with another couple and drive off campus. They never went very far—either sexually or geographically—but those weekend voyages into the world beyond their sheltered environment became as stimulating and as potentially dangerous as foreplay.

On April 4, 1968, Martin Luther King, Jr., was shot and killed in Memphis, Tennessee. While it shocked the nation, his death didn't impact many of those at Pilot Point—civil rights weren't exactly a priority—but for Mack, it was a seminal moment. King's brutal death had crashed through the walls of his quiet ivory tower, leaving a gaping hole. Bobby Kennedy's death showed Mack how to fill it.

Mack had read about it in the local paper: Bobby Kennedy was going to speak at Texas Christian University in Fort Worth. Curious, Mack enticed Maribel and several of their friends to go.

Thousands of people jammed into the stadium, mindless of the long lines and security checks. It was a troubled time, and people were seeking answers. An ocean away, a war few wanted continued to be waged. Soldiers were dying by the thousands but America couldn't seem to get the upper hand. Unthinkable as it seemed, the army that had saved the world almost twenty-five years before was losing.

At home, there were protests about the government's policy in Vietnam, loud enough and violent enough to convince President Lyndon Johnson not to run for another term. And there were race riots. Throughout the country, cities like Atlanta and Chicago and Detroit were burning. There were beatings and killings and lootings and, in a final act of hate, the assassination of Martin Luther King, Jr.

Their seats were high, toward the back of the stadium.

They could barely see the man they had come to hear, but it didn't matter. Kennedy might have appeared like a tiny speck in a sea of faces, but the force of his message described him as a colossus. Mack was mesmerized and not just by the powerful oratory. It was the essence of the speech that engaged and captivated the restless spirit of the young plainsman. This man had an agenda, a program to stop the rioting and the killing that was destroying the nation, an approach to ending the war and bringing America's sons and daughters home, a vision of a prosperous and peaceful future. John Kennedy had issued the charge for the crusade to save the soul of America. Robert Kennedy clearly intended to pick up that mantle and move the crusade forward.

Mack's friends were impressed, but dubious. They were strict Methodists. Kennedy was Catholic, and even though the Pope had held no sway in JFK's administration, the suspicion of influence lingered. If Maribel, who by this time was in love with Mack, had any doubts about Kennedy, the look on Mack's face erased them. He was enraptured.

During the entire ride back to Pilot Point and for weeks afterward, Mack rhapsodized about Kennedy. Unbeknownst to everyone but Maribel, he returned to Fort Worth and signed up to help in the presidential campaign. In Mack's mind, there seemed little question about Kennedy's securing the Democratic nomination. When he raised the subject in the dorm or the student lounge, he found— not surprisingly—that most of his friends claimed little interest in politics. When he pushed the issue, unable to believe anyone could be indifferent during these times, they confessed that their religious upbringing made them fearful of Kennedy's liberal bent.

"What he's talking about is beyond labels," Mack argued. "He wants everyone to do something. He wants us to pool our talents and work for the good of the country. If we work with him, we can change the world."

The problem was that most of his friends at Pilot Point liked the world just the way it was. When on June 6, 1968, that world allowed Sirhan Sirhan to assassinate Robert Kennedy in California, Mack knew he would never lead a ministry. He would never teach philosophy. He would never stand by when he could take part. He would never accept the status quo if change was needed. And he would never follow if, by leading, he could make a difference.

On June 6, 1968, Mack Kenton decided to devote himself to public service.

On June 7, he received his draft notice.

Mack agonized about what to do. He cared deeply about his country, but his religious beliefs and his conscience told him there was no way he could carry a weapon and kill another human being. He could not and would not go.

With the encouragement of Maribel and his entire family, particularly his father, he went to the draft board and declared himself a conscientious objector. At the end of the interrogation process, during which everything he had said or done in the past several years was questioned, it was decided he was sincere in his discomfort and was released from his duty to serve.

That fall, Mack returned to Pilot Point a changed man. He had defied the demands of his government, and while his peers might have applauded his courage, something else had happened: He had challenged the system, stood up for his convictions, and won. By refusing to fight alongside his countrymen, he may once again have fallen short of perfection, but he had tasted power.

After graduation, he and Maribel were married. Instead of returning to Iowa and studying for the ministry, the newlyweds were scheduled to leave for Cambridge, where Mack was to enter the Harvard School of Government.

Eustus Kenton wished his son well on his marriage, but he felt betrayed and said so.

"You were meant for the Lord's work," Eustus intoned, barely able to contain his scorn.

"Maybe this is what the Lord means for me to do," Mack said.

"Don't you dare tell me that God put you on this ignoble path!" his father boomed. "You've been seduced by the devil and, mark my words, son: one of these days you'll pay dearly for your weakness!"

After graduate school, Maribel wanted to move to Oklahoma to be near her family. Mack, who had never fully recovered from his father's rejection, insisted they return to Iowa. As a compromise—and probably as a subliminal act of self-protection—they settled in Des Moines, rather than Otho.

Over the years, Eustus's harsh premonition often came back to haunt Mack, especially when, on several occasions, he strayed from his marital vows. Or when, in the name of ambition, he compromised on certain positions that might have improved the lot of the needy. But the time those words clanged the loudest was after Mack recognized that he had indeed been seduced by the devil.

She was beautiful and enchanting and sensuous beyond his wildest imaginings. Under her spell he did terrible things. He abandoned Maribel and his children and ignored the teachings of his church. Ego made him weak, lust made him vulnerable, and she took advantage of both. Eventually, he ended the relationship, went back to Maribel, and made work his penance, but he could never fully wash the sin from his hands.

When the first kidnappings occurred and Elton Haynes announced he was stepping down, a fire that had been smoldering in Mack's soul ignited. This was more than a political opportunity or a personal challenge. This was the call of clarions.

It was his destiny to respond.

☆   ☆   ☆

March madness was a term most often applied to college basketball. Celia felt it better described the new primary schedule for presidential elections. Within one month, thirty-two states, including electoral behemoths like California, Texas, New York, Ohio, Michigan, Illinois, and Florida, would vote for their favorite candidate. Ten of these elections would take place on a single day—Super Tuesday. By April first, the likelihood was that the tops of both tickets would be decided. And, Celia thought, the entire national press corps would be hospitalized for exhaustion.

In a week that took her from Georgia to Louisiana, Missouri, Maryland, and South Carolina, the toughest leg of the trip was the weekend stop in Florida. The day started with a morning rally in Tallahassee, moved on to a miniparade at Disney World in Orlando, a luncheon with big contributors at the Breakers in Palm Beach, a stop at the Orange Bowl for a halftime appearance at a University of Miami/University of Florida at Gainesville football game and then, later that night, another rally at the Miami Convention Center with Gloria Estefan as the headliner. Blessedly, the next day, Sunday, was free.

Though she was beat and could have used a long sleep on a deserted beach, Celia was going to visit her father. She tried to speak to him at least once a month, but over the past several years, their visits had become sporadic. If she missed this opportunity, it would be months before she could get back.

From the Hyatt on S.E. Second Avenue, she drove across the bridge that spanned the Miami River, cut over to Brickell Avenue, and headed west. It was early, but traffic was fierce. Between the elderly's chronic disregard for stop signs, signals, and turning lanes, and the younger generation's penchant for speed and reckless abandon, driving in Miami had become hazardous to one's health.

She turned off Douglas Road, thankful she had survived. Deliberately slowing to a near crawl, she indulged herself, drinking in the lush splendor that was Coral Gables. Celia's windows were closed, yet she inhaled deeply, as if the rich scent of the flowers blossoming around every house could permeate the tinted glass. She took a quick left, drove down four houses, and stopped across the street from the house where she had spent most of her childhood.

Celia looked up at the three windows of what had once

been her room with its dormer poking out from the main roof, topped by a small roof of its own. Celia used to pretend she was a princess and this was the turret of her castle. She recalled the hours she used to spend looking out at her domain, watching the rain splash just beneath her window, feeling the sun trying to bake through the brick tiles that kept the cool air in, the heat out. She could still see the soft white eyelet that had draped her windows and the crisp white coverlet of Battenberg lace. She could almost feel the coolness of her rosebud sheets and the cushy comfort of her pillows. She had loved that room. Small tears welled in Celia's eyes as she put the car in drive and eased out into the street. They had been so happy in that house.

Hugo waited for her in the doorway of another house in another neighborhood, several blocks—and a world— away from the first. Even at seventy, he was a striking figure, tan and nattily dressed in his ubiquitous white suit and straw fedora. Unlike many of her Atlanta-based relatives, it had never been hard for Celia to understand how a refined woman like Nell Dickerson might have fallen for the likes of Hugo Porter.

"Hey, pretty girl," Hugo said, as Celia mounted the steps, offered her cheek for a kiss, and sank into one of her father's bearlike hugs.

"Hiya, Pop. How're you doing?"

"Hangin' in!" He laughed, his body shaking with the effort.

Celia smiled, but only on the surface. People used that expression all the time; Hugo had meant it as an honest assessment of his circumstances. Celia hated the thought that her father was simply hanging in. He wasn't a hanging-in, just-getting-by kind of guy. Hugo Porter had always been fueled by a sense of adventure. It was what defined his essence. Nothing excited him more than the heady triumph of discovery: new places, new foods, new people. When CORAL AIR, a small charter company, was in its heyday, it was nothing for the three of them to take off on what Hugo called, "Saturday-Sunday-safaris." They'd pick a place on a map, pack an overnight bag, and go.

When Hugo led Celia inside, her nose wrinkled at the musty smell that greeted her. The air conditioner was whirring, but she sensed he had put it on for her; she guessed he couldn't afford to keep it running all the time. She had offered to send him money dozens of times, but each time, he refused. He thanked her and assured her he was okay. It was mostly cargo, now, but CORAL AIR was still up and running, he reminded her.

He hung his hat on a hook by the door. Celia noted that his head was barer than the last time she had seen him and that his fingers were bent from arthritis. When he removed his jacket, she saw that his shirt hung on him, as did his trousers. This suit must have been ten years old, donned for the occasion of his daughter's visit. She was touched by the gesture, saddened by the visible reality of his impoverishment, a stark reminder of an unhappy time.

They talked, mostly about the election. Hugo had always loved the excitement of politics, but his interest had remained local—who ran Miami, Cuba, Haiti, Mexico, and the islands that drew the largest amount of American tourists. Who got along with whom directly affected his business. This presidential cycle interested him only because his daughter was covering one of the candidates, and his niece had been married to the other one.

"Why aren't you reporting Ben's campaign?" he asked.

"I would have liked that, but unfortunately, I didn't get to choose," she explained. "Actually, Edwards is considered the plum assignment."

Hugo's turquoise eyes fixed on his daughter. "So why do you look as if you were just handed the booby prize?"

She leaned over and kissed his cheek, rewarding him for his intuition. "Because, you clever fellow, Dean Walsh is using me."

She offered him a condensed version of the meeting in Titus Mitchell's office, after which Hugo said, "Forget about Walsh and those other camera hogs. You just get out there and do your job. This is your big break. It doesn't matter how you got it, it's what you do with it that's going to count."

Celia nodded, feeling as if she was five years old again. In a way, it was nice. No one had taken care of her in a very long time. She looked around the room, noticed a picture of her and her mother. It had been taken on the porch of their old house. Nell, dressed in a frothy white dress, was brandishing a gleaming trophy and grinning. Celia stood next to her, self-consciously posed in a white dress with a blue sash that proclaimed her Little Miss Pompano.

"I still miss her," Hugo said softly.

Celia patted his hand. Even after all these years, his love for her mother remained strong. "Me too."

She wondered, and not for the first time, if she'd ever find anyone to love her as fiercely as Hugo had loved Nell. It was probably the one thing about her mother's life she had really envied. As for the way Nell had loved Hugo, Celia doubted it would happen to her. She had tried to find a man like her father, but the world seemed devoid of men who, to use her mother's words, "were both daring and caring."

"She'd be mighty proud of you, Celia."

"You think?" Celia's smile was small and insecure.

Hugo nodded, but his smile had faded. "I worried when you were in the Gulf and in Bosnia."

Celia shrugged. "It's part of the job."

"I also worry that you're alone." He eyed her carefully. "Got a man in your life?"

"Not at the moment," she confessed.

"Too bad. You're like your mother. You need to be loved."

"I suppose." Celia was thirty-nine years old, and she never remembered talking about such personal things with her father. She didn't know if she was amused or embarrassed.

"You need to find a man who's not bowled over by how

damned gorgeous you are. A guy who loves you for what's in here," he said, tapping his head, "and here." He tapped at his chest. His eyes fixed on her as he gently caressed her cheek. "The outside's just a bonus, baby. The inside's the real deal."

Odd, Celia thought, as he studied the little girl in the picture. For so long, the only thing that seemed important was the outside.

Celia won her first beauty contest at four years old; Nell had entered her as a lark. Celia wasn't clear on precisely when these pageants became an obsession with her mother, but before she knew it, Nell was scouring the papers, searching for every opportunity to parade her daughter before a crowd.

As for Celia, it felt exciting then, to put on a pretty new dress and have people fuss with her hair, to walk across a stage and have people applaud when she smiled, to get a bouquet of flowers, a crown, a silky banner, and her picture in the newspaper. It was nice to take home a gleaming trophy, even nicer to hear Daddy talk about his "shining star" and Mommy brag about her "precious beauty."

Soon, either Hugo was flying the two of them all over the South, or they were on buses and trains, heading for contests for the coveted title of Princess This or That, or Little Miss Something or Other. It didn't matter who was sponsoring the event; if there was a crown and, more important, a cash prize, Nell and Celia Porter were there.

Most of the time, Celia won. On the few occasions when she didn't, Nell never commented or criticized, but she seemed down for days afterward, prompting Celia to try that much harder the next time out. The last thing Celia wanted was to disappoint her mother.

Once, on the way home from Birmingham, when Nell looked particularly tired, Celia asked why they bothered.

"Because God gave you a double gift," Nell had said, wearily stroking Celia's cheek. "You're beautiful and you're smart, and that sets you apart from those who are merely ordinary."

"Is that important?" Celia asked. "Not to be ordinary?"

Nell laughed at her daughter's naïveté, then turned thoughtful, her eyes closing for a moment while she quietly recalled the times she was ignored in favor of her two older, more stellar siblings. "I would say that being ordinary is the absolute worst thing you can be."

By the time Celia hit her teens, she had a room filled with trophies and ribbons, a scrapbook loaded with newspaper articles and photographs. For a while, it seemed as if Nell's enthusiasm had waned, but then, at thirteen, Celia was sent north to spend the summer in Atlanta with her mother's sister, Avis Coburn.

Ostensibly, this visit was so that Celia could spend time with her cousin, Felicia. While the two young girls had a wonderful time together, Celia couldn't shake the feeling that something was off. When she returned to Miami, her suspicions heightened. Her father looked aged and worn, as if he had barely survived a life-defining crisis. Nell seemed different as well. Quiet and withdrawn, she was possessed of an unfamiliar intensity Celia found unsettling.

It also appeared that Nell had mapped out Celia's future while she was away: a string of beauty contests leading up to the Miss America Pageant, in Atlantic City. The key, according to Nell, was the Junior Miss title.

"You win that, and Miss Miami is a shoo-in. From there, it's not even a full step to winning Miss Florida."

It frightened Celia that Nell spoke of these contests with an inexplicable sense of urgency, and an air of calculation. There was no joy in the discussion of which pageants they were going to enter, no laughter, no fun planning what to wear and what to say. These outings had become markers along a path to a place where Nell was headed. Celia was simply the vehicle for her journey.

* * *

Celia was sixteen when she discovered the reason for her mother's strange behavior and her mysterious trip to Atlanta three years before: Nell had breast cancer. At that time, Nell had undergone a lumpectomy and follow-up radiation. Her apparent recovery had allowed her to hide her condition from Celia, but when the cancer returned, it was further advanced and far more aggressive. Mastectomy was certain. The only question was when to start the chemotherapy and how strong to make the dosage.

When Celia was told, she was devastated. She wanted to quit school and stay by Nell's side throughout the ordeal.

"I can nurse you better than anyone," she said, fighting the fear that had translated itself into a constant feeling of nausea.

"You have school and the Junior Miss Pageant," Nell reminded her.

"I can do both of them next year, when you're better."

"No! Do them now!" Nell insisted.

Celia would have continued to protest if Hugo hadn't reminded her how important these contests were to Nell. "Whenever you win, she feels as if she's won, too. She could use a win right now, Celia."

The first three days after a chemotherapy treatment were the worst. Hugo took Nell to the hospital, waited while she was transfused with the chemicals, and took her home, staying until Celia came home from school. Then he headed off to the airport to check on things at CORAL AIR, leaving Celia to nurse her mother. Without a single complaint, Celia fixed Nell's dinner, fed her, helped her to the toilet, and held her head while she vomited.

On the fourth day, Nell was weak and pale, but able to regain some semblance of normalcy. It was during those interim periods that Celia indulged Nell's obsession with the Junior Miss Pageant. Together, they filled out the entrance applications and scoured department-store catalogues looking for the perfect dress. They had picked out several, but before they could send away for any of them, the matter had become moot. Avis Coburn flew in from Atlanta and took over.

"Hugo told me you two have been holed up in here so long you're growing mold!" Avis said, trying not to gasp at the sight of her younger sister.

"That's not true," Celia said. "Mom's doing great. Aren't you, Mom?"

"I'm fit as a fiddle." Nell tried to do a quick two-step, but if she hadn't grabbed the wall for support, she would have fallen on her face.

Celia winced. Avis looked away.

"I guess the Olympics will have to wait," Nell said, trying to buoy their spirits.

"You're doing fine," Avis said, kissing her sister's forehead, careful not to move the scarf that hid her baldness. "Just fine."

Avis took Nell's arm and led her toward the couch. When they were seated and she was certain her sister was comfortable, she asked about the surgery.

"When do you go into the hospital?"

"Another month or so." Suddenly, Nell laughed. "There's a method to their madness. They pump you full of chemicals and make you so sick and so fatigued that the idea of lying unconscious on a table for a couple of hours seems like a terrific idea!"

Celia and Avis laughed, too, but the sound was hollow.

"Hugo said you're entering the Junior Miss contest," Avis said to Celia.

"She's going to win!" Nell's smile was filled with a light Celia had feared the cancer had extinguished.

"Well, of course she is! We Dickerson women are famous for our beauty. Aren't we, Nell?"

"Maybe once upon a time . . ." Nell said wistfully, aware of the silky blond hair that had fallen out in clumps and the full, womanly breast that would soon be gone.

"*Still!*" Avis said with conviction. "Why, if there were a contest for Miss Chemotherapy USA, you'd win hands down, darlin'!"

"Forget about me," Nell said. "Let's talk about Celia and the pageant."

"Precisely why I'm here."

Avis jumped up from the couch, ran into the hall, and came back carrying several cartons from Rich's Department Store. "Since I am a definite part of Celia's genetic pool and, therefore, have a stake in this title, I am insisting on providing her dress."

Nell and Celia protested, but mildly. Within seconds after Avis opened the boxes and pulled out the frothy confections she had selected, mother and daughter were too entranced to object. When Hugo came home, the Dickerson sisters insisted that Celia model each one for him. He knew better than to think that his opinion counted for anything, so after Celia had paraded about the living room in five equally scrumptious gowns, he threw up his hands, and said, "They're all gorgeous!"

"Of course they are," Avis said with feigned indignation. "It's not every day my niece competes for the title of Junior Miss!"

The night of the America's Junior Miss Pageant was one Celia would remember for the rest of her life. As she stood with the other four finalists, her eyes sought those of her mother, who sat in the first row, next to Avis. The contrast rattled Celia: Avis was stunning in a peach-colored silk suit, her blond hair confined in a neat ponytail, her neck and ears gleaming with South Sea pearls. Next to her, Nell looked frail and old. Avis had wrapped her head in a magnificent floral silk scarf and had bought her a lucious pink silk suit, but Nell's complexion was wan, and even though the suit was only two weeks old, it hung on her ravaged frame.

As each runner-up was announced, Celia prayed she wouldn't hear her name. Never before had she wanted to win as badly as she did now. Her heart pounded as the emcee held up the final card.

"And now, ladies and gentlemen, our first runner-up, the lucky young woman who will take over the Junior Miss title if something happens to our winner, the recipient of an eight-thousand-dollar scholarship, the lovely Miss Daisy McClintock from Nashville, Tennessee.

"Which means that America's Junior Miss is the representative of the Sunshine State, Miss Celia Porter of Miami, Florida!"

Celia stood as still as she could as the previous year's Junior Miss draped the satin sash over her shoulder, pinned the crown on her head, and handed her a dozen roses. Her eyes never strayed from Nell's. When the music for her victory stroll began, she started down the runway as she had been taught, but when she came to where Nell and Avis were sitting, she broke with tradition and stopped.

"I love you, Mom," she said, as she bent down and handed her mother her roses.

Avis steadied Nell, who had risen to receive the bouquet. Flashbulbs popped like firecrackers. With Avis's arm around her, Nell summoned every ounce of strength she had and stood tall as her daughter completed her walk and took her place on the throne for the start of her year-long reign.

Two weeks later, Celia left for the first stop on her tour of the United States, with Avis as her chaperone.

Two days after that, Nell Porter underwent eight hours of surgery.

Despite the surgery and the follow-up chemotherapy, Nell's cancer continued to spread. When she died, Nell was buried in Atlanta, next to her mother. Hugo had wanted her to be buried in Miami, near him, but Nell had insisted. She wanted him to get on with his life, not spend it visiting a grave.

Before the services, Hugo requested a private moment with his wife. Though the casket was closed for the condolence visits, it was opened briefly so Hugo and Celia could say their good-byes.

Hand in hand, they stood alongside the flower-draped casket, weeping, drowning in their own pool of remembrances. Hugo kissed his wife's cold lips and then placed his wedding band and a gardenia by Nell's clasped hands. They were her favorite flower. He had given her one the day they met. It seemed only right to give her one now.

Hugo stepped to the side, allowing Celia to move closer to Nell. Celia couldn't stop sobbing. Hugo wrapped his arm around her and pressed her against him.

"You were the best thing that ever happend to her," he whispered, his own voice shaking. "Don't ever forget that."

Celia nodded and took a deep breath, trying desperately to control herself. It was the hardest thing she ever had to do. Looking down at her mother, seeing the gaunt face and nearly skeletal frame, it was almost impossible to believe that once, this woman had been beautiful. Celia closed her eyes, forcing herself to recall Nell in the good years, when her hair was thick and blond, when her skin had had that peachy cast that had marked her as a true Southern belle.

Opening her eyes, she willed herself to hold on to that picture, to block out the horrible reality of what that cannibalistic disease had wrought, to smother the fear that had selfishly risen in her heart that this same thing might one day happen to her.

"There are an awful lot of beautiful angels in heaven," she said softly. "Which is why I want you to take these with you."

As carefully as her trembling hands would allow, she laid her Junior Miss sash and crown on Nell's chest.

"They need to know just how special you are." She kissed her fingers and gently touched Nell's lips. "Godspeed, Mom."

* * *

It was late when Celia returned to her hotel room after having dinner with Hugo. Clay Chandler was waiting.

"Visiting Daddy?" he asked, with deliberate sarcasm.

Inside, Celia recoiled. Finding someone in her room was unsettling enough; knowing how familiar Clay was with her history nearly made her lose her composure.

"It's no business of yours whom I visit," Celia said, slamming the door, hiding her discomfort behind a display of anger. "Why you're in my room and how you got here is my business, however."

"How is simple." He held up a key and dangled it infuriatingly. "The why is also simple. I want you to stop trashing my candidate."

"What!"

"I've been studying the General's coverage and you know what? You are the fly in the ointment. Everywhere the man goes, you throw an irrelevant question at him and throw him off message. If I didn't know better, I'd think you were being paid by the Knight camp to sabotage us."

Celia's reaction was instantaneous and heated. "That is the most outrageous thing I've ever heard!"

"Presidential campaigns bring out the outrageous in all of us, or didn't you know that?" His tone was not only patronizing, but deliberately so, which made it even more galling.

"I don't know why I'm dignifying your accusation with an answer, but I am not being paid by anyone other than my network. And in case *you* didn't know, presidential campaigns usually involve more than one issue."

Clay shook his head. "No, my pretty. This election is going to be won or lost on the hostage issue. Not the economy, not crime, not health care or welfare or abortion. Hostages. Plain and simple. So don't do stupid things like asking Scottie to comment on a proposal by one of his minions that would require welfare mothers with more than two children to be sterilized."

"He has opinions on everything else. Why not that?"

"It's not important, that's why."

"To those women, it's very important."

"It's not central to the election." Clay was growing impatient. His round, hyperthyroid eyes bulged, making him look like a frog.

"It is when the candidate has commented in the past that he supports such legislation."

Clay leaped out of his chair, his carefully constructed calm shattered by Celia's lack of deference.

"Oh, for Christ's sake, Celia! He said that in answer to a question put to him at a small, inconsequential Christian League convention in Virginia two years ago."

"How many people attended that convention is immaterial and I would hardly call the Christian League inconsequential. Scottie Edwards was their keynote speaker. He had his picture taken with his arm around the living symbol of the Radical Right, Gray Pryor. And he loudly and vociferously advocated state-sponsored sterilization."

Clay tugged at his tie. His lips tightened into a thin line. "So he said it. He was put on the spot. What the hell difference does it make?"

"It's called accountability, Clay. Was Edwards lying to them? Or is he lying to us?" Celia had learned that the best way to confront a radical was to use his own words against him and not allow extreme comments to go unchallenged. "He can't court the far right one minute and woo the middle the next. Eventually, he's going to trip over his own lines."

Exasperated, Chandler moved toward the door, his displeasure obvious. "Do everyone, especially yourself, a favor and give up the crusade, Celia. Just report on what you see and hear. Not what you think or remember or you've looked up or been fed by some grunt in the home office."

"What if," she countered, refusing to be cowed, "for reasons you'd never understand—like journalistic integrity—I continue to insist upon honesty and full disclosure. What are you going to do about it?"

Clay leaned in close. With the back of his hand, he traced the line from her temple down to her chin. She shivered with disgust. "You muck around in his past," he said, making no attempt to disguise his threat, "and we'll have to muck around in yours."

Celia had married Buddy Brown because he was tall, dark, very handsome, and madly in love with her. Also, she thought it was what she was supposed to do. By her senior year at Boston University, half her class and most of her friends were engaged. Felicia's wedding to Ben had been two weeks after graduation, Georgie's to Lyle Mercer only a few months after that. Zoë was the only unattached among them, but Zoë was different. She had her eye on a career. Celia had her eye on a title: Mrs. Somebody Wonderful.

If there was a negative to Buddy, it was Iowa. Whenever Celia had dreamed of living happily-ever-after, it was in New York or Paris or Los Angeles. Ames, Iowa was never even part of a daydream. Yet that's where the new Mr. and Mrs. Brown settled. After Buddy had completed his master's, he had been offered a job at the Iowa State University as an economics instructor.

Celia tried, but she never fit in. She wasn't like the other faculty wives. She wasn't a student or a mother. She didn't like teas, tailgate picnics, or county fairs. Buddy never complained. As he told her over and over again, he considered himself a lucky man to have such a beautiful wife.

Celia was restless. Her first choice was to work at the *Des Moines Register,* but there were no openings, not even for cubs. She applied to the local television and radio stations, offering to do just about anything, but there, too, she came up empty. Disappointed and bored, she took a job in Younkers Department Store selling cosmetics and perfume.

Christmas Eve day her counter was besieged by husbands desperate to buy last-minute gifts for their wives. Celia was too busy making a pitch for a gold compact to a wary insurance broker to notice another man, observing her.

Finally, she turned her attention to him.

"Are you looking for a gift for your wife?" she asked as she reached down to ready another compact and lipstick.

He nodded, then twisted his head to one side and squinted at her for one unsettling moment. "I'm also looking for a weather girl for KIOW's evening news. Think you might be interested?"

"Excuse me?"

"I'm Harry Birns, news director over at KIOW."

Celia couldn't decide whether this was a legitimate offer or an elaborate come-on. As if divining the cause of her skepticism, the man handed her his card.

"I'll take the gift set. You take my card and please, call me after New Year's. I swear on Santa, this is an honest-to-goodness job offer."

Celia started work the second week in January. At first, she found it embarrassing to stand before a large map of the United States discussing rising and falling barometers and the flow of the jet stream with a plastic grin on her face. Even worse, was having to attach magnetic weather symbols to the smaller map of Iowa like a kindergarten teacher dressing a classroom bulletin board.

After six months, she made an appointment to discuss her job with Harry.

"I feel dumb," she said.

"You don't look dumb."

"It's not about looks, Harry. It's about making the weather into something other than a sideshow."

Harry leaned back and massaged his chin. Since Celia had come on board, ratings were up. True, he had made other changes in the presentation of the news, but she was part of the formula. He didn't want to lose her. Besides, she was making sense.

"What've you got in mind?"

"Let's upgrade our presentation by decreasing the show and increasing the business side of the weather. There's a large segment of our population whose businesses depend on the weather. Farmers. Ranchers. Store owners.

Truckers. Why not do stories on how the weather affects them? If it snows, send me out to talk to truckers stranded on the highway. If it rains for days on end, let me interview the farmers whose crops are in danger of being ruined and homeowners on the rivers in danger of being flooded out. If it's brutally hot, let me talk to the people frying on the street. Let me do something other than look pretty!''

Harry said he wanted to think about it. Celia decided to give him a push.

The next week, a huge winter storm was due to blow in from the northwest. Expecting predictions of snowfall amounts and warnings to stay off the roads, Harry was stunned when instead, Celia gave all the meteorological particulars and then quoted Henry Wadsworth Longfellow:

> Out of the bosom of the Air,
> Out of the cloud-folds of her garments shaken,
> Over the woodlands brown and bare,
> Over the Harvest-fields forsaken,
> Silent, and soft, and slow
> Descends the snow.

Harry groaned. KIOW's phone lines were jammed. He was certain the callers were advertisers canceling their contracts. But he was wrong. KIOW's weather spot quickly became the talk of the town. It wasn't unusual to hear people in coffee shops or beauty parlors or around office water coolers talking about Celia Porter's ''Eye on the Sky'' segment. Whether it was a tape of her leading local tribes onto a sun-dried field to do a rain dance or standing in the midst of a blizzard commiserating with commuters or, during a disastrous rainy season, quoting the English humorist, A.P. Herbert:

> The Farmer will never be happy again;
> He carries his heart in his boots;
> For either the rain is destroying his grain
> Or the drought is destroying his roots.

Ratings soared, and Celia became a local celebrity. Unfortunately for Buddy and Harry, her popularity spread well beyond Iowa's borders. Station managers around the country began to take notice of the bright and beautiful weather girl from Des Moines. When KMIA in Miami contacted her, they offered her both evening news segments, the chance to branch out onto larger, non–weather-related stories, and a full-blown publicity campaign heralding the return of their local star. It was an offer she couldn't refuse.

She and Buddy divorced, her star did indeed rise higher, but her glitter attracted two people she would have been better off avoiding: Harris Ralston, the man who would become husband number two. And Clay Chandler.

☆   ☆   ☆

The airways were filled with it: Late Friday night—Eastern Standard Time—twelve French citizens were kidnapped from their embassy in Lebanon. Seven were women. Fifteen million dollars had been demanded as ransom. Elton Haynes scheduled a press conference. Scottie Edwards scrambled for airtime. Mack Kenton flew to Washington to caucus with his foreign policy team while his communication staff tried to book an appearance on ABC's *Newsmakers*.

Ben, who had been called to do NTN's *Sunday Headlines*, arranged for a Senate colleague from New Jersey to fill in for him at a fund-raiser in Connecticut and ordered his top strategists to Philadelphia. With the first round of the March primary crunch only three days away, many of them were in the field doing advance for upcoming events. Allowing them time to fly in, the meeting had been scheduled for late afternoon on Saturday.

Zoë arrived first. Ben had flown in only minutes before from a New England Women's Political Caucus breakfast in Maine followed by an address to a medical symposium in Baltimore focusing on breast cancer. From the start, Zoë, Jed, and Ben had agreed on an aggressive pursuit of women. Not only were they one of the most powerful voting blocs, but their agenda was clear: choice—either pro or con—health care, education, and gun control. Women were caretakers and voted accordingly.

Ben and Zoë chatted for a few minutes, going over who would be in attendance and how Ben wanted to proceed. Then he took her on a tour of his house on Chestnut Hill.

It was exactly what Zoë would have expected of Felicia. Grand in scale, luxuriously appointed, it reeked of old-line money and carefully cultivated taste. As if reading her mind, Ben told her he had wanted to sell it after Felicia died, but couldn't.

"This house was never mine. It was given to Felicia by her parents. When she died, it was left to her children. Avis and her brother, Dewitt Dickerson, are the executors of Felicia's will. They felt Keeley and Ryan had a right to continue to live here, surrounded by memories of their mother."

"Did they want you to be continually reminded of Felicia as well?" Zoë could have kicked herself. She sounded jealous and petty. If Ben noticed, he didn't let it show.

"Probably," he said, "but I decided not to take a stand on this issue. Keeley and Ryan had had enough taken away from them."

Loretta Knight intruded on what could have become an uncomfortable moment, greeting Zoë like a long-lost relative.

"Ben told me you were still the most gorgeous woman he'd ever seen," she said, oblivious to her son's raised eyebrows and the faint coloring of his cheeks. She hugged Zoë, then held her at arm's length. "He's right. You're still spectacular."

"And you are still incorrigible." Zoë laughed, returning the older woman's embrace.

"Can you spare her?" Loretta asked her son.

"One cup of coffee or until the others arrive. Whichever comes first." Ben offered Zoë a sly smile, and said to his mother, "She is indispensable, you know."

The two women strolled arm in arm toward the kitchen,

laughing and chattering like girlfriends. They had connected the moment they met; even after her romance with Ben ended, Zoë and Loretta kept in touch. They were still catching up when Ben's children bounded into the kitchen. Keeley appeared startled to find her grandmother chumming it up with a woman unknown to her. Loretta, noticing the pinched expression on Keeley's face, introduced them. It was obvious that while Keeley didn't recognize Zoë's face, she had heard the name before.

"What a pleasure it is to meet you," Zoë said, extending her hand. Keeley took it, but cautiously. "You're as beautiful as I'd imagined you'd be."

"Thank you." *So are you,* Keeley thought, but kept it to herself.

"Grandma says you're a Red Sox fan," Ryan said.

"And proud of it!"

"That's almost as bad as rooting for the Phillies." From his expression, it was clear he wondered if she was suffering from dementia.

Zoë and Ryan bantered baseball until Keeley telegraphed some kind of signal to him, and they made an abrupt exit.

"Don't take it personally," Loretta said, her brows knitted together. "Keeley's wary of every woman who comes near her father."

"It must be awful for her to think of someone taking her mother's place."

Loretta nodded, but clearly, that wasn't her total concern.

"She's slipped into a role that's a little too grown-up for her. She tries to be Ben's hostess, his companion, and sometimes, his confidante. It's not good. She's only fifteen."

"What does Ben say?"

"When his father was killed, he saw himself as my protector. He was the man of the house. Keeley thinks she's the woman of the house. To him, it's the same thing."

Zoë's expression became thoughtful. "He once told me

that because his dad's death was so sudden and so horrifyingly impossible to understand, he lived most of his life in constant fear of losing you the same way."

"I know that," Loretta said quietly. "I tried to reassure him and make him feel secure, but some events are simply too overwhelming."

Zoë agreed. There was a simmering anger inside Benjamin Knight that would never abate. It was what made him a dedicated activist; also, it fueled his infamous outbursts of temper. The murders of his father and brother had become an element of Ben's personality that was truly beyond his control. Like a chronic disease, the pain persisted, impervious to any of life's analgesics. Some days were better than others; no day was pain free.

"He's a wonderful father," Loretta was saying. "He's home for dinner almost every night. He goes to every school play, every parent-teacher conference. He misses very few Little League games." She laughed. "He actually did a stint as a Girl Scout leader." She laughed again. "The lobbyists positively hate him. He doesn't hang out like some of them do, going to dinner with this one or that one. And if he goes on vacation, it's with his children. You won't find Ben flying off on junkets or ski trips or golf outings."

Zoë was impressed. On a senator's schedule, involvement like that was quite a feat. It was also quite rare.

"They don't have a mother," Loretta continued. "As much as he loves his work, Ben was determined they wouldn't be fatherless as well."

"No," Zoë said quietly. "He knows better than most what that's like." She leaned over and patted Loretta's hand. "You must be awfully proud of him."

"I am." The older woman nodded. Her eyes misted for a moment, but then a big grin covered her face. "I'm mighty proud of you, too. Look what you've done with yourself! From what Ben tells me, you should be running the State Department."

"I don't know about that," Zoë said.

"He said you predicted this crisis. That you warned them at State and not only did they ignore you, they punished you."

Zoë nodded. "Questioning the judgment of the president and the secretary of state is not exactly the best route to the top of the career ladder. I told them someone they had dismissed as inconsequential was dangerous."

"You were right."

"This is one time, Loretta, I would have given anything to be wrong."

Benjamin Knight was eight years old when his father and brother were gunned down in the street. It was a Sunday afternoon. Kirk Knight had taken his family to Shibe Park to watch the Phillies-Dodgers game. It had taken twelve innings and six pitchers, but the Phillies won and the Knights were anxious to celebrate.

Before they left the ballpark, Kirk bought his two boys—Robbie and Ben—pennants and ice-cream cones. By the time they headed for the lot where they had parked their car, the crowds had thinned. They were standing on the corner of Lehigh Avenue and Twenty-first Street waiting for the light to change when suddenly, a red car careened around the corner. The tires squealed. The car seemed to be standing on two wheels. Loud, thumping music spilled out into the streets, demanding attention. Just as the Knights turned to the source of the ruckus, two young black boys leaned out the windows and started shooting.

Ben heard the sounds, but since guns were not a part of his everyday world, it took a minute to react. Within that minute, his father and his brother were mortally wounded.

The rest of the night was a blur of howling sirens and anxious voices and beeping machines. He tried to concentrate on the moment, but his mind insisted upon replaying the scene outside the stadium: the sight of his brother's chest gushing red, the strange angle of his father's head and neck, the awful sound of Robbie's agonized screams, the more horrifying sound of his father's silence.

He remembered sitting in the patients' lounge with his mother, being questioned by the police. Loretta recalled little. Ben was able to supply the color and make of the car, though not the year, as well as two numbers on the license plate. Yes, it was a Pennsylvania plate. No, he didn't know whether the numbers he recalled were in sequence. No, he couldn't describe the shooters. Was there anything unusual about them? How they looked? What they were wearing?

"One of them was wearing a Yankee hat."

"How'd you notice that?" one of the officers said, grateful for the information, nonetheless thinking it strange that in the midst of a barrage of bullets, this young boy would notice a baseball cap.

"It was a Phillies-Dodgers game," Ben said, as if it should be as obvious to them as it was to him. "You don't wear a Yankee hat to a Phillies-Dodgers game."

"Maybe they weren't at the game," the other officer said, testing Ben.

Ben remained firm. "They were coming from the parking lot." His eyes pooled, and though he struggled to hold them back, tears streamed down his face. "The car was red and all souped up. I like cars, so I guess I couldn't help but notice it." He wiped his eyes, but the tears continued to come. "Why didn't I see the guns?" he asked the officer next to him. "If I had, I could have warned my father and Robbie. I could have told them to watch out. I could have . . ."

The policeman took the young boy in his arms and held him close. "Don't," he said, trying to quell the boy's tremblings of guilt. "There was nothing you could do, son. Nothing."

In the weeks that followed, many other voices echoed the policeman's sentiment. But Ben refused to believe he was without blame. Ben had seen the car. His father had died instantly of a bullet to the brain, his brother had died on an operating table after five hours of surgery.

No matter what anyone said, or how often they said it, for the rest of his life, Ben would continue to believe that he could have, more importantly, *should* have done something.

It was well past nine when a dark blue car parked across the street from Ben's house. The driver didn't get out. Within seconds, two other anonymous cars slid against the curb several houses down in either direction. Those drivers also stayed put. Ten minutes later, an ordinary taxicab pulled up in front of Ben's house. Two men climbed out of the backseat and the taxi drove away. A tall man walked briskly to the door where one of Ben's Secret Service agents waited; the shorter man lagged behind, his eyes darting from side to side. When both men entered the house, the door closed quickly behind them.

Zoë was standing in the hallway, and the tall man went straight for her. They embraced warmly, kissing each other on both cheeks and exchanging greetings in a language Ben assumed was Hebrew. Again, he found himself marveling at Zoë's linguistic talents.

"Ben, this is General Zev Shafir," Zoë said, "Zev, this is Senator Benjamin Knight."

The two men shook hands. Zoë continued with the introductions, including Zev's bodyguard, Moishe, and when they were completed, nodded to Ben, who led the way into his library. As they entered, Ben noted the way the general's piercing blue eyes scanned the richly paneled room, surveying the space, assessing danger zones. Not surprisingly, he took a seat in a corner away from the windows, facing the door. Moishe positioned himself in the doorway so that he could guard against anyone coming from inside the house, or out.

Zev Shafir was in his early fifties, a *sabra* born in Haifa when Israel was still called Palestine. A former air force pilot, he had risen to the rank of general during his lengthy tour as part of an élite unit within the Israel Defense Forces trained in counterterrorist activities. Now, he headed a division within the famed Israeli counterintelligence agency, the Mossad.

In April, the Israeli Prime Minister Hershel Goldfeier was due to visit the United States. While here, in addition to meeting with Elton Haynes, he would pay the customary calls on the various presidential candidates. Zoë had already arranged for a bilateral with Goldfeier immediately after his meeting with Haynes. In a town where power was often defined by perception, your place in line was important.

This private conference with General Shafir was a coup primarily because it was not customary. Zoë had suggested it because Zev's area of expertise was Russia and because Zev had participated in the daring raid on Entebbe.

That episode was of particular interest to Ben, and he asked if Shafir would mind recalling it.

On Sunday, June 27, 1976, Air France flight 139, flying from Tel Aviv to Paris via Athens was hijacked. Two of the terrorists who boarded the plane in Athens were members of the German Baader-Meinhof gang of urban guerillas. The other two were Arabs claiming membership in the Palestine Liberation Organization. In the aircraft were 256 passengers and twelve crew members. The plane refueled at Benghazi, Libya, and then continued south, landing at Entebbe in Uganda. There, they were joined by additional PLO terrorists as well as units of the Ugandan army who moved the hostages into the old terminal building at the airport.

The hijackers demanded the release of fifty-three convicted terrorists. They flew the non-Israeli passengers back to France, but kept the Israelis prisoners.

"Shimon Peres was minister of defense then," Shafir said. "What was of paramount importance to him was that Israel refuse to submit to the terrorists. He felt it would set a dangerous precedent."

Ben nodded. That was the same attitude underlying American policy.

"General Gur," Shafir continued, "said he would not recommend a military operation unless he personally concluded that the risk was reasonable and the proposal was feasible.''

Ben was rapt. There were so many similiarites between the two situations. The major difference was that in Entebbe, all the hostages were in one place.

''My friend, General Shomron, was chief infantry and paratroop officer. When he heard they had separated the Israelis and non-Israelis he began to plan the release of the hostages—without any instruction from his superiors.'' Shafir's jaw hardened. ''Dan likened that separation to the selection process used by the Nazis in the camps.''

Ben could almost hear the unspoken *Never Again*.

''As the air force commander, I knew our Hercules aircraft could reach Entebbe, but in order to get home, we would have to refuel at the Entebbe airport.''

Sam Trout rubbed his forehead as if the stress were his. He had followed the Entebbe rescue as it occurred. It had amazed him then. Listening to Shafir, he felt the same sense of wonder now.

''The one weak point was landing the first aircraft with out arousing suspicion. If we could do that, most of us felt we had a one hundred percent chance of success. With luck, there would be no casualties.''

''How did you resolve your weak point?'' Ben asked.

''The operation was scheduled for Saturday. Friday night, General Gur and I flew in a Hercules to make certain that it was capable of a blind landing. We already knew that the weather would be good and that the night would be dark without any moonlight.''

''At the same time,'' Zoë added, ''intelligence was being gathered from the non-Israeli passengers in France about the daily routines, the habits of the guards, locations of various conveniences, et cetera.''

''We had four planes in the air at 15:30. We were flying seven hours when we came within range of the Entebbe control tower. We had planned it so that the first aircraft could dovetail behind a scheduled British cargo flight, thereby avoiding arousing suspicion.'' Shafir's lip curled upward briefly. "We came behind the British plane just as the captain was asking for permission to land. We glided in, slowed, and the advance party jumped out while we were still taxiing. Within minutes the other three planes were on the ground as well.

"Fifty-seven minutes after the commencement of the operation, the first aircraft loaded with the hostages took off from Entebbe. We suffered only one casualty, Lieutenant Colonel Yoni Netanyahu."

Ben ruminated over what Shafir had said, mixing it in with facts already known and operations he had experienced in Vietnam.

"I was always impressed with the speed and sophistication of that rescue," he said. "My experience in the field of battle taught about the importance of assuring definite margins of safety. You guys had no safety margin at Entebbe. Every single element was interdependent. The slightest error, the slightest lack of coordination and everything falls apart and lives are lost."

Ben didn't have to mention the failed attempt to rescue American hostages in Iran in 1980. He could see by the faces of his countrymen they were thinking the same thing. It had been poorly planned.

"Entebbe was the culmination of years of training for such eventualities on the part of our counterterrorist unit as well as other commando forces." Shafir's tone said that he had intuited their thoughts. He wasn't gloating, he was sympathizing. "We may be the younger nation," he said, "but we are far more experienced when it comes to terrorism."

He looked around the room, drawing the others in. "We've had our successes, but don't think we haven't paid a price for our policies." Again, he caught Zoë's eye. Her eyes clouded. "In 1974, a school in a northern Galilee town was taken over by Arab terrorists. We stormed the building and killed the intruders, but twenty-two children also died."

Every American face registered horror at the sudden realization of exactly how precarious the situation was. No one there wanted to be responsible for the death of a child.

"What's your assessment of our current problem?" Zoë asked Zev, voicing everyone's concern.

"Our government has already made attempts to speak to Durgunov on behalf of the United States. As expected, our efforts were rebuffed." His lips spread across his teeth, but one would never have called it a smile. "Durgunov is a rabid anti-Semite."

"Do you know what his ultimate plan is?"

Shafir shrugged. "We used to have someone in place within his organization, but no longer."

"What's your general knowledge of the man?" Ben asked.

"Our intelligence says that his geopolitical agenda is based on the imperialistic concept of the Last Push South."

Ben looked confused. Zoë, who was fully engaged again, explained. "Durgunov's view of Russian history is that all bad things, like plagues and wars and invasions, have come from the south. For him, the south is some vague entity made up of Iran, Afghanistan, Transcaucasia, and Turkey. This region presents a danger to Russia because their inter-ethnic warfare could spread north to Russia."

"So what's the Last Push?" Sam asked Shafir.

"Durgunov's plan for peace on the Eurasian continent is to incorporate these southern nations into a friendly empire . . ."

". . . called Russia," Ben said, completing the thought.

Zoë nodded. "Exactly."

"What he suggests," Shafir continued, "is that the United States, western Europe, China, and Japan follow his example and make their own push south. You would grab up Central and South America. Europe would conquer Africa. Japan and China would take control of the lands south of them. The spheres of influence would run north to south. With no overlaps, we could expect peace and prosperity for all."

"If this weren't so serious," Sam said, "it would be funny."

Shafir fixed on Ben. "He claims this will take place in

an atomosphere of the greatest tolerance and respect for the cultural and human dignity of all involved.''

"But . . ."

"Some groups might have to be properly pacified."

"I'm only a candidate," Ben said. "I don't even know if I'll win my party's nomination, but one way or another something has to be done about this man. He's picking off innocent people as if they were clay pigeons." Ben's face was an honest display of anger and frustration. "You're the expert, General. What should we do?"

"You do what the Israelis do," Shafir said. "You start planning and you start now!"

☆   ☆   ☆

CNN anchor Brian Price's face was grim as he reported on the latest Red Rage escapades.

"Late this afternoon, at an undisclosed meeting point, the French ambassador to Lebanon delivered fifteen million dollars to a representative of Red Rage. There is some speculation that the man is an emissary of Yegor Durgunov, but that has not been confirmed. Two hours later, the twelve hostages were transported from an unknown hiding place believed to be somewhere in the Taurus Mountains to Beirut, where they were handed over to the ambassador. From there, they boarded a plane for Paris. They are expected to land at Charles de Gaulle airport within the hour. When they do, we will take you there, live."

To enrich his report, Price had gathered a panel of government luminaries to discuss the latest development. One of the panel members was Scottie Edwards. His face filled the screen.

"How do you feel about the actions of the French, Mr. Secretary?" Brian Price asked.

Edwards shook his head and spoke slowly. "I've said it before, and I'll say it again: You don't reward the enemy."

"That may be true on the traditional battlefield, General, but the French got their citizens back in less than a week. They're safe and sound while American women and children are still in the hands of terrorists."

"Believe me, my heart goes out to the families of our hostages, but, often, military experience teaches painful lessons. I know it's hard for civilians to accept, but there are times when the security of the many has to take precedence over the rescue of the few. This is one of those times."

"What if one of those hostages were your wife, or your child? Would you bargain then?"

Edwards rubbed his chin, his expression one of extreme conflict. Michael Dukakis had lost an election when he was asked a similiarly loaded question about how he would react if his wife, Kitty, were raped. Dukakis had responded coolly, mechanically, and without passion. That was hypothetical and about rape, Edwards reminded himself. This was real and about foreign policy.

"No," he said firmly. "I wouldn't."

On the other side of the world, Yegor Durgunov watched a replay of the interview on CNN. When he heard Scottie Edwards's reply, he laughed. It was a sound void of mirth.

"He might not bargain for his wife or his kid," he said to the aides gathered around him. "But if his own ass was on the line, he'd negotiate with the devil himself."

Again, he laughed. Again, it was not a pleasant sound. "I should know."

Elton Haynes clicked off the television in his second-floor office and poured himself a drink. The same panel discussion that had amused Durgunov had infuriated the president.

"I'd love nothing more than to deflate those overblown egos. How dare they comment on my performance when they know perfectly well my hands are tied?"

Chip Thompson, Haynes's chief of staff, loosened his tie, opened the top button of his shirt, and let his boss vent. There was nothing to say because the president was right: he was stymied. Despite several secretive diplomatic inquiries, they had come up empty. Red Rage disclaimed any knowledge of the Mad Hatter, as Haynes called Durgunov, insisting that the United States concentrate on meeting their demands; only then would the hostages go free.

Thompson had nosed around the Capitol to see if there was a chance Congress might agree to a military strike, UN intervention, or some kind of third-party negotiation, but the opposition was enjoying Haynes's predicament too much to budge. Chip had reminded Frank Boyle, the majority leader, that most of the hostages were women and children. Boyle reminded the president's chief of staff that "tragic as this situation is, national policy can't be changed simply because the American public is having a difficult time.

"If we buckle under to this lunatic," he said, "you'll have madmen with ransom demands coming out of the woodwork."

"If we don't, we'll have women and children coming home in body bags!"

Boyle never flinched. He simply turned and walked away, leaving Thompson stunned by his complete absence of compassion.

Of course on CNN, and then later on *Newsline*, Boyle put a different spin on it. He congratulated Scottie Edwards on having the courage to speak the truth on national TV—no matter how callous it sounded. And then, as if someone had pressed a button to start a recording, he repeated the party line. He reiterated Edwards's military record as if it contained *the answer*, insinuated several references to Jimmy Carter's failed efforts as contrasted to Ronald Reagan's success, and then cleverly turned a discussion on an international crisis into a campaign speech for his party's poster boy.

Chip could have lived with that. He had been in and

around Washington too long not to know how the game was played: no matter how serious the issue, the underlying motivation was always a win for the party. What he couldn't abide were gratutious character assaults. Questioning Elton Haynes's leadership was expected; Edwards's entire campaign was based on doing what the president couldn't do. But Boyle had stepped over the line when he insinuated that the president lacked courage.

"Too bad those kids aren't old enough to vote," he mumbled as he too fixed himself a drink. "Maybe then, someone in this godforsaken town would give a shit about what happens to them!"

Elton Haynes seated himself across from his friend. He looked up at the gilded bronze and cut-glass chandelier that once hung in the Green Room, then down to the Persian Kirman rug brought in for George Bush. Finally, his gaze returned to Chip.

"When I have absolutely no chance of resurrecting my presidency, the other side will demand a change in policy and," he said, shaking his head, "will take me to task for not suggesting it sooner."

"But lives are at stake!" Thompson declared angrily.

"Inside the Beltway, old pal, the only thing that's at stake are careers. And while we all talk about wanting to make people's lives better and safer, the truth is, politics doesn't always have a heart." Elton tipped his glass to Chip, his face filled with resignation. "Especially in an election year."

Arlo Reid's face glowed with unabashed pride as he presented Scottie with a huge check made out to the "Friends of General Prescott Edwards."

Scottie's eyes widened at the amount, then narrowed when he looked at the signature: Harlan Fletcher, President of the American Gunowners Association.

"This is awfully generous, Arlo."

"Mr. Fletcher is a big supporter of yours, General." Arlo

clasped his hands behind his back, spread his feet at-ease style, and faced his superior. ''He assured me that his entire organization is at your disposal.''

Scottie nodded. Over the years, he and the AGA had enjoyed a comfortable relationship: He had backed many of the positions advocated by the wealthy lobby; they had supported him with their legendary financial largesse. They disagreed only on the matter of making assault weapons readily available. As a soldier, Edwards preferred that those items remain under the control of the military. When he promised to avoid making public statements pro or con, they continued to contribute to his cause.

''Harlan doesn't give without getting,'' Scottie said, fingering the check gingerly as he waited for the other shoe to drop.

''He asked if you would address the AGA convention in Spokane.''

It was rare that Arlo asked anything of him, but this put Scottie in a quandary. While the AGA convention was, on the face of it, simply a gathering of gun enthusiasts, it tended to attract antigovernment Patriots from all across the county. The last thing Scottie wanted was to be seen as presiding over a rally of extremists that preached an antidemocratic gospel of hatred and separatism while hiding behind the Bible and the second amendment to the Constitution.

Once, several years before, he had asked Arlo about his affiliation with the Patriot movement. Arlo denied any complicity with the white supremacists and anti-Semites who dominated the membership, but he did claim a common concern about the path the country was taking. He was disillusioned, he had said, about the way government seemed to be expanding and encroaching upon people's lives. He was disappointed in trade agreements that robbed Americans of jobs. And, most of all, he agreed with those who feared a federal goverment dedicated to eliminating a citizen's right to bear arms.

''We're patriots in the true sense of the word,'' Arlo had

explained. "Most of us have donned this country's uniform and have been willing to die for the America we believe in. But we're not willing to live in a country that forgets about the individual liberties granted us by our Founding Fathers."

Scottie remembered worrying about the fervent glint in Arlo's eyes and saying so.

"You, sir," Arlo had countered, "are a patriot to your core, which is why you have my loyalty and the support of my brethren. We know you're one of us."

Scottie, noting a revival of that glint, put the check on a nearby table and approached Arlo cautiously. "I hope you didn't commit us to anything," he said. "I'd hate to disappoint the AGA."

Arlo's posture remained rigid, his expression definite. "I told Mr. Fletcher I had to review the dates with the campaign scheduler."

Scottie nodded. His expression remained one of reservation.

"The event is closed to the press, General. It's attended by thousands of Patriots," he said, pressing his case. "All of whom vote."

"I hear you, Arlo." Scottie conceded as gracefully as he could. "I'd be happy to address them, but I must insist that they be firm on their insistence of no media."

"Mr. Fletcher assured me . . ."

"He assured you that no one from the mainstream press would be allowed in. I don't want anyone from the Patriot press covering my speech either. Is that clear?"

"Yes, sir!" Arlo snapped his feet together. He nearly saluted. "Perfectly!"

"Run it by Clay and the scheduler. When it's okayed, let me know when and where."

"You won't be sorry, sir," Arlo said as he exited.

"I hope not," Scottie said.

☆ MARCH ☆

The "Knight for President" headquarters was a converted textile mill in Manayunk at the top of Main Street, overlooking the Schuylkill River. Ben had chosen the site for sentimental reasons: his grandfather had owned one of the mills that once distinguished this neighborhood; the house he had lived in with his father and brother was only a few blocks away.

The ever-burgeoning, mostly volunteer, staff was spread over three floors of large, open space—no walls, no private offices, no cubicles, no conference rooms, no executive bathrooms. Just a free-for-all area filled with donated desks, computers, TVs, and communications equipment.

The first floor was home to the mail room, administration staff, finance personnel, and delegate liaisons. If they made it out of the convention, and Ben was the party nominee, there was space for a campaign memorabilia store. The second floor housed state operations, media, schedulers, travel, and advance—both site and press. The War Room, which was the nerve center of the campaign, anchored the third floor. Aside from Jed Oakes, who was the undisputed ringmaster, there was the communications director, the chief of staff, the political director, their various staffs, surrogate scheduling, and the beginnings of an opposition research department trained for rapid response. If Ben became the party nominee, this group would expand.

Desks were set up bull-pen style, seeming to float in the wide-open space, yet connected in groups. Televisions were everywhere, with staffers monitoring the networks as well as various cable channels. Another group tracked the wire services, another regional press. There were those who collected the news and those who analyzed it—not only what was said about or by Ben, but also about and by every other candidate. One small group did nothing but watch C-Span; another surfed the Internet.

Jed Oakes was centered in the hub of this organized chaos. It was a few minutes after 9 P.M. and the polls had just closed in most of the eastern seaboard states. Empty coffee cups, half-eaten sandwiches, open cartons of Chinese food, and snack wrappers littered the area. Televisions were blaring. People were shouting across the room. Telephones were ringing nonstop. A huge map of the country mounted on a movable wall was being watched carefully. Within the heavily outlined boundaries of each state, were listed the number of delegates at stake, the time the polls closed, and the name of the field operator in charge. It was too early for actual voter counts, but field aides were phoning in exit poll numbers. It wasn't an exact science, but if done correctly—and Hal Kingsley had trained his crew well—it was a fairly accurate barometer.

Jed propped his boot-shod feet up on his desk, leaned back in his chair, raised his arm, and tossed a crumpled ball of paper across the floor into a metal wastebasket. "Falling into the Kenton camp, the great state of Idaho."

He looped three paper missiles, one after the other, into the air toward a second wastebasket. "And into the Knight camp, Colorado, Georgia, and Maryland."

As the results dribbled in, the states were flagged: red for Ben, blue for Kenton. According to early reports, Ben was expected to take Maine, Minnesota, Connecticut, Washington, and Vermont. Kenton would pick up Utah. Added to Idaho and his previous wins in Iowa, Arizona, and South Dakota, he could claim a good showing. Ben was ahead in delegate strength, but this was hardly a romp.

"What's happening in the hinterlands?" Jed shouted, his voice jagged with anxiety. Someone shouted a response, and Jed barked at Sarah Jenks, demanding a repeat rundown of Ben's schedule. Each time the results of another race came in, Jed asked for a review of upcoming events. Things were too close for Ben to waste time where it might not produce the biggest harvest.

"Tomorrow morning, Don Imus. Immediately after, the Four Horsemen of the Apocolypse"—Sean Quinn's nickname for the four Democratic hopefuls—"are taping a debate to air on Larry King. That afternoon, Ben does Buffalo, then flies back to the Big Apple for a major rally. Thursday's Detroit. Friday morning San Francisco. Friday night, L.A. Saturday in Dallas. Sunday, New Orleans. Monday, it's on to Boston."

Jed made a mental note to check the dates with Georgie. In the past few weeks, they'd managed one rendezvous. Better than nothing, he reminded himself.

Sarah flipped through a stack of papers on her desk. "We've sent surrogates to Oklahoma and Mississippi. Maribel Kenton's family is well known in Oklahoma, and their church is strong in both those states. We felt it was better to channel Ben's energy elsewhere."

"Gimme the local draw."

"In New York, he's on stage at Radio City Music Hall with the theater folk. Sort of a Ben does Broadway kind of thing. Mayor Hoskins will be there, too."

Jed made a face. Broadway stars were good; theater people came off as more serious than Hollywood types. Hoskins was good news/bad news. The mayor was popular with some groups, hated by others and every now and then, indulged some self-destructive tendency for stand-up comedy. Jed made a note to have someone check his speech for possible offenses.

"Okay, who else?"

"Otis Jefferson in Detroit."

Jed's expression went from a scowl to a rare blend of excitement and respect. Otis Jefferson was a strategist's dream: the highly popular African-American mayor of Detroit was a former outfielder/slugger for the New York Yankees, the Cincinnati Reds, and, during his last years on the field, the Detroit Tigers. He was a potential Hall of Famer, an honors graduate of the University of Michigan, a Vietnam vet and an army reserve colonel who had commanded a battalion of tanks during the Gulf War. Better, he and Ben had served together in Vietnam.

"San Fran's a mix of local politicos, leaders of the gay community and some wine guys from Napa. The site's great, and some Nob Hill deep pockets have already pledged major bucks, but L.A.'s the biggie. We've got the Hollywood Bowl. Spielberg and Ovitz are chairing. Paul Reiser's emceeing. Streisand's headlining. All the Hollywood big wigs are expected. National media's going to knock themselves out covering this one, if for no other reason than they want to hear Streisand sing."

Jed scanned the sheet of Super Tuesday primaries. "What about Miami? Aren't we doing anything there?"

"We would have, except everyone's favorite Latina couldn't make it," Sarah said.

"Why not? Florida has 152 delegates! We should be doing events in Gainesville and Tampa and Jacksonville. What's the story here? Are we writing off the whole damn state?"

Jed's nerves were frayed. Those who had worked with him before ignored his testiness. Those who hadn't trembled.

"The Senator can't be everywhere," Sarah said. "We've tried to maximize his exposure. Miami works if the local draw is a major magnet and Fabia wasn't available."

From the desk where she and Sam Trout were analyzing

voter trends, Zoë listened carefully. Fabia, it appeared, was quite the celebrity in these quarters.

"And where is the estimable señorita?" Jed asked.

Sarah was growing exasperated. "Off in some jungle saving the downtrodden, I suppose."

"Save her for the general election," Sam told Jed.

"If we ever get there!"

Zoë was disappointed that she wouldn't get a chance to meet Fabia Guevera. The idea of getting to know the woman Ben had been involved with after Felicia intrigued her. Because, to be honest, Ben intrigued her. He had always been intensely driven, but he had grown into a profoundly complex man with a number of shadows that wouldn't stand still for examination. Despite her firm avowal to remain at arm's length, the more time they spent together, the more Zoë wanted to know who Ben was.

It was late when NTN's election night coverage went off the air. Celia was drained from trying to squeeze an element of excitement out of the Republican primaries. While there had been several other names on assorted ballots, in effect, Scottie Edwards had run unopposed. As for issues, the only one worth tracking was gun control. In the wake of another post-office killing spree, the revelation of the rise in militia movements, and the current hostage crisis, even those who proudly claimed membership in the American Gunowners Association were softening some of their positions.

There seemed to be a growing revulsion about violence. It showed in the decline of the blood-gore-bullets-and-beefcake movies and the increased popularity of light romantic comedies. While some daytime television talk shows and most radio call-ins still relied upon shock and schlock, nightly news shows were beginning to retreat from the "if it bleeds, it leads" axiom of programming. The public was turned off by their own dark side, and it showed, in television ratings, box office sales, and at the polls.

Celia, Dean Walsh, and several others left the studio exhausted, but too wired to sleep. Walsh suggested they grab a drink at the Mayflower Hotel, just around the corner on Connecticut Avenue. The bar was busy, despite the late hour. Sprinkled amid the conventioneers and tourists, Celia spotted other journalists: pencils from the *Washington Post* and the *Washington Times,* several little feet from the regions in to cover the elections and in a corner, surrounded by a bevy of fans, Mr. Big Foot himself, Sean Quinn.

In spite of herself, Celia found her gaze drawn to him. His jacket hung over the back of his chair. His tie was loosened, his collar button undone. His shirt was wrinkled from hours under hot lights. He looked a bit rumpled, but there was something incredibly sexy about his dishabille. Annoyed at herself, she turned away from him and back to her colleagues, all of whom were dissecting this first Super Tuesday.

As Dean presided over the discussion, Celia sipped her amaretto slowly, letting the almond liqueur glide down her throat. It pleased her to hear that around this table, at least, the conventional wisdom favored Ben.

"Let's see how he does on Thursday," Clark Aiken said, referring to the New York primary only two days away. "If he pulls a majority there, he's got the big mo!"

"Polls have him way ahead." Celia had remained careful about her enthusiasm for Ben's campaign, but this was a fact, not wishful thinking.

"In the bigger cities," Walsh cautioned. "But Kenton's farm background and Sunday school image play well in the rural areas. He could pull it out."

Inside, Celia groaned. She knew Kenton in a way none of them did. There was more to this primary battle than anyone, including Ben, realized.

"Good evening, competition." Quinn stood behind Anthea Ogden's chair and smiled down at the NTN crew. His gaze lingered for a moment on Celia before addressing Walsh. "Well done, anchorman. I thought your take on the electoral mood was spot on. Our guy was lost somewhere in the middle distance." He shook his head. "How one interprets a large turnout during a crisis as a sign of hopefulness and not desperation is beyond me. The man had to have cotton stuffed in his ears not to hear the public's primal scream. And thanks," he said, with a gestural tip of the hat to Walsh, "for using my Horsemen sobriquet. You didn't give me credit for it, but hey! You didn't grab it for yourself either."

Walsh responded with a shrug of bonhomie.

Aiken was growing agitated at the friendly banter. Clark's dislike of Quinn was obvious, but his rabid jealousy of anyone whom he felt had exceeded him was well-known, so no one flinched when he went on the attack.

"Would you mind telling us how you managed to be so informed about our broadcast while filing your own reports?"

"Talent and versatility," Quinn answered. He enjoyed the bait and trap between adversaries. Probably because he was better at it than most. He especially enjoyed it with Aiken.

"So what's the bet?" Walsh asked, splaying a hand in the way of an invitation.

It was so smooth no one took much notice, but with one quick move, Quinn had commandeered a chair, slid in between Walsh and Celia, insinuated himself into the group, and ingratiated himself by offering to buy the next round. Aiken gulped the last of his drink and ordered another.

"Edwards is a lock, but the Dems can look forward to a brokered convention."

Celia frowned. Quinn's political instincts were keen.

"Neither Kenton nor Knight is going to stampede."

"Who's the buyer? Who's the seller? And what's the price?" NTN's news producer asked.

"Right now, it's anybody's guess." He pondered. "My gut tells me Knight's going to pull it out. Kenton's going to be awfully close, but no cigar. As for the price of shifting his votes? Second slot on the ticket.''

Aiken disagreed, probably just to be ornery, but the debate lasted through yet another round of drinks, the exits of Anthea, Walsh, and their producer. It was one-thirty in the morning when Aiken surrendered. Begrudgingly, he thanked Quinn for the drinks and left.

''And then there were two,'' Quinn said. His green eyes reached out and grabbed onto hers. His mouth eased into a languorous smile. ''You were awfully quiet tonight.''

Celia shrugged. ''I didn't have anything to add.''

''That's a first.''

''Then relish the moment.''

Quinn's smile widened. ''I am,'' he said quietly.

A light curtain of silence descended, a mood somewhere between comfortable and expectant.

''Another drink?''

Celia shook her head. ''I'm just about amarettoed out,'' she said, surprised at herself for returning his smile.

He studied her face, her pale blue cashmere sweater, her cleanly manicured hands, which were laced beneath her chin. Inside, Celia squirmed. He had a way of looking at her that made her feel as if he was undressing her. Other men had incited that same awareness, but they had provoked an outraged discomfort. Quinn was producing another feeling altogether.

She sipped her drink, reminding herself how tired she was. If she were more awake, she thought, he wouldn't be able to arouse these emotions.

''You're a beautiful woman, Celia Porter,'' he said, as if this were the first time that had occurred to him.

Celia acknowledged the compliment with a quick nod. Talk about her looks bored her.

''I'll bet that's a problem.''

''I beg your pardon?'' Suddenly, she was far from bored.

''In this business, people tend not to take beautiful women seriously.''

''Isn't that the truth.'' She sighed.

Years before, frustrated that no network would give her a desk, Celia had begged for a job at National Public Radio. There, where looks weren't an issue, she had covered everything from civil wars in Africa to the war on poverty in Detroit to the continuous battle in Congress between the two sides of the aisle. It was those five years on the radio that had solidified her reputation as a reporter, five years of an audience judging what they heard from a voice, not what they saw on a screen.

"No offense intended," Quinn was saying, "but Anthea Ogden's a dog. People will listen to hard news from her because they're not distracted by her face."

Celia didn't respond. She wasn't about to knock a female colleague, particularly about her looks. There were dozens of cases of women being fired from broadcasting jobs for gaining a few pounds or turning gray or acquiring the natural puffs and lines that come with aging. Celia had heard it a hundred times: Men gained character; women got old.

Quinn swallowed the rest of his drink. "Most news producers would give someone as pretty as you the soft news. Entertainment. Weather. Human-interest stories."

"Been there. Done that," she said.

"I know," he said in a way that told her he was more than mildly familiar with her past. "I give Titus credit. Giving you Edwards was a gutsy move." He laughed. "Aiken must have blown a few corpuscles over that one!"

She remained impassive. If he was fishing, he'd have to work hard. She wasn't going to jump on the hook.

"How'd Walsh take it?"

"He was all for it." *In a way. . . .*

"On the outside, maybe, but in here"—Quinn pointed to a spot in the center of his chest—"where his ego lives, he's shaking."

"And why is that?"

"Because impressive gray matter and incredibly gorgeous is a powerful combination." He grinned. "Come to think of it, I'm jealous."

"I think you're pretty, too, if that helps."

"It does. Thanks."

They shared a laugh, and suddenly, Celia felt slightly madcap, as if she would give a "why not" to a suggested barefooted splash in the Tidal Basin à la Fanne Foxe and Wilbur Mills.

"It's late. How about if I escort you home?" His smile was becoming hypnotic.

"Sure," she said, knowing she was anything but sure.

It had started to snow. Several inches had fallen, and the streets were blanketed with a downy cover of sparkling white, glistening beneath the streetlamps of Connecticut Avenue. As they reached the curb, a taxicab skidded, sliding across three lanes trying to get to them.

"What say we walk?" Quinn chuckled, shook off the cab, linked Celia's arm through his and headed north.

"I'm on...."

"The corner of New Hampshire and Q." He leaned down, his breath warm on her face. "As in Quinn."

"Or quisling," she said pointedly.

"Whew!" he grumbled. "Are you ever going to forgive me?"

She granted him a sideways glance and a tentative smile. "I haven't decided yet."

"Okay," he said, as if digesting her response. "Yet is better than never."

A gust of wind swirled snow about their faces. Neither of them was wearing a hat. Quinn lowered his head and held a gloved hand over his ear. Celia hiked up her coat collar and turned into Quinn's chest. His arm slid around her waist and held her tightly, both of them bracing against the storm. Her face was cold and damp, but inside she felt as if a furnace was being stoked.

They were a block from her apartment when suddenly he let go of her, reached down, and came up with a loosely packed ball of snow. He reared back and tossed it at a fire hydrant, delighted when he scored a hit. She had continued walking. Once she was safely ahead of him, she balled some snow and tossed it at him, landing it against his right shoulder. Within seconds, the battle was joined, each of them fully engaged. By the time they reached Celia's building, they were soaking wet, covered in snow, and giggling like children.

Beneath the awning that shielded her front entrance from the elements, they stomped snow from their boots and tried to shake it from their hair. Their eyes met, the laughter stopped, and, for a few moments, they stood frozen in a self-conscious hush. Quinn removed his gloves, stuffed them in his pockets and combed Celia's short blond hair with his fingers, slicking it back off her face. Her eyes watched him as he studied her. His hands lingered in her hair, as if he hadn't decided what to do next. A drop of snow fell from somewhere against her cheek. Quinn drew her face close to his, kissed the cold from her cheek, then slid his lips onto hers. Celia allowed herself to sink into his arms, which had moved from her head to her back. As he pressed her close to him, her breath caught in her throat. She laced her arms around his neck, feeling fully charged yet unbelievably weak.

His hands cupped her face. He drew back and stared deep into her eyes. Though his desire was clear, again he seemed hesitant, questioning. Reluctantly, he dropped his hands.

"I'll see you tomorrow."

His voice was hoarse. She didn't trust hers, so she simply nodded. Quickly, before she could respond, he turned to go. They both knew it was the right thing to do.

They both also knew there would be a next time.

☆　☆　☆

As Otis Jefferson folded his arms around Zoë and kissed her cheek, he had to fight off his wife, Jonetta, and their two children.

"You can just wait your turn," he said, holding up a hand to stop the onslaught. "I knew her first. I get to hug her first!"

Zoë nudged him playfully, pulled away, and went on to embrace Jonetta and each of the children. When everyone had been hugged and kissed and giggled over, Zoë drew back, narrowed her eyes, and gave Otis a long, hard look.

Six-foot-three, 220 pounds. Daily workouts had helped his body retain much of its athletic tone. He wore his hair short now, and slicked back, its neatness reflecting the well-groomed look of his signature mustache. His eyes, always so riveting and incisive, had gained a few parenthetical lines over the years, but they still gleamed with the indomitable can-do spirit that defined the man.

"I don't know, Otis," she said, shaking her head.

He looked himself over, checking his suit as if he expected to see a missing button or a half-open zipper. "What's the matter?"

A deliberately lazy smile crept onto her lips "You are still one of the hunkiest men I've ever met!"

Otis grinned, relieved and flattered. His son, Dannel, and his daughter, Raina, groaned.

"You're not as good-looking as Jonetta and the kids, of course, but hey! Who is?"

Jonetta, a stunning woman with short wiry black hair, a mocha complexion, and a figure that was enviably lean and fit, flashed her husband a "so there!" look, took Zoë's arm, and led the way into the living room. Ryan Knight, together with Dannel and Raina, followed along behind. Keeley hung back.

Ben was visiting a senior citizens' home in West Bloomfield. Earlier, in Pontiac, he had addressed a group of autoworkers. Then he visited the newly renovated trauma center at an inner-city hospital, where he was scheduled to make a statement supporting Otis's program to get guns off the street. When he finished there, he was expected at the mayor's mansion, where he would visit, shower, and change for the rally at Cobo Hall in downtown Detroit.

Keeley Knight couldn't wait for her father to show up. Maybe then, this meeting of the Zoë Vaughn fan club would be adjourned. Keeley had been really excited when her father said she and Ryan could come to Michigan with him. It had been much too long since the Knights had seen the Jeffersons. She and Raina were the same age, as were Ryan and Dannel. They didn't get together often, but their reunions were always easy and familiar, always fun.

Keeley had been surprised to learn that Zoë knew Otis and Jonetta. Keeley didn't know nearly as much as she'd like about this woman who had suddenly insinuated herself into Ben's life. Loretta loved her; she had made that clear. Ryan was taken with her; he was silly and impressionable and anyone who could quote baseball statistics was a hero to him, so his opinion didn't count. But Sam Trout had begun to sing her praises almost constantly. Jed Oakes, whose biting sarcasm amused Keeley, had nothing but nice things to say about the estimable Ms. Vaughn. And now the Jeffersons—all of them—were fawning over her.

"She's a terrific lady," Otis said, coming up behind Keeley, looking over her shoulder into the living room. "If you gave her a chance, you'd probably like her."

Keeley flushed. She couldn't believe Otis had intuited her thoughts so precisely. Worse, that her dislike of Zoë was so obvious. Keeley prided herself on her ability to disguise her feelings; as the daughter of a politician, she never wanted to reveal anything her father preferred to keep private. She arranged her features in a noncommittal mask and sought to cover her embarrassment with studied composure.

"As a rule," she said, "I try not to get too involved with people who work for Daddy. Other than Sam, of course."

Otis nodded and pursed his lips. "That's very wise. But there are exceptions to every rule."

"What's so exceptional about her?"

"I could give you a list, but probably her standout quality, the one I point out to Raina all the time, is that she's succeeded in an area that doesn't exactly open its arms to women. The State Department is a good old boys' club, and they don't like people who think that should be changed."

"I heard she was fired." A tinge of triumph underscored Keeley's words.

"Don't believe everything you hear. Zoë's a woman of very strong principle and keen intelligence." He tilted his head, looking slightly befuddled. "Some men get real threatened by that kind of woman."

"My father didn't."

"No," he said. "To his credit, I think he found her brains as attractive as the rest of her."

Zoë laughed, drawing Otis's attention. She was sitting on one of the couches looking like the coed she was when he met her: one leg tucked beneath her, her arm draped casually over the back, dressed in a long-sleeved black sweater, a mid-calf woolen jumper, opaque hose, and short leather boots. With her tangle of curls caught in a loose ponytail and her face alive with laughter, she looked vibrant and youthful and refreshingly attractive. A sideways glance told him Keeley was doing some appraising of her own.

"She's pretty," Keeley said charitably, "but she's not very elegant."

"That was your mother's style," Otis said quietly. "And Felicia did elegant better than anyone I've ever known."

Keeley's mouth twitched in agreement. Otis put a hand on her shoulder. "Zoë isn't anything like your mom."

Keeley turned and faced the large man, her blue eyes wide with emotion. "You never liked her, did you? You thought she was a bigot."

Otis was stunned by her bluntness. He wished he could dismiss her accusation with the wave of his hand, but he could see that would never do.

"I thought she had some preconceived notions that were narrower than I would have liked."

He could never tell this adoring child that he had considered her mother a plantation princess who refused to adjust to the idea of a mixed society. Or that he believed her to be socially myopic, her associations governed solely by class and color. Or that he thought Ben had made the biggest mistake of his life when he followed his ambitions instead of his heart.

"And Zoë?" Keeley demanded.

This conversation was roaming into dangerous territory. Much as he'd like, Otis could find no quick detour. "They're not rivals, Keeley. Felicia was your father's wife and the mother of his children."

"And Zoë?" she repeated, doggedly.

Otis sighed. "To answer your first question, Zoë is one of the most broad-minded, color-blind people I know. As for the second? Once upon a time, your father was madly in love with her."

Keeley ruminated on that for a bit, watching Zoë, looking away, reminiscing about her mother, studying Zoë again. "What about now?" she asked. "What are they now?"

"Old friends and colleagues. Nothing more."

Keeley offered him an unconvinced smile. "Would you like it to be more?" she asked suddenly.

"I'd like your father to be happy, Keeley. He's been alone a long time." He glanced at Zoë, a shadow passing over his eyes. "So has she." He turned back to Keeley. "If they found their way back to each other, yeah! I would like that a lot."

She knew it wasn't his intention, but Otis had made Keeley feel selfish. She wished she could explain her feelings better, but it was complicated and embarrassing. She didn't want Ben to be alone. She wanted him to be happy. But she was afraid. What if he did fall in love again? What if he got so wrapped up in another woman he forgot all about his home and his daughter?

Just like Felicia had.

Zoë watched the proceedings from the wings. Normally, she preferred to be in the audience. People often applauded out of habit or politeness. From the stage, if it was loud, it was good. Amid the throng, it was easier to know if a response was automatic, superficial clapping or a reaction born of emotion and conviction.

As she listened to Otis address the packed hall, it was easy to see why he was so popular. He was an up-front guy who spoke with the easy confidence of someone who had been on the other side of the podium, believed that the power of his office could never corrupt him, and knew that his constituents believed that as well.

The people of Detroit—both black and white—loved him. Blacks, because he was one of their own who had made good and come back. Whites, because his years as a baseball player had given him a credibility other politicians couldn't claim. His years in the army as a reservist bolstered his reputation as someone who "didn't go along, but got along." And as mayor, he was known for trying to heal the city's wounds by making everyone feel they were as important as everyone else.

When he introduced Ben, Otis went through the standard list of reasons why "this is the man I believe in," but it was when he called the Senator from Pennsylvania the "white Knight who helped save my black butt in Vietnam," the audience went wild. Zoë watched the two men embrace. It was so warm and genuine it moved her to tears. She listened to the crowd and watched their faces, wishing she was down on the floor among them to hear what they were yelling, even more, what they were mumbling to themselves.

Ben's speech was rousing, made even more so because of his deep feeling for Otis. He spoke of their days on the battlefield, particularly those few days in May 1969 when U.S. and South Vietnamese forces battled for control of Apbia Mountain, which lay one mile east of the Laotian border.

"They called it Operation Apache Snow," he said. "Our job was to cut off the North Vietnamese so we could stop them from menacing Hué to the north and Danang to the south."

He looked over at Otis, whose face had taken on a somber aspect. He, too, was remembering.

"Otis and I were part of the 101st Airborne Division, which parachuted smack into the middle of a well-fortified Communist stronghold. There were a thousand of us and four hundred South Vietnamese, all fighting our way to the summit. There were heavy allied air strikes. Artillery barrages. And ten infantry assaults."

Again, he looked at Otis. His voice was raspy. "It was on the eleventh attack that we finally captured the mountain. We lost fifty-six men. Four hundred and twenty were wounded. And we took the lives of nearly six hundred North Vietnamese."

He glared into the crowd, demanding that they respect all of those who fought and died, including the enemy.

"Because of the severe loss of life, Apbia Mountain became known as 'Hamburger Hill.'"

Ben then turned his nightmare into an example. He spoke of the importance of Americans learning to rely on each other, regardless of ethnic or racial or economic differences.

"Otis Jefferson and I didn't grow up in the same neighborhood. We didn't have the same friends or the same enemies. We didn't speak the same language or like the same movies or feel the same way about the American dream. Otis Jefferson and I were on different sides." He gulped back a knob of honest emotion. "Vietnam put us on the same side."

The audience stood, many of them misty-eyed, as they gave him a thunderous ovation. Smoothly, skillfully, he quieted them and segued from the long ago to the here and now, relating the danger he and Otis had faced in Vietnam to the danger the American hostages were confronting today.

"We fought an unknown, largely invisible enemy," he said. "So do they. Their captors look like ordinary people. But they're not. They're fanatics blinded by devotion to a cause. I don't know what that cause is or to whom they swear their allegiance, but their prisoners are school-children who don't understand their zeal. They don't understand their anger. Yet they're victims of both.''

Zoë couldn't help studying Keeley and Ryan during their father's speech. A lump formed in her throat as she saw love and pride and respect and, perhaps, awe gather in their eyes. She didn't blame them. At that moment, she thought Ben Knight was special, too.

When the speeches were over, the entertainment began. Chairs were pushed back to make room for a dance floor, and a band took the stage. Otis's staff had organized a Motown extravaganza with Smokey Robinson, Gladys Knight, and a few younger groups. Zoë led the kids to their seats. Jonetta, Otis, and Ben joined them.

When the music started, Zoë's face broke into a grin. This was the music she had grown up with—the oldies-but-goodies from the sixties—and she loved it. Before long, she and Jonetta were up on their feet, rocking and rolling with the best of them. Ben and Otis stood also, clapping their hands and hooting. Their teenaged children couldn't decide if they were perplexed, impressed, or humiliated.

Suddenly, the band played something that had Zoë going through all sorts of strange gyrations. She slapped her thighs, clapped her hands, jerked her thumbs in each direction like a hitchhiker, rolled her hands over and started again. In spite of herself, Keeley was intrigued.

"What's that?" she asked, trying to follow along, but getting hopelessly confused.

Zoë laughed. "The hand jive. Here, I'll show you." She went through it a few times until Keeley caught on. In minutes, they were jiving and dancing, laughing at each other's mistakes, and having a wonderful time.

The party was getting hotter. Throughout the hall, people were dancing or clapping as they watched others recall their youth. Otis grabbed Jonetta and took her out onto the floor. The crowd backed off. It wasn't the first time they'd seen their mayor and his wife dance, but never with such enthusiasm. They formed a circle, thumping their hands and shouting encouragement.

"You gonna leave me out here all by myself?" Otis said, pointing to Ben, daring him to come on out.

People starting chanting "Ben! Ben! Ben!" With a chuckle and a shrug of surrender, Ben grabbed Zoë's hand and joined the Jeffersons on the dance floor. Of course while Otis and Jonetta were doing Detroit, Ben and Zoë were pure *American Bandstand* Philly. If she had thought about it, Zoë would have been amazed that after all these years, she could still follow Ben, but she wasn't thinking. She was twirling, spinning, pushing off this hand, turning under that arm, having an absolutely fabulous time. For a second, it did flash through her mind that their friends at Harvard had once dubbed them "Boston's answer to Bob and Justine," the Philadelphia locals who had become celebrities during *American Bandstand*'s heyday.

She didn't notice the strobes or the video cameras. Her eyes were on her partner. He was older and wearing a suit instead of a sweater, but in her mind's eye, time had evaporated. There was no gray in his hair, no tug at his skin. There were no lines on her face, no gravitational pulls on her frame. They were young and happy and in love, with more hopes than disenchantments, more successes than failures, and more of life ahead of them than behind.

When the music slowed and he took her in his arms, the illusion grew more intense. Nothing was real except the two of them. Everything—the hall, the band, the people, even Keeley and Ryan—became unwelcome intrusions in her fanciful web of revived memory. Only Otis and Jonetta fit, because they had been there, yet they, too, had shed their current reality. Through Zoë's filtered remembrance, Jonetta's hair was long and bushy, Otis was larger and less refined. The song was brief, but each moment became an instant of suspended time, a magical interval within which there was no history to relive, no future to create. It was only the two of them, there, in that moment.

"Just like old times," Ben said when the music stopped.

Zoë thought his voice sounded shaky. She wondered if he, too, had one foot in the past and one in the present.

"I enjoyed it," she said.

"Me too." He squeezed her hand and then, with great reluctance, released it.

As he did, the world intruded, reminding them who Ben was, where they were and why. Quickly, they separated, she heading off to join Ben's press secretary and help spin the event, he getting to the business of shaking hands and high-fiving his supporters. Neither believed their fleeting minute of intimacy had been noticed and if it had, had been accorded any significance. They were wrong.

Ryan had seen his father's hand linger over Zoë's and smiled. Otis saw the regret in his friend's eye as they parted and felt hopeful. Keeley had seen the emotion on both their faces and felt strangely conflicted.

There was someone else who had shown great interest in the warm exchange between the Senator and his foreign policy advisor. He was the same man who had snapped dozens of photographs of them dancing, the same man who was about to call Clay Chandler and tell him what he had.

Otis, Ben, and Zoë sat huddled around a table in Otis's library, drinking coffee and discussing the campaign.

"Technically, we won New York," Ben said, fatigue carving deep lines in his face, "but just barely. Kenton's coming on. If we don't grab the majority on Tuesday, this candidacy is in trouble."

"What does Hal say?" Otis hated the fact that polls dominated so much of the political process.

"His numbers say we look good everywhere but Oklahoma and Mississippi. Florida's a toss-up. So is Louisiana, but there's a big rally in New Orleans on Sunday." A wry

smile crossed Ben's lips. "These things are all so unpredictable. Between now and Tuesday the *Enquirer* could claim
I'm married to an alien, Kenton could be named a saint,
Elton Haynes could pull off a miracle, or Durgunov could
blow up the world."

"God forbid," Otis groaned.

"It's not beyond his capability," Zoë said, half to herself.

While the two men had been counting delegates, Zoë
had been pondering a rumor that had been fed to her, a
rumor that something was going to happen within the next
few days. She had relayed that information to Ben, who
had opted to interpret it with a worst-case scenario.
Prompted by the curiosity her comment had aroused, Ben
explained the situation to Otis, who then looked to Zoë
for her take.

"I think he's going to throw us a bone."

"Like what?" Ben asked.

"My guess is he'll release a hostage." Her green eyes
darkened. "Or a body."

Ben lowered his head and kneaded his forehead. Otis
drummed the table with his fingers.

"I can't sit by and do nothing," Ben said. "Zoë introduced me to an Israeli general who said some things that
really set me thinking."

"Who's the general?"

"Zev Shafir."

Otis smiled and whistled like a kid who had just hit his
first grand slam. "That man knows his stuff!" When Ben
appeared surprised, Otis explained. "My reserve unit had
several joint training sessions with Israel. A bunch of years
ago, I did a six-week commando course with Shafir as my
instructor."

Ben didn't hear Otis say to Zoë, "Remember? That was
when you were posted in Israel." He didn't see Zoë's
pained expression or Otis's look of regret. He had
retreated into his own thoughts, trying to piece together
how he felt about what was going on, what Zoë had predicted might happen, and what, if anything, he could do.

"Shafir said we should be planning a rescue operation now." Oblivious to the silent drama being played out between his companions, he continued his monologue. "I wholeheartedly agree, but I have no authority to mount a mission. Elton Haynes is the Commander in Chief. I'm not."

"You have to think as if you were." Zoë had forced herself to shake off whatever memories Otis had revived, and her tone was firm and unflinching. "You may not have the power to activate troops, but that doesn't mean you shouldn't be thinking about possible tactical maneuvers."

"True, but I'm not a military strategist either."

"No," Otis said, "but I know someone who is and who probably would be more than willing to design an offensive." Ben and Zoë stared at him expectantly. "Harry Cadman."

His audience of two smiled. Harry Cadman had been the commanding general during the Gulf War. He was retired now, but word was his life of leisure was less than satisfying.

"I served under Cadman," Otis said. "He and I were friends before Desert Storm and we've remained friends since. What if I call him and arrange a meeting?"

Ben pushed back his chair and began to pace. "If he agrees, we can't afford any leaks," Ben said. "Aside from looking arrogant and presumptuous, it's dangerous. I don't know what Haynes has in the works, if anything, but the last thing I want is to jeopardize any effort to free those people."

"If we keep this between the three of us, there won't be any leaks," Zoë said with complete confidence.

Ben nodded. In matters like these no one was above suspicion. He knew he could trust Otis with his life; he already had. He believed he could accord Zoë the same faith. As for anyone else, it was better to err on the side of caution. He couldn't afford to make a wrong call.

Otis leaned back in his chair, his arms folded across his chest. "I'll make the initial contact. If Cadman agrees, we arrange a secret meeting." Ben looked skeptical. "And then we pull off a version of the old shake and fake," he said, referring to a maneuver used frequently during their paratrooper days. A group on the ground staged a distraction. A helicopter dropped a few dummies in a clearing far from the actual drop sight, drawing the enemy away, making it safe for the real paratroopers to land.

"It'll be just like old times," Otis said.

Ben's eyes found Zoë's. When he said that to her earlier, the memories had been warm and pleasant, and he gladly would have returned to those old times. Now, those same words had been spoken in a completely different context, evoking a wildly contrasting response. Ben loved Otis, but those two years in the army had not been good times. His memories of Vietnam were not warm and pleasant. And he never, ever wanted to go back.

☆　☆　☆

The girl wandered into the American Embassy in Riga, clearly disoriented. She blinked furiously; even the dim light of the embassy foyer was too bright for her eyes. She looked about eight years old, but it was hard to tell. Her clothes were ill fitting and unclean. The colors clashed, the shirt was too big, the pants too small, there were rips here and there, and the sweater more than two sizes off. Her hair was matted and pressed against her head, as if she had been wearing a woolen hat for quite some time. What struck the guard most was her skin tone—white tinged with the dull gray of ill health—and her gait— clumsy and uncertain, moving one step at a time, but hesitating between each step, as if she had to be granted permission to put her foot down.

"Can I help you, young lady," he said, smiling, bending down so he could look into her eyes. They appeared vacant, yet her entire mien was one of someone on alert.

She handed him a note. Automatically, he fingered the paper for a possible explosive device. It was a single sheet, no envelope. He opened the note. *RED RAGE* jumped out at him. Immediately, even as his stomach lurched at the possibility, his eyes scanned the child's body, looking for any suspicious bulge.

"It's awfully warm in here," he said. "How about giving me your sweater?"

She stepped back, clutching the huge woolen rag to her body.

"Okay," he said, holding up his hands, surrendering. He picked up a nearby phone and kept his eyes fixed on her.

Within seconds, three soldiers bounded down the stairs. The guard raised his hand. They slowed their pace, coming through the metal detector and, in effect, surrounding the child. The guard handed the senior officer the note: *This is the first political prisoner to be released. If our demands are not met, and soon, it will be the last. Red Rage.*

The officer passed the note to his assistant, bent down and spoke softly. "What's your name?"

Her eyes appeared to scan his uniform. For an instant, her face softened, but then the terror returned. She didn't know who he was, what he wanted, what she was supposed to do. And what would happen to her if she didn't do it right.

The officer pointed to the American flag standing to the left of them. "Do you know what that is?" She nodded. "Good." He smiled and nodded approvingly. "This place," he said, using his hand to indicate the building in which they were standing, "is like being in America. You're safe here."

She ran for the corner and hugged her knees to her chest, cowering. Another call was placed. Soon, a woman joined the group, a vice-consul with a warm, engaging nature. Quickly assessing the situation, she joined the girl on the floor, careful not to sit too close or appear at all threatening. It took an hour before she could get an answer to a single question: "What's your name?"

"Molly Crookshank," the little girl whispered.

* * *

Ethel and Rob Crookshank looked older than the last time they had been seen on camera; the harrowing months since their granddaughter's abduction had taken their toll. Seated next to each other on the couch in their living room, surrounded by campaign staffers, cameramen, lighting and sound technicians, the two appeared small and frail.

"She's coming home," Ben said to Ethel, whose hand was clutching his. His face was somber, his voice gentle. Ethel nodded. Rob was fighting back tears, trying desperately to appear brave and in control. "Have you spoken to your son?"

A wobbly smile emerged. "He's in Latvia now."

"How is Molly?"

Rob covered his face with his hand in an attempt to smother his sobs. Ethel turned to her husband and patted his cheek in a gesture so tender and loving, Ben felt a stab of profound envy and incomprehensible sadness. For his mother, because a senselessly aimed, selfishly fired bullet had deprived her of the tightly knit companionship the Crookshanks shared. For himself, because he worried that, like Loretta, he would live out his life without a partner, without that spiritual oneness only a lifetime of shared love could produce.

"She's not good," Ethel said, her hand clutching Ben's. "The doctors say she's suffering from post-traumatic shock syndrome. Like soldiers get."

Ben nodded. He knew it well. He had had his own bouts with nightmares and sweats and unremitting depression.

"My son and daughter-in-law are flying home with her." She stuck a trembling finger underneath her glasses and wiped away her tears. "They said we shouldn't expect too much. They said she's like a different little girl." She swallowed hard. "Not our happy-go-lucky Molly."

Ben grimaced. Molly had been emotionally abused, that

much was certain. He prayed that she had not been physically tortured or sexually violated.

"The doctors know how to handle this, Ethel. They'll be gentle with her." He tried to smile. "Honestly they will."

Rob looked at him, begging for assurances Ben couldn't truly provide. He gave them anyway.

"She's going to be fine, Rob," Ben said, reaching over and squeezing the older man's hand. "You'll see. In no time, Molly's going to be just fine!"

"That's it!" the segment producer said.

The camera stopped rolling. Lights were shut off. Microphones were removed. And the crew began to pack up. There was a sudden flurry of activity, and though they tried to be respectful, voices were raised and people were jostled as equipment was moved out of the small room to a waiting truck. The Crookshanks looked lost and confused, prisoners on their own couch, too burdened by grief and worry to fight the melee.

Ben watched the pandemonium created by his campaign circle around these two elderly people, and felt sick. A horrible thought had insinuated itself into his consciousness: Red Rage had kidnapped an eight-year-old child to bring attention to their crusade. They had used her for their own ends, regardless of her rights or her feelings or the consequences of their actions. He had invaded the Crookshanks' home as well as their privacy for the sake of his candidacy. He could tell himself how much he cared—which he did—and how concerned he was about this family and what had happened to them. But he had jabbed at their dignity, probing their hearts until Ethel and Rob had bared their innermost feelings. And why? To create good television. To get a bump in the polls. To garner a few more votes in his march to the White House.

Not for the first time, Ben wondered—no matter how nobly one painted the end—how one justified these means.

* * *

Anthea Ogden shoved a microphone under Mack Kenton's chin and asked what he made of this goodwill gesture by Red Rage.

Kenton's pale gray eyes looked into the camera. His face was composed, almost ethereal. "Having Molly Crookshank delivered from evil was a blessing from God. But the devils who took her in the first place don't understand what goodwill is. If they did, they would have released everyone."

Anthea smiled to herself. It was the perfect sound bite: a feel-good statement that advanced no policy, revealed no insight as to what might—or should—happen next, and earthy enough to make it onto every broadcast.

Anthea was a cynic, prone to believing the worst about anyone within the political arena. Her years in Washington had led her to think that everyone from lobbyists to activists to members of Congress to presidents were serving their egos first, their pocketbooks second, their long-term self-interest third, and the public, fourth—if at all.

Anthea had been following Mack Kenton for weeks and in that time had gained a begrudging respect for the farmer from Iowa. He may have fit her cynical mold perfectly, but he had crafted an image so wholesome and above the fray that even Anthea had begun to wonder if perhaps he was the exception.

Contributing to her wonderment was Kenton's reputation as a man of contradiction; in politics, that should have been a negative, inspiring epithets like "waffler" and "flip-flop," but it seemed to work in his favor. He positioned himself as a religious man, which in today's label-crazed climate should have placed him on the right, but his stand on domestic social programs for the poor and the disenfranchised placed him squarely on the left. He toed a hawkish Republican line on the need for maintaining America's defense capabilities, yet was a well-known dove.

To voters in search of America's absolute middle, Mack Kenton appeared to be The Man.

Still, there was something weird about him. In a process that normally encased candidates within a tight bubble, Kenton remained more of a loner than most. His campaign included the usual herd of handlers, yet none could claim closeness to the boss. They were believers. They were employees. But they weren't friends.

On the stump, he liked town meetings—"a good way of exchanging ideas without the filter of the media"— tolerated baby kissings, plant visits, and early-morning commuter handshakes, but so loathed the grip-and-grin photo sessions with thousand-dollar-a-plate contributors that he often ran out before the first camera strobe went off.

With reporters, it was worse. He was off-putting, even insolent at times, as if Anthea and her brethren had no right to ask him questions he didn't wish to answer. Once, on the campaign plane, when she had found herself alone with him, Anthea had wondered aloud about the wisdom of his recalcitrance.

"You know, Congressman, if you don't mind my saying so, your, uh, negative attitude toward the press is counterproductive. If you would only be more cooperative, we could help you get your message across."

He had looked at her as if she had suggested he give his speeches in the buff. "You just don't get it, do you?" he sniffed with utter disdain. "This campaign is not about my attitude or the bruised egos of the press corps. It's about ideas and how to get America back on the right path. If you want to help us do that, fine. If you don't, that's your choice."

Kenton's wife, Maribel, seemed nice enough on the infrequent occasions when she was trotted out, but there, too, Anthea sensed something was off. Theirs was supposed to be the perfect marriage, the middle-America model of what family values were all about. Maribel stood by his side, the very picture of love and loyalty, projecting the worshipful smile and awed expression of someone who felt truly blessed to be Mrs. Mackenzie Kenton.

He spoke of her devotion and her sacrifice, how he could never have made it without her, how thankful he was that she was the mother of his children and the woman God had chosen to be his helpmate. But they never touched. Their eyes never fully engaged. And every now and then, Anthea was certain she noticed a dolorous cloud of blue pass over Maribel's practiced stare.

Kenton could stomp his feet and cry foul and dismiss the rumors of his philandering as "hideous slime invented by the prurient press," but Anthea would have bet her laptop that Maribel was a woman with an aching heart. And an empty bed.

☆   ☆   ☆

Celia had passed annoyed a long time ago and was well on the way to furious. Not only was Scottie Edwards ignoring her, but Clay Chandler was positively relishing her frustration. He was standing off to the side, looking like a Galapagos tortoise in his bulky, hooded green parka, but there was no escaping his insufferable grin. Each time Edwards passed over her and gave the nod to another reporter, he snickered. And Celia fumed.

They were standing at the base of Vail Mountain, where General Edwards had skied in an event to raise money for NOMORE!'s Save the Parents project. Kate Siegel had initiated the program to help pay some of the costs incurred by those involved in bringing NOMORE!'s no-parole agenda to the attention of their state legislators.

Behind them, skiers came down the flagged runs in pairs, racing against each other and the clock. Some were pretty adept. Most found themselves struggling just to stay on their feet. The sun was shining. The sky was that special blue that only seemed to come to Colorado skies. White banners emblazoned with the red NOMORE! logo flapped in the wind. And hundreds of fans who had gathered behind a bright yellow string fence shouted encouragement to their favorite celebrities, groaning when someone tumbled off course or missed a flag.

Edwards, his face pink from the biting cold, his white hair taking on a silver cast against the majestic backdrop of snowy peaks, was repeating his "thanks to the Lord" speech for the safe return of Molly Crookshank. Leaning against his skis, his goggles turned to the back of his neck and looking every inch the experienced schusser, he was dressed in a royal blue jumpsuit stamped with designer insignias and a pinny with his racing number on it. Celia thought he looked sporty, but far too cavalier for the circumstances. Chandler had goofed on this one.

"We have Molly back," Edwards was saying, "but she is only one of many." His eyes narrowed and his posture straightened. He was at attention. "Maybe it's time for us to take a few prisoners," he brayed.

"Don't you think a comment like that is reckless and inappropriate?" Celia raised her voice so loud he couldn't ignore her.

Edwards glared at her. "We have women and children in captivity. What is inappropriate about demanding that something be done to obtain their freedom?"

"Making that demand while hobnobbing in a posh ski resort, for one," Celia retorted. "Suggesting that we commit American troops to an action that might put them and our hostages in jeopardy without full knowledge of the facts, for another."

Quinn, standing to Celia's left, smothered a laugh. She had bested Edwards, and everyone knew it. Edwards mumbled some platitudes about the nobility of NOMORE!'s cause and how his presence here was prompted by his love of children and his abiding concern for their well-being, but his balloon was descending. Even his closing sound bite came off as too little, too late.

"As Kate Siegel, the founder of NOMORE!, often reminds us: Until all our children are safe—from enemies abroad as well as within—none of us can rest."

Tony Archer, Celia's producer, had to restrain himself

from hugging her. "That was a major coup, sweetcakes," he said, his face aglow with the triumph of the moment. "You had that pompous one-star scrambling for cover."

"Today," Celia said, leading Tony away from Edwards's minions. "Tomorrow, they'll pay us back by giving someone else the sound bite and us frostbite."

"Nope." Tony shook his head. "This is Saturday. Super Tuesday is two news days away. They might not care if they piss off the pencil from the *Vail Daily*, but they're not going to mess with NTN's rising star."

Celia protested humbly, but inside she was crowing. NTN's *Nightly News* was moving up in the ratings, and, if fan mail was an indication, Celia was part of the reason. Only a week earlier, Titus Mitchell had called to congratulate her on a piece about Edwards's abysmal record on social issues. But then, Celia recalled, after patting her on the back, Titus had poked her in the ribs by mentioning Anthea Ogden's investigation into a questionable real-estate investment Mack Kenton had made during the late eighties and Clark Aiken's piece about Ben Knight's so-called ties to Cuban special interests. This afternoon's verbal victory was a one-shot deal. What Titus wanted was a story with very long legs.

As she and Tony started back to their hotel, she noticed Clay Chandler leaning against a wall of snow, his arms folded across his chest, his eyes fixed in a belligerent stare. Even from a distance, she could feel the heat of his anger. She returned his gaze without flinching, but inside, she was roiling.

"Whew!" Tony whispered as they walked by. "That man is scary."

"More than you know," Celia scoffed.

"What's his gripe?"

"He believes that once upon a time, he was grievously wronged, and the world owes him an apology."

"Wronged how?"

"It's a long story, but basically, he was unfairly scapegoated so that some higher-ups in the Justice Department could salvage their own reputations. He believes he was robbed of his future.''

"Was he?"

Celia pondered for a moment. "Yes, I guess he was.''

"Hey! That would make me nasty,'' Tony admitted. "I give him credit. He picked himself up and got on with it. I don't like the guy, but he worked his way up from chump to champ. You have to admire that sort of dedication.''

Celia could not agree because she did not admire Clay Chandler. She knew him too well. What Tony saw as dedication, Celia defined as directed rage. What Tony thought was resilience, Celia recognized as an obsession with revenge. And what Tony might have perceived as ambition, Celia saw as a way of attaining enough power so that everyone who had so much as slighted him would feel the pain and suffer the humiliation he had.

As she and Tony arrived at the hotel and went their separate ways, Celia shuddered. Tony could afford to be generous. He wasn't on Clay's list of intended victims. She was. Clay had vowed to hurt her, and she had no doubt that, given the opportunity, he would.

But, she decided, she was not going to be Clay's scapegoat. She was not going to be bullied into backing away from her job. This assignment was her shot at the big time, and she intended to make the most of it. Whether Clay Chandler liked it or not.

Rick found Kate sitting by the fire in the lounge at the Sonnenalp. Here and there, people were winding down from the day's activities with a quiet drink; the awards program had been over hours ago, so most of the guests had gone to bed. Rick had come from Kate's room, where he and Ethan spent time catching up. When he had left his son, Ethan was asleep, his face wreathed in a smile of contentment.

"He's an incredible kid," Rick said, sliding into the chair next to her. Kate nodded, but continued to stare at the fire. "It was great spending these few days with him. And you."

She didn't respond. It had been this way from the minute he had arrived. Whenever they were together, Kate was all business, going over schedules with him, telling him what was expected of him, where to be when, whom to speak to about what. When Ethan was around, she was warmer, but barely. They might have been strangers.

What disturbed Rick even more was the presence of Stan Jeffries. He was everywhere: on the slopes, in the dining room, in meetings with Kate and the crew from Vail Associates. Not only was it clear from their body language that they were comfortable—although not necessarily intimate—with each other, but Ethan had mentioned that Stan had suggested Kate join his firm as a consultant, working part-time. Ethan thought it was a good idea.

"Mom needs to do *her* thing," Rick's wise son had said.

On its own merits, Rick also thought it was a good idea. If asked, he would have encouraged her to go back to the law. It was getting more involved with Jeffries he didn't like.

A waiter asked if he could get them anything. Rick ordered stingers for the two of them. Kate said nothing. It was as if her brain had shut down and was receiving no external signals. The room was lovely, just the kind Kate preferred, with large cushy chairs, a stone hearth, kalanchoe plants in brass cachepots, and baskets of mountain greenery. The fire was hot, yet Kate was shivering.

"Are you all right?" He leaned over and placed his hand on her arm. Her eyes were glistening. Seeing how upset she was, Rick felt guilty thinking how beautiful she looked, but she did, with her cheeks all rosy and her eyes so moist, her auburn hair swept back in a loose ponytail and her long, lean frame, curled into a sinuous coil.

"I wish someone could find Mira," she whispered.

He felt as if she had taken a heated poker and lanced his heart with it. He took her hand and laced their fingers together. He, who made his living with words, could find none to express his desolation and his regret.

The waiter, sensing he was intruding, quickly placed their drinks on the table in front of them and left. Kate wiped her eyes with the back of her hand and for the first time since he sat down, faced her husband.

"The Crookshanks are very lucky," she said. "I'm happy for them."

Rick nodded. "Me too. Molly's been through a terrible ordeal . . ."

". . . but she's alive and home with her family."

Rick handed Kate her drink. She sipped the minty concoction slowly, welcoming the memories Rick had hoped to revive. She and Rick had acquired a taste for this blend of brandy and white crème de menthe during the early years of their marriage. It had been such a wonderful time. They had two children and a passion for each other that seemed boundless. Sometimes on a weekend after they had tended to Mira and put baby Ethan in his crib, they would order in a pizza, mix up a few stingers, climb into bed, eat, drink, and make love until they were deliciously exhausted.

"I miss you, Kate," he said. "I miss us. Who we were. What we had."

Her eyes met his. They were soft, but with an edge that made him uncomfortable.

"Who we were was a family, Rick. A mother, a father, and two children. Now there's a mother and one child. That's who the *us* is today."

Rick would have preferred her to scream at him, to hit him, to do something other than calmly recite the facts as she saw them. He would have preferred anything to being confronted with the truth.

"We still share that child," he said, pleading his case. "We share NOMORE! And a history."

Kate's expression never changed. "We don't share Ethan, Rick. I mother him. You send money and call when you can. We don't share NOMORE! I run it. You contribute what you can. And as for sharing a history? That didn't stop you from moving out. And it's not going to get you a free pass to move back in."

She placed her drink on the table, rose from her chair, and without another word, went to her room.

He remained in the lounge for a long time after Kate left, thinking what she had said and what he had done to provoke such quiet rage. He had no defense. She was right about everything, except the one thing she didn't say: that he didn't love her. On that count, she was wrong. He loved her very much; he had left because he hated himself.

Though he hadn't deserved the time to heal at his own pace, in that sense, the separation had served its purpose. While his grief over Mira would never disappear, nor his anger, through therapy and hundreds of sleepless nights he had arrived at a difficult peace. He understood that life went on and that was as it should be. He understood that often, during a time of such emotional upheaval, terrible mistakes were made and feelings were trampled. On some level he even understood that, according to statistics, most marriages suffered irretrievable damage when faced with the kind of tragedy that had hit the Siegels. But Rick didn't want to be a statistic. He didn't want to be alone anymore. He wanted his family back.

Earlier, he had told Ethan he wanted to move home.

"Then you'd better come up with a whopper of a campaign, Dad," he'd said. "Because you've never had a tougher client than Mom."

Now, Rick nodded. Ethan was right. This was the campaign of his life. But he'd never lost a battle he really wanted to win. And this one, he wanted to win most of all.

Celia was jotting down leads she thought might be worth pursuing in her quest for dirt on Chandler and/or Edwards, when a knock on the door startled her.

"Just a minute!"

Force of habit prompted her to turn off her PowerBook and slip it into a drawer before answering. When she opened the door, she was surprised to see Quinn standing there holding a bottle of red wine and two glasses.

"You really should have been in the bar tonight," he said, walking past her before she had a chance to decide whether to offer an invitation or slam the door in his face. "Everyone was talking about how you aced the General." He put the bottle down, took a corkscrew from his pocket, and set about his task. "I think you're on your way to becoming a legend."

"I think you're on your way out," Celia said.

Secretly, she was delighted to hear that the boys finally had something good to say about her. She wasn't displeased to see Quinn either, but she was in her nightclothes and he had a bottle of wine and there was no denying that something electric was buzzing about this room.

Quinn ignored her dismissal and handed her a goblet of wine. "To you," he said, clinking his glass with hers.

Over the rim of his glass, his green eyes contemplated the beautiful woman before him. She was wearing a short, champagne-colored nightgown and a long, delicately floral robe. Her hair was brushed softly behind her ears. Her face was pale and polished with a just-washed glow. She had never looked more enchanting.

"You were awesome today," he said, his mouth spreading in an appreciative grin. "Actually, you're even more awesome right now. That down-filled whatever you were wearing really doesn't do you justice." He clucked his tongue and shook his head in disapproval.

"Didn't I ask you to leave?" Celia said.

"You did. I refuse."

"And why is that?"

"Because I want to stay. That should be obvious by the wine and how charming I'm being."

"Ah! So that's what this is: *charming*. I'm so glad you told me. I wasn't sure."

He took her hand and led her to the couch.

"If I'm being charming," he said, encouraging her to sit and sip her wine, which she did, "you should be cordial."

"Got it." She saluted.

"Good."

"Now what?"

"Now, we drink and we talk and we try very hard to get along."

"Why?"

"Because I think we're attracted to each other—*real* attracted—and I don't want you using me as your sexual boy toy."

Celia laughed in spite of herself. "Perish the thought!"

Somehow, Quinn managed to look indignant and very self-righteous. "I want you to want me for my mind," he said, "not just for my body, which, in case you're interested, is quite fabulous . . . for a man my age."

It surprised Celia how endearing she found him. Instead of coming on like some road-show lothario, he was courting her, and she liked it. Intrigued but wary, she sat back, put her emotions on alert, and practically dared him to woo her.

Smoothly, he segued away from them to a discussion about Vail and skiing and the glory of the Rocky Mountains. Now and then, he replenished her wine. As they talked and she relaxed, her mind began to wander, as did her eyes. He did look wonderful in his cashmere sweater and jeans. He was so glib and so droll. And the wine was excellent. And his body did look fit and . . .

She would never know what possessed her, but suddenly, she put her glass down on the table, put his there as well, slid next to him, sat on her knees, took his face in her hands, and kissed him, hard. As their mouths touched, she felt a thunderous rush. He moaned, letting her know he had felt the same charge. She shook off her robe. His hands slid down her back and around to her breasts, heating the silken fabric that separated their flesh. She gasped, her breath catching in her throat. He kissed her ear and then her neck and then followed the line of her negligee. Her breasts begged for attention, but again, he sought her lips. Celia thought she would burst from wanting him.

Her hands tugged at his sweater. He pulled back and looked at her. His eyes were intense, filled with the flames of his own passion and a question. She smiled in response.

"I thought you'd never ask," he said gruffly, as he pulled the sweater over his head.

Impatiently, she undid his belt and watched as he shed the rest of his clothes. He hadn't lied to her. He was magnificent. She reached for him, needing to feel his lips on hers, his flesh against hers. As he sat, he removed her negligee and lifted her onto his lap. Her legs snaked around him. When he looked at her, he thought he would stop breathing, she was that magnificent.

His eyes never left her face as his hands caressed her. Slowly, tenderly, he voyaged across her skin, feeling the satiny surface of her body, the hard excitation of her breasts, the warmth that only need can generate. She bit her lip as his mouth grazed her chest. She inched forward, her hands finding him and holding him, feeling the insistent power of his desire.

Suddenly, he laid her down, guiding her beneath him, glorying in the view he had of her. Straddling her, his hands cupped her breasts, reveling in their perfection. Her hands massaged him, taunting, teasing, moving up his chest and down to his thighs and then, only for a moment, to the place he needed her most. He descended slowly, almost unwillingly. She was so gorgeous that looking at her was nearly as erotic as touching her. She smiled as if she knew, pulling his mouth onto hers, encouraging him to move closer to the heat.

With a desperation that demanded completion, he protected himself, and then they came together. She arched her back and gasped as he filled her. Whatever electricity had buzzed about them before, ignited them now, charging them with a passion that enveloped and enthralled and carried them to a place neither had ever been before.

When it was over, Quinn brushed a lock of hair off her face and smiled, then bent down and kissed her. "So what now?"

Celia sighed. What she wanted was to spend a week in bed with him. What she said, was, "You're going to go to your room. I'm going to stay in mine. And we're going to take it nice and slow."

He shook his head and made the sound of a buzzer. "Sorry. Wrong answer." She started to speak. He put his finger on her lips. "We're going to finish the wine and finish our evening together."

"But what about . . ."

"I'll leave before the rooster crows and the busybodies get their noses stuck in our business, but until then, the hell with them. Let's concentrate on us!"

Fear about whom she could trust suddenly intruded on Celia's reverie. Her eyes darkened as they searched his.

As if he was able to read her thoughts, Quinn said, "I'm not going to hurt you, Celia. Unless you tell me differently, this is not a one-night stand. Okay?"

If only he knew how much she wanted to believe him. "Okay," she said. If only he knew how terrified she was that she had just made another dreadful mistake.

☆ ☆ ☆

Georgie climbed back into the golf cart and proceeded to record the scores: four for her, four for Scottie Edwards, five for J.R., and six for her father.

"Gimme a five," he said. "I wasn't really concentrating on that putt. If I had, it would've dropped."

"It didn't drop. You had a six."

"Doggone it, girl! This isn't the U.S. Open. That damn putt was within the leather. In my regular game, that's a gimme."

"It was six feet from the cup, but all right. I'll give you a five," she said, suppressing a laugh. "With a star."

"What the hell's the star for?"

"To remind you that it's not an honest five." She penciled in the number and starred it. "And that you're a terrible cheat."

"Am not."

"Are too."

Roy Hughes grumbled all the way to the next tee, but when his daughter went to hit her drive, his mouth relaxed into a proud smile. She really was his favorite. Aside from her beauty and her brains, both of which were considerable, was her savvy. That was the trait Roy admired the most—her savvy. Georgie's instincts were always on the money. It was Georgie who had insisted that her family resign from their former country club—which was luxurious, but exclusive: no blacks, no Jews, and no single women—and join this semiprivate facility. At the time, Roy and the others had bucked, and mightily so. The Hugheses might have been civic-minded, but they had never let public service interfere with private indulgence. Georgie had told them to do as they wished.

"I, however, shall play my golf where I'm wanted and respected."

Naturally, the others had followed. In the end, of course, Georgie had been right. When Wade ran for the Senate, his opponent's various memberships were headlined in all the papers. Not only did the fool belong to an all-white, all-Protestant, only-men-as-members golf club, but he carried cards from several other politically incorrect establishments as well.

Roy watched Edwards take a few practice swings. Then, playing to the small audience that was following them around, Edwards consulted with his caddy, threw some grass up to test the direction of the wind, and changed clubs.

What a pompous jerk, Roy thought. When he had first called Edwards to invite him to play a round before a scheduled fund-raiser, Edwards had made a point of making certain that the club didn't exclude blacks or Jews or women or any other vocal minority.

"I *am* running for president," he said. "I'm sure you understand. I have to be very careful not to offend."

"I have a son who's a United States senator, sir, a daughter who's a member of the House of Representatives and, in case you have forgotten, I am a former governor of this great state. I wouldn't belong to anything but an open club!"

Edwards's tee shot plunked into a sand trap to the left of the green. Roy had a hard time hiding his delight. Georgie poked him in the ribs.

"The golf god punishes those who take pleasure in other golfers' pain," she said.

"Yeah, yeah." Roy grabbed his five iron, took a practice swing, addressed an apology and a small prayer to the golf god, and hit his drive. Someone had listened, because his ball landed six feet from the cup. When Scottie Edwards shouted "nice shot," Roy responded with a modest nod.

They were on the eleventh hole when Georgie's mood unexpectedly soured.

"Daddy, I've got to leave Lyle."

"What the hell are you talking about?"

"Lyle. Me. Our marriage. It's been over for years, you know."

"I know no such thing."

Georgie stopped the cart, forcing her father to look at her.

"Yes, you do. You'd have to be deaf, dumb, and blind not to see the distance that exists between us, and you are none of those things. It's unbearable, Daddy. And I want out!"

Roy shook his head. She was right. He had known there was trouble and that this would come up sooner or later. He had hoped it would be later.

"Listen, sugar. There's nothing I want more in this world than for you to be happy, but . . ." He was about to plead Lyle's case, but the look on Georgie's face squelched the impulse. "Your timing's off. You've got a tough reelection campaign, and we're looking to hook your brother to a national ticket. We can't afford any negative publicity now."

"It's worse staying married to him."

"In what way?"

"I'm always making excuses for him, explaining where he is, why he's never where he's supposed to be. Not only to the public, but to the twins. I hate it!"

"What brought on this thunderstorm?" Roy asked, concerned at the flush on her cheeks.

"That call I took at the turn?" Georgie said. "That was Lyle telling me he couldn't make the dinner tonight. He's going to be tied up," she said, mimicking her husband's tone. "Tied up, my ass!"

Georgie got out of the cart, pulled a club out of her bag, and went to her ball. "I don't know who she is, but I hope after she ties him up, she whips the hell out of him." Having said that, Georgie smashed a three wood straight down the fairway.

When she returned to the cart and her father had hit his ball, she bit back the tears that threatened.

"I know this isn't the time or the place to discuss this," she said. "I'm sorry. I just feel so frustrated and angry and ... empty."

Roy patted his daughter's hand. Despite what she thought, Roy had never been blind to Lyle Mercer's shortcomings. He knew Lyle was an ambitious man eager to attach himself to the Hughes name and the power that came with it, but Roy didn't object to ambition—he had more than a dollop of it himself. More important, Lyle's ambition hadn't been empty. He had proved himself a capable businessman, time and time again, which of course, was what had endeared him to his father-in-law.

Suddenly, Roy felt guilty. He had heard the rumors about Lyle and other women. Having fished in other ponds more than once during his own marriage, Roy was hesitant to judge. Then the rumors had increased. Roy had thought about confronting Lyle, but Georgie didn't seem terribly bothered. He thought perhaps she didn't know, or if she knew, didn't care. Perhaps it was a phase that would blow over. Looking at Georgie now, he knew it wasn't a phase. She knew. And she cared.

"Why didn't you tell me how you feel? Why didn't you leave him?"

Georgie hesitated. At that instant, Roy understood.

"Aside from the fact that I was afraid you'd view it as an act of treason, I was stupid," she said, her voice resonating with profound regret. "I trusted him and told him some things I shouldn't have."

Roy had suspected as much. "You just hang in there, baby, and don't you worry," he said, his feelings about Lyle doing a swift one-eighty. "After the elections in November, I promise: you can dump him, shoot him, or keep him. Whatever you want."

Georgie nodded and tried to concentrate on her golf game, but Roy could see how miserable she was.

I'll make it up to her, he told himself. *Whatever this lizard knows about my daughter will pale in comparison to what I'm going to know about him.*

Olivia Mercer was in the den, her rangy body draped across the couch. A telephone was pressed against her ear. A bowl of popcorn sat within easy reach, a half-empty soda can on the coffee table. As Georgie walked in, her daughter's throaty laugh filled the room.

"He's such a jerk," Olivia said, running her fingers through her highlighted brown hair. "Then again, Tami is totally clueless. She wouldn't know he was lying if his nose pulled a Pinocchio right in front of her."

Georgie smiled. If they ran a contest for the world's most typical adolescent, Olivia would win. She was completely absorbed in the antics of her friends, the activities of her hormones, and her looks. She believed that the Neiman-Marcus catalogue was required reading, the telephone was equivalent to a life-support system, and Ralph Lauren was the most important man in America. She did well in school, but only incidentally. Gossip and teenage intrigue held a much higher spot on her agenda than did biology or algebra. And at eighteen, her mood ping-ponged between loving and hostile, depending on the hour.

Olivia hung up, swung her legs around, and sat up, facing her mother.

"Tami Sexton is beyond!" she intoned, her expression one of utter incredulousness. "I don't know how she makes it through the day."

"Some days I wonder how anyone makes it," Georgie said, suddenly exhausted.

"Grandpa wear you out?"

"No. Actually, we had a fun game."

"Did he cheat much?"

"Same as always."

Olivia giggled. Roy may have terrified the other grandchildren, but like her mother, she had always had a key to his soft side. "How much did he win?"

"About twenty dollars, but it wasn't the money he enjoyed. It was the look on Scottie Edwards's face as he handed it over. Grandpa positively relished the moment."

"As only he can," Olivia said knowingly.

"Right." Georgie nodded, then rubbed her eyes.

"You could use a power nap."

"No time. I'm hosting that fund-raiser for Edwards."

"Is Daddy going?"

"No." Georgie held her tongue. It bothered her how much a habit that had become. "How would you like to come with me?"

"Love to, but I've got Cookie's party tonight." Olivia shrugged, trying to look as if she would have gone if she could have. They both knew she loathed all political functions, save family victory parties, particularly her mother's. "Maybe Hunt will go."

"Maybe Hunt will go where? With whom? To do what?"

Both women turned as Olivia's twin, Hunt Hughes Mercer, loped into the room. As tall as his sister and bearing the same aristocratic bone structure, his eyes were the same light gray-blue as Georgie's; Olivia's were on the navy side, like Lyle's.

"I have to introduce Scottie Edwards tonight at a rally. Your father can't go, and I don't really want to go alone."

"Dad have a business meeting?" Hunt asked, unwilling to hide his sarcasm.

"So he says."

"Yeah. Right."

"Don't start, Hunt." Olivia's eyes narrowed. Her stance had turned protective. She hated when Hunt battled with their parents. Nine times out of ten, it turned ugly within minutes.

"Chill out, Liv. Mom looks frazzled enough. She doesn't need my input."

"I do need an escort, however," Georgie said, returning to the subject at hand.

"If it were something cool, maybe, but I don't do son-of-the-candidate gigs."

"What's the big deal?" Olivia asked, completely exasperated.

Hunt glared at her. When he spoke, it was with exaggerated patience. "The big deal is that two seconds after we arrive, the esteemed congresswoman from the Fifth District will be into a full tilt meet-greet-and-eat, and I'll be left standing by the door like some rent-a-jerk." He shook his head. "Uh-uh. No way."

"Never mind," Georgie said, walking toward the door. "Forget I asked."

Olivia watched as her mother climbed the stairs to her bedroom. "You just can't give her a break, can you?"

"I don't see you signing on as a member of the entourage."

"I have an appointment."

Hunt issued a disbelieving grunt, slumped onto the couch, and finished what was left of Olivia's soda.

"She looked so sad."

"You'd look sad, too, if your husband was fucking half the state of Texas."

"Don't be crude."

Hunt leaned forward, rested his arms on his legs, and looked at his sister, dropping his tough-guy pose and turning soft, as he always did with her.

"I'm not being crude, Livvie. I'm telling it like it is. You just don't want to hear it."

Olivia's voice was small. "No, I don't."

Hunt reached out and took her hand. "You have to stop thinking of them as Ma and Pa Perfect. He's a money-hungry, skirt-chasing lowlife, which has turned her into an ambitious, power-hungry tool of the GOP," Hunt said.

Olivia grimaced, knowing that in this case, GOP was not the Grand Old Party, but Hunt's less-than-complimentary nickname for their grandfather: Grand Old Patriarch. As brittle as he sounded, however, Olivia felt the tears hiding behind the harshness. No matter how different they seemed, they were twins. They didn't need words to communicate; they relied on what Hunt called "twin telepathy."

"Why do you hate them so?"

"The problem isn't how much I hate them, it's how much they hate each other. If they weren't so intent on running away from each other, maybe they'd be here for us."

Olivia's voice was quietly reprimanding. "When you really needed her, Hunt, Mom was there for you. In a major way."

Hunt nodded, chagrined, but only slightly. True, his mother had been a rock during a difficult time, but Hunt's young, bruised ego still saw her as much a cause of his problem as part of his cure.

Hunt's drug habit had started the way most addictions start, slowly and unwittingly. Hunt had believed he wasn't the type to become addicted, that smoking a little dope was no different from drinking a few beers, that he could control his desire for the high. He was wrong on all counts.

From the moment she arrived at the police station until she checked him into the Wilcox Clinic just outside Fort Worth several days later, Georgie never left his side. While she acceded to the rules of the center and stayed away during Hunt's detoxification and the initial phase of his recovery, when the therapist asked if she would participate in his family group sessions, Georgie was there.

Even in the midst of his angst, Hunt understood how much his mother had risked baring the intimate details of their home life to an audience of strangers. Some or all of it would have made juicy fodder for those who might want to trade on it after they were released. He was an angry young man, and he spared nothing.

"You don't give a shit about my recovery," he screamed at her one afternoon. "You're only here because it looks good for the voters." He stood and bowed before the group. "Ladies and gentlemen, feast your eyes on Congresswoman Hughes's new poster boy for her crusade against drugs."

Georgie said nothing; her gaze never wavered from his face. Suddenly, Hunt laughed. It was the sound of someone in excruciating pain.

"It just hit me! Thanks to all this great publicity, *I* might be the key to your winning reelection. Me! Not your brother the senator or your brother-in-law or your super-precious father, the greatest governor of all time. Me! Ordinary, nonpolitical, unaccomplished, unimportant Hunt Mercer."

Georgie had never realized how much her son resented her father. The knowledge stunned her.

"Just think. You might have to be grateful to me for this one, Mom. What a bummer." Hunt slumped back into his chair and dared her to refute his diatribe.

The therapist looked from one to the other. When he started to speak, Georgie held up her hand.

"First of all, Hunt, you are neither unimportant, unaccomplished, nor ordinary. It is true that you are not wildly interested in things political, but who could blame you?

Considering the family you come from, you've probably had a stomachful.

"As for gratitude, I'm already grateful to you, for many things, most of all for filling my life with all the little pleasures that only a son can give to a mother."

She leaned forward, stretching toward him as if by changing her body position she could bridge the chasm between them.

"In my mind and in my heart, you and Olivia have always come first. Obviously, I've done a poor job communicating that. I've allowed you to believe that my work and other family members take precedence over my children. They don't."

Hunt's fingers curled into fists, relaxed and tightened again. Georgie saw moisture gathering in his eyes. She also saw how hard he was fighting against any show of emotion.

"You're my little boy, Hunt. My one and only son. That makes you very special. You've got to believe that."

"I believe that if your father said, 'jump,' you'd ask how high." His voice vibrated with resentment.

"You couldn't be more wrong," Georgie said, thunderstruck by the irony of the accusation. "I am my own person, Hunt Mercer, with my own goals. Do I love my father? Damn right I do! He's worked hard to earn my love and respect, and so I'm more than happy to give him his due. You've never had to earn my love, and you know it! That's been yours since the moment you were born. But I don't respect easily."

Her voice labored over a lump in her throat. "You deserve respect for many things: for swallowing your embarrassment and taking the boos of the crowd when you were a Little League pitcher and struggled on the mound. For standing up at a public debate when you were ten years old and telling my opponent he couldn't say mean things about your mother. For always defending and protecting your sister."

She paused, gathering her courage.

"For telling your father he couldn't yell at me in front

of you or call me names." Her voice stumbled. It was getting harder to get over that lump. "You sure as hell had my respect then. But taking drugs is a needless, senseless, self-indulgent cop-out, Hunt, and you'll get no respect from me for that!"

She had silenced him then, but two years later, while Hunt was drug-free he still was seeing a therapist, still seeking answers.

Markham, the Mercers' driver, prided himself on his loyalty, so when Georgie asked him to take her where he had taken Mr. Mercer, he complied, but reluctantly.

"Wait here," she said, as she walked into the small, out-of-the-way hotel.

It didn't take long for her to weasel Lyle's room number and the spare key from the desk clerk. When she opened the door, she found Lyle sitting on the edge of the bed, lost in a fog of sexual ecstasy.

Georgie's calm belied the fury simmering just below the surface. "I only stopped by to deliver a message: there's a seat for you at Daddy's table at Scottie Edwards's fundraiser. He expects you to fill it."

"And whatever Roy Hughes wants . . ."

"He gets," Georgie said emphatically.

"Lucky man," Lyle said, nodding at his companion. "I have to go elsewhere for what I want."

"That's too bad." Georgie shrugged. "But if pleasure-seeking is such a bother," she said blithely as she closed the door. "Go fuck yourself!"

Georgie hated being chauffeured. It reminded her of when her father was governor and she was driven everywhere, including to school. In the beginning, she had asked to be let off several blocks away. She had wanted to fit in, and arriving at an elementary school in a big black limousine was not the way. For weeks, she thought she had managed to be Georgie Hughes, regular kid. Then, one afternoon, she and a bunch of her friends had walked out of the building only to find a limousine waiting by the curb. Her father had decided to surprise her. He didn't see her because he was asking a group of students if they knew his daughter.

"Gorgeous little girl about so high. Shiny black hair. Prettiest blue eyes you've ever seen." When he spotted her, he pointed. "There she is! Sweetest rose in Texas."

Georgie remembered how every face had turned toward her in total amazement. She hadn't known whether to hug her father, hate him, or cry.

She felt caught now, just the way she had then, exposed as someone other than who she had said she was. How could she condemn Lyle when she couldn't erase the memory of being in bed with Jed the night before?

As her car pulled into the driveway of the Adolphus Hotel, Georgie shook off her remorse. She hadn't gone to that motel because she was devastated at the thought of losing her husband's affection; she had come to terms with that years ago. She had gone because she feared she was turning into an habitual victim, someone who saw everything through the grainy, enslaving filter of "what would happen if . . ." It was time to fight back.

As she walked into the lobby and headed toward the ballroom, she was accosted on all sides by admirers. People shouted her name and rushed to shake her hand. She smiled, straightened her shoulders, held her head high, and made her way to the holding room, where her father and Scottie Edwards were waiting.

Despite her calm, worries lingered. If she humiliated Lyle by leaving, he would retaliate; pride dominated his nature. But what was the worst thing that could happen? That she would have to face her past?

She tried to tell herself she was prepared for the effects of disclosure, but in truth, she wasn't sure how large a wave it would create. It could turn out to be little more than an embarrassing ripple. Or it could surge and become a rip tide that pulled her under an ocean of accusations and recriminations.

She had seen it so many times. Incidents accumulated importance when they became secrets. The longer those secrets remained submerged, the more they festered and swelled. It was the poison that concerned Georgie, and the pain. It had devastated her then and, despite her best efforts, had barely diminished over time.

Shake it off, she told herself. *Hang in until November. Then, Lyle won't matter. I'll make a life with Jed and the twins.*

Suddenly, the fluttering in her stomach tightened into a substantial knot. What if it did matter? Could she really predict what Jed would think? Or how Hunt and Olivia would feel? What would happen to Roy? And Wade? Their careers? Her career?

For much of her life, Georgie had been so protective of her privacy, she hadn't thought beyond that. With a flash of horrifying clarity, she realized that privacy was the least of it.

If Lyle made good on his threat, she could lose everything.

☆   ☆   ☆

The next day was Super Tuesday. Ten states, including electoral behemoths like Florida and Texas, would hold their primaries. Monday, in each state where the race between Mack Kenton and Ben Knight was a toss-up, the late editions of every local tabloid carried a picture of Kenton, Maribel, and their three children waving as they left Sunday church services—along with a benign piece about Kenton's stand on the issue that played best in that locale. Juxtaposed to that Rockwellian portrait, was an old, unflattering picture of Ben Knight and Fabia Guevera as well as a new picture, taken in Detroit, of Ben and Zoë Vaughn dancing cheek to cheek. The headline screamed: FOREIGN POLICY? OR FOREPLAY?

The accompanying article rehashed Ben's romance with Fabia, the allegations of interference, the possibility of payoffs, and the implication of serious wrongdoing on Ben's part. Then it moved on to Ben and Zoë. It glossed over the brevity of their early relationship, making it sound long-term, insinuating that her being named as his foreign policy advisor had less to do with her diplomatic credentials and more to do with the continuation of their affair.

According to sources who insist upon remaining nameless, at the time of her resignation from the State Department, there were a number of rumors that on a number of occasions, Ms. Vaughn had formed intimate attachments with foreign men whose trustworthiness was deemed questionable by those in the intelligence services. One man suggested that her resignation had been demanded in order to protect our national security.

Zoë slammed the paper down on the table. Hot tears stung her eyes.

How dare they? she raged, her fingers curled into tight fists. Overwhelmed by the unfairness of it all and exhausted by her own fury, she plunked down on her couch, laid her head back, and closed her eyes, waiting for a sense of calm to return.

How naive you are! she thought. *You know the game and you know the rules.*

Elections were about power, and winning was everything. If the truth had to be sacrificed, it was. If one reputation had to be savaged to maintain another, it was. Politics was hardly a gentleman's sport. More often than not, it was a no-holds-barred contest in which facts were distorted. Rumor became reality. Innuendo and illusion replaced accuracy and authenticity. And the long-term needs of the public were subordinated to the more immediate ego needs of the candidate.

Zoë stared at the newspaper, this time with the cold composure that comes from finally acknowledging a battle with a formidable foe. The same person who had tormented Dixon Collins had planted this story and for the same reason: to ensure silence.

Up to now, she had said nothing publicly about what had happened in Moscow. But Scottie was nervous. If this hostage crisis wasn't resolved and Ben survived the primaries, he was guessing that Zoë might feel compelled to come forward with what she knew. Scottie couldn't afford for that to happen. Which was why the people who had worked with her had been demoted, transferred, or harassed to death. And why she had just been Borked.

What depressed Zoë was that she had warned Ben that something like this would happen. Sooner or later, Clay was bound to raise the issue of Zoë and Ben's former relationship. Which would allow Scottie to recall some embassy scuttlebutt about Zoë. Which would prompt someone on the campaign staff to reach the startling conclusion that if they trashed her, they could discredit Ben without appearing to attack him directly. Between Scottie's need to keep her quiet and Clay's hatred of Ben, there was no doubt about that plan being approved immediately. If the trashing was effective enough, Ben's campaign would never get out of the primaries, Scottie would have the easier opponent in the general election, and Zoë's credibility would be so thoroughly tarnished that anything she said about Durgunov and Red Rage and Edwards would be suspect.

"I'm not going to let you win this one," Zoë vowed. "If you want to play dirty, General, that's fine. I've got plenty of mud to sling."

Suddenly, Zoë's mind was racing, retrieving facts, planning a strategy, estimating her chances of success. In preparation for her posting in Moscow, she had done an exhaustive background check on the ambassador under whom she would be serving. Since his predecessor, Prescott Edwards, had moved from Moscow to Washington as secretary of state, she had thought it prudent to run an equally meticulous check on him. Her reasons were simple and innocent: She had wanted to know everything about both men so she would be able to deal with them effectively.

In the course of her investigation, she discovered that Scottie Edwards had a pile of dirty laundry he had done his best to hide. Unfortunately for him, it was the kind of story that never could be buried completely. Zoë had debated using it as barter during her difficulties with him at State, but she hadn't had time to gather the necessary evidence. Without witnesses or undeniable proof, the whole matter could have been thrown back in her face, making her look like a liar or worse.

Now, however, Zoë felt emboldened, as if her finger had just depressed a trigger halfway. If she pulled all the way, she could blow Edwards's campaign out of the water. Tempting as it was, once again, she decided the timing wasn't right. This revelation couldn't come from her; it could boomerang and hurt Ben. An investigative report by a respected member of the legitimate press, however, couldn't be dismissed as something invented by the dirty tricks operation in the opposing camp, especially if the report was complete with facts and dates and corroborating evidence. Clay and Scottie and their entire staff could jump up and down, scream, shout foul, and deny it until election day. But the public would know it was the truth.

And that would hurt Edwards more than anything else.

After a round of frantic conference calls, it was decided that Otis and Zoë would work the evening news circuit. Coached by Jed to maintain an "all-out offensive on those who reveled in rumors rather than talking about issues," both did their jobs well.

Otis chastised the media "for stooping to the level of supermarket smut-sheets," ridiculing those who would "make dish from a dance."

Zoë ignored the swipes at her reputation and shrugged off the controversy as "a pitiful, cowardly attack on Senator Knight's candidacy."

"Whoever planned this," she said to Clark Aiken, "wasn't brave enough to challenge the Senator's policies. Probably because that would expose the weakness of his own positions."

"Who do you think's behind this?" Aiken asked. "Do you think Representative Kenton set this up? Or either of the other two Democratic candidates?" When Zoë didn't answer right away, Aiken filled the void just as she had wanted him to. "What about General Edwards?"

"I'm not certain who's responsible for this campaign of disinformation, but I assure you, it's nothing more than smoke and mirrors."

"A story like this has to hurt," Aiken said, looking to press the emotional button and enliven his piece. "Whoever planted this wanted to savage your reputation."

Zoë checkmated his move with a quick and clever spin. "What hurts is that someone used an untruth about me and the Senator to try and manipulate the public. Is it any wonder people are fed up with politics?"

Aiken was tempted to applaud; her cool was admirable. Instead, he asked again if she had any idea who was behind it all.

"If I had to guess," Zoë said, looking directly into the camera, keeping her tone even, "I'd say the man behind these scurrilous tales about Senator Knight has something in his own past he's trying to hide."

Scottie Edwards lay sprawled on the couch in his room at the Adolphus watching a replay of the evening's news reports. An aide had taped both the early and late editions while Scottie was jawboning at the Hughes fund-raiser. The Hughes clan had raised over a million dollars for his campaign. As she had done in New Hampshire, Georgie Hughes had rallied the troops until they were in a near frenzy. Scottie should have been ecstatic. Instead, he gulped his drink, his blue eyes nearly black with anger.

"If she thinks she's going to play head games with me," he groused, "she's making a big mistake."

Emily Edwards rose from a chair near the couch and turned toward her husband, her face void of any discernible emotion. "It's you who made the mistake, Prescott, and if she doesn't call you on it, you can bet the White House, someone else will."

Calmly, without any sympathy or remorse for her husband's predicament, Emily left him alone with his past and went to bed. Edwards sighed, rewound the tape, and watched it again, wondering which secret Zoë was alluding to: The one Emily knew about? The one Zoë knew about? Or the one he thought no one knew about.

After the last interviews had been given, including appearances by Otis and Zoë on *Newsline*, Ben, Otis, Sam, Jed, and Zoë headed over to the Willard. The throng of reporters who had waited for them outside the television studios and followed them to the hotel tossed questions at both Ben and Zoë about their past and possible future. Ben stopped and moved to the side. The reporters flocked like pigeons. Otis took Zoë's arm and, flanked by Sam and Jed, led her inside and to the elevators.

"Ms. Vaughn and I dated in college," Ben declared in an open-faced manner that said he had nothing to hide. "We have seen each other twice in over twenty years. Once at a funeral. Another time at an American Embassy function. Neither one constitutes a romantic setting."

"How about now?" someone shouted.

"Now, Ms. Vaughn is a foreign policy advisor. She is highly qualified for the post and to imply that the only reason she has the job is because she is a woman with whom I was once involved is insulting to her, to me, and to women in general."

He parried several more verbal lunges and then, maintaining his congenial mien, bade them good-night. Once inside the hotel, he went straight to the elevators on the

Pennsylvania Avenue side and up to the fourth floor, where he quickly entered a large suite. Waiting for him were Otis, Zoë, and General Harry Cadman.

"It was good of you to come, General," Ben said.

"When Otis told me what you guys wanted, I decided he was right. You need me." Cadman laughed, a hearty guffaw that invited companions.

Harry Cadman had retired a four-star general. At the time, he claimed it was time to give the younger generation a crack at the top ranks. The real reason was that his wife had been diagnosed with breast cancer, and he wanted to be with her. After a rough bout with the disease, it appeared as if she would be fine. Harry, on the other hand, was said to be dying of boredom.

Ben offered Cadman a seat, placing himself on the opposite couch. Otis and Zoë pulled up chairs to complete the tight circle.

"I assume you know what we want to do."

Harry nodded. "Rescue those poor hostages."

Ben looked sheepish. "This conversation is premature at best, arrogant at worst."

Cadman's reply was blunt. "I don't know what's going on behind closed doors, but the president simply isn't getting the job done."

"It's possible something is in the works and under very tight cover," Zoë said.

"I hope there is a plan, and I hope to hell it works." He shrugged. "But if it doesn't, or worse, if there is no plan, by the time you're sworn in, the hostages' time just might have run out."

Ben kneaded his forehead, wondering—and not for the first time—how wise it was to start down this path.

Cadman watched Ben ruminate. He understood the young man's conundrum, but he was a general, and to him there was one rule and one rule only: you go after your own.

"I know General Shafir quite well," he said to Ben, hoping to allay some of his concerns. "I also understand the delicacy of the situation, but if we can find out where these hostages are being held, by whom, and how many, we can chart a strategy to get them out with a minimum of casualties. It'll take highly trained commando units, but it can be done." He reached over and placed his hand on Ben's knee. "And it should be done."

Ben nodded. "I agree." He looked at Otis and Zoë, both of whom gave their assent. "Nonetheless, I'm nervous about this, General."

"You should be. We're talking about sending young men and women into battle. If you did that easily, you'd be no better than the thugs holding our women and children prisoner."

When Ben joined the others in the smaller side of the suite, they filled him in on the reports from the field: The consensus was that they had doused the flames.

While the others analyzed the relative effectiveness of such late-hour damage control, Ben and Zoë, as they had during the meeting with Cadman, avoided making eye contact. Both knew the day's events had raised a question that needed to be asked. At the first lull in the conversation, Ben decided it was his responsibility to do the deed.

"I wish you didn't have to go through what you did today, but since someone seems determined to drag up anything and everything about everyone associated with me, is there anything in your past, other than us," he said, staring into her pale green eyes, watching a shadow pass over them as he spoke, "that we should know about?"

Zoë's eyes never left his. "Yes. I spent several months in a hospital suffering from a nervous breakdown."

Silence greeted her stark confession. Otis rose from his chair, walked behind her, and protectively placed his hands on her shoulders. Jed and Sam stared at each other, visibly shaken. Ben appeared to be the calmest person in the room, perhaps because this revelation didn't surprise him as much as it did the others. Twice, he had witnessed her battling with ghosts; they had to come from somewhere.

He leaned forward to listen as Zoë spoke. Beneath his unruffled exterior was a growing sense of dread.

"In 1984," Zoë began, "I was posted at our embassy in Israel. During my tour there, I met, fell in love with, and married a man named Avi Yaacobi."

Ben felt an unreasonable rush of jealousy course through him. He hadn't known about a husband.

Otis squeezed Zoë's shoulder. Though she didn't look up at him, she nodded. He had known Avi. They had met and become friends when Otis trained with the Israelis.

"He was a cardiac surgeon." She paused. A quick, proud smile flickered across her lips. "He was quite brilliant. World renowned, in fact."

Again, she paused. Her gaze sought Ben's. "He operated on Mira Siegel."

Ben's eyes widened. He had known about the surgery to repair the damage to Mira's heart. He recalled Kate and Rick telling him how incredible the surgeon was.

"Did I meet him when I was in Israel?" he asked, remembering a photograph in Amalia Trilling's apartment of Zoë and a handsome young man.

Zoë shook her head. "He was operating the night of the embassy party. I tried to get the two of you together during your visit, but you were there such a short time, and your schedules never seemed to coincide."

"Avi was a hell of guy," Otis said, his voice filled with an emotion Ben didn't yet understand.

Zoë lowered her head and stared at her hands. She appeared to be gathering strength. Ben found himself growing anxious, almost fearful of what she was about to say. His colleagues were downright panicked.

"In December 1985, Avi and I decided to spend the holidays with Amalia in Italy." She looked away, unwilling to let anyone see the grief that had pooled in her eyes. "I was seven months pregnant."

A heaviness spread throughout Ben's chest. The sorrow

washing over Otis's face didn't relieve his sense of doom. Even Jed and Sam looked affected by the mournful aura that had permeated the room.

"We left Florence a few days after Christmas. We wanted to take our time driving to Rome where we would catch the flight for Tel Aviv. El Al makes you check in several hours before, so we got to the airport early. I was sitting at a table waiting for Avi. He was at the ticket counter checking us in."

Her voice had become an empty monotone; she was reciting facts. Her eyes and the pinched expression on her face, however, showed that somewhere deep in her subconscious, she was reliving events—terrible, life-altering events.

"Suddenly, everything went haywire. Grenades began bursting all around me, creating heat and noise and smoke. And death. Masked men were firing submachine guns into the crowd. People were screaming. Bodies were falling. Next to me, something exploded. I felt myself being lifted out of my chair and thrown across the floor. I don't remember feeling any pain, although I must have. I only remember yelling for Avi."

The color drained from her face. Her eyes closed, as if she couldn't finish the story without returning to the moment. Ben watched her carefully. His face was damp, hers was dry. He wondered how many tears she had shed between that day and this. Otis moved around the couch and took a seat at her side. Quietly, he folded one of her hands in his.

"When the noise stopped and I thought it was safe, I started to crawl toward the counter. There was blood everywhere. Parts of bodies. Babies crying. People dying. When I found Avi, he was lying in front of the counter." She inhaled sharply. "Half his head was gone."

Ben groaned softly.

"The authorities said a grenade had gone off inches from where he had been standing," Otis explained. "That same day, the same horror took place in the Vienna airport, all orchestrated by a renegade group of Palestinians headed by Abu Nidal.''

Sam Trout's complexion had paled. Jed Oakes had buried his head in his hands, which were shaking. No one had expected this.

''I must have fainted because I don't remember anything until I woke up in a hospital. Amalia was there. So was my mother.'' Zoë's lip trembled as she opened her eyes and looked at Ben. This time, she allowed a few tears to fall. ''They wanted to be with me when the doctors told me I had lost my baby. And that I could never have another.''

She wiped her eyes, took a deep breath, and swallowed her sadness. When she spoke, her voice was hoarse from straining to keep her grief at bay.

''I spent several weeks at a hospital in Rome recovering from my injuries. When I could travel, I returned to Israel to visit Avi's family. And to bury our child next to him.''

She stopped and again closed her eyes, revisiting that place and that time. Lost in the black eddy of her memories, she appeared to swoon. Otis put his arm around her, and, for a minute, she rested her head against his chest; he had accompanied her to Avi's grave. He understood the unique heaviness of this remembrance.

When she was able she sat up, gently caressed Otis's cheek and resumed. ''With the approval of my parents, Amalia checked me into a hospital in Switzerland. I was there for three months. When I came home to Washington, I continued therapy.''

She surveyed her audience, one by one. They looked ravaged, but this was no time for sympathy or muddled thinking. Zoë summoned an eerie serenity that closed around her like a shell.

''When Ben first came to Boston,'' she said to Sam, ''I told him it might not be in his best interest to have me on his staff. If any of you, or all of you, feel I am now or could be a detriment in the future, there'll be no hard feelings. For the sake of Ben's candidacy, I'll gladly step aside.''

Ben started to speak, but Sam held up his hand. He was the hard nose of the group. It was important that Zoë knew exactly how he felt.

"I was impressed by your brains and your savvy before," he said, somewhat gruffly. "But I'm overwhelmed by your courage, Zoë."

He hesitated, clearly checking his emotions. When he was certain he was in control, he pointed to Ben, his eyes still firmly fixed on Zoë.

"I love that man as if he were my brother. I would never do anything that would hurt him, even if it meant I had to hurt someone else."

Zoë nodded as if she understood what he was about to say. Ben thought about interrupting, but stopped himself. Sam would do the right thing.

"I have no problem with you being part of our team," Sam said. "If anything, I'm honored."

Zoë smiled, but only briefly. "I thank you for that vote of confidence, but let's remember, gentlemen, my medical history makes me vulnerable to labels like 'unstable' and 'unsteady.' Those could hardly be considered admirable qualities in someone giving foreign policy advice to a potential president."

"Did the State Department know why you were in that hospital?" Jed asked.

"Of course. In fact, after I returned from Switzerland, the therapist I went to was recommended by someone at State."

"Well, hell! They sent you to Moscow," Jed said. "If they weren't nervous about you then, the American public shouldn't be nervous about you now!"

Zoë laughed. What she loved most about Jed was his ability to distill everything, even the most complex of issues, down to a single, simple notion.

"Scottie Edwards would love nothing more than to tag me as irrational," she reminded him.

"Uh-uh." Jed shook his head. "To do that, he'd have

to explain why he thought so, and I don't think he wants to do that."

Otis looked at Ben, who had risen from his chair and was pacing the room. Otis's tone was quiet, curious. "You haven't said anything, my man. And unless the world has turned upside down for sure, you've got an opinion."

Zoë hadn't realized how nervous she was about what Ben would say. As she waited for him to speak, she could feel moisture gathering in the palms of her hands.

"What's Avi's connection to General Shafir?"

Sam, Jed, and Otis all registered surprise. To them, Ben's question seemed like a non sequitur. Zoë recognized it as typical of Ben's incisive intellect and emotional radar. When Zev and Zoë and he were together in Otis's house, Ben must have picked up on something he didn't bother with then, but wanted explained now.

"Avi was Zev's nephew."

"Are you and he close?"

"Very."

"Did the Mossad provide you with information during your tour in Moscow?"

"Now and then."

"Was your mysterious source one of them?"

"Yes."

The others looked from Ben to Zoë, waiting for an explanation. There was to be none. Ben nodded. He was satisfied. Zoë was grateful he was willing to leave it at that.

He paced a few moments longer. Everyone watched in silence. Otis leaned back, rested his head against his hands, and waited, a faint but knowing smile hiding beneath his mustache.

Ben stopped and faced Zoë. "I wish I had known about this before," he said. His eyes caught hers and held them. "I know what unexpected tragic loss feels like. I would have been there for you in whatever way possible."

"Thank you," she said, looking away, not willing to trust herself in front of the others.

"As for helping or hurting the campaign," he said, lifting his voice to brighten the mood, "you already know what I think."

Zoë smiled. Relieved, the boys gave her a unified thumbs-up.

"But how far this campaign goes is not up to me," Ben said. "Tomorrow, we hear from the voters. Then we'll know whether we're on our way to the convention. Or on our way home."

Ben won six out of the ten Super Tuesday primaries. Wilcox and Ujvagi dropped out of the race. The following week, Ben picked up Illinois, Michigan, and Ohio. Still, Kenton plodded on. When he managed to garner thirty-five percent of the vote in California, he vowed to take his fight to the convention floor.

When Clark Aiken asked what Ben thought about that, Ben grinned, and said, "Bring 'im on!"

☆ APRIL ☆

The flag at the White House flew at half-staff. Sunday morning tours were canceled. The staff had been alerted that there were to be no calls and no visitors. Upstairs, Beth and Elton Haynes remained secluded in their bedroom. Their breakfast sat untouched, their newspapers unopened.

Beth Haynes had seen her husband cry only twice before: at the births of his children. Watching him now was painful. Elton sat crumpled in a chair like a deflated balloon, his head buried in his hands, his face ashen. Though Beth had advised against it, he had demanded that they watch the morning news broadcasts. With masochistic insistence, he listened to the story being repeated again and again. Each time he heard it, each time he looked up and confronted the gruesome pictures, his depression deepened.

At least once during their tenure, most presidents find themselves impaled on the horns of a mighty dilemma. The books of modern history are filled with chapters born of agonized decisions: Hiroshima, Korea, Cuba, Vietnam, Iran, Bosnia. Even if he secured the safe return of every last hostage, there would be those who would praise him and those who would deride him, because no solution comes with guarantees and each solution involves gambling with other people's lives and the possibility that some of those lives will be lost.

Despite extraordinary cooperation by the international community, all diplomatic efforts to date had failed. The State Department appeared to have run out of options. The families of the hostages had become increasingly vocal with their demands for an immediate and satisfying resolution. Public outcries were growing louder, their impatience agitated by a media so crisis-obsessed they were in danger of drowning in the flood of their own analyses. Adding to the morass were the many members of Congress who had declared themselves family guardians and—in the name of grieving Americans—made it part of their daily routine to accuse the administration of everything from basic ineptitude to cold-hearted abandonment.

Yet while the scope of those scrutinizing his efforts was broadening, Elton's choices were narrowing, and time had become a formidable enemy. When the CIA reported they had received information that several of the hostages were being held in a small village high in the Zagros Mountains of Iran, it seemed like the break everyone had been waiting for. The president called a meeting of his National Security Council. After a lengthy discussion, it was decided that Haynes would call Borofsky personally to ask if he would intervene on America's behalf. At the same time, intelligence services would seek to verify the original sightings. If Borofsky refused, and it was assumed he would, the military would be called in to effect an immediate rescue. For months, the Joint Chiefs of Staff had been working on several different strategems, each designed around a specific set of circumstances. Haynes ordered the chiefs to fine-tune whichever offensive fit this situation and begin to position their troops.

When Borofsky turned the president down—citing the delicacy of his own problems with Durgunov and pleading personal political vulnerability—and it was confirmed they had indeed uncovered a prisoner enclave, Haynes called another meeting of the NSC. Despite the risks inherent in staging such an operation, and mindful of the fact that this was only one cluster of hostages and that others might pay for the rescue of a few, it was decided that some action was better than no action at all. With the approval of his advisors, and a heavy heart, President Haynes issued the order to proceed with the mission.

Several hours before dawn on the appointed day, from aboard the USS *Roosevelt* in the Persian Gulf, a squadron of F-16s took to the air to fly cover. They were followed by two Super Stallion helicopters bearing marine gunmen and reconnaissance scouts. Staying out of range of any possible radar scopes, they made their way up the coastline in the receding darkness. At sunrise, several miles before Bushire, the crisis action team swiftly turned inland. Even in the fresh light of a new day, the gray-walled, mud-brick houses and tall minarets of Iran's coastal towns appeared faded and drab. Circumventing the more heavily populated city of Shiraz, the team burrowed deep into the mountains, heading for their site point.

It was a tiny settlement squeezed into the navel of a peaked mass. Surrounded by mountains that kept out the rain and kept in the heat, the valley floor was narrow and not yet green. Primitive, mud gray houses with flat roofs and few windows surrounded a square dominated by a mosque. Narrow, unpaved lanes twisted in and around a series of walls, making the small village look like a maze.

The first Stallion landed. Fully camouflaged marines spilled onto the ground, racing to secure the perimeter. As the second Stallion descended from the clouds, it caught a patch of clear morning light, making the lumbering craft an inviting target. Suddenly, the silence was broken by small-arms fire that began to wink off the helicopter rotors. Forced to veer off course, the huge copter landed too close to one of the mountains and was unable to open its tailgate. Quickly, it shuddered back into the air, searching for another landing site. Before it could touch down, the recon team reported that they had flown into a trap. The entire village was deserted, except for a well-trained, mightily determined battalion of Red Rage warriors equipped with SAMs, a stash of machine guns, and sophisticated antiaircraft artillery.

Everyone made it back to the *Roosevelt* safely, but the mission was deemed a complete and utter failure. Not one hostage had been saved; much of the prestige of the United States had been lost. And then, for no other reason than to put an exclamation point to their victory, an American soldier was murdered, his brutalized body tossed onto the steps of a church in Bucharest. Pinned to his chest with one of his service medals was a note: *I am not a victim of Red Rage. I was killed by my government's arrogance and my president's stupidity.*

Scottie Edwards took his outrage to the airwaves, publicly declaring Haynes's handling of the matter a disgrace to the military and a disaster for the hostages.

"Elton Haynes should be ashamed of himself! He was willing to sacrifice American lives for the sake of flattering headlines and better poll numbers. He bungled the job, and, because of his ineptness, a fine young soldier was butchered!"

Mack Kenton also deplored Haynes's carelessness, but he went a step further, accusing him of falling prey to the demands of a bloodthirsty media.

"The president is supposed to lead his flock to the higher ground, to do everything within his estimable power to effect a noble conclusion to this ignoble tragedy. His job is not to give in to the base cravings of an industry that feeds on blood and profits from violence."

Lamar Basalt led the attack from the Hill. Not only did the senator berate the president for his obvious military failure, but he condemned him for authorizing such an action without consulting the Congress.

"Whatever happened to the concept of advise and consent?" he bellowed, his face florid with righteous indignation.

Elton Haynes accepted the harsh criticisms and personal attacks, particularly from Edwards and Kenton. It was expected, and, he supposed, grimacing as the dead soldier's body appeared again on the television screen, deserved. They were his political rivals; they would have been fools not to tromp all over this debacle.

Benjamin Knight was also seeking Elton's job, and therefore equally entitled to take advantage, but Ben was an old friend, a frequent advisor and confidant. When Elton saw that Ben was the scheduled guest on *Sunday with Dean Walsh,* he—naively perhaps—looked forward to a brief respite. From Ben, he told himself, he would get an intelligent, but tempered assessment and a well-articulated, but mild reproach.

When Ben hesitated to rebut Clark Aiken's verbal vivisection of his competence, Elton was stung. Even more devastating was to witness his friend's struggle to find an answer to Dean Walsh's question, "Bottom line: What does this botched rescue mean to the ultimate outcome of this situation?"

"It certainly lessens the possibility of a negotiated solution."

Anthea Ogden, leaning forward in her chair like a runner at the ready. "Are you saying that nothing short of a full-scale military invasion will resolve this?"

"I'm saying that the situation has grown more complicated."

Clark Aiken's tight-lipped, self-assured smile faded. "Has this disaster damaged United States credibility as a world power? Do we appear too weak to effect a solution?"

"Even against a two-bit renegade like Yegor Durgunov?" Anthea added.

Again, Ben seemed uncomfortable. "I would reject the notion that we've lost our standing as a superpower as the result of one failed mission, but there is no question that Elton Haynes has tied his own hands."

The unanimous silence was stunning, and it made Beth furious. As she stomped around the room, raging about self-serving palaver and pompous armchair pundits and the rabid disloyalty of political men, Elton Haynes simply wiped away a new spate of tears. He knew what was coming. And he knew it was the truth.

"By allowing himself to walk into their trap," Ben said, with chilling boldness, "Red Rage has added one more hostage to their list: the president of the United States."

☆ MAY ☆

Kate marched into the hearing room flanked by Stan Jeffries, Ethan, and Rick. As they took their places at the long table accessorized with microphones, drinking glasses, and pitchers of water, Kate turned and looked into the audience, seeking a few friendly faces as a balm for her nerves. Seated directly behind her and appearing emotionally armed for the battle was the core of her support group: Bob and Ronnie Kramer, their daughters, Lisa and Jessica, her parents and in-laws. They all nodded to each other, mumbling words of encouragement and good luck.

Kate looked to each side and counted the number of cameras and journalists cramming the front of the room. She knew several and acknowledged them with a wave or a tilt of her head. Scanning the crowd, she spotted other parents whose children had been victims of paroled sex offenders, other spouses of women who had been raped and murdered, all wearing the NOMORE! white ribbon and red teardrop. They had come to Washington for the same reason Stan Jeffries and the Siegels had come, to testify about the responsibility government had to its women and children and the disastrous consequences of a careless system.

Several rows back, Kate noticed two of her closest friends, Celia Porter and Zoë Vaughn. The sight of them brought a smile of thanks to her lips. With their schedules, she never expected to see them here. Although, she thought, feeling blessed to have women like this in her life, they had been by her side throughout this ordeal. As they had told her many times, they loved Mira. This fight was their fight, too.

Next to Celia sat Keeley Knight, wearing both a NOMORE! button and a ribbon. She waved to Kate who smiled back.

Kate turned away from Zoë, Keeley, and Celia just as her other champion, the sponsor of the legislation before this panel, Georgie Hughes, entered the regal chamber and quickly made her way to her seat at the double-tiered, elegantly paneled stage where the House Judiciary Committee met. Several aides hovered, showing her papers, giving last-minute briefings and, probably, an up-to-the-minute guesstimate on how the vote looked. Georgie had told Kate she felt confident of a majority—few politicians would argue on the side of sex offenders.

One by one, the thirty-five members of the committee filed in, each accompanied by a flock of assistants. Mack Kenton, the ranking member, took his place next to the chairman and immediately buried his nose in a sheaf of papers. His visage was grim.

"I would have thought Kenton was on our side," Rick whispered to his wife. "He looks anything but friendly."

"He's playing to the cameras," she said, studying the congressman from Iowa. "If they're taking pictures, and he hopes they are, he wants the country to see a serious man taking a serious issue seriously."

Rick chuckled at her undisguised sarcasm. "You sound like a trial lawyer assessing a potential jury member."

"I have had some experience in that area," she reminded him.

Rick addressed Kate's profile. "I heard a rumor that you've returned to the law."

"Part-time."

"With Stan Jeffries's firm."

"They made me an offer I didn't want to refuse."

Rick nodded. He wondered what other tempting offers Stan had made Kate. "Are you enjoying it?" he asked, swallowing his jealousy.

"Very much."

Stan Jeffries leaned over and asked Kate something, detouring her attention and annoying Rick. This man was becoming a burr. Rick had hoped this trip to Washington—this appearance as a family—would make it easier for him to tell Kate that in a few months, he was moving back East. The preliminary work on his new series was nearly completed. Script revisions and other business matters could be handled by phone and fax. And he had signed on to run the advertising for Ben's campaign. The timing, for him at least, seemed right. How Kate would feel was another matter.

While the chairman of the committee counted heads and looked at the back of the gallery to see if the doors had been closed, Georgie smiled at her witnesses. Ethan grinned back at her and waved. It didn't matter that in this venue she was known as Congresswoman Hughes. To him, she was Aunt Georgie, the woman who had taught him to ride horses on her family's ranch and taken him white-water rafting in Colorado.

The meeting was gaveled to order. The first hour was taken up with speeches by the chair and representatives from both sides of the aisle about the rapidly rising rate of violent crime in the United States. Kate thought Georgie's speech was the most powerful. Then again, it focused on Mira.

"I knew Mira Siegel," Georgie said. "I knew her as a beautiful baby who gurgled and cooed and as a delicious toddler who was curious and eager to explore the world around her. I also knew her as a fighter. Mira was born with a heart defect that severely restricted her activity. I watched her struggle to play with friends. To ride a bike. To dance ring-around-the-rosy. To climb stairs or throw a ball.

"When she was four years old, her parents took her to Israel where she underwent a risky operation to repair the valves of her heart. She spent an entire summer in a hospital bed, in pain much of the time. Yet nothing diminished this child's spirit. Each day, instead of complaining, she found something to clap her hands about. Over the years, as I watched her take charge of her life, gleefully embracing things she hadn't been able to before, I found her courage, her stamina, and her complete lack of bitterness something to clap *my* hands about."

Kate's throat tightened when she saw tears welling in Georgie's eyes. Rick reached for her hand beneath the table. She let him take it.

"It's a crime to abuse any child. It's a sin to kill any child. But for me," Georgie said, "these crimes and these sins became intensely personal when the child abused and killed was Mira Siegel."

She swallowed, gathered strength, and continued.

"We're supposed to be a compassionate nation that cares for our children and worries about their future. But, ladies and gentlemen, some of our children may not have a future because our justice system has stopped caring about a criminal's past. That cannot continue!"

Ethan leaped out of his seat and applauded. At first, the audience, unaccustomed to spontaneous displays of raw emotion, was stunned. Within seconds, however, all had joined him.

A period of witness interrogation followed, most of it quite benign. One by one, the various representatives asked Stan, Kate, Rick and, once in a while, Ethan, questions about life since the heinous crimes that had brought them here and what they thought the government should do to prevent further incidents. It was when the chair recognized Representative Mack Kenton that the tone changed.

After some preliminary questions, Kenton folded his hands and leaned forward, as if to announce that he was about to dig into the real meat of the issue.

"Mr. Siegel, I understand you are heading the creative team doing the ads for the Benjamin Knight presidential campaign."

Rick's eyes narrowed. "I am."

Kenton nodded and scribbled something on the notepad in front of him. He leaned back in his chair, asked something of one of his aides, and nodded somberly at her answer.

"I believe your sister, Ronnie Kramer, is one of the financial officers of the Senator's campaign. Is that correct?"

"It is," Rick said, the "what of it?" unsaid but definitely hanging in the air.

Kenton looked past him, toward the back, directing the camera's eye at Zoë. "And Ms. Vaughn, Senator Knight's foreign policy advisor, whom I see here today, she is . . .?"

"A longtime friend of the family. My parents, my in-laws, my brother-in-law, my two nieces, and my son are here as well," Rick said, his voice dripping with derision. "Is there a point to this roll-taking, Congressman?"

Kenton glared at Rick and then turned to Kate. "Mrs. Siegel, it's been reported that you were present at several meetings of the New Jersey 'Knight For President' finance committee, as well as at a large fund-raiser for the Senator. It has also been brought to our attention that representatives of your NOMORE! organization have been helping the Knight campaign by supplying membership lists. Is that true, Mrs. Siegel."

Kate forced herself to strain the hostility she felt from her voice. "Yes, Congressman, it is."

He shook his head and shrugged as if she had just said something self-incriminating and ominous. His gaze found the camera, to which he addressed his next statement.

"Under ordinary circumstances, I would have supported

this measure eagerly. I have three children myself, and, Lord knows, I would do anything to protect them, but I have to wonder if this particular bill is the way. In the House, it's being sponsored by my esteemed colleague, Congresswoman Hughes, who has been visibly stumping for General Edwards. The Senate version has been proposed by none other than presidential hopeful, Senator Benjamin Knight, a law-school classmate of Mrs. Siegel's and a close personal friend of the family's. Since the Siegels have not been shy about their support of his candidacy, and Congresswoman Hughes has been quite open about her support of General Edwards, I'm forced to wonder if this NOMORE! PAROLE is a laudable piece of legislation or a one-cause-fits-all bit of political manipulation.''

"That is so low and twisted, it's beyond being merely offensive," Rick blurted loudly into his microphone, coming halfway out of his seat. "It's downright sick!''

Kenton ignored him as well as the sneers being directed at him from the gallery. His primary audience remained the one on the other side of the cameras. "What a terrible shame that this bill has been tainted by the stain of politics.''

"Then it is you who have stained it, Mr. Kenton," Kate declared, her voice booming throughout the room. "And it is you who should feel shame at what you're doing.''

"And what is that?" Kenton demanded, waiting for the chairman to bang the gavel demanding order and silence, flustered when he didn't.

"Using a legitimate piece of legislation as a bat with which to beat up on your opponents. This bill is not about politics, sir. It is not about you or Senator Knight or General Edwards or even President Haynes.''

Her face was flushed. Her jaw was tight. Her eyes were blazing.

"This bill is about my daughter, Mira Siegel. An eleven-year-old girl who was raped and murdered by a man who had sexually abused several other young girls before her. It's about Polly Klaas and Sara Anne Wood and Megan

Kanka. It's about Sylvia Jeffries, a wife and mother who was raped and tortured and murdered by a man who had been jailed twice for rape, yet released so that he could rape again.

"But most of all, Congressman Kenton, it's about reworking a system that allows sexual predators to reenter society as free men, while making innocent women and children prisoners of fear."

An edgy silence pervaded the hall. From the gallery as well as from his colleagues on the panel, Mack Kenton became the focus of emotional responses that ranged from stony glances to expressions of pure disgust. Meanwhile, every camera in the house was pointed at Kate's face, which was a portrait of quiet outrage and thundering dignity.

"I think you need to go home and reread the wording of this legislation, Mr. Kenton," she said softly, but deliberately. "Judging by your statements this afternoon, it seems quite obvious that you've missed the point."

Kenton thought about rebutting, but Kate wasn't finished.

"And while you're home," she said, her eyes fixed on his, "give your three children a hug and imagine how you'd feel if something happened to one of them. Maybe that will compel you to reorganize your priorities and help you to understand that Mira's bill is about saving lives, not about saving your political career!"

That evening, Keeley accompanied her aunt Celia to Zoë's for a celebratory dinner. She was surprised at how modest the apartment was. The five-room flat overlooking Rock Creek Park had good bones, as Felicia might have said, but it was small and more hodgepodge than haute, decorated with a unique slapdash style Zoë must have honed over years of living in exotic places. Keeley found it intruiging.

The entrance foyer resembled a giant photo album, the glazed vanilla walls tatooed from floor to ceiling with simply framed photographs of dignitaries Zoë had met during her years of service. In the living room, built-ins displayed an impressive collection of books and objets d'art. Keeley liked Zoë's office, with its leather-topped partner's desk and pale striped walls, but her favorite room was the bedroom. There, a striking four-poster bed commanded immediate attention. With its slim, mahogany spindles, plain rice-paper canopy, simple, tucked-in quilt, and mountain of silky pillows, it was feminine without being fussy—much like Zoë, Keeley supposed.

Along one wall was a series of shelves housing a collection of small dolls dressed in various native costumes. There were dozens of them, representing all the places Zoë had been. Some nationalities Keeley guessed easily; others were harder to place.

"She's from Peru," Zoë said.

Keeley was examining one doll's woolen skirt, lightly fingering her long braids and brightly colored, saucerlike hat.

"It's been four centuries since Pizarro and the Conquistadors vanquished the Incas, yet if you travel into the interior the people still look much the same as they did in their heyday."

"You like traveling, don't you?" Keeley said as she replaced the Incan doll.

Zoë nodded. "I like learning, and travel is one of the best teachers."

"Is there anyplace you haven't been?"

Zoë laughed. "The world is a very big place. What I haven't seen could fill another wall of shelves."

"Why did you buy dolls?" Keeley asked. "I mean, why not stamps or books or something, I don't know . . ."

"More grown-up?"

"I guess."

A cloud eclipsed Zoë eyes, darkening them for a moment. "I started buying them for my children," she said quietly. "I had hoped to teach them about the history and culture of our neighbors through these dolls."

"I didn't know you had children," Keeley said.

"I don't."

Keeley didn't know what to say. A sense of relief had washed over her, which she found confusing. Why should she care if Zoë had children? Also, an unmistakable aura of sadness had suddenly overwhelmed the room, a feeling so powerful Keeley could almost touch it.

"Unfortunately," Zoë said cautiously, as if the words were flames searing her tongue as she spoke, "I can't have any."

"I'm sorry," Keeley said with a sincere rush of sympathy.

"Me too." Zoë forced a smile to her lips. "But it is nice to have friends around who remind me of where I've been and whom I've met." *And what might have been.*

Zoë didn't have to say it; Keeley heard it. If there was one thing she was sensitive to, it was grief.

Offering Zoë a moment's privacy, Keeley went back to studying the dolls. It surprised her to note that when she first had looked at these shelves, they had seemed so full and inviting, so alive with the prospect of tales to be told. At second glance, she saw the lonely spaces in between the souvenir figurines. It was an emptiness she recognized, the kind that came from a terrible loss: huge at first, narrowing over the years, but remaining deep and ingrained, the kind that couldn't be erased or smoothed over or filled.

"Thanks for introducing me to your friends," she said, somewhat awkwardly.

"It was my pleasure."

Keeley nodded and backed out of the room. "Yeah. Well, thanks again."

A host of emotions gathered in Zoë's throat as she watched Ben's daughter take her leave. "Anytime," she whispered into the air. "Anytime."

Jed Oakes couldn't decide between the poached salmon or the filet, so he took healthy portions of both. "I don't know if Kenton was having a nervous breakdown this afternoon or committing political suicide," he said as he pushed the grilled vegetables to the side of his plate, making room for a mound of potato salad, "but either way, he made my day!"

"He underestimated Kate Siegel, that's for sure." Quinn grabbed a glass of wine and followed Jed into Zoë's office. Every seat in the living room, and half the floor, was occupied.

"More to the point, he overestimated himself." Jed grinned as he plunked his body down in the chair behind Zoë's desk. "But it had to happen. Sooner or later, highfalutin', self-righteous assholes like Kenton have to trip over their own arrogance."

"Is that an Oakesism?" Quinn asked.

"Just one of many brilliant takes on the political scene, my friend. Listen and ye shall learn."

Quinn chuckled and went back to his dinner. For a while, the two men ate in companionable silence. They weren't friends, but they had been thrown together often enough over the years to be comfortable in each other's presence. Also, each respected the other's intelligence.

As a campaign operative, Jed viewed the press with what he considered a healthy cynicism. His theory about the workings of the national press corps was that they had grown lazy. They waited for some*one* to come up with an original thought and that became the press line of the day—an immutable, implacable, unchangeable, oft-repeated perspective.

Jed liked Quinn because he harked back to an earlier time in political reporting when the newshounds were less knee-jerk in their coverage of a candidate. Instead of hopping on the ten-second-sound-bite-of-the-day bandwagon, Quinn took a wider view, questioning the thrust of an entire week. In addition, he knew the rules. If Jed told him, "I'm on background," Quinn wouldn't attach Jed's name to a story. If Jed said he was on "deep background," he would use Jed's thoughts, but not his exact words or his name. If he didn't want anything used, Jed had to state flat out that anything said was "off the record."

"You think your man has it sewn up?"

Jed shrugged. "Nothing's ever a hundred percent. Today should have killed Kenton, but who knows how many potential primary voters were watching and out of those who were, how many care?"

"Can Knight take Edwards in the general election?"

Jed's fork stopped in midair while he considered his answer.

"It depends. When it comes to a wonk's head for policy, an affinity for people and steady-as-she-goes leadership, Ben's the man. But if this hostage thing gets much worse, the public may get so bloodthirsty they won't care about the brain or the heart, they'll go for the guy with the helmet."

The men ate silently for a minute or two. Then Jed leaned across the desk.

"Maybe you can clear something up for me. Off the record. Why isn't General Macho touting a military solution to this quagmire? All I ever hear from him is that Haynes is a jerk who doesn't know what to do. Where's the big gun's game plan?"

"I don't know that he has one." Quinn sipped his wine, his bushy eyebrows furrowing. "I have to admit, Oakes, I've been struck by the same incongruity: Why would a military man be advocating a nonmilitary solution? The reason Edwards jumped out front in the initial polls was that people thought he would know exactly what to do. Yet instead of screaming 'bomb the bastards,' he gives mind-numbing speeches about how he learned leadership slogging through the jungles of Vietnam."

Jed shook his head, astounded by the foibles of those who ran for national office. "I guess sitting down and conceiving a realistic plan's just too much to expect. That would mean taking a concrete position that could be proved right or wrong before the election. And while that may be good citizenship, it's bad politics."

Quinn agreed. "Why go out on a limb that Haynes or Knight or Kenton could saw off, when he can play it safe?"

Jed groaned. "Look, I think Edwards is an empty uniform, but in all fairness, this hostage thing is nasty, sticky stuff. It's hard to blame anyone for trying to make points without inciting that whacko Durgunov. Shit! When we saw the body of that soldier . . . we went over every speech just to be sure it wasn't something *we* said."

"Still," Quinn said, "I can't shake the feeling that we're missing something."

With wineglass in hand, he meandered about Zoë's office, checking out the pictures hanging on the walls and dotting the shelves as he spoke.

"I'm of the theory that character creates patterns, and, unless there's something cockeyed going on, most people stick pretty close to their line."

He stopped, as if this conundrum was too difficult to allow walking and talking at the same time.

"Edwards has a long history of salivating over the prospect of marching into battle. Knight has a history of preferring compromise and conciliation. So how come Knight's the one doing the saber-rattling, and Edwards is making nice?"

"I hadn't thought about it in exactly those terms, but you're right. Something is definitely wrong with this picture."

"Speaking of pictures . . ." Quinn's mouth lifted in an amused smile as he lifted a photograph off a bookshelf. He brought it to the desk and showed it to Jed. "Quite the quartet."

They looked different. The clothes said the photograph had been taken eons ago. But there, linking arms, their mouths caught mid-laugh, were Georgie, Celia, Kate, and Zoë.

"Were you aware that they'd known each other this long?"

Jed peered through the door as if to confirm that the

four women chatting it up in the next room were indeed the same women in the picture.

"I know Georgie because I managed two of her campaigns," he said casually. "I know Celia because she's a political reporter. I met Zoë a few months ago and Kate, only briefly before tonight. I had no idea they were ancient buddies." He snorted in amazement. "Whew! That is one heavy-duty bevy of beauties!"

"It certainly is," Quinn thought, looking at the picture again. As he and Jed wandered back into the living room, he couldn't help but be fascinated. Women were much more open than men. They confided in each other, supported each other and, if need be, protected each other. Here were four extraordinary women who had been friends since their youth. What intimacies, he wondered, had they shared over the years. And how many secrets had they promised to keep?

Hunt Mercer eyed Keeley Knight as she snaked her way through the crowd. He had known her forever, but he didn't think he'd ever noticed her before . . . *really* noticed her. Maybe it was because they hadn't seen each other in a long time, but he couldn't get over how terrific-looking she was! Blond and pale, with soft brown eyes and a wide, inviting mouth. With her no-makeup face and loose, easy hair, she reminded him of Olivia, except that Keeley rarely smiled; Olivia's lips seemed stuck in an infuriatingly cheerful curl.

"Guess what they're discussing," she said as she joined him in the portal separating the entry and the living room.

"Duh!" Hunt said, crossing his eyes and affecting a stupid face. "Politics?"

Keeley laughed. Hunt felt rewarded, as if he'd just accomplished some singular feat.

"Your mom was awesome today," she said.

Hunt looked at Georgie, who was talking to Celia, and nodded. "Yeah. She did good."

"Do you like coming to the House and watching her do her thing?"

"This was my first time."

Keeley's mouth dropped. "Are you serious?"

"Yeah." Hunt ran his hand through his hair and shifted his weight from one foot to the other. His gray-blue eyes fixed on Keeley's face with an unnerving intensity. "I used to hate her *thing*," he said with brute honesty. "I hated that she was here while Livvie and I were in Dallas. I hated that she had a life I wasn't part of. And I hated the fact that she was happier here than at home."

Keeley had expected a "yes" or a qualified, "sometimes." She hadn't anticipated an outburst. Fascinated, she probed further. "So why'd you come today?" She could practically see him working his answer through.

"Because I knew this was important to her. And like I thought I'd give her a break." A sheepish grin, flickered on his lips. "I'm always dissing her. I figured the least I could do was see whether I was on target or off base."

"And?"

He shrugged and splayed his hands, clearly surrendering. "The lady's got the moves." Again, he looked at his mother. "She really put it out there. I was impressed."

"You should be."

Her tone and her expression were so I-told-you-so parental, Hunt grunted. Then, he folded his arms across his chest and leaned against the wall. "You get off on being the Senator's daughter, don't you?"

"I get off on being Ben Knight's daughter," she snapped. "Just being a congressional brat is far from a good time."

"What's the worst part?"

Keeley never hesitated. "The loneliness. And," she said, unconsciously biting her lip, "like I'm afraid something's going to happen to him."

Hunt didn't say so, but he worried about his mother, even more so after seeing her today. She was an outspoken woman. There were a lot of angry men who thought their problems were caused by outspoken women. The last thing Hunt wanted was for his mother to become the symbol for what some thought was wrong with America.

"What if he loses?" Hunt asked.

"He has a life," Keeley said with a shrug. Her eye caught sight of Zoë, who was trying on the Baltimore Orioles baseball cap she had given Ethan. "Who knows. Maybe he'd find a wife."

"Some people are better off solo," Hunt said.

"I used to think so," Keeley said cautiously, as if she was exploring new territory and hadn't decided yet whether it was habitable. "But someone I admire a lot told me I was being selfish."

Otis's words continued to haunt her: *If you gave her a chance, you'd probably like her.*

"So," she said with deliberately exaggerated brightness, "I'm working on a major change in attitude."

"And we're going for, what, exactly?"

"Accepting."

"Accepting's never been my strong suit. But Livvie majors in accepting. She even claims to love Lyle the vile."

"Hunt!" Keeley's shock was almost Victorian. "He's your father."

"That doesn't mean I have to like the guy. How would you feel if your father was cheating on your mother with every piece of available flesh that came his way?"

Keeley turned her face away, but not before he saw an unexpected look of anguish take hold of her features.

"How dumb was that. I'm sorry," he said, misinterpreting. "Your mom's dead, and I'm talking trash. Forgive me, Keeley. I've got this jerk gene that sometimes just takes over."

"It's okay," she said, knowing that it wasn't okay, that he had hit a nerve. But it was something she couldn't, and wouldn't, talk about. With anyone.

Hunt persevered. "How about if I fight my way through the mob at the buffet and grab dessert for the two of us? Will that make up for my colossal lapse?"

She tried to smile. When that failed, she simply nodded. "It's no big thing, Hunt. Really."

"Yeah, right."

As she watched him dash through the living room like a football player on his way to a touchdown, she couldn't help pondering the notion of atonement. It wasn't as simple as Hunt had tried to make it. Some lapses were more significant than others and had consequences that pushed redemption far beyond a simple act of penance. The real problem, she decided catching her reflection in the glass covering one of Zoë's photographs, was that most often it wasn't those who were guilty of the lapse who paid. It was the ones they left behind.

☆ ☆ ☆

While her fellow reporters kept their eyes glued to the General, Celia watched Emily Edwards. It was unusual for her to be at a campaign stop—she made no secret of her loathing for the stump—and even more unusual for her to be buoyant, but this was Seattle. Perhaps being in her hometown had brought out the best in the candidate's wife. She was shaking hands and talking to voters as if she did this every day and enjoyed it, neither of which was true. Celia had concluded a long time ago, however, that it wasn't the campaigning Emily hated; it was her husband.

At the final stop of the day—scheduled to make the late news on the East Coast, the early-evening news in the Pacific time zones—Scottie was to deliver a speech damning the environmental regulations that he claimed strangled the fishing and lumber industries. Also, he intended to beseech Congress, in light of this current international crisis, to rethink the federal budget and increase defense appropriations. With the Boeing Company one of the largest providers of jobs in Washington state, his message was an easy sell.

His advance team had set up an "America the Beautiful" photo-op at Alki Beach Park: the General standing in front of the concrete pylon that marked the birthplace of Seattle,

Puget Sound glistening in the background, a line of American flags flapping in the breeze, and, with a clever arrangement of camera angles, views of both the Cascade and the Olympic mountains rising in the distance. When he reminded his listeners of his wife's roots, somehow making it sound as if one of her forebears had been part of Arthur Denny's pioneering party, and moved on to talk about growth and progress and the need to remove governmental restraints on business—"Big business creates jobs. No business creates unemployment."—the site worked. When, however, Edwards castigated his opponents as tools of the EPA surrounded by some of the country's most glorious vistas, he sounded disingenuous to some, foolish to others.

Celia faithfully recorded his comments, but without enthusiasm. Having grown up in Florida, where the sugar industry had contributed greatly to the alarming rise in water pollution, she didn't see the EPA as the enemy. When the rally was over and she had filed her story, she decided to do some shopping before returning to her hotel.

Celia loved Seattle, maybe because it stood in such stark contrast to Miami. Both were places where water and sky and land converged in a burst of scenic splendor, but their differences were as sharply defined as their similarities. Miami had the Keys. Seattle had the San Juan Islands. Miami had humidity and hurricanes. Seattle had rain and fog. Miami had South Beach and salsa. Seattle had Pioneer Square and Starbucks.

Despite a light drizzle, Celia took her time wandering around Pioneer Square, the quaint cobblestone triangle where historic rubbed shoulders with funky. She meandered into a few of the galleries, where she bought a turned wood bowl and a piece of Pilchuk glass, and browsed in some of the clothing shops. She had stopped for a latte when she spotted Clay Chandler and Emily Edwards outside an art gallery a few doors down. They appeared to be arguing. Celia inched closer, keeping her face toward the store windows, her head low behind the collar of her rain-coat.

"Don't give me a hard time, Emily," Clay was saying in a condescending tone that insinuated an ominous ". . . or else." "You're going to the banquet. You're going to say a few words and shake hands with the folk. You're going to gaze adoringly at your husband. And you're going to pretend to love every minute of it. Because you're a trouper."

"And you're slime," Emily said, plainly unintimidated. "You're also inept. Not only is it stupid and careless of you to indulge my husband's indiscriminate libido, but it's hardly necessary. Believe me, he's got a whore in every port."

"She's a secretary. The General simply wanted to redo tonight's speech."

"And I'm Mary, queen of Scots!" Emily scoffed.

Celia looked at their reflection in the window and saw that Emily's face was rigid with disgust. Clay's eyes were darting about, worried that they might be overheard.

"You're overreacting, Emily. It's not what you think."

"What do you take me for?" Emily hissed. "A fool? I know Scottie Edwards better than anyone. I'm the mother of his children and the keeper of his house, which means I know where all the dirty laundry is."

Even from where she stood, Celia could see how nervous Clay was.

"I'm sure that's true, but I don't think we should be airing it in public, Emily."

She squinted at him the way a fisherman studied his catch, gauging whether to throw it back or chop off its head.

"Fine," she said, "but mark my words, Chandler. If my husband gets caught with his pants down, I'll make damn sure it's your ass that gets the boot!"

Emily Edwards turned and walked away with a confident gait, leaving Clay chastened and disconcerted. From the side, two campaign aides who had maintained a discreet distance fell into step with their charge. Celia waited for Clay to spot her. When he did, his round, frog face flushed.

"What the hell are you doing here?"

"Taking in the view," she said. "Isn't this the most fabulous city? I love it! Wherever I go, I see something interesting or meet someone interesting or hear something *very* interesting."

"You print any of this . . . "

"And you'll do what? Deny it? It won't matter. This is the kind of story that doesn't require absolute proof. Innuendo alone will give it legs longer than the hooker you sent up to service Edwards!"

He grabbed her coat, his eyes bulging. "I've worked too hard and too long on Edwards's campaign to have a worthless face like you ruin my chances at the big time." He pulled her within an inch of him. His breath was stale and acrid. "I warned you, Celia. You fuck with me, I'm going to hurt you. Get it?"

She yanked herself free of his grasp, but kept her face close to his. There was no way she would back away. Not when the "gotcha" was in her column.

"What I get, Clay, is that you don't give two damns about Scottie Edwards's run for the White House. You're not managing his campaign, you're working out some twisted vendetta against Ben.

"As for your threats, whatever you think you have on me, you have. But you, Clayborne Chandler the Third, have not exactly been a model Boy Scout. And, if I might state the obvious, neither has your General. My guess is there's enough garbage floating around about both of you to sink a battleship. Now get out of my way!" she said as she pushed past him and marched toward the business district, the roaring heat of his stare on her back.

She couldn't imagine why this phrase popped into her head just then, but it was something she had heard Hillary Rodham Clinton say when someone in the press asked her how she handled the blistering, often venomous criticism directed at her. "I take it seriously," she had said, "but I try not to take it personally."

Clay Chandler's malevolence had to be taken seriously, because it affected his targets personally. Which was why it felt so good to have an edge.

And why Celia was more determined than ever to find the smoking gun that would blow him away.

"I don't know where our candidate was off to this evening, but thank goodness they barred the press," Celia said to Quinn over an entree of salmon in a sauce of sake and chili oil. "I don't think I could've remained conscious during another one of his speeches."

"Oh, I think this one would have held your attention." Quinn flashed her a sly grin. He leaned across the table and whispered, "Just before I picked you up, I got a call from one of my spies. The General's at some armory outside Spokane speaking to a bunch of guys outfitted in camouflage gear."

Celia's fork stopped in midair. "Scottie Edwards is keynoting a paramilitary convention?"

"So it would appear." Quinn busied himself with his Alaskan halibut.

They had flipped a coin for restaurants. Quinn would have been happy slurping oysters and sloshing beer, but Celia favored something more atmospheric. She won the toss, choosing a lovely spot in Pike Place Market that was big on candlelight and views.

"I knew he was against gun control and had occasionally served as a mouthpiece for the AGA, but I never pictured him consorting with antigovernment extremists. I don't like the man, but Scottie Edwards never struck me as the paranoid patriot type who sees a conspiracy around every corner."

"I think it's that creepy sidekick of his who frolics in the woods with the militia guys," Quinn said.

Celia nodded. "Now that you mention it, Arlo does have

that vigilante air about him. But why would Edwards agree to appear before a group of crazies?''

"It's an election year. And those crazies make up a part of his base. Don't forget, Celia, the AGA is sponsoring this little gathering. They probably gave Edwards a gigundo check. This speech is their payback.''

"Maybe, but . . .''

"Can we just enjoy our dinner, please?''

She smiled, happy to oblige. Things had been so rushed since the House hearing, they hadn't had any time alone. It did seem a shame to waste even a minute of it on Edwards.

"I hadn't realized you went so far back with Georgie Hughes, Kate Siegel, and Zoë Vaughn," Quinn said, after a few minutes of companionable silence.

"So how'd you find out? Did you decipher our secret password?''

"I saw a picture of the four of you at some kind of party.''

Celia nodded. "Ben's wedding to my cousin, Felicia.''

"It looked as if people had been cut out of the photograph.''

Celia nodded again, this time as if the reason should have been obvious. "I guess Zoe didn't want a picture of the happy bride and groom." She paused as if mentally counting heads. "She must have cut Clay Chandler out as well, but who could blame her! He's so totally reptilian.''

Quinn played with his fish. "What's Georgie's husband like?''

"Why do you want to know?''

He shrugged. "I'm a political reporter. She's becoming a very visible Congresswoman. He's the invisible man. I'm curious.''

Observant and naturally suspicious, he added silently, recalling how Jed Oakes had gone warm and fuzzy around the edges when he and Georgie had talked, how connected they had looked, intimate almost.

"If you think you smell a story, blow your nose," Celia warned.

"They're never together."

"Lyle runs Hughes Oil & Gas. While Georgie does Washington, he does Dallas."

"Is their marriage happy?"

"They've had their ups and downs, but what couple hasn't?"

"Their son, Hunt, was into drugs for a while, wasn't he?"

"Yes, but that tale's been told. What are you fishing for?"

"Nothing," he claimed. "It's my nature to be nosy." He flashed her an impish smile. "It's what I do."

"Well, don't do it with me," she snapped. "I don't give up my friends, Quinn."

He held up his hands, surrendering, but not without noting how harsh her response was, how protective. *What wouldn't she give up?*

"Back off, Fido," he said. "I wasn't going to bite. I was only sniffing."

"Well, sniff some other tree, okay?"

"Okay. I got it. I'm off it." When she continued to glare at him, he pulled a rose from the centerpiece and handed it to her, his face awash with contrition. "Forgiven?"

She debated, then relented. "For now."

With an elaborate salaam, he lowered his forehead onto the table, as if waiting for her benediction.

Celia stifled a smile and touched his shoulder with her rose. His response was to reach beneath the table and slide his hand up her skirt and along her thigh. Suddenly, the waiter appeared at his side.

"Is everything all right, sir?" he asked.

Quinn sat up, assured the young man he was fine, and asked him to refill their wineglasses.

"At least you had the decency to blush," Celia laughed when the waiter was gone.

"Yeah, well, don't think I was embarrassed being caught copping a quick feel. I can blush at will, you know."

"Right!"

Celia finished her salmon and sipped the crisp chardonnay, encouraging the tastes of the fish and the wine to mingle on her tongue. She sipped again and closed her eyes, sinking into a deliciously mellow mood.

Quinn, as he always did when they were together, marveled at how lovely she was. Many women relied upon animation to spark their eyes and their lips. Celia was stunning in her stillness.

"I thought I was the one who had wandered into the middle distance," Celia said, resting her hand on his. "You look a little lost. Want to tell me where you went?"

"Xanadu. Valhalla. The Elysian Fields." He shrugged slightly, entwined their fingers and laughed softly. "I don't know, Celia. Whenever I'm with you, I feel as if I've been spirited off to some pleasurable paradise."

"Is that a problem?"

"Could be."

"Why? How?"

He drew her face close to his. "Because I can't think about anything except being with you and making love to you and waking up next to you and making love to you again. Because you fill my head and my heart with feelings so powerful, they're beginning to take over my life. Because, in spite of all my defense mechanisms and emotional safeguards, I'm falling madly and wildly in love with you."

Celia was drowning in his green eyes, sucked in by the strong undertow of his emotion. "I don't see that as a problem," she said in a voice too tremulous to rise above a whisper.

"I don't do love well," he said, his face pinched. Quinn didn't own up to negatives easily.

"Oh, I disagree." She kissed him softly, skimming his lips with her tongue. He started to respond, tensed and pulled away. She retreated to her wine.

"I thought I was in love once before," he said. "I was young. Probably too young. We got married and vowed to be together forever. It didn't take long for my bride to come to the sad conclusion that I was more in love with my ambition than I was with her. I was rarely home, and, when I was, I was preoccupied with where I was going next. Our forever lasted three years."

Needing something to look at other than the expression on Celia's face, he swirled his wine around in his glass.

"I married twice," Celia said, quietly. "Once because I thought the guy was so grounded, I'd be spared the roller-coaster ride. The second time, because the guy was so rich, I thought I'd be secure and, therefore, ecstatically happy. I wasn't."

"What went wrong?"

"I never loved either of them."

"How do you know?"

"Because I know how I feel about you."

She said it so matter-of-factly, it unsettled him. He sputtered inanities for a second or two, until she placed her hand over his mouth.

"Don't get yourself in a state," she said with a tender smile. "I'm not proposing to you, okay?"

He chuckled uncomfortably, then quickly turned pensive. "Though it shocks the shit out of me to tell you this, I've actually considered taking that aisle trip with you."

If he thought she was going to get mushy, he was mistaken. Instead, Celia grew contemplative.

"We're being thrown together almost every day in the heat of a presidential campaign," she said, more sensibly than he would have liked. "For all we know, it's political passion we're feeling."

"I don't think so," he said, with a slight leer.

"You may be right, but we won't know until the election's over. Now's not the time to be making life-altering decisions."

He feigned dismay. "You mean you don't want to make an honest man out of me?"

"I'm not sure anyone can make an honest man out of you," she said, her face devoid of the humor he thought should accompany that comment. "Which is why, my darling Irishman, I'm not looking for, asking for, or even thinking about, a commitment from you."

"Tell me what I missed," he said, truly confused.

"I may love you, Quinn, but I'm not sure I trust you." He looked hurt, yet not surprised. She hastened to reassure him. "I don't want us to stop seeing each other. I just want to take it in stages."

"Am I on probation?"

"Not at all." How could he be? she asked herself. As much as she needed to believe she could rely on him, if she were honest, she would admit that it was the aura of adventure and the uncertainty his personality generated that made him so exciting.

"Then would you mind telling me what stage we're at?"

"We're at the go-with-the-flow-and-see-where-it-takes-us stage. Okay?"

He grinned, clearly relieved that they had come to some agreement. "As long as it takes us to your bed, I'm flowin', baby."

"Whenever you're ready," she said, as he called for the check.

Later, after they had made love and Celia had fallen asleep in his arms, Quinn reviewed their evening. As she snuggled nearer and he felt the warmth of her body against his, a chill ran through him. He truly loved this woman— he didn't doubt that—but he feared he had spoken the truth when he had said he "didn't do love well."

She was right not to trust him.

☆ JUNE ☆

The Jacqueline Kennedy Garden was dressed in its June colors, all pale pink and deep green, its flowering shrubs and lush plantings glowing beneath a warm summer sun. The First Lady stood at a podium and finished delivering an address to Never Too Late, a group of retired teachers who donated their services to local schools and community centers. A small, grassroots organization taking root in America's inner cities, they provided education for adults who wanted to learn to read or sharpen skills that might help them get a better job, or youngsters who had dropped out and wanted to get back into school.

Beth Haynes closed by quoting one of the founders of Never Too Late, Loretta Knight: "When it comes to education, America has to start saying *never*. You're never too old to learn. We're never too old to teach. Things are never so difficult they can't be turned around. And as long as you're willing to try, you're never too late for school!"

The applause was loud and heartfelt, particularly when the First Lady called Loretta Knight to the podium and encouraged her to take a bow. Later, while the guests were walking to a small tent set up on the adjacent South Lawn where tea and muffins would be served, Beth Haynes posed for the cameras with Loretta, Benjamin Knight, and his two children, Ryan and Keeley. She fielded a few questions, then invited the gaggle of reporters to join her for some refreshment.

"Come," she said, guiding her group out of the garden, onto the walkway leading to the lawn. "Speak to some of these wonderful people. Avail yourselves of their experiences. You might come away with a clearer notion of the real spirit of volunteerism, which is alive and well and thriving in America."

As was traditional with modern First Ladies, when her husband took office Beth Haynes had selected a cause to champion. For her, it was updating the old-fashioned notion of volunteering. Not simply women pushing magazine carts in hospitals or ladling soup for the homeless, but men coaching inner-city teams, or becoming big brothers to fatherless boys. Seniors teaching everything from auto mechanics to small-business management to those with an interest, but no funds. College students helping out at day-care centers or old-age homes.

It was Beth's answer to the current rage of complaining about the decline in the quality of services and the unraveling of the fabric of our society, while at the same time, railing against the intrusion of government in our everyday lives. The problem, as she defined it, was that the loudest complaints were coming from couch potatoes who favored "Monday morning quarterbacking to dirtying themselves on the field."

While she had agreed to the phrase, "GIVE SOMETHING BACK" as her primary slogan—punchy, pithy, and perfect for buttons, tee shirts, and sound bites, her media consultant had said—every now and then, despite cautionary warnings from anguished aides, she could be seen sporting a second button: "PUT UP OR SHUT UP!" It shocked many and angered some, but for most, it was a welcome splash of cold water completely in keeping with the forthright reputation of the First Lady.

"Also," Beth said, on this two-button morning as she herded her flock into the tent, "think how unique it would be to put a positive, feel-good piece in your papers and on your newscasts. How uplifting and reassuring it would be for your viewers."

Most of them laughed, murmured, "Yeah, yeah," stuffed a few Danishes in their mouths, and went about their business. They never noticed Beth look over her shoulder and nod to Ben Knight, who slipped away through the door leading to the ground floor corridor. Quickly, he made his way down the hall to the Map Room, a small reception area Franklin D. Roosevelt used as a situation room to follow the course of World War II.

Elton Haynes was alone, seated in a graceful red wing chair in front of the fireplace. When Ben had requested this off-the-record meeting, the president, happy to forgo a photo-op and dreary questions about who he thought might succeed him, graciously agreed to a private rendezvous—no attending staff, no aides, no recordings, no notes. Just the president and the senator who wanted to be president.

Ben entered, shook Elton's hand, and accepted his host's offer of coffee and breakfast rolls. He made his selection from a silver tray set on a Chippendale sideboard and joined the president at a small table set for two.

"The First Lady's speech was inspiring as usual," Ben said, amiably.

Haynes smiled. "She'll be pleased you thought so." He clasped his hands and tented his fingers, seeming to appraise his guest. "Your family looks good, Ben. How are they handling the campaign?"

"It's tougher on them than they'll admit. Thank you for asking."

Elton chuckled. Ben thought he detected a touch of bitterness.

"Been there, done that, as they say." Elton nibbled on a dry bagel, his attention distracted. "We forget that decisions we make for ourselves have enormous consequences for our families. Often their lives are changed in significant ways they might not have chosen for themselves.''

He looked tired, Ben thought, older than when he took office. *Will that happen to me?*

"You know that old saying 'Be careful what you wish for, because it just might come true'?" Ben motioned that he did. Elton smiled briefly. "I'm certain that was coined especially for people running for president."

"Is this your way of urging me out of the race?"

"Absolutely not. You're the best man for the job, Ben."

"Other than you, sir."

"At this juncture," Haynes said, frustration tugging at his features, "I'd probably say including me."

Ben started to protest. The president held up his hand.

"This is a tough job, far more difficult than you can possibly imagine." A profound disappointment settled in his eyes. "It's feeling responsible twenty-four hours a day, every day, for the conduct of every American's life. Are they safe? Are they taking home a paycheck? Is there enough money in that paycheck to take care of their families? Are they well? If not, will health care be available? And that's on the days when there's no crisis, no American heads on the block." He issued an exasperated sigh. "I tell you, Ben, it's endless."

"You can only do your best, sir."

Haynes agreed, but his shoulders drooped from the weight of his office. "When you live in this house, your best is rarely good enough."

Ben squirmed in his seat, uncomfortable at his friend's distress, dismayed at his president's uncertainty, nervous about the fate of the hostages, and frightened that he was looking into the harried, aging face of his own future. *Was it really worth it?*

"My foreign policy advisor has suggested I go to Europe and meet with our allies," Ben said, getting to the point.

"Smart move."

It was neither unusual nor presumptive for a presidential candidate to pay his respects to the leaders of allied nations, just as it was not uncommon for a prime minister or a president visiting the United States during a national election cycle to receive a hopeful. The world moved too rapidly to wait out results. The sooner ties could be established and rapport created, the better.

"Even smarter getting Zoë on your team. She understands the dynamics of international politics better than most." Haynes shook his head ruefully. "She was one of Edwards's biggest blunders."

"I agree."

"She's arranging your meetings?"

Ben nodded. "I wanted to inform you of those plans and ask if this trip presented you with a problem?"

"You are a rare specimen, Benjamin Knight. Most men in your circumstance would either be ignoring my existence or trampling all over my body every chance they got. You're respectfully tiptoeing around me."

Again, there was that sadness, as if he had a terminal illness and felt sorry that his condition was making others shy away. For a moment, however, it faded, allowing a brief, but welcome return of Haynes's sense of humor.

"Except for your appearance on Walsh's Sunday show. That time, one of your track shoes left an imprint on my neck."

Ben laughed, somewhat self-consciously. Then his face sobered. "As a concerned American and as your friend, I deeply regretted the failure of that rescue mission."

Elton's complexion turned gray. The image of that soldier would haunt him for the rest of his days. As would the faces and voices of the hostages' relatives, with whom he'd met on several stormy occasions.

"If it's not too presumptuous to ask, is there another operation in the works?"

The president considered his answer. If Ben had been declared the nominee of his party, he would have been entitled to limited security briefings. Until then, giving him access to certain information would have been a breach.

"We've eliminated the possibility of a military strike."

Zoë had predicted that. Aside from the obvious inherent danger to the hostages, Elton's advisors wanted to avoid the equally disastrous risk of another failure.

"We've brought in Reginald MacDuff, the assistant UN Secretary-General to negotiate on our behalf." He paused, clearly measuring whether or not to continue. "And we're pursuing several other avenues of communication."

Ben grimaced. He knew the code. That was politispeak for *arms for hostages*. Haynes must have decided to take a page from Reagan's book, even though it broke the law, went against policy, was certain to offend our allies, and infuriate Congress, to say nothing of the public.

"With all due respect, sir," Ben said, probing carefully, "has the Pentagon weighed the effect of a series of well-timed commando raids against communicating with someone as unpredictable and power-hungry as Yegor Durgunov?"

"You haven't experienced the anguish of the families," Haynes said. "You haven't had to look into their eyes and listen to the terror in their voices and count their tears as you're feeding them sugar pills and mumbling inanities like 'We're doing everything possible.'"

"I am hardly naive, Mr. President, and I sympathize with your predicament, but your administration has gone on record as disapproving of Reagan's backroom dealings. You deplored the Iran-Contra mess. More to the point, you assured the public there would be no rewards given to these terrorists."

"I thought that with the help of Russian President Borofsky, we could resolve this matter quickly. I was wrong. We tried to effect a rescue, and it failed. The public is screaming for action, and, believe me, they don't really care how we do it. They just want the hostages released!"

A myriad of emotions washed over his face, from frustration to embarrassment to resignation to determination.

"Sometimes, Ben, we have to tell them what they want to hear and then go out and do what they want us to do."

With nothing further to say, Ben offered his support. "I

understand, Mr. President. And if I can help in any way, please let me know."

Elton rose slowly. "You can encourage our allies to remember that we're their friends and Red Rage is the enemy. And," he said, gripping Ben's hand firmly in his, "you can pray for me. Just as I'm going to pray for you."

Zoë, Ben, Sam Trout, Sid Guest, Cliff Benson, Ben's staff foreign policy assistant, and Adam Schwartz were gathered in Ben's Senate office to go over the details of his trip. Zoë began the briefing on time and proceeded with her usual crisp efficiency.

"I suggested this diplomatic jaunt for several reasons: Not only will the photos play well back home, but Ben needs to assess the feelings of each of these leaders about Durgunov, Red Rage, the plight of America's hostages, Borofsky and President Haynes's handling of the crisis." Looking directly at Ben, she said, "You should also try to find out what they might be willing to do to assist in bringing about its end."

Having painted the broad strokes, Zoë laid out a list of goals for each bilateral, ran through a suggested Q-and-A, and provided insights about the men Ben would be meeting.

"Lord Stanton, the British Foreign Minister, is a good friend to the United States. He's sensitive to the tension created by Britain's increasing closeness to its European Common Market partners. The British don't want to have to choose between us and the ECM. It's important to make it clear you don't think that's necessary."

Ben nodded, scribbling frantically. Though Zoë was providing dossiers for each vist and would be traveling with him, he was an inveterate note taker.

"NATO's a perennial worry. So is the Middle East. Britain's oil supply depends on stability in that region.

"In Paris, you'll meet with the new French president." Zoë's eyes rolled. "Claude D'Artain is as arrogant as they come. You will not have an easy time with him. The French ransomed their hostages and don't want to be told they did the wrong thing. You can raise the subject—he expects you to—but avoid harsh rebukes."

She flipped the pages in her notebook, running her finger down a list of single words which served as prompts. Zoë didn't like to walk around with these kinds of comments in writing and she didn't need to read from a research report. She knew her facts cold.

"Otto Lassmann, the German chancellor, can't wait to meet you. He couldn't stand President Rumson and he loathes Scottie Edwards." She tried, but couldn't stifle a satisfied smile. "Since reunification, immigration's his number one problem. He's also very concerned about Yegor Durgunov's rantings about reclaiming land Germany stole from Russia."

"What's Lassmann like?" Ben asked, slightly dazed at the depth of her knowledge.

She smiled. "He's terrific! You'll enjoy being with him. I must warn you, though, the man loves to eat and drink. And German food isn't exactly heart smart," she said, having noted Ben's proclivity for low-fat foods. "Like it or not, you're going to have to chow down on bratwurst, potatoes, and kraut."

Ben grimaced. Zoë laughed. "We'll pump your arteries later."

"Not fair." Ben turned to a fresh sheet of paper. "Okay. Turkey."

"I had a two-year posting in Turkey, so I know the foreign minister very well." Her brows furrowed. "He's very upset that children were taken from the base at Ankara. Aside from granting increased access to bases there and diplomatic cover for any military operation we want to launch, he's offered guides to lead troops over the mountains to raid possible prison sites in Iraq."

Ben underlined that in his notes. "Generous of him."

"Yes and no. The Turks are battling the Kurds over demands for a separate Kurdish state. Both sides want our support, so don't make any promises and don't feel pressed. Turkey needs American money. They'll do whatever we want.''

"I assume NATO and GATT are on every table," Sam said.

Zoë nodded. "Europe is always concerned about the level of America's military support. As for GATT''—the General Agreement on Tariffs and Trade—"there are several hot buttons: product standards, intellectual property laws, cooperative strategies in areas such as environmental technology, aerospace and biotechnology. And the big bugaboo: market-access problems in Japan.''

Ben tipped his chair onto its rear legs, folded his hands behind his head, and laughed. "Can I bring a crib sheet?"

"She's the crib sheet," Sam said, pointing to Zoë.

Ben's eyes fixed on hers as if he was seeing her in yet another light. "So she is."

Zoë's gaze remained controlled and focused. "Gentlemen, this trip has many stops but only one objective: to instill confidence in our European allies about a Benjamin Knight presidency."

She looked from one to the other, noting the seriousness of their expressions. With exaggerated solemnity, she rose from her chair and tucked her notes into her briefcase. Then, she looked Ben squarely in the eye and gave him a thumbs-up.

"Piece of cake!" she said.

☆   ☆   ☆

Amalia Trilling's sixteenth-century villa was several miles north of Florence. An imposing three-story structure set on a sweeping expanse of sunny landscape high in the Tuscan hills, it presented itself as a lavish palliative for those who wished to escape life's annoyances, even if only briefly. Behind its elegantly somber facade were numerous guest suites, a remarkably decorated ballroom, an exquisite parlor once called the "gossip room," an enormous living room distinguished by elaborate frescoes, and at the back end of the property, an open-air theater where plays and musicales had been performed since the mid–fifteen hundreds. For Zoë, who had been introduced to the Villa LaRocca during her year in Bologna and had spent a great deal of time there since, a short stay was just what she needed.

Zoë was exhausted from hopscotching around the various capitals setting up meetings, making arrangements for support staff in each venue and, along with Ben's press secretary, establishing contact with the appropriate media. While Zoë worked the advance, Ben stayed behind to shepherd the NOMORE! legislation through the conference procedure. Once a compromise had been reached and he was certain the bill would be passed by both houses and be on President Haynes's desk before the month was out, he flew to London. Zoë accompanied him to each city as diplomatic liaison and protocol deputy.

Throughout, she and Ben remained alert. Neither one wanted to be caught in another pseudoscandalous photograph. They both knew that within a larger context even the most innocent gesture could be cropped to a shot brimming with innuendo. Enjoying a laugh along with an entire room became "sharing a private joke." Putting their heads together at a meeting to quietly exchange opinions became "whispering sweet nothings." Leaning toward each other to provide a three-second bio on those coming through a receiving line became "stealing an intimate moment." The public never saw the crowd, only the couple.

When the bilaterals were over, Sam Trout, Stan Guest, and several others stayed behind to do follow-ups: confirm dates for meetings in the United States, provide information requested on Senate bills affecting imports and currency rates, arrange for communications access in the event of another hostage-taking or other unforseen occurrence. Ben joined Keeley and Ryan in Paris for a quick weekend before coming to Villa LaRocca for several days of much deserved R and R.

Zoë, Amalia, and Tobias Kohl were lounging on the terrace, reviewing the needs of their expected house-guests—Gianni Viabella, Zev Shafir, Harry Cadman, and their wives—when the limousine bearing the Knights pulled into the gravel driveway. Within minutes, the butler had guided them around the house to the terrace, where Amalia embraced them as if they were family. Ben introduced his children to Toby, whose warm, avuncular manner immediately put them at ease, and then watched with amusement as Ryan ran for Zoë, who bent down to absorb his running embrace. It pleased Ben even more to see an unedited smile dash across Keeley's face as Zoë welcomed her to Italy.

While their luggage was being unloaded from the car and placed in their rooms, a tray of refreshments was brought out. The adults listened as the youngsters recounted their whirlwind tour of Paris as well as their quick stop in Rome and the ride up from Florence.

"I wanted to shop on the Ponte Vecchio," Keeley said, playfully glaring at her father. "Daddy said we had no time."

"Men never have time for the bridge," Amalia said with a dismissive wink.

"Because on that bridge, time is money," Toby said in the manner of one who knows.

"Okay! Okay!" Ben said, surrendering. "Before we leave, I promise, we'll shop 'til you drop," he said, mimicking his daughter's favorite expression. "Or until I'm broke. Whichever comes first. How's that?"

Keeley and Amalia shared a triumphant look. "Fair."

"Bless you both," Ben said.

"The press on your trip was excellent," Toby remarked to Ben. "How did your private sessions go?"

"They were informative, sometimes difficult, but on the whole, extremely productive." Ben pointed at Zoë. "Due in large part to that woman sitting right there."

Everyone turned to look at Zoë, making her blush.

"Everywhere but London—where I'm relatively fluent

in the language," he said, sparking smiles all around, "she functioned as translator, policy advisor, and personal confidante. She was amazing!"

Amalia flashed Zoë a we'll-talk-later look. Zoë was too busy shielding herself from the spotlight to respond.

"You have no idea how incredible it was to have complete confidence in the transcription of information. Sometimes, when the translator is supplied by the host, I wonder whether I'm being paraphrased or misinterpreted or what. With the estimable Ms. Vaughn by my side, I had no such fears."

He bowed his head in gratitude. She shook off his praise, but his words had greatly impressed his children.

"You can talk in French and Italian and German?" Ryan said.

Zoë smiled and nodded.

"As well as Spanish, Russian, Hebrew, and Turkish," Amalia added.

"It was a matter of survival," Zoë said, wishing the focus would shift to someone else. "In the foreign service, if you become proficient in a language, especially a difficult one like Turkish or Russian, you get a few extra dollars in your paycheck. And when you work for the government, every little bit helps!"

"How do you keep them straight?" Keeley asked.

"I have to bone up before sessions like the ones I attended with your father, but once the conversations start, I can clear my head of everything but that language." Keeley was wide-eyed. "It's taken years to learn how to do that, however," Zoë said,

"It wasn't simply the languages," Ben continued. "You know the players and how to get things done. A couple of times you jumped in and saved my butt. Don't deny it."

"I'm a career diplomat," Zoë reminded him. "Saving the butts of American senators is part of the job description."

Ryan giggled. Keeley was amused, but far more interested in her father's reactions. It was rare that he went on like this. He was truly wowed. Again, Otis's words came back to her: *he found her brains as attractive as the rest of her.* She could remember her father telling her mother how stunning she looked and how pretty the house was and how nice the party had been, but she couldn't ever remember him complimenting her on a substantive accomplishment. Or speaking about her to others with such obvious admiration and respect.

"What else do you do in your job?" Ryan asked. "When you're not bailing out guys like my dad?"

Zoë laughed and tugged on the brim of his cap. "In its simplest form, I tell the countries I'm sent to what I think they should know about the United States, and I tell the U.S. government what they should know about the country I'm in. The president and the State Department need that exchange of information so they can make friends for America."

"So being a diplomat is a really important thing."

"Being a *good* diplomat is very important," Ben said to his son. "And Zoë is that."

Again, Keeley took note of Ben's expression. *Once upon a time, your father was madly in love with her,* Otis had said. Was he falling in love with her all over again?

That night, after an early dinner, Zoë and Toby offered to take Keeley and Ryan on a tour of the villa. Ben and Amalia preferred to linger over their coffee. After a few moments of idle chatter, Amalia's elegant brow furrowed.

"Mack Kenton came to see me," she said.

"I'm not surprised. You're a formidable presence in the party, Amalia. Not to mention your Midas touch when it comes to fund-raising."

"His visit was not the surprise. It was his response when I informed him that I had committed my resources to your campaign."

"I assume he was less than pleased."

Amalia rested her elbows on the table and delicately

entwined her fingers. "That would be putting it mildly." For a moment, she appeared to be examining her manicure. "Is he . . . I don't know how to put this . . . balanced?"

Ben considered the question. "Sometimes he appears to push the envelope a bit, and the press has taken to labeling him as a bit eccentric, but truly, I wouldn't know."

"Are you friends? Do you travel in the same circles?"

Ben shook his head. "We're colleagues. We met when we were both in the House. I moved on to the Senate, and, frankly, Amalia, I don't hang around the Capitol, so my circles are small. From what I understand, Kenton's are, too. He's a family-church-work kind of guy who doesn't party much."

"How about the rumors of extramarital activities?"

"There are those," Ben said, "but again, I wouldn't know." He paused. "When he first came to Washington he did do the circuit. In fact, I think the Kentons were at a couple of Felicia's dinners. Why do you ask?"

"Because when I told him I believed you would be the party's nominee and the country's next president, he laughed, but not in a way that contained any humor." Amalia's expression grew somber. "Then he took off on a strange tangent, talking about how things are never as perfect as they seem. I asked him to explain, and he told me to wait for the convention."

"He probably meant that I'm not as smart as I think, and his people believe they can turn enough delegates to deny me a first-ballot nomination."

"And if that happens?"

Ben shrugged. "We hit the floor running and hope we convert more votes than they can."

"And if it goes several ballots and it's still unresolved?"

"The convention turns into *Let's Make a Deal.*"

Amalia's expression darkened even more. "I think that's the moment he's waiting for." Ben appeared quizzical. "At one point, I recall him saying that when 'everyone was gathered together in a place called Armageddon,' he'd come out the victor because he had good on his side. Do you have any idea what he's talking about?"

"No."

"I don't like the sound of it, Ben."

"I'm not exactly crazy about it myself."

"I hate to ask this, but does he have anything on you?"

"Nothing that hasn't been chewed over in the press already."

"Would he smear Zoë to get to you?" Amalia's love for Zoë was etched on her face.

Ben was moved by her affection. He reached over and touched her hand. "That's Edwards's game, and, believe me, I'm doing everything I can to protect her."

Amalia smiled and squeezed his hand. "Now let's figure out how we're going to protect you."

Ben shook his head. "Why waste a beautiful evening worrying about Mack Kenton? He's simply playing politics."

"I wouldn't dismiss him."

"I'm not." A broad smile enlivened his features. "I'm sitting in an exquisite villa with a magnificent woman, looking forward to a wonderful few days with family and friends. I refuse to spoil a moment of that bliss by obsessing about what Mack Kenton may or may not have up his sleeve."

"You're right. While you're here, you enjoy yourself!" Amalia smiled and then sobered again. "Just be ready for him."

"Don't worry," Ben said. "I can handle whatever he throws at me."

Ben's confidence was reassuring, but Amalia wasn't appeased. There had been something ominous in Kenton's eyes, a look that said he was going to throw Ben a hardball stitched with the unimaginable.

The next night, Amalia and Toby hosted an enormous gala in honor of their friend, Senator Benjamin Knight.

Guests included the American ambassador to Italy, the mayors of Florence and Rome, Israeli general Zev Shafir, retired American general Harry Cadman, Tom Hanks and Sally Field, who were filming in Venice, Gianni Viabella, his uncle, Silvio, and Alberto Baldinelli, from the Secretary-General's Office at the United Nations.

During cocktails in a stunning room of tapestries and painted wooden panels, Ben struggled to maintain his focus. As a veteran of the campaign trail, he was able to carry on a sociable conversation while pursuing other thoughts, which was a good thing. While his chat was amiable and intelligent, his concentration wandered like a leaf to light, finding Zoë wherever she was. Currently, she was holding court in the center of the room, gabbing in Italian with Gianni Viabella, his uncle, and Signore Baldinelli. Ryan stood at her side, clearly fascinated.

Ben was touched by the way she included his son, bending down to translate for him, coaching him so he could say a few words and feel part of the tête-à-tête. He was less delighted by the way Viabella hovered over her. His posture appeared so proprietary, so entitled. As he had many times before, Ben wondered about their relationship.

Harry Cadman interrupted his thoughts. "How'd your meetings go?"

Immediately, Ben cleared his head. Harry Cadman was not making idle chatter. "I spoke to the president before I left. They have no plans for a military operation." Cadman nodded. Ben assumed the general's Pentagon sources had told him the same thing. "I think he's trying to work an exchange."

Harry's face screwed into a mask of complete disgust. "I'll never understand that. Why give arms to people who've already used arms against us? They kidnapped our citizens and would love nothing more than to blow our collective butts off the face of the earth. Giving them weapons that would help do that strikes me as bare-ass stupid!"

Ben didn't disagree.

"How about our allies?"

"The French are still defending themselves for paying a ransom. Their attitude is 'We took care of ours, you take care of yours.'"

"Vive la France!" Cadman said, shaking his head.

"The British are anxious to resolve the situation. Since I'm not even a candidate as yet, Lord Stanton remained circumspect when it came to making any future commitment, but he made it clear that he lacked confidence in Haynes's ability to bring about a satisfactory resolution."

"And he's afraid that if Red Rage can't push us, they'll snatch a few Brits as a squeeze."

"Exactly."

"How about the Germans?"

"The Germans, the Turks, the Spanish, the Italians— they all believe Borofsky's a paper tiger, Durgunov's a lunatic with an agenda, and no one is safe. In the course of our discussions, I suggested several options. No one could comment officially, of course, but it is as we suspected: a large-scale commando rescue operation was numero uno on everyone's hit parade."

Cadman wasn't surprised. "It's too soon to have any concrete conversations," he said, "but when you're officially on the ballot, I'm going to schedule a sit-down with an old friend of mine, Chuck Mallory."

Ben's blue eyes came alive with interest. Chuck Mallory was the general in charge of the United States Rapid Response Force.

"Chuck and I go way back," Harry said. "He was one of the pilots in that abortive expedition to free the hostages in Iran, back in '80. I remember hearing a lot about him around that time, because he had voiced a number of objections to the planned mission that the brass didn't want to hear. When it failed, I was sent to persuade him not to say 'I told you so' to the press."

Harry's large jaw slackened, and his eyes narrowed. "He was grieving for the eight Americans who had died on that damn desert and didn't give two hoots about the press or Carter's popularity in the polls. Frankly, neither did I, which is why we got along. We talked for a long time about what went wrong and why. Eventually, I convinced him it was in the best interests of the country, the army, and our hostages if he didn't air our dirty laundry in public. He was patriotic enough to agree."

Harry's mouth spread in a broad, self-satisfied smile. "When his name came across my desk as one of the applicants for head of the RRF, I put all of my considerable weight behind his nomination."

"If I recall, there were a number of people who held that botched mission against him."

"Let's just say that some of the ranking members of our armed forces don't like rewarding those who were right when they told you something was going to go wrong."

Ben couldn't help being struck by the similiarity to Zoë's predicament with the State Department.

"Mallory owes you." After so many years in Washington, Ben was familiar with the unspoken protocol: A career saved is a debt owed.

Harry shrugged. "What's important here is that having been part of one fiasco, Chuck's entire career has been dedicated to planning and executing successful missions. The man knows how to get the job done. And if we need him, he will."

Harry winked, patted Ben on the back, and, as casually as if they had been discussing their favorite Chianti, strolled off in the direction of his wife.

For a minute or two, Ben stood off to the side, digesting the essence of what Harry had said. If Ben became the nominee, he would enlist the help of General Charles B. Mallory and together, they would set a plan into motion to free the American hostages and destroy Red Rage. Ben's head reeled at the prospect.

He closed his eyes and rubbed them, chasing ponderous thoughts that had no place at this party. When he opened them, the first thing he saw through the pin dots of light gave him a rush. Zoë had entered his field of vision. Wearing a halter-topped, softly skirted dress of midnight blue silk, she was magnetic and irresistibly distracting. He couldn't keep from staring at her, from counting the number of golden ringlets in her hair or the lashes framing her hypnotic pale green eyes or the way her ripe lips enticed when she spoke.

"She is rather spectacular."

Gianni Viabella came up alongside Ben, and together they quietly appraised the provocative woman in blue. Zoë was chatting with Zev Shafir and an odd-looking young man. She seemed distressed. Her observers didn't seem to notice.

"She overwhelms a room just by being in it, which in Italy is difficult to do when one is as understated as Zoë."

Ben appeared loath to participate in this discussion. Gianni persisted anyway.

"Did you know that since 1980, I've proposed to that glorious creature every other year?" Gianni said.

"I had no idea."

"It's become something of a ritual. I propose. She refuses. I pout. She moves to another posting. Time goes by. I track her down and propose. She rejects me. I pout. And so on." Gianni laughed at the ridiculousness of it all. Then, he stroked his chin, his aspect becoming one of innocent curiosity. "Is that how it was with you?"

"I never proposed."

"Too bad," Viabella tsked. "She would have accepted you."

"Really."

"Then, definitely. Now, perhaps." Gianni grinned like a child eager to divulge a secret. "Of course, you'd have to work at it a bit."

"Is there a point to all this?"

"The point, my friend, is simple." He draped his arm around Ben's shoulders and piloted him toward a window in a quiet corner. "While it's painful for me to admit that someone else might succeed where I have failed, it's become quite obvious that you and Zoë have an attraction for each other. As a man whose life revolves around attractions, I'm both fascinated and dismayed by your . . . how shall I put it? Reserve?"

Ben knew when he was being goaded, so he checked his response.

"How could you not go after a woman like Zoë?" Viabella demanded. "Is it some American male thing? Or is it this race for the White House?"

Ben wasn't certain Viabella was expecting a serious answer, but that's what he offered. "I hurt Zoë once. I don't want to do that again."

"Oh, I know better than you how badly you hurt her," the Italian said, his face flushed with awareness. "I met her shortly after she and her broken heart arrived in Bologna."

Ben winced. "We were young," he said, reflecting back. "Both exploring possibilities, trying to find our way in the world. I made the mistake of getting caught up in who I thought I wanted to be." His expression turned pensive. His eyes darkened with regret. "For a while, I forgot who I was. That's when I lost her."

"Is that what's happening now? Are you too caught up in who you want to be to pay attention to what is?"

Ben shook his head. "If anything, I'm holding back precisely because I don't want to drag Zoë into something as uncertain as my life. She's had more than her share of upheaval. The last thing she needs is a romance with a man whose future is up for grabs."

"Do you love her?"

"It's a distinct possibility," Ben said with a self-conscious smile. "But there again, is it the intensity and closeness of the campaign that's providing the charge, or is the real thing?"

Gianni waved his hand dismissively. "You think too much. You need to feel more." He grinned. "You need to be . . . more Italian!"

Ben laughed. Gianni joined in, then sobered.

"There were times during our glorious history when Zoë and I were lovers. During her posting in Italy and again, a few years after the death of her husband." His face warmed with pleasant reminiscences. "Though I definitely didn't agree, she thought we were better suited as friends, which is what we are today."

That admission was meant as a conciliatory gesture. Ben accepted it as such.

"You mean a lot to her, Gianni. She makes that very clear."

"I hope so."

They shared a momentary silence as each ruminated about what was, what might have been, and what could be.

"I was very jealous of you once," Gianni said. "I fell in love with Zoë the minute I met her, but she wasn't interested. She was in love with someone else. It took me a long time to make her forget you."

He glanced out the window at the fading sunset, smiling wryly at the undeniable appropriateness of such a symbol.

"I'm jealous of you now," Gianni said to Ben, "because I still love her. And I don't think she ever really forgot how much she loved you."

"I never would have recognized you," Zoë said as she greeted the man standing alongside Zev Shafir.

She tried not to stare at the horribly disfigured face of Anatoly Chertoff, but it was difficult. The victim of a car bomb, his skin was pale and paper thin, stretched over facial bones like a sheet of kitchen plastic wrap.

When Zoë first met Anatoly years before, he was sturdy and nice-looking, a serious young man who was having a clandestine affair with Maura Silver, one of Zoë's embassy attachés. Maura was a talented linguist from Evanston, Illinois, with an incisive intellect and an instinct for foreign policy. She had been in Russia five years when Zoë arrived. Aside from being Zoë's language tutor and friend, Maura had been instrumental in compiling much of the information contained in Zoë's classified reports on Borofsky. She was also one of those former staffers Zoë had been unable to locate.

Zoë met Anatoly through Maura; their relationship was also clandestine, based as it was on the secret exchange of information. Anatoly had been on Yegor Durgunov's staff. He had joined before the Soviet Union had broken up, when it was easy to claim that he had renounced his religion and owed allegiance to no one but the state. Over time, after putting Anatoly through a number of grueling loyalty tests, Durgunov came to accept the bright newcomer as a trusted aide, allowing him a closeness that made Anatoly's primary task a lot easier: Anatoly was a Mossad informer.

"Someone on staff must have made me," he said, as if he needed to explain the reason for the bomb.

"You're lucky you survived."

"Maura wasn't as fortunate," Anatoly uttered quietly.

At first, Zoë didn't think she'd heard him correctly. When his expression confirmed that she had, she reeled from the news. Zev slipped his arm around her waist to steady her.

"What happened?" Her voice trembled with grief.

"I really don't remember much." His eyes pooled. It upset him to be asked questions he was unable to answer. "I'm suffering from amnesia caused by post-traumatic shock. What little I do know was pieced together by Zev and my doctors and my Russian contacts."

Zoë touched his arm. His body shook, as if he was stifling a sob. "You've been through a great deal, Anatoly. Go slowly."

He nodded glumly and began. "When I told my superiors I suspected that my cover had been blown, they ordered me to Tel Aviv. I told them I wouldn't leave without Maura, so they granted permission for me to bring her along. Through a courier, I got word to her to come to my apartment."

He paused as he pieced disconnected memories together.

"We had done this dozens of times before. She took a taxi to a building on the next block, walked up to the third floor, stayed there until she was sure she wasn't being followed, then wended her way downstairs. The basement of that building had a passageway that attached to the basement in my building," he explained.

"The plan was to wait until the tail end of the rush hour. Then we were to drive to a secluded spot outside of town where we'd change cars and head for the airport. We thought if we stayed in my apartment, we might be easy targets."

He laughed with the ironic humor of one who had walked toward the light and come back.

"I had followed procedure and secured the area. I was certain we were safe."

He looked confused again and embarrassed, as if somehow he could have prevented this atrocity. Zev took over.

"Maura went downstairs first. She got into the car and scrunched down on the floor beneath the dashboard. Anatoly waited half an hour before leaving the building. By then, Maura was nervous and scared and eager to get out of Moscow. When she heard Anatoly's footsteps, she must have put the key into the ignition. When he opened the door, she turned the key. The force of the explosion threw him away from the car. If it hadn't, he would have burned to death."

"Like Maura did." Anatoly's tone was so mournful it hurt. "If General Shafir's people hadn't shown up, I would have been nothing but a pile of ashes."

Zoë felt sick.

"They saved my life and put me on a plane to Tel Aviv. I've spent the last ten months in a hospital."

"We had a tail on him. For backup," Zev said, explaining the presence of two agents. He kneaded his forehead and cast a look of apology in Anatoly's direction. "They had gone over the car and it had come up clean."

Lamentation lined Zev's face. It was rare that the Mossad failed to protect one of its own.

"The bomb was in the trunk of the car parked in front of Anatoly's, and it was massive. The ignition in Anatoly's car had been rigged to function like a remote."

Zev's jaw tightened as he looked at the tragic consequences of his agents' oversight.

"Why didn't I hear about any of this?" Zoë was visibly shaken.

"Car bombings in Moscow aren't as unusual as one would like to believe. The press and the Moscow police assumed it was the Mafia. Those who tried to kill me assumed they had succeeded."

"When did this happen?"

"Last April."

The same month the first hostages were abducted.

"Was this because they suspected you were with the Mossad?"

Zoë knew that was the logical conclusion, but she couldn't avoid linking Dixon Collins's suicide, the attempted murder of Anatoly, and the implied threats against her to the unimaginable possibility that all this was somehow connected to the hostages.

Anatoly shrugged as he and Zev exchanged uneasy glances.

"Anatoly was never an operative. He was an informer."

"To someone like Durgunov," Zoë said, "that's traitorous enough."

"True. But we think it was more than that. Tell her," Zev encouraged, patting the young man on the back.

"Do you remember when Secretary Edwards came to Moscow in April '91 to meet with Borofsky?"

"How could I forget?" Zoë frowned as she recalled the visit. "I was excluded from those sessions. I assumed it was because I had already delivered my findings and my disapproval of Borofsky was on the record."

"As was your condemnation of Durgunov."

Zoë was confused. "Why would that matter?"

"He was present at one of those meetings."

Zoë's breath caught in her throat. Edwards consistently

denied ever meeting Durgunov. Borofsky publicly disavowed him at least once a week.

"It was held late at night in a farmhouse outside of town," Anatoly said. "There were the three of them, their aides, and their translators. I came with Durgunov. Edwards came with a Colonel Reid and Maura, who served as his interpreter."

"What did they talk about?" Zoë asked.

"At first it was a lot of diplomatic mumbo jumbo, about what was good for Russia was good for the United States. That kind of thing. Then the conversation shifted onto how different American administrations viewed foreign policy. How some insist on tying their policies to whatever aid is given, while others take a more laissez-faire approach. It was when Durgunov and President Borofsky started questioning the secretary on how he would handle things if he were president that they dismissed us."

"They continued without translators?" Zoë was dumbstruck. She had never met a diplomat or government official who was willing to conduct the business of state without linguistic backup.

Anatoly understood her disbelief, but assured her that what he had told her had occurred.

Suddenly, another thought struck Zoë, one that buckled her knees. Maura hadn't said a word about that meeting. Zoë doubted she ever would, but Edwards hadn't trusted her. Just as he hadn't trusted Dixon Collins. So he had protected himself. Or someone else had protected him. For the first time, Zoë feared for her own life.

"That meeting was very incriminating," Zev said, stating the obvious. "The three of them present themselves to the world as enemies. Yet at least once, they convened like friends."

Zoë remained distracted. There was so much she needed to know: Had Edwards already decided to run for president back in '91? Was that why he had entered into an unholy alliance with Borofsky and Durgunov? Had the Russians offered to finance his campaign? It was certainly possible.

But was it possible that he had conspired to steal an election by creating this hostage crisis? Was he so desperate for power that he would broker American lives with a crazed despot like Durgunov? Edwards wasn't her idea of a patriot, but she had never viewed him as a traitor either. And what had he promised in return? Why would Borofsky and Durgunov join forces with each other, let alone with Edwards?

"Knowing there was a meeting isn't enough," she mumbled, talking more to herself than anyone else. "We'd have to know what they said."

Suddenly, she looked at Anatoly. Zev had brought him here for a reason. "Do you know what they discussed after you left?"

Anatoly hesitated. When he spoke his voice was so muted, Zoë had to strain to hear him. "Yes and no."

"The Russians made tapes," Zev said quietly.

Zoë's mouth dropped open in shock. Her head pounded with possibilities. "Wasn't the room swept?"

"I'm sure it was, but no one would have patted down Durgunov, and he was wired."

"Does Edwards know about this?"

"We don't think so. We don't think Borofsky knows either."

Zoë tapped her foot and stared at the floor, running various scenarios through her head. "Are they complete?"

"Word for word, from beginning to end. Not only would they reveal Edwards for the fraud that he is, but they might provide your president with an excellent bargaining chip for the hostages."

"What was your interest in all this, Zev?"

Shafir's brow knotted with concern. "When Durgunov's quirky imperialism broadened to include the Middle East and, more specifically, the elimination of Israel, he became a problem for us. An American politician with a shot at the White House agreeing to that kind of disastrous policy makes it a catastrophic problem. Those tapes may not delineate a plan or prove collaboration on an exact policy, but they show a willingness to go along or worse, to look aside."

"Stealing them was my parting gesture." Anatoly's scarred face twisted into a triumphant smile.

Zoë rejoiced, but only for a moment. People close to her had been hurt or killed because of that meeting. The tapes wouldn't change any of that. They could, however, help the hostages. But, Zoë realized, if Zev had gained possession of them, he would have turned them over to his government, which in turn would have shared them with President Haynes. If that had occurred, Elton never would have exited the race. At the very least, he would have discredited Scottie Edwards. He hadn't.

"Do you have them?" she asked Zev hopefully.

"No."

The word thundered in Zoë's brain, dispelling any dreams she might have had about a quick and positive resolution. Again Anatoly's face was clouded by a pathetic expression of shame, as if he had failed both Zoë and Zev.

"I don't really have any memory of that day. The doctors are working with me, and it's coming back, but my recollections are vague and incomplete." Zoë smiled, encouraging him to continue. "I know I had one set of tapes on me."

"By the time we got to him, they were burned beyond repair," Zev said.

"Did you make copies?" Zoë asked with her fingers crossed.

Anatoly shrugged. "I'm sure I would have. Just as I'm certain I would have tried to pass them to an authorized receiver. The problem is I can't remember if I mailed them, dropped them, or handed them over. Nor can I recall who I used as a contact. All I know is I didn't have much time."

"They weren't found in any of our drop boxes. Nor did any of our on-site operatives claim receipt." Zev strained to keep his voice free of frustration.

"Did you check with our people?" Zoë asked. It was not uncommon for information services to aid each other.

Zev nodded. "Since Maura was involved, we thought Anatoly might have used her, but your guys say no."

"Wouldn't there have been a list?"

"Sometimes informers have last-ditch emergency contacts, people they know they can go to without worrying about being questioned or betrayed. Those names would be committed to memory. They'd never be written down."

From across the room, Toby Kohl caught Zoë's eye and smiled. She smiled back, but inside she wanted to scream.

Zev tried to assuage her agitation without raising her hopes.

"Our best guess is that Anatoly mailed the tapes to someone outside Russia. That would explain why no one on the ground has them or can find any trace of them."

"Why hasn't the receiver come forward? It's been months."

Zev's expression was a mirror of Zoë's anxiety. "The mailing address might not be a primary residence or office. It might be a secret box that's only checked occasionally."

Zoë groaned.

"Sooner or later, someone is going to open that package. When he does," Zev assured her, "we'll hear from him, and we'll get those tapes."

"I hope so," Zoë said. "A lot of lives depend on it." *Including mine.*

The air was soft and redolent with the scents of summer: freshly cut grass, newly budded flowers, and a breeze still warm from the afternoon sun. On the lawn, beyond the terrace and the garden, several rows of chairs had been set up. Boxwood hedging—neatly clipped—defined the outdoor theater and directed the eye toward two large, Baroque arches which framed the stage. One held a statue representing tragedy, the other, comedy. Behind the slightly raised platform bathed in subtle lighting, was a stand of tall cypress trees and a comforting blanket of open sky.

As Zoë took her place at the far end of the second row, she closed her eyes and breathed deeply, allowing herself to be captured by the illusion that she was in one of Titian's voluptuous gardens and not on the grounds of a modern estate. Her encounter with Anatoly and Zev had been disturbing. The memories it revived and the visions it initiated had been difficult to shake, despite a delicious dinner, several glasses of wine, and lighthearted, thoroughly enjoyable conversations with Harry Cadman, Silvio Viabella, and Nella Shafir. If she could just escape into the music, she might be able to suppress the darkness and come out of the concert refreshed.

Gianni, ever the protector, noticed her pinched expression and seated himself next to her. "Was my uncle that tedious?"

She was laughing before she even opened her eyes. "He was delightful."

"Then why are you displaying the symptoms of a grade-four headache?"

"One glass of wine too many, I think."

He shook his head. "That's not possible. In Italy, it is against the law to get headaches from wine, no matter how much you drink."

"I'll try to remember that," Zoë said as she saw Ben and his children leave the house.

She watched them make their way toward their seats, impressed at what a handsome family they were. Ben, tanned and rested, looked fit and lean and very much in control as he strode across the lawn, stopping every few feet to shake hands and exchange greetings. Over the past few months, she had watched him bewitch enormous crowds with the same easy charm he was dispensing to this small group. Possessed of a quiet sureness, Ben drew people to him like steel to a lodestone, connecting with everyone from the ordinary to the most extraordinary.

Keeley was lovely, Zoë thought, a flaxen, fair-skinned replica of her mother, with the quick mind and social skills of her father. Zoë couldn't deny a certain envy as she watched Ben beam with fatherly pride as Keeley exchanged pleasantries with the mayor of Florence and his wife. His hand rested protectively on his daughter's back as he guided her from one well-wisher to the next. His other hand held his son close to his side.

Zoë smiled to herself. If Keeley was the well-schooled, well-disciplined socialite-in-training, Ryan was the gyro, the never-ending swirl of curiosity and energy, uncertainty and fear that was the essence of boyhood. Now, however, Ryan seemed skittish and displeased. As Keeley took her seat, he searched the audience. When he found Zoë, he whispered something to his father. Ben listened, looked at Zoë, gave her a slightly embarrassed smile, and shrugged as Ryan broke ranks and ran to her.

"Can I sit next to you?"

"Of course," Zoë said.

Gianni laughed and moved over one, making room for the worshipful boy. "Don't you want to sit up front with your father?"

"No," Ryan said. "If I sit up there, I'm like, you know, on display. Everyone watches everything I do. What if I don't like the music and I yawn? Or I can't sit still. It could make my dad look bad, and I don't want that. If I'm here, they'll all watch Keeley and I can chill. You understand?"

Gianni responded with appropriate seriousness. "I understand completely. That's why I'm sitting near Zoë. So I can chill."

Amalia had arranged for the chamber music ensemble, I Musici, to perform. Before introducing them, she wandered among her guests, handing out golden helmet "Knight for President" pins and making certain everyone's needs had been attended to. Then she strode out to the stage, stood between her grand arches, and introduced the famous ensemble.

Zoë was enchanted. She adored Baroque music, particularly Bach and Vivaldi, so their program of *Brandenburg Concerti* and two of Vivaldi's *Four Seasons* suited her. When they started to play, her mind inadvertently drifted back to those long-ago days at Harvard. She recalled that Ben, who favored the robust compositions of Beethoven and Tchaikovsky, had never been able to understand her fascination with what he called "fussy music." Yet, as she had explained to him, it was precisely the fussiness of Baroque music that she loved: the feathery daintiness of the sound, the intriguing complexity of a contrapuntal fugue, the quickened tempi of the first and third movements, contrasted with the sober mood of the andante second.

"It's so girly-girly," he had said one night when she had brought a recording of Handel's *Concerti Grossi* to his apartment.

"I'm girly-girly," she had replied.

"That you are," he had said, pulling her to him. "In fact, you're the girliest-girl I know."

Zoë sighed in spite of herself, caught up in the frothy memory of a night when she thought their lovemaking—and their love—would go on forever.

The music must have triggered the same recollections for Ben, because in the middle of the first Brandenburg, he turned and stared at her. His face was caught in a swell of emotion, one that had tightened his jaw and flamed his eyes. An unbidden surge of heat coursed through her body. She flushed and told herself she was reading something into nothing, that his glancing back had been out of concern for his son, that she felt warm because she still hadn't shaken off that extra glass of wine or the afterglow of a reminiscence. Yet every instinct told her that what she thought she had read in his eyes—an undeniable, unquenchable yearning—was very real and incredibly intense.

For Ryan, the program exceeded his store of stamina. Shortly after the intermission, his eyelids began to droop. Zoë let him rest against her. It wasn't long before he was fast asleep. Gently, she laid his head in her lap and stretched his feet across Gianni, who chivalrously covered the boy with his jacket. By the time the encores had been played and the guests began to disperse, Ryan lay cuddled in Zoë's arms.

"I had a feeling this might happen." Ben sounded apologetic, but he couldn't keep from smiling at the sight of his son napping so cozily in this stunning woman's lap. "You're both very kind."

"All my life, I've fought against being what you Americans call a couch potato," Gianni said, playfully aghast. "So what have I become instead? A couch!"

"And a comfortable one at that!" Ben laughed as he prodded Ryan onto his feet. "If you don't mind, I think I'll take him up to bed."

As Gianni retrieved his jacket, he noticed the look Ben gave Zoë, as well as the one she gave him in return. If ever a couple needed a break, he decided, they were it. Since it was evident that Keeley had also noticed this exchange and was experiencing a mild attack of pique over it, he offered to take her for a nightcap.

"Nothing lethal, Papa Bear," he said to Ben, winking at Keeley. "Perhaps a spritzer under the stars."

Ben caught the look of adolescent ecstasy in his daughter's eyes and granted her permission to go.

"Ryan's grown quite attached to you," Ben said as he walked a sleepy Ryan up the stairs to the third floor.

"He's a terrific kid. So's Keeley, even though I'm sure she doesn't believe I think so."

He laughed, grateful that Zoë didn't resent his daughter's overprotective bent.

"You've done a great job with them." Her smile was drowned by the wave of longing in her voice.

"It's amazing," she said several steps later. "You've been hit by two unbelievably horrible tragedies in your life, yet you managed to come through both of them stronger than ever."

He stopped, angry at the self-reproach he heard in her voice and the self-doubt he saw in her eyes. "It helps to have someone to hang on to while you navigate your way through the pain."

She looked away, but not before he saw her lips quiver. He wanted to pursue the matter, but with Ryan stumbling along beside him, it was awkward. When they reached Ryan's room, Zoë opened the door for Ben, but instead of going in where she felt she didn't belong, she left father and son to each other and went to her room alone.

The hall outside the corner suite on the second floor was quiet. Amalia's guests had either departed for their hotels in Florence or their quarters at Villa LaRocca. Zoë nestled against a pale, ivory silken headboard, relying on a cluster of candles and the full moon outside her window for light. Ever since she first befriended Amalia and began staying here on a regular basis, she had thought of this room with its sweetly flowered wallpaper, fringed cornices, painted ceiling, and finely painted antique furniture, as hers.

This bed, with its elaborately carved and gilded canopy, had been her refuge, even during her darkest hours. Tonight, she craved the sanctuary she found there, the sense of shelter she found tucked between the elegantly tied drapes and lavish bedcoverings. Hugging her knees to her chest, she laid her head back, closed her eyes, and listened to the lilting strains of a Bach violin sonata on the stereo.

She hadn't realized how thoroughly alone she had felt until this evening when that young boy had attached himself to her. When his warm breath had tickled her neck, it was as if the thick layers of isolation she painstakingly had built up over the years had balled together and crashed into her chest, reducing her carefully constructed existence to rubble. Suddenly, the padding around her heart was gone.

Loss was a terrible thing, so much more than the opposite of winning. It was having something taken away. It was being deprived or presented with an unfillable void. When Avi and her unborn child died, loss had overwhelmed her.

For months, it engulfed her, dragging her down like a mighty rip tide. She had flailed at it and screamed at it and tried to swim away from it, but, despite her best efforts, the loss had remained oceanic.

Zoë had responded by closing up like a threatened clam, shutting everything that pulsed with life's essence inside a hard, impenetrable shell. Since she couldn't fight it, what she had to do, she decided, was to suppress it and eliminate the possibility of ever encountering that kind of monstrous pain again. That meant smothering her emotions and relying solely on her intellect. It meant not allowing herself to fall in love or get too close or feel too connected. Alone was better, because alone was safer.

For years, it worked. Her job was complicated and could, if she allowed it, absorb most of her waking hours. It lacked the permanence that encouraged relationships and it kept her far away from friends and family who might ask too many questions or pry too deeply or expect too much.

But then tonight, Ryan Knight had snaked his arms around her waist and rested his cheek against her chest. Alone suddenly felt very lonely indeed.

Why couldn't she be like Ben? she wondered. Or Loretta? Or Kate? They had suffered immeasureable losses, yet they hadn't become hermits.

What's wrong with me? Zoë asked the empty space around her. *Why can't I move on?*

There was a knock on her door. She didn't feel like talking to Amalia, so she ignored it, preferring to soak in this bath of self-pity she had drawn for herself. Whoever it was persisted, forcing her out of bed. When she opened the door, she was surprised to find Ben standing in the dusky hallway.

"I wanted to thank you for taking care of Ryan."

"I enjoyed it."

His blue eyes fastened on her like a vise, tracing the movement of candlelight across her face.

"I waited to say good-night to Keeley before coming to say good-night to you."

He leaned against the doorframe, his face a breath away. The faint scent of his spicy cologne wafted past her nose, fuzzing her brain like an opiate.

A smile crawled across his lips. "Do I hear that fussy music you're so crazy about?" he asked.

She nodded, noting the way the backlighting sharpened his features, making him appear even more striking.

"I would've thought you'd have gotten your fill this evening," he said, staring at her shamelessly.

"I guess not." Acutely aware of her state of undress, she moved her arm across her chest. "Did Keeley have fun with Gianni?"

"Uh-huh." He perused her like a man with a thirst, his penetrating gaze moving from a tumble of honeyed curls to soft, celadon eyes that hadn't looked away, to ripened lips that pursed as if to ask a question. Or receive a kiss.

"I'm glad. She's . . ."

His mouth was on hers before he stepped inside. The door closed behind him, and he folded her into his arms with an urgency that startled her. His kiss echoed that imperative, growing deeper and more passionate. While Zoë's mind might have considered a mild protest, her body mounted no defense. Instead, she relinquished control and clung to him, moving so close she could feel his heart pounding in his chest. Somehow, it wasn't close enough. The door his young son had cracked open earlier had been flung wide, and all the emotions she had suppressed over the years came spilling out in a rush of desire.

"I love you, Zoë," he said, holding her face in his hands so she could see his eyes when he spoke those words.

They sounded different than they had so many years before. Better, she thought.

"And I need you."

"I need you, too," she said, a sob catching in her throat. It was the first time in years she had owned up to the demands of her body and her heart.

He grabbed her and drew her to him, feeding on her like a starveling. She pushed his jacket down his shoulders and off his arms, undid his tie, and started to unbutton his shirt, but stopped. Ben's hands had begun to travel up her sides to her breasts. She gasped as he touched her, feeling her entire body tremble from the exquisiteness of the sensation. She had forgotten how wonderful love felt.

He caressed her, relishing the voluptuousness of the flesh beneath his fingers. She enticed him to explore freely while she removed his shirt, undid his belt, and did some scouting of her own. She found him firm and pulsing with excitation. Indulging her own need as well as his, she pressed against him. He moaned as again, his mouth covered hers.

When their cravings demanded another venue, he lifted her in his arms and carried her to the bed. Gently, he laid her down in a pool of shadows, watching as a ray of lambent moonlight twinkled against the filmy white fabric of her negligee. She rose onto her knees, springy tendrils falling onto her face and shoulders. He stripped quickly, unashamed of his eagerness. Though equally impatient, she slowed things down, langorously pulling her gown over her head, elevating the act of disrobing into one long, luscious, erotic stroke. He groaned when the soft light of nature's lantern bathed her body. Never had he seen anything so lovely.

His desire was evident, but it was the emotion blazing in his eyes that truly seduced Zoë. This was more than sex for him. This was what he had said it was: love, pure and simple.

As he descended into her open arms and she felt his nakedness meld with hers, she wanted to cry with delight.

"You're still the girliest-girl I know," he whispered, as if intuiting her thoughts.

"It's the music," she said, eliciting a smile.

"It's growing on me," he said, as his mouth began to follow his hands.

Zoë wriggled beneath him, surrendering to the boundless bliss of his lips on her flesh; Ben had always known how to arouse her. Her appetite for him was no less insatiable than his was for her. She couldn't bear for his lips not to be on hers or for his hands to be idle. Nor could she bear to deny herself the joy of her own explorations. When, finally, he joined his energy with hers, she exalted in the rapture of feeling inexorably bound to him, even if only for one miraculous instant.

After, they lay next to each in a contented haze, their legs still entwined, their spirits loath to separate. Zoë's head rested on his shoulder. Her fingers toyed with the hair on his chest. His hand was tenderly combing her hair. It all felt so right.

"I love you," he whispered as he bent down and kissed the top of her head. "And if you'll have me, I'd like to marry you. Tomorrow if possible."

Zoë sat up and stared at him, incredulous.

He grinned at her, amused by her surprise. "Is tomorrow too soon? Okay, how about the day after the election? Win or lose."

When she didn't respond, his smile faded.

"You can't tell me you don't love me," he said. "I won't believe you. Not after this."

She retreated to the other side of the headboard and covered herself with a sheet. "I do love you," she said. "But . . ."

He shook his head. "Sorry. There are no buts. We played that game years ago and wound up losing each other. I have regretted it every day since. Which is why I'm rushing right from I-love-you to will-you-marry-me without passing Go or collecting two hundred dollars."

He had expected a smile. She was still projecting concern.

"Is it the idea of taking on an instant family? Okay. I can see where that might be overwhelming. But Ryan already worships you and Keeley will come around."

Zoë's heart ached. She wanted to tell him that tomorrow would be perfect for a wedding, that she would marry him anyplace, anytime. But she couldn't. Not after what she'd heard tonight.

"Are you worried that this is a déjà vu romance? That I have this twenty-some-odd year hangover I simply can't shake?" Ben's voice was soft, but anxiety underlined every word.

As she buried her face in her hands and fretted about how she was going to do what she had to do, she tried to erase the images flashing before her: Dixon Collins hanging from a rope. Anatoly Chertoff's charred features. Maura Silver's body being melted by flames. When she looked at him, the specter of terror must have insinuated itself onto her features, because Ben jumped to an incorrect, though understandable conclusion.

"Are you afraid you might lose me the way you lost Avi?"

"Maybe," she said, thinking quickly. She would allow him to travel down this road; it was one she thought he could accept. "I can't deny that's made me rather cynical about the notion of happily ever after."

His fingers grazed her cheek. "If I could suffer some of that pain for you, I would. And if I could promise you nothing would ever happen to me, I would. But I can't. Avi is a part of your past, and tragedy is often a part of life, Zoë."

Zoë might not have accepted that from anyone else, but she did from Ben.

"You and Avi loved each other. You were going to have a child together. What happened is horribly sad, but it's yesterday. I'm here today, and I want to be here to love you tomorrow and all the days after that."

Tears dribbled onto her cheeks. Ben kissed them away.

"I loved you when you were eighteen years old, Zoë, but I didn't really know what love was then." A shadow eclipsed the light in his eyes. "I know what it is now. It's how I feel every time I hear the sound of your voice or spot you from across a room. It's how I feel when I watch you charm the president of France or comfort my son or fence with my daughter. It's how desolate I felt when I didn't have you lying naked in my arms and how ecstatic I feel now that I do.

"For years, I've felt as if I was searching for something I'd lost. Once or twice, I thought I found it, but it was always a cruel illusion." The pain of old wounds manifested itself in his eyes. "Even with you," he continued, "I didn't trust my feelings right away."

His honesty was impressive. And seductive.

"When I began to think I was seriously falling in love with you, I balked. I told myself to write it off to that campaign trail Cupid that creates lovers of convenience."

They both smiled. It was hardly an unheard of phenomenon.

"It was when you began dominating my thoughts and my dreams that I realized the truth. You're the part of my life that's been missing. I want you to marry me, Zoë, because I need you to complete me."

Zoë felt as if a bullet had just shredded her insides. She, too, had felt incomplete and unfinished, like a doll whose seams had come undone. She too had been searching for that spark that would restart her life. Then Ben had come to Boston. From that night on, she had felt the wounds healing. Day by day, stitch by stitch, even without knowing it, he had been putting her back together again. Yet now, she was about to pull both of them apart.

"I can't marry you, Ben."

"Tomorrow or ever?" he said, alarmed and annoyed. Ben liked answers, and she wasn't giving him any that made sense.

She climbed out of bed and quickly threw on a robe. "We'll talk about it another time." Her tone was curt, final.

Ben started to dress, but slowly. Her body was tense. Her eyes were vacant. Something was very wrong, something more than simply the discomfort of having to reject a marriage proposal.

Rather than confront the devastation she had caused, Zoë walked to the window and turned her back to the room. As she looked out into the pitch of night, she wished she could scream at the gods who were making it impossible for her to grab the happiness being offered to her.

Anatoly's revelations had changed everything. They made it clear that her problems went way beyond the fallout from a policy disagreement. Scottie Edwards believed she knew more than she did. She didn't know how far he would go to ensure her silence. All she knew was that she had to push Ben as far away as possible. .

When he came up behind her, slid an arm around her waist, and pulled her back against his body, she had to fight every impulse she had not to bury herself in his arms.

"I don't know why you're doing this," he said, his breath warm against her face. "But sooner or later we're going to be married. I love you, and I'm willing to bet my life that you love me, too."

As she heard the door to her bedroom close, she wept. Because she did love him. And she wouldn't let him bet his life.

☆   ☆   ☆

Sometimes Celia wondered whether her job was to report the news or manufacture it. Titus Mitchell had just spent twenty minutes puzzling about why Celia's newscasts had been so "blah," as he put it. Celia had reminded him that this was the lull between the primaries and the convention, that little, if any, real news was generated during this phase of the process, that the public was bored with politics and needed a breather before the next onslaught. He remained unmoved by her logic.

Back at her desk, she let off steam by shuffling papers and grumbling about the constant, unremitting pressure of gathering news. She was still bemoaning her fate when the FedEx package arrived. It was from Clay Chandler: photographs, a background report, suggested follow-ups, and a handwritten note urging her to tell the world the truth about Zoë Vaughn.

"If you don't," it said, "I'll have to tell the world the truth about you. And yours."

Celia seethed at his audaciousness. *How dare he threaten her? Who did he think he was? Who did he think she was?* She considered tossing the package into the trash, but curiosity got the better of her. Piece by piece, she studied the contents, her discomfort mounting. There was a story here— possibly a big story—but one that presented her with a Solomonic dilemma: Did she report this and boost her career at the expense of her friends? Or did she allow loyalty to rule the day, take a pass, and risk reprisals from her superiors and retaliation from Clay?

Suddenly, she was reminded of Anthea Ogden's question: *Can you report on people close to you with an unbiased eye?* And her answer: *I will track any legitimate story to its honest conclusion, whether it's about Ben or Georgie's brother or Zoë Vaughn or anyone else. If it's newsworthy and it's the truth, I'll go after it no matter where it leads.* She had meant what she said at the time, but then, the matter had been rhetorical. Clay had just made it relevant.

The pictures were of Zoë and a horribly scarred young man Chandler claimed was a former aide to Yegor Durgunov. They were seen huddling in the VIP lounge at the airport in Rome. According to the accompanying dossier, the man, known as Anatoly Chertoff, had been a guest at a party in Benjamin Knight's honor at Amalia Trilling's villa. He had departed the next day for Rome escorted by Zoë Vaughn, and was seen boarding a flight to Tel Aviv.

Celia agonized about what to do. A reasonable first step might be verifying the facts. With that in mind, she tracked down Zoë in Boston. After the usual preliminaries, Celia explained she was trying to corroborate something that had come across her desk.

"A photographer snapped you and a Russian doing a tête-à-tête at da Vinci," she said, hoping she sounded more relaxed than she felt. "According to the source, this guy's a former aide to Durgunov."

"And?" Zoë's voice turned frosty.

"And I guess the appropriate questions are: What were you doing with him? What were you talking about? Is Ben negotiating some sort of October surprise with Durgunov?"

"Don't do this, Celia. Take my advice and leave this story alone."

"I wish I could, but it was dumped on my desk, and if I don't air it, someone else will."

"You don't understand. There could be serious consequences," Zoë insisted, anguished. "Not only could this damage Ben's campaign, but lives are at stake." *Mine included,* she wanted to add.

"That's why I called," Celia pleaded. "So that you could tell me it's nothing, and I could drop it with a clear conscience."

Zoë's persistent silence confirmed Celia's initial impression that this story warranted attention.

"Who sent you these pictures?" Zoë demanded, kicking herself for not seeing the photographer. "Was it Clay Chandler?"

"You know I can't tell you that."

"Then this call is on the record?"

Celia hesitated, but both women knew there was no turning back. "Yes," she said. "It is."

"In that case," Zoë responded curtly, "no comment."

The click of the phone resounded in Celia's brain. For a time she stared at the phone, hoping Zoë would call back and either provide her with the information she needed or grant her permission to follow the story, no hard feelings. The call never came.

When Celia contacted Ben, he vaguely recalled meeting Anatoly Chertoff at a reception, but insisted he hadn't spoken more than a few words to him and knew nothing of his past associations. "Unfortunately, he was distinguished more by his scars than his résumé."

"What about Zoë?" she asked. "She was seen driving out of Amalia's villa with him and having a rather intimate conversation with him at the airport. What was she doing with an aide to Durgunov?"

"You'll have to ask Zoë that," Ben snapped.

"I already did. She gave me a big fat 'no comment.' "

"Because that's all this deserves."

"Please, Ben. Tell me what's going on."

"It's nothing," Ben warned. "Don't buy into it."

Celia understood Ben's stonewalling, but the tension in his voice—and Zoë's—made it obvious: This was news.

Two days later, Celia and her crew headed for Miami to begin on-site preparations in advance of the convention. Deciding what to do about Clay's double-edged donation had occupied most of Celia's weekend. Her biggest concern was that by declining to refute the evidence—circumstantial though it was—Zoë had given credence to the assumption that she was working out a deal to free the hostages when it would be most beneficial to Ben's election.

Celia tried to work it from a number of different angles, but however she slanted her piece, it didn't look good for either Zoë or Ben. Then again, this had come from Clay. No matter what she decided to do, he came out the winner.

She was still ruminating about that particular point when she pulled up outside her father's house and stepped out of her car into the sizzling heat. She choked as the heavy air clogged her lungs. She had forgotten how miserable summers in Miami could be. Thankfully, Hugo had the air conditioner running and a pitcher of iced tea waiting.

They talked about the weather and Hugo's health and life on the campaign trail and how much she disliked Scottie Edwards, both as a man and a presidential candidate. It was when the conversation turned to Ben Knight and whether or not Celia thought he could win that she said "I have to ask you something."

"Anything."

"Someone gave me an intriguing lead."

"About . . . ?"

"Ben and Zoë and the lunatic who's believed to be behind the hostage-taking."

"Sounds serious."

"It's probably more of a perception problem than a substantive issue, but yes. It's serious."

Hugo shook his head, trying to understand why life was so complex. "And if you put this on the air, you'll look good. Two of your closest friends will look bad."

"Precisely," Celia said, once again amazed at his perspicacity. "I'm not afraid of Clay Chandler, but I really care about Ben and Zoë. The last thing I want to do is . . ."

"What does Clay Chandler have to do with this?"

Celia hadn't meant to mention Clay, but his name had popped out of her mouth involuntarily. Lately, she felt his presence lurking wherever she went.

"He's not happy with my coverage of his candidate. He's threatened me a couple of times, including in the note he sent with the packet. Frankly, I think it's a lot of hot air." She waved her hand as if to prove that Clay wasn't a worry. "He's never gotten over the fact that I don't find him even remotely attractive and that I'm a friend of Ben's or that . . ."

"What has he said to you, Celia. Exactly."

"He told me that if I didn't get off Edwards's case, he would destroy me. And mine," she said, hating the thoughts that were roiling inside her brain. She looked her father squarely in the eye. "What's going on? What do you know that he does and I don't?"

Hugo wrestled with how much to tell his daughter. There was so much about his past that he regretted. Some sins he had managed to keep from Celia. Others she had witnessed. This, he was certain she knew nothing about. Clay Chandler, unfortunately, knew every detail.

"I think I know what gun he's holding to your head." Hugo paled from the weight of his burden.

"Whatever it is," Celia said softly, "you can tell me."

"You know how bad my debts were after your mother died."

Actually, she didn't. She had been young and wrapped up in her own grief. She only knew that things were hard.

"The hospital bills were enormous. CORAL AIR was nearly bust. I owed back taxes. I borrowed from everyone I knew trying to pay off my debts, but the more I borrowed, the deeper the hole I dug for myself." Hugo lowered his eyes, unable to face her. "And then I flew a charter for Harris Ralston."

"Harris Ralston? My Harris Ralston? That loathsome, slimy pig of an ex-husband, Harris Ralston?"

Hugo chuckled in spite of himself. "The very same. It was shortly after you married him. He asked me to fly some cargo to St. Thomas. It was a good charter, so I did. I flew a bunch of charters for him over the years, most of them on the up-and-up."

"Most of them?" Celia cringed, knowing that if Harris was involved, it had to be immoral or illegal or both.

"I made a number of runs to El Salvador and Nicaragua."

It took a minute before Celia caught on. "Guns? You were running guns to the Contras?"

"I didn't know it at the time." He rubbed his eyes. "I suspected it, but honestly, I needed the money, and Harris paid very well. Since Clay and Harris were asshole buddies back then, I'm sure Clay knows all about it."

"And if Clay were to decide to go to the authorities?"

Hugo shrugged. "It depends on what the statute of limitations is on a federal offense."

Celia felt caught in a cyclone of emotion. She was upset for her father, outraged at her ex-husband, disgusted with Clay Chandler, and annoyed at herself for not seeing what was going on when it was going on. She felt fairly certain Clay would never file any formal charges against Hugo; no doubt he was a partner in one or more of Harris's enterprises. But if he leaked the story to the press, it was possible that her father would be prosecuted. At the very least, his reputation would be ruined.

"Don't worry, Daddy. It'll be all right." *I'll kill that bastard,* she thought as she gave Hugo a hug, furious that Clay would menace her father this way. "I won't let him hurt you."

"It's I who've hurt you," Hugo said.

"You did what you had to do. My only regret is that you couldn't tell me how bad things were."

Hugo patted her cheek. "You'd already had enough bad things happen in your life. They were my problems."

"And you solved them," she said with a wry laugh as they walked to the front door. "I can't say I'm thrilled with your solution, but what the hell! It is what it is."

"You don't think Chandler will do anything, do you?"

"No. He just gets a kick out of tormenting me. But you know what? I'm a Porter! I don't torment easily."

Hugo kissed her cheek, opened the door, and grimaced as a wall of heat slammed into their faces. The temperature was over a hundred degrees.

"Well, there's April in Paris and Miami in July," he quipped as if the torrid weather were their only concern.

"Right now, I'd rather be in Philadelphia," Celia joked as she kissed him good-bye and walked to her car, her heart as heavy as the humid air.

Clay Chandler had boxed her into a corner, and she didn't like it. He handed her a major story, one that would garner national recognition and get Titus Mitchell off her back. Reporting it would alienate, and possibly ruin, two of the people closest to her. Not reporting it might incite Chandler to leak potentially disastrous information to the press about Hugo, ruining both her father and her. Despite the efficiency of her car's air-conditioning system, Celia was sweating.

Slowly, she wended her way back to her hotel. In the midst of her peregrination, she recalled a bit of campaign catechism: if someone had to take a fall, better a staffer than the candidate. Ben had dismissed meeting Chertoff as incidental. Since no one had come forward to dispute that, his involvement was a one-day story. He could come out of this muddied, but viable. Zoë had been photographed with Durgunov's aide. That, plus her State Department history, created a potential breeding ground for speculation. The only way to innoculate against such virulent bad press was a strong statement.

Celia raced to her room and called Zoë again. She ran through her logic and pleaded for a quote. Something. Anything. Again, Zoë refused.

For hours, Celia debated. The choices were: save the candidate by sacrificing the staffer, or save the friendship by sacrificing her father. At the end of the day, Celia saw she had no choice.

The minute Zoë opened the door, she knew something was terribly wrong. Although nothing in her small foyer was disturbed, everything else was. Her apartment had been ransacked. Drawers had spilled their contents onto the floor. Closets had been emptied, cushions rearranged, furniture overturned. Books lay strewn on the floor, many of them opened, their pages wrinkled or torn.

As she reviewed the damage, hot tears rilled down her cheeks. This was not a simple break-in; this was a search-and-destroy mission. Slowly, she moved among the debris, mourning the invasion of her privacy. She straightened a table, righted a chair, and harvested the remains of a Japanese teapot.

As she tucked a cushion into the corner of her couch, two pictures flashed across her mental screen. The first was Scottie Edwards, his arm around Yuri Borofsky, waving from the center of Red Square. She had seen it on the front page of the *Herald* while flying from Rome to Washington. The accompanying article placed Edwards in Russia at the same time she and Ben were in Italy.

The second picture, of her and Anatoly in the El Al lounge, had been flashed on every TV screen from Rome to Raleigh with commentary by none other than Celia Porter. She could still hear Celia's voice describing Anatoly's past association with Yegor Durgunov, the presumed head of Red Rage. She heard Ben disclaim all knowledge of conversations between Zoë and Anatoly. She heard Amalia berate Celia for demanding the names of those who had attended her soirée. And she heard Celia wonder what—if anything—Zoë Vaughn and Anatoly Chertoff were plotting.

One didn't have to be a genius for this pillage to make sense. While Edwards was in Russia, he must have learned about the tapes Durgunov made and panicked. Seeing the snapshots of her with Anatoly, he must have assumed that she had a set of duplicate tapes or something equally damning. He must have sent his personal pit bull, Arlo Reid, to check it out. When Arlo didn't find anything, he trashed her place—just to make a point.

Zoë fumed as she picked up the pieces of her doll collection and placed the precious debris in a box. As she laid the fractured arms and legs alongside each other, she knew most of her shattered keepsakes were beyond repair. They were as damaged as her friendship with Celia.

Zoë tried to maintain perspective about that, but it was difficult. She understood it was the height of the political hunting season and everyone had their rifles loaded for bear. She admitted that Clay Chandler's maneuverings had been artful. She even suspected there was an insidious, underlying reason that he had given the story to Celia rather than Dean Walsh or one of the other anchors. But bottom line—Celia had betrayed her.

Slowly, she went about the task of putting her home in order. As she swept glass into a dustpan and rehung the pictures that lined her foyer, she studied a recent one taken of her and Ben with the British Prime Minister outside Number 10 Downing Street in London.

When the story had hit the airways several days earlier, she offered Ben her resignation. He refused to accept it. He did insist that she explain Anatoly's presence, his connection to Zev Shafir, and his relationship with her. She provided a cursory accounting. She told him about Maura's job at the embassy and Anatoly's work as an informer for the Mossad, but she omitted the meeting between Edwards, Borofsky, and Durgunov and the tapes. Until they were found, scrutinized, and authenticated, the less Ben knew, the less danger he was in.

Thinking about the tapes suddenly gave Zoë pause. In effect, by exposing Zoë's meeting with an associate of Durgunov, any future revelation she might make about Edwards's convening with the enemy had been neutralized. Celia couldn't know that. But Clay could. Exactly how much did he know? And when did he know it? Had he sent this package under orders, without being fully aware of its implications? Or had he been in on this scheme from the start?

The only thing to do, Zoë thought, was to fight back in a way both Clay and Scottie Edwards would understand. She had to cut the legs off this story immediately. The best way to do that was to distract the press with something equally juicy.

Determined now, she went to the phone. She had been sitting on Scottie Edwards's nasty little secret far too long.

"How about meeting me at i Ricchi in an hour," she said.

Wary of bugs and taps, Zoë gave no reason for her sudden invitation. Sean Quinn didn't need a reason. He could smell a good story a mile away.

THE
CONVENTIONS

☆

☆ JULY ☆

The middle of July was not the best time to visit Miami; on a good day, the weather was hot and steamy. Nor did it seem an apt location for those who called themselves conservatives to rally their cause in a city that was generally acknowledged as America's edge, both geographically and morally. Still, there were those who thought the Republicans had made a good decision choosing it as their convention site because they felt Miami's trendy image might add a little excitement to the Grand Old Party's party.

Several days before the actual start of the convention, delegates from all over the country began arriving for the preliminary conferences and caucuses that would decide procedures, rules and the all-important platform. As the hotels in the area filled up, carpenters and electricians worked feverishly to convert the Miami Convention Center into a patriotic playpen for thousands of loyal partisans in flag-colored clothes and elephant hats.

At the hotel next door, in a luxurious, sun-filled penthouse suite that afforded a view of downtown Miami as well as the Miami River, Prescott Edwards, Clay Chandler, and Arlo Reid greeted their very special guests: Roy, Wade,

Branston, and Georgie Hughes. After they had shared a glass of champagne, exchanged pleasantries, and toasted the man who several nights later would be nominated without challenge, the Hugheses seated themselves and waited for Scottie to ask Wade to join the ticket.

While the General sweet-talked her father, Georgie kept an eye on her brother. She could only imagine how Wade felt. If her feelings were roller-coasting between excited, frightened, exhilarated, and nervous, he had to be a wreck. Despite their spasms of sibling rivalry, she admired Wade. He was bright and able and, most important, honestly concerned about the future of his country. She felt good about what was about to happen.

For months, the family had campaigned for this moment, and she had no doubt that they had succeeded in convincing Edwards of Wade's worthiness. She had done her part by speaking at numerous Edwards fund-raisers, grabbing every opportunity to lobby the General about the wisdom of balancing the ticket with someone whose domestic expertise was well documented and whose name was well-known.

"I know it's customary for this part of the process to be completed before the party convenes," Edwards was saying, "but I wanted to be sure I was making the decision that was in the country's best interests."

He sipped his champagne, replaced his glass on the table alongside him, leaned forward in his chair, and laced his fingers together. Georgie thought Roy would explode. Edwards was being coy. Roy hated coy.

"While we considered numerous candidates, Governor, your family holds a unique place in the fabric of this nation. The Hughes name has long represented service to America, and, for that reason, I would consider it a special pleasure to share our ticket with a Hughes."

Roy flushed fittingly and sputtered his appreciation for the kind words. Georgie bit back a smile. Her father had a hard time being grateful to anyone for anything. He had worked at it—appearing grateful was an important part of a politician's repertoire—but he never seemed to get it right. Even now, there was a look in his eye that said: "You should be thanking me."

"I've campaigned with Georgie all across the country," Scottie continued, "and I have to tell you: She's a natural! The public loves her!"

Roy looked confused. Branston stuck a finger in his ear, as if he was suffering from sudden wax build-up. Wade shifted uncomfortably in his seat, his expression alternating between confusion and hysteria. He looked like a puppy in need of a walk.

"I think I missed something," Roy said, looking from Scottie to Wade to Georgie.

"Forgive me if I didn't make myself clear." Scottie rose and crossed the room to where Georgie was eyeing him cautiously. He smiled, his blue eyes twinkling. "I feel as if I'm proposing marriage. In a way, I suppose this is not too dissimilar." He bowed gallantly. "What I'm asking, Congresswoman Hughes, is if you would consent to be my running mate."

"What!" Wade was on his feet. Roy nudged his son to stop him from saying or doing anything foolish. Roy hadn't fully absorbed the what or why, but he had the basics: Edwards hadn't picked the Hughes Roy had in mind, but he had picked a Hughes.

"It's going to be a tough campaign," Scottie was saying, "but these are tough times. America needs leadership and guidance and comfort through this terrible crisis. Together, I think we can give them what they need."

Georgie stood and faced the man who had just asked her to be part of history. Though shaking from this extraordinary turn of events, her attitude remained calm, her voice steady.

"It would be a privilege to run with you, General Edwards. I'm truly honored that you would think I'm worthy of the opportunity." Then, quite unexpectedly, she giggled. "I'm also positively bowled over," she said, catching sight of the apoplexy that had siezed control of the Hughes men. "As are the rest of my family."

Edwards smiled, partly because he had put a big one over on Roy Hughes. "I can see that."

His demeanor sobered as he approached Wade.

"I don't mean any disrespect, Senator Hughes. I know that you, your father, your brother-in-law, and your sister had you in mind for this position and believe me when I say that you are more than qualified.

"But these days, the American voter is a restless animal. He's angry and distrustful and suspicious of anyone who's ever even visited Washington." He pointed to Georgie. "I've watched this woman walk into jungles crowded with those wild beasts and tame them. She talks to them and they weep. She sings to them and they smile. What I'm hoping is that she'll appeal to them enough to make them come out in November and vote us into the White House!" Scottie hesitated, as if waiting for applause.

"I'm sure she'll do just that," Wade said stiffly. "Naturally, we'll all support the ticket and work for you and Georgie in whatever capacity you think would be helpful."

"That's mighty generous of you . . ."

"I'd like to be among the first to congratulate Congresswoman Hughes," Clay said, loudly interrupting Scottie's fence-mending.

He painted a smile on his face and raised his glass as if in a toast. Georgie noted that the smile was halfhearted and his sincerity was as flat as his champagne. She also noticed a look of irritation as he waited for everyone to take their seats, as if they were conspiring to steal time from his part of the program.

She, for one, couldn't wait to hear what he had to say. While they camouflaged their feelings well, the truth was she and Clay didn't like each other, never had. In the beginning, it was a conflict of personality; she found his unpleasant. Later, it became a choosing of sides. If Clay Chandler had one hard-and-fast rule it was that if you were a friend of Benjamin Knight, you couldn't be a friend of his. Georgie's loyalty to Ben was fierce.

"I want you to know, Georgie, that I fully support the General's decision." A perfunctory smile vaulted across his mouth. "You're an experienced, talented campaigner, someone who I believe could be a valuable addition to the ticket."

Georgie acknowledged the strangled compliments with a pleasant nod.

"I do have some questions, however."

"Ask away."

"We don't know for certain who our opponent is going to be, but it's possible that Ben Knight will come out of the convention as his party's nominee."

Georgie was attentive and wary, but kept silent.

"He's a good friend of yours."

Still, she said nothing.

"In the heat of the campaign, will you be able to attack him?"

"On the issues? Absolutely. As for personal attacks: I don't believe in them."

"How would you feel if he attacked you?"

"If it was on the issues," Georgie responded, "I'd fire back."

Scottie and Arlo exchanged satisfied glances. Clay's expression remained impassive, save for one second during which Georgie detected a triumphant twitch of his eyebrows.

"I'm glad you raised the subject of issues," he continued. "Would you mind refreshing us about where you stand on taxes, welfare, abortion, gun control, and the hostage crisis?"

Georgie's eyes never left his. This interrogation was an empty exercise; her views on all these subjects were well documented. Something else was going on.

"I'd like taxes lowered and the budget balanced. Welfare needs to be drastically reformed. I'm against abortion as a means of birth control, but I believe in a woman's right to choose. And even though I own several guns and fully support the second amendment right to bear arms, I have no problem with proper registration procedures and waiting periods. I am not even opposed to the notion of testing. We don't issue driving licenses without behind-the-wheel tests. Why put guns into the hands of people who don't know how to use them?"

Scottie's smile was broadening.

"As for the hostages, I have no expertise in that area, so I look to the General. He is renowned for his courage on the battlefield, his savvy at the negotiating table, and his intimate knowledge of the way the diplomatic wheels grind. I would probably support whatever position General Edwards espouses," pausing so that everyone would know that she did have her own prerequisites, "assuming its premise is the safe return of our citizens."

Scottie's head bobbed in obvious approval as he accepted her benediction. Even Clay proffered a congratulatory nod. So far her performance was perfect.

"I see only one potential problem," he said, still playing devil's advocate. "The party platform supports a right to life amendment. How do you reconcile your personal view with the political stand of the man heading the ticket?"

"My opinions on that subject are already on the record. To deny them or drastically alter them now would make me look like a political panderer or a moral fence-straddler. I'm neither."

There was a stridency to her voice. Clay might have pressed her, but feared she was growing impatient with his grilling.

"Now if you don't mind," he said, quickly shifting gears, "let's get down to the business of announcing the General's selection. We'd like to hold a press conference at noon tomorrow so we can make the early news cycle. If your husband and children aren't in Miami, get them here. If they have any objections to your running, get them on board."

"Aye aye," Georgie said with a crisp salute, smothering

the small voice warning her that this situation played right into Lyle's hands; it would be just like him to bargain for his cooperation.

Clay scowled at her mockery, but continued running down his checklist. He turned to the Hughes men.

"Naturally, we want the distaff members of the clan present for this momentous occasion." He displayed his breeding by smiling quickly, then refocused on Georgie. "Needless to say, I want your children looking wholesome. No earrings. No thigh-high skirts. No oddly colored hair or spiky Mohawks. And nothing that even looks like drugs."

Georgie's face tightened. "Don't you ever dare say anything like that to me again. As the manager of this campaign, you can tell me where to stand and to some extent, what to say. But my children are off-limits. Do you understand that, Clay?"

Chandler physically rebounded. Her reaction was so swift and so volatile it threw him off stride. Before he had time to frame an apology, Scottie Edwards bounded to his feet.

"Georgie, my dear. Please don't take offense. Sometimes, Clay obsesses on the details and loses the forest for the trees, so to speak. He didn't mean anything. He couldn't possibly. I've met your children, and they're marvelous examples of American youth."

He took her arm and suavely steered her toward the door. "Why don't you call them and give them the wonderful news." -

He ushered the Hugheses into the hall and with a conciliatory grin, tipped an imaginary cap to her. "Have a nice evening, Madam Vice President."

Georgie swallowed her indignation, shook hands with Edwards, and bade him good-night. She signaled to her father to follow suit. By the time the door of the elevator reopened, tempers had calmed. Branston announced he was going to the bar. Wade agreed to join him, but before they parted, he turned to Georgie.

"I'm happy for you."

It wasn't an enthusiastic endorsement, but considering the circumstances, Georgie viewed it as generous.

"I didn't lobby for this, Wade. I was promoting you all along."

"I believe you." His eyes affirmed that he did.

Georgie's eyes narrowed. "Who do you think suggested me for the number two slot?"

The question was posed to all of them. Roy answered almost immediately. "Chandler." Branston and Wade registered uncertainty.

"Normally, I'd have said Edwards," Roy explained, "but he's too traditional to go for a female veep. Chandler must have convinced him that while this was an election based on strong-arming a global menace, there was more to the presidency than bullying a bully. Georgie's supposed to soften the General's harder edges."

"Makes sense." Wade was eager to agree. It assuaged his ego.

"Only on the face of it," Georgie said, still ruminating. "The crux of this is not why Edwards bought it, but why Clay sold it."

Roy stroked his chin while he mused. "You've got a point, sugar. He was never a big fan of yours."

"But Ben is."

"I'm not following," Branston said.

"It was all that crap about personal attacks versus issue assaults," she hissed, her composure slipping as realization dawned. "Clay didn't propose me because I'm capable of giving the ticket geographical, philosophical, or gender balance. I'm in this enviable position because of one simple fact: I'm Benjamin Knight's good friend."

The three men looked confused. Georgie refreshed their memories about Clay and Ben's long-standing quarrel. She also pondered Celia's airing a negative piece on Zoë. Suddenly, it seemed an unlikely coincidence.

"Don't you get it?" she said, beginning to pace. "This isn't a presidential campaign anymore. This is a carefully staged, nationally televised jousting match conducted for the private pleasure of one man!

"Will friendship override ambition?" she asked as she struck a Shakesperean pose—chin elevated, eyes aflutter, one hand to her chest, one pointing skyward. "Will Ben stab Georgie in the back? Will Georgie lance Ben in the groin? Tune in tomorrow for the next installment of Clay Chandler's Personal *Family Feud!*" She practically growled with disgust.

As she resumed her pacing, Roy concurred. "He's betting Ben won't hit hard at the ticket because it would reflect badly on you. Edwards, meantime, can hit as hard as he wants."

"That's warped," Branston ventured.

"To say the least." Whatever feelings of exoneration Wade might have had faded as he watched his sister wrestle with her anger over the notion that she had been made a pawn. "You think Edwards knows he was manipulated?"

Roy snorted. "He doesn't give a shit. His gut—and probably his pollster—say Georgie's a good call. That's all that counts."

"I *am* a good call!" Georgie's outburst startled them. "With all due respect," she said, bowing to her brother, "I make an outstanding candidate! I've got the record. I've got the background. I've got the name. And I've got the talent on the stump."

Her eyes glinted with flinty determination. "In spite of himself, Clay picked the best person for the job!"

"You know what," Wade said, surrendering with a smile, "I think he did."

"I'm going to win this sucker," Georgie declared, "and when I do, I'm going to kick that son of a bitch out on his ass!"

Georgie, Wade, and Branston clasped hands and raised them in a defiant victory salute. Roy choked on his pride. When Georgie turned to him seeking approval, a broad smile illuminated his face.

"Go, girl!" he cheered.

"We may be slightly flabbergasted by this turn of events, Georgie," Branston observed with a chuckle, "but we're family. And we're behind you all the way!"

"That's a fact!" Roy joined his hand with theirs and chortled loudly. "And if you think we're flabbergasted? Wait 'til Georgie tells Lyle!"

By early evening, Lyle and the rest of the family had arrived from Dallas. Acceding to her wishes, there was to be no public announcement until she had broken the news to Lyle and her children. Lyle's first question was "What's in this for me?"

"That depends," she told him flatly, "on how well you behave. I'm not the one in charge of handing out the goodies. Scottie Edwards will pick his cabinet and his ambassadors. If you're a good boy, you might wind up with something. If you're not, and you do anything to hurt his chances of winning the White House, you can bet your latest bimbo that the only cabinet you're going to visit is the one where the pain medicine is kept."

That elicited a promise of cooperation. Both of them knew it was minimal and conditional.

Hunt and Olivia were genuinely thrilled. Both made an on-the-spot decision to postpone their entrances to college so they could campaign for their mother.

"I'm so proud of you, Mom," Olivia said as she hugged Georgie. "I can't wait to get out there on a thousand college campuses and tell everyone what an awesome V.P. you'll make."

This was a major concession coming from a child who made a practice of running the other way whenever she was asked to attend a political event. Georgie understood that Olivia's commitment was one made of love, which was why the sacrifice was so appreciated.

Hunt's reaction surprised her. Not only was he completely positive and emotionally supportive of her candidacy, but quite vocal about wanting to do whatever he could to assure her election. Still, Georgie sensed a second thought.

"I'm concerned about security," he admitted, thinking back to his conversation with Keeley Knight. "There are whackos out there who think you should shut your mouth, go home, and bake cookies."

Olivia made a face. "They never tasted Mom's cookies."

Georgie chuckled, then sobered. "The Secret Service will assign a team of agents to me. I'll be well protected."

Hunt nodded, but the look of an unresolved doubt remained.

"What else?" Georgie asked.

"Am I going to hurt you?"

She caressed Hunt's cheek. "Never."

"I mean, because . . ."

"I know what you mean. My answer stands. I'm beyond proud of you, Hunt. You overcame a drug habit. It took a lot of hard work and discipline to get clean, and it takes even more to stay clean. Anyone who doesn't want to vote for me because my son made a mistake, paid for it, conquered it, and fights a private battle every single day of his life, can stuff it!"

Roy Hughes was also concerned about Georgie. "In case I didn't make it clear before," he said, stealing a moment alone with her late that first night, "I'm awfully proud of you, Georgina." He kissed his daughter's cheek, not bothering to hide his love or his awe. "Still, I am worried about you."

"The Secret Service . . ."

"No, not that way. You were planning to leave Lyle after the election. This puts a crimp in that plan."

Georgie's silver blue eyes filled with a mix of wonderment and frustration. "Most gifts are tied with a string," she said softly.

"This is an incredible opportunity, baby."

She nodded, leaned nearer to him, and patted his knee.

She knew what this candidacy meant to him. "It's also a terrible trap. Once we announce, I'm tied to a man I loathe."

"And you have to stop seeing the man you love."

Georgie stared at her father. "I should have known."

Roy chuckled, but his laughter stumbled over feelings of guilt and regret. "Damn straight you should have known!"

"How do you feel about . . . him?" Georgie felt like a sixteen-year-old asking for her father's approval, but, she supposed, some needs never diminished.

"Does he love you?" She nodded. "Then he shows remarkably good sense. Is he good to you?"

"Very."

"Then hang in there. We'll work this out. You'll see."

He took her hands in his and looked at her face, marveling as he always did at her loveliness. It disturbed him to note that at a moment when she should have been flying, she looked strained.

"Have you told him yet?"

She shook her head. She hadn't worked up the courage.

"You can file for divorce after the election. The public's a lot more tolerant than you think."

"If Lyle weren't as vindictive as he is, I'd agree with you. But he's not going to go quietly, Daddy."

A Cheshire cat smile licked Roy's lips. "Maybe not, but he is going to go."

"What have you done?"

"It's not what I've done. It's what Lyle's done. It seems he felt he wasn't making enough money with Hughes Oil & Gas. So he paid some investment banker to tip him off about which companies planned to gobble up other companies and when. He bought stocks ahead of the transactions, sold fast, and made humongous profits. Problem is, insider trading is illegal. If someone turns him in, he could wind up wearing an orange jumpsuit for a very long time."

Georgie considered her father's bulletin. Again, she should have known. Once she had said she wanted to leave

Lyle, Roy must have investigated him within an inch of his life.

"I don't know. Maybe." She rubbed her temples, weighing angles and possibilities. "As long as he's my husband, in the public's mind, I'm tainted by his wrongdoings. He might just get off on being my bête noir."

"Don't you worry, darlin'. As long as the spotlight's on, Lyle's gonna bask." Roy patted her cheek. "You just enjoy your moment."

"Whoa! I think the skin on my boots just got goose bumps," Jed said when Georgie told him about Edwards's bombshell.

For privacy's sake, she used the phone in Roy's room. He conveniently arranged to go down to the lounge for a drink with Lyle.

"That's the good news."

"I already know the bad news, darlin'. You and I are back on the shelf."

A weighted silence traveled across the phone wires.

"I need you," she said. Her voice was small, yet large enough to break his heart.

"You just say the word, and I'm there." She was silent, but he knew she was nodding. She knew he would do anything for her. "Of course, it probably wouldn't look too good to have Edwards's veep slobbering all over Ben Knight's campaign manager."

She laughed. He tried to join in, but couldn't.

"Frankly, I'd throw caution to the winds and fly down tomorrow just to give you a hug, but they might have their spies out. That Chandler can be a nasty dude. I heard he orders female V.P. candidates for breakfast."

"I don't know about that, but he is the one I'm worried about."

"After Lyle, of course."

"Of course." She wished she could tell him about Roy's snooping, but if this phone wasn't secure, it was bad enough she was speaking to her lover. She didn't need to add her husband's crimes to the pot.

"You nervous, babe?"

"A little."

"Don't be. You've got the stuff, and you know what to do with it."

She wanted to say, "Only because you taught me." Instead, she said, "Are you okay with this?"

Jed struggled to find a voice that would maintain the illusion that he was handling this unexpected turn of events.

"Hell no, I'm not okay," he declared rather loudly. "With you running against me, I'm gonna have to put in some serious time. Not only that, but I'm gonna have to work the ass off your good friend, the Senator."

He heard her chuckle softly, which was all he wanted. She needed to feel good about what she was doing. She needed to feel confident and sure of herself. Besides, he felt miserable enough for both of them.

"But," he said, unable to keep all his feelings at bay, "make no mistake about it, sweetheart. Come November, I'm gonna whip you."

"You think so, eh?"

"I have to."

"Why's that?" Georgie asked, expecting another Oakesism.

"Because I love you to pieces, Georgie girl, and I'm scared that if you win, I might lose you."

Georgie waited until her tears had dried before placing her second call.

"The announcement's being made tomorrow," she said to Zoë, "but I wanted to tell you myself. I'm Scottie Edwards's running mate."

"You're what!"

Georgie laughed. "The veep. The number two. The

second banana. A heartbeat away. Me: Georgina Hughes.''
She giggled again. "Can you believe it?''

"No,'' Zoë said, truly overwhelmed. "I mean, yes, of
course I believe it. I'm stunned, that's all. Who would have
thought that old goat would have made such a brilliant
choice? You're a fabulous candidate! In fact, if I were
to indulge in a moment of selfishness—you're much too
fabulous. You're going to give that skunk a major goose!''
She groaned, gleefully. "Oh, who cares! I'm delighted for
you!''

Georgie smiled into the phone. Zoë's ebullient congratulations were sincere and most welcome. "Thanks. I knew
you would be.''

"Yeah, well, don't expect me to sound this excited in
public,'' Zoë teased. "From here on in, I'm not going to
have one nice thing to say about you.''

"I fully expect you to beat up on me,'' Georgie said,
"but before you put on the gloves, I want to clear something up.''

Zoë already knew where Georgie was headed.

"Back in New Hampshire you and I had a conversation
about what we'd do if we found ourselves on opposing
sides.''

"We agreed to disagree,'' Zoë said. "And to abide by
Paddy Vaughn's Pub Rules.''

"Right. No hair pulling, no knocking the foam off a
freshly drawn brew, and no pillow talk.'' Georgie allowed
her words to sink in. "As of tonight, there's only one pillow
on my bed.''

Zoë's heart hurt. She knew how painful it was to push
away the man you loved. "Only for the duration of the
campaign, I hope,'' she said.

"We'll see.'' Georgie's voice was scratchy, like a needle
skipping a groove on an old 45 record. "Will we be friends,
no matter what?'' Georgie asked, voicing a fear both had
thought of, but neither had wanted to raise.

"Absolutely,'' Zoë said reassuringly. "I can handle losing
an election. I wouldn't be able to deal with losing you.''

As Georgie hung up she realized that both Zoë and Jed had worried about losing her. She found that troublesome, mainly because of something Jed once told her: "When the only thing that's important to you is winning, the first thing you lose is yourself."

Georgie pondered that for most of night. By morning, she had resolved to keep her eye fixed on the prize, but not to lose sight of who she was when she began the race. And who she wanted to be when she finished.

☆   ☆   ☆

As the welcoming speeches droned on, Celia worked the floor, conducting interviews with delegates. She asked the usual questions: "What do you think is the most dominant issue facing this convention?" "How did you get to be a delegate?" "What would possess you to put an elephant hat on your head?" But the real buzz was the stunning announcement that Georgie Hughes was Scottie Edwards's pick as a vice-presidential nominee. Though the press conference held the day after her selection had been open to everyone, Celia had scored a coup with an exclusive interview that would air the night of the nominating speeches. What she was doing now was taping a filler piece to be inserted into the convention coverage when the producer felt the tempo was lagging.

The Texas delegation was crowing about Georgie's nomination. The consensus from New York, Massachusetts, California, and Illinois was that it was a brilliant move. The Rust Belt states, the Heartland and much of the South were split. Moderates, especially those familiar with her record, approved. The more conservative voters weren't certain that in a time of international crisis, a woman was the best candidate.

"The General needs an adjutant, not a wife," one man asserted.

"Edwards could have picked Howdy Doody," another said, reflecting the opinion of many who viewed this as a one-issue election. "I'm looking at the top of the ticket and from where I sit, no one's going to beat the General. Not as long as some lunatic's holding hostages!''

It didn't surprise Celia that the female vote wasn't unanimous.

''I don't know if I'm comfortable with a woman a heartbeat away from the presidency,'' an elderly woman from Indiana worried.

''Are you saying you don't think a woman could be president?''

The woman sensed that Celia disagreed, but she believed what she believed. ''Men can't have babies. And women can't run wars.''

A younger woman saw Georgie as a level head in a potentially chaotic time. ''Women are never in a hurry to send their children into battle. She'll think long and hard before committing troops.''

After several ''She's nothing but window dressing,'' Celia found two men and a woman who were of the ''It's about time'' opinion to round out her segment.

As she was wrapping up, she caught sight of Quinn chatting with Hugo. Two mornings ago, before the demands of her job would eat up all her spare time, she had brought Quinn to meet her father for breakfast in the Grove. If any part of her brain persisted in denying that Sean Quinn was Hugo redux, it conceded that morning. The two men were utterly simpatico. They practically ignored her as they rambled on about where they'd been, where they'd like to go, what they'd learned from their travels, where they found adventure today.

Now, the two men were standing in the aisle behind the Florida delegation, behaving like old friends. She watched as they shared a joke, slapped each other on the back, and shook hands when Quinn left to join his network's anchor. Celia smiled from within the NTN broadcasting booth.

Her smile faded when she spotted Clay Chandler hurrying through the arena, his head down, his face buried in his notes. Hugo turned just as Clay did, and the two men collided, then righted themselves. When they looked at each other, recognition came in seconds. It was not the most joyous of reunions.

Even from a distance, Celia could tell that the conversation had not been pleasant. Clay was his usual unctuous self, preening and gloating in that oleaginous way he had. Hugo stood tall and chuckled slightly, as if he found Clay's braggadocio amusing. When they parted, Clay seemed disappointed. Hugo turned toward the broadcast booth, caught Celia's eye, and gave her a thumbs-up.

She grinned just as the red light blinked.

"Good evening ladies and gentlemen," she said, suppressing a laugh. "And welcome to sunny Miami Beach, home of this year's Republican National Convention."

Since the hotels in and around the Convention Center had been reserved for delegates, the press corps had bivouacked on Miami Beach. The pencil press spread itself out among several Collins Avenue landmarks, while the networks each commandeered a hotel and established their own beachheads, so to speak. In addition to his room at the Eden Roc, Quinn also had taken a rendezvous suite at one of the newly renovated hotels on Ocean Avenue in South Beach. It was there that he and Celia escaped when the gavel closed the convention for the evening and the weary wended their way to a bar or a bed.

"Were you brilliant tonight?" he asked as he lowered the lights, turned the air conditioner on high, and poured them each a drink.

Celia slipped off her shoes, removed her suit jacket, and practically collapsed onto the bed.

"Maybe not brilliant," she said, draping an arm over her tired eyes. "But certainly very good. And you?"

"I'm always brilliant."

"Forgive me. I forgot."

He tucked a few pillows behind her back and handed her an amaretto with a lot of rocks. Even at night, Miami was obscenely hot this time of year. He had stripped down

to his shorts almost the minute they walked into the room.
He poured himself a vodka and tonic and gulped it as if
it was water. He added more ice, a little more vodka, and
sat on the bed, facing her.

"How'd your interview with Madam V.P. go?"

Celia grinned. "It was fabulous. She's fabulous. The
whole thing is fabulous. Of course, I'd be happier if someone other than Scottie Edwards was at the top of the ticket,
but I won't quibble." Her grin got wider. "I still can't
believe it! My friend Georgie. Vice president of the United
States. Whew! It's enough to take my breath away."

Quinn unbuttoned her blouse, took an ice cube from
his drink, and slithered it from under her chin down to
the cleavage between her breasts.

"You take my breath away," he said.

He removed her blouse and unhooked her bra, tossing
both to the other side of the bed. Taking another ice cube,
he drew cold, wet swirls on her warm flesh, tracing the
pale swell of her breasts and the darker areola that centered
them, watching as the clear liquid dribbled into the vale.
He took an ice cube from her drink and touched it to her
lips. She sucked at it gently, fixing her doelike eyes on him
as the sweet, almond liqueur teased her tongue. Quinn
covered the other half of the cube with his mouth, sucking
at it until the two of them had melted the ice and found
each other.

As it always was with them, arousal was instantaneous. It
seemed as if they couldn't be alone without feeding their
voracious carnal appetites. They tried to take things slowly,
but that came later, the second time they made love, or
the third. It was as if everything else—running into each
other at work, days spent apart, meals, cocktails, telephone
calls, and other nonphysical encounters—was merely a
form of subliminal, extraerogenous foreplay, tortuous,
secretive caresses that heightened desire to such a pitch
that any contact at all became explosive.

"Now what were we talking about?" Quinn said when
the beast of their passion had been subdued.

They were lying next to each other, individual portraits of contentment.

"Something unimportant, I'm sure," Celia mumbled.

Quinn raised himself onto his elbow and looked down at her. She could feel him staring. Reluctantly, she opened her eyes.

"What's the matter?"

"Nothing, I guess."

His vagueness was upsetting. "What does that mean?"

He made light of it with a quick shrug of his shoulders, but his expression continued to transmit concern.

"Was it something my father said to you tonight at the convention?"

Instead of answering her, his fingers probed her right breast. They moved without sensuality, rather with purpose. Just under the nipple, his fingers stopped.

"Before, I thought I felt a lump," he said. "Here it is."

The color drained from Celia's face. He took her hand, but she snatched it back, refusing to confirm or deny his discovery.

His voice was quiet. He didn't want to frighten her or anger her. "I'm not a doctor, but I think this needs to be checked."

"It's a cyst," she insisted as she slid to the other side of the bed, grabbed her clothes, and began getting dressed.

"It probably is. It's just I never felt it before."

She spun around and glared at him. "Oh! Wow! Thank you, Dr. Quinn. I didn't know you were a nationally recognized expert on breasts and their various lumps and bumps."

"I'm concerned. That's all."

"If I want your concern, I'll ask for it!"

She ran from the room and slammed the door before he could stop her. She didn't return his calls that night, and the next day she refused to speak to him.

Quinn didn't care about being the bad guy as long as she visited her doctor. His biggest fear was that her fear wouldn't let her do that.

☆ ☆ ☆

Georgie felt as if she had been taken out of the real world and locked inside a fun-house hall of mirrors. Few things were exactly as she expected them to be. Rather, she was confronted with exaggeration, distortion, flattery, images that looked good one minute, twisted the next, and even a few off-guard glimpses at a side of herself she had never seen before.

Over the past several days, she had been closeted with speech writers, media advisors, campaign personnel, schedulers, and wardrobe consultants. She had posed for dozens of photographs, granted as many interviews as time would allow, and answered zillions of ridiculous questions about everything from, "Would you switch your loyalty from the Dallas Cowboys to the Washington Redskins", to "Would you bomb Red Square if Borofsky continues to refuse to help gain the release of America's hostages?"

Her hotel room looked like a florist's showcase, crammed with elaborate arrangements from close friends as well as people whose names she'd never heard before. As quickly as they came in, they went out, donated to local hospitals. The ones she saved: a bouquet of yellow roses from Ben— *"Care to change partners and dance with me?"* Tropical exotics from the Siegels— *"Who woulda thunk it? We would!"* An orchid plant from Zoë— *"You'll always be top of the ticket to me."* A vase of flaming birds of paradise from Celia and Hugo Porter— *"Vice is nice!"* And a spray of blue-bonnets that didn't need a card.

Last evening, after Scottie Edwards had been officially nominated as the party's candidate for president by the roll call of the states, her name was placed in nomination by her father. It had been a moving tribute to her many accomplishments in the public arena, including the diffi-culties of being the lone female politician in a male dynasty of political achievers. Laced as it was with intimate anec-dotes and paternal accolades, it became the highlight of the convention, overshadowing the flag-waving, aggressively partisan keynote speech delivered by former President Rumson.

Since tradition dictated that neither of the nominees make an appearance at the convention hall until the following night, when they would deliver their acceptance speeches, the Edwardses and the Mercers had enjoyed a private dinner in the General's suite. Afterwards, the two couples were joined by children, grandchildren, and assorted friends, who gathered in front of a television to watch the evening's festivities. They, in turn, were watched by a camera crew charged with the task of recording their every gesture.

Georgie swallowed two headache tablets and took a last look in the mirror. Tonight she would deliver her acceptance speech. Clay had been riding herd on the writers to get them to produce a fifteen-minute deification of Prescott Edwards, with a few thoughts by Georgie Hughes. Late this afternoon, Georgie took one of the writers aside and rewrote the testimonial. She neglected to run it by the campaign manager.

She ran a brush through her thick black hair, softening the heavily lacquered helmet the hotel's hair salon had created. When it didn't look like it would repel bullets, she relaxed. Her makeup looked good, but she knew it would be enhanced later by professionals so that it photographed well. Her dress, a simple sheath of Republican red, had already been camera-tested and approved. The neckline was plain and could have used a strand of pearls, but Georgie preferred her bluebonnet pin. To draw attention to her face, which was what the wardrobe consultants wanted, she wore a pair of large, elegant earrings: pearls surrounded by sapphires.

Her fingers touched the delicate pin. That first night, after she had hung up with Jed, her heart had ached so, she actually toyed with the idea of rejecting the General's offer, serving Lyle with divorce papers, and letting the chips fall where they would. As she lay in her bed, less than three feet from Lyle, all she thought about was ending her marriage and being with Jed. In the dark, her need for him became overwhelming, like a magnet drawing her to conclusions that, in the light of day, seemed rash and unlikely.

Her blue eyes turned away from her reflection. When she didn't call Edwards and decline, and didn't call her lawyer about a divorce, she had felt ashamed. The lure of the office had proven too great.

Which was precisely what Emily Edwards had told her last night during the seconding speeches for the General. Aware that there would be no escape once the roll call began, Emily had invited Georgie to have a private cup of tea in her bedroom. The woman's candor was startling, particularly when Georgie asked if Emily was excited about her husband running for president.

"I find the whole process quite bizarre. The public wants heroes in the White House, yet most of the time, the real heroes don't run and the men who do border on megalomania."

Georgie's mouth dropped open.

"Think about it. If you met someone at a party who stood on a chair and declared that he had all the answers and was meant to be the master of the universe, you'd lock him up. Right?"

Georgie was amused, but refrained from comment.

"How is that different from a man who stands on a soapbox and announces that not only *could* he be the leader of the free world. But he *should* be!"

Georgie chuckled, but couldn't refute the central point of Emily's argument. Georgie had thought about that same thing many times. Millions of little boys—and now some girls as well—were told they could grow up and be president of the United States. Most of them preferred the idea of being firemen or cowboys. Yet some held on to that thought, allowing it to shape the conduct of their lives. Certainly, the notion of leadership had molded Roy's life. And Wade's career. And Branston's. And, she supposed, on some level, her own.

"You and your husband don't have much of a marriage, do you?" Emily said, after a spate of small talk. She was blunt, yet there was no criticism in her voice. When Georgie flushed, Emily laughed.

"Takes one to know one, my dear. You try very hard to hide it, and I'm sure with most people you're successful, but to me, it's quite clear you can't stand him."

"We've had our ups and downs," Georgie confessed, unwilling to reveal the true state of her union.

Emily laughed, but in a knowing way that didn't insult Georgie. If anything, it was a gesture of kinship.

"Scottie and I passed ups and downs years ago," she said, sipping her tea as if they were discussing the perils of caffeine. "That was after we'll-stick-together-for-the-children's-sake. Now, we're going through the civil-at-all-costs phase. All I ask is that he's discreet and that he confine his activities to girls who've reached their majority."

"Why do you stay with the General?" Georgie asked, feeling oddly drawn to this woman.

"I like the power. If Scottie's elected president, I become the First Lady. Why would I give up the chance to wield such awesome power just because the man I married is an ego-bloated, lying, cheating piece of shit?"

She rolled her eyes at the mere thought of such insanity. Then she took Georgie's hand and squeezed it.

"Grab the power that's being offered you, Georgie Hughes! And when you're comfortable wielding it, throw your husband out and find yourself someone who loves you to pieces. Unless," she said archly, "you've found him already."

Even now, as she prepared to take the stage, Georgie hated the cynicism that had prompted her to wonder if perhaps the entire conversation had been a fishing expedition. In case it had, she had kept Jed's name a secret.

Her fingers grazed the pin again. Emily was right about one thing: power was the ultimate charm. Just days ago, she had thought Jed was all she wanted and that if she could have him, nothing else mattered.

But, she thought as she walked out onto the stage and watched thousands of people rise to their feet in a thunderous ovation, *I too, must have a touch of megalomania.* Because as her admirers stomped their feet, clapped their hands and shouted her name, she raised her arms in triumph, knowing that while she loved Jed, tonight mattered.

Power mattered.

". . . as a mother, I worry about the welfare of all children. As a woman, I fear violent assertions of male domination. As a member of Congress, I've been frustrated by the limits of power, but I've also learned the difference between authority and effective leadership."

Otis Jefferson, comfortably sprawled on the couch in Ben's library, gave an appreciative nod. The camera zoomed in on Georgie Hughes for a close-up.

"This election comes at a time when we have innocent people being held hostage. Many, including President Haynes and our opposition will offer solutions based on their experiences. Some will tout their record of military service. Others will showcase their years of public service. I take pride in standing alongside a man who represents a life of service to the American people, a man I believe will not only bring about the resolution of this current crisis, but prevent incidents like this from ever happening again."

Hundreds of EDWARDS/HUGHES placards danced in front of the podium as chants of "Georgie! Georgie!" filled the convention hall. Georgie indulged the crowd for a minute or two, then moved in close to the microphone, her eyes looking straight into the camera.

"I know there are those who distrust politicians and disbelieve their promises. You've been disappointed in the past. But you won't be disappointed in the future with a president and vice president whose primary concern is security: whether it's sleeping peacefully at home or going to school or doing our nation's work abroad. General

Edwards and I take pride in being private citizens and public servants. But our biggest pride is in being parents. Which is why we believe that when the question is asked, 'Do you know where your children are?' everyone in this land should be able to say 'Yes. And they're safe!' "

"It was a good speech," Otis said, heartily joining in the applause. "I'd say you've got your work cut out for you!"

"I'd say you're right!" Ben laughed as he muted the sound on the TV. The demonstrations would go on for a while. "The woman is dynamite!"

"Speaking of dynamite women . . ." Otis said. "Where's my favorite diplomat these days?"

Ben groaned. He had known Zoë would become a topic of conversation. "Avoiding me," he said, as he began to pace.

"Did you do something to provoke such a negative attitude?"

"I proposed."

Otis's eyes boggled. "And she said no?"

Ben leaned against a bookcase, folded his arms across his chest and nodded his head, still amazed. "Turned me down flat and refused to discuss it." He kneaded his brow, exhausted from weeks of trying to make sense of something that to him, made no sense. "She loves me, Otis. And I did everything I could to convince her I loved her."

Otis was confused. "So what do you think it is?"

"I get the feeling something's spooking her."

"You're running for president. She's already lost one husband to fanatics."

"I brought that up. She said yes, that was part of it. But trust me, Otis, it's a cover for the real reason."

"Which is what?"

"I have no idea!" Ben raised his arms and his voice in frustration. "She's wary of Edwards and with good reason. The guy's made trashing her career his life's work, but really! Whatever the hell went on between them is history."

"History has a funny way of rising up and smacking you in the face," Otis reminded Ben.

"True."

"Maybe she just doesn't want to complicate the campaign," Otis conjectured. "She's a pro, Ben, which means she's not going to allow herself to become an issue. The public wants to know what you'd do about the hostages. Not where you'd take your bride on a honeymoon."

"I said we'd wait until after the election."

"Is it the kids?" Otis asked.

"I don't think so. She and Ryan have a thing for each other. As for Keeley's hostility, Zoë tries not to incite it, but she's not put off by it either. She actually said she thinks Keeley's terrific." He shrugged at the irony. "I just keep telling myself Zoë loves me and that whatever it is will resolve itself. I haven't given up on us, Otis. Not by a long shot."

"How do things look for the convention?"

"As up in the air as my love life. But," Ben said, brightening, "since you've brought it up, let me tell you why I wanted you to stop by after your meeting with our illustrious mayor."

"You want me to sing the national anthem." They both knew he was tone deaf.

"Hardly," Ben replied

"You want me to deliver the keynote at the convention."

"Sam suggested Bill Rutledge from California."

Otis conceded. Not only was Rutledge an incredible orator, but he headed a state rich in electoral votes. "Nominating speech?"

"I've asked Kate Siegel to do that."

"Brilliant choice. So I get one of the seconding speeches?"

Ben shook his head, laughing at his friend's feigned dismay.

"Miss Congeniality?"

"How about second line on the ballot?" Otis stared as if Ben were speaking in tongues. "Vice president. Running mate. When I say something you understand, blink twice."

"Have you gone totally off the deep end?"

Ben grew serious. "I don't think so, Otis. I need a running mate who's known to the public as an honest, hard-working man who has the strength, the guts, and the intestinal fortitude to take on whatever problems face the country. You're that man. I also need someone I can trust. And there's no one I trust more than you."

Otis shook his head, truly stunned by Ben's request. "Have you forgotten I'm black?"

"Most of the time I don't think about it, but no, I haven't forgotten."

"There are millions of Americans who think about race all the time, Ben. The Simpson trial proved that."

"There are millions of Americans—both black and white—who think Colin Powell is a hell of a guy," Ben countered.

Otis considered both statements. "I just don't think you should be rolling the dice on whether this country is ready for an African-American a heartbeat away from the presidency. You should be going with a sure thing."

"I'm going with the man I feel would do the best job for me and for the country. There will always be racists, Otis, but there are plenty of people who've accepted the reality that America is an ethnically diverse nation. Some might not love it that way, but they've learned to live with it." Ben smiled. "Just like we did."

Scottie Edwards was nearing the end of his acceptance speech when the television station broke away for a special bulletin. Dean Walsh, looking unusually grim, faced the camera.

"We interrupt this program with an important announcement. At approximately 6:00 A.M. Moscow time, an assassination attempt was made on the life of Yuri Borofsky, president of Russia. Though details are sketchy, it appears that a band of well-armed men attacked the president's car as he was leaving his apartment in the Kremlin. President

Borofsky was shot in the chest and rushed to a hospital, where he is in surgery. Doctors remain cautious.''

Scottie was given the news in the midst of a raucous balloon shower. Arlo Reid wormed his way through the throng crowding the podium and whispered into Scottie's ear. The General's arms stopped waving, frozen in a vee above his head. His heart thundered in his chest as his eyes darted about the arena. Suddenly, instead of a sea of supporters, he saw an assassin lurking behind every placard.

"Get me out of here!" he muttered, a cold halo of sweat beading his brow.

Arlo inched close to Scottie, bumping him so he knew Arlo was armed. "Stand behind Georgie. If there's anyone here, and I don't think there is, they're not going to shoot her to get to you."

The convention finale was scheduled to last twenty minutes, but Scottie couldn't take it any longer. Holding Emily's hand on one side and Georgie's on the other, he hoisted their arms in a traditional victory salute, held that pose until he thought his skin would jump off his body, then exited the stage.

Back in Scottie's suite, Clay Chandler erupted

"What the hell happened? Did you suffer a spontaneous lobotomy?" His face was so puffed and red he looked like an overripe tomato. "You left the networks with ten minutes of nothing but convention hall bumpkins as a backdrop for their in-depth analyses of your speech."

Clay glowered at his boss, showing no concern about whether or not he was embarrassing him.

"Instead of talking about how inspiring you were and how leadership positively oozes out of every pore, they're speculating about heart attacks, diarrhea, indigestion, cold feet, and whether Haynes might include you in the presidential delegation attending Borofsky's funeral if the guy dies. What they're *not* talking about is the Edwards/Hughes ticket!"

"I'd had enough." Scottie's voice was clipped. His jaw

was clamped as tight as his fists. "Now if you don't mind, I'm tired."

His tone indicated there would be no further explanation. A confused staff complied with the General's request to empty the room. Neither Arlo nor Clay budged. Emily walked over to Scottie, caressed his cheek, and put her hands on her husband's arms. Though it appeared a wifely bracing, it was Emily's way of shutting the others out.

"Since I know you couldn't care less about what happens to Yuri Borofsky, it wasn't the tragic news about his health that turned your complexion to chalk," she hissed, locking her gaze onto his. "What exactly did your rottweiler say that prompted you to walk off the podium in front of millions of viewers?"

His eyes were blank, as if he had lost the capacity to reason out even the most elementary response. Emily was tempted to liken his expression to the proverbial deer in the headlights, but his hands were frosty and trembling. His fear was genuine. Quickly, she ran through a list of possibilities: from Haynes making a deal to release the hostages to Scottie's treasurer absconding with millions in campaign funds. He shook his head, she scratched hers. Since the only thing Scottie feared was that which he couldn't control, Clay couldn't manipulate, or Arlo couldn't silence, Emily suddenly suspected that instead of a complicated political tangle, it was the erupting of a tawdry situation they all thought they had contained.

Her grip on Scottie's arms tightened as she saw her dreams being dashed by his stupidity. "Tell me it isn't a page out of your inglorious past catching up to you," she said, her eyes filled with disgust.

"No," Scottie said. *Not yet,* he thought.

Throughout the week, Scottie Edwards danced on a tightrope, defining his abrupt behavior at the convention as the result of shock and heartfelt concern.

"I found it difficult to celebrate when elsewhere in the world terrorists had attacked a personal friend and long-time ally of the United States."

According to the polls, the public bought it. Two weeks before the Democrats picked their candidates, the Edwards/Hughes campaign could claim 60 percent of the vote.

President Haynes spoke to the nation from the Oval Office, expressing his wishes for the Russian president's speedy recovery and publicly decrying the attempted assassination "as the work of demagogic cowards who feared the spread of democracy and freedom." Privately, he dispatched an envoy to meet with Durgunov's negotiators to demand an explanation as well as an accounting of the American hostages.

Lamar Basalt took to the floor of the Senate and ordered the cessation of aid payments to Russia as well as a hold on all wheat shipments until it became clear who was in charge.

"I will not allow American generosity to blindly gift those with no regard for the laws of international conduct and decent behavior!"

Mack Kenton exhorted the American public to pray for Borofsky and for the lost souls of those who would commit such dastardly acts.

"Now is not the time for President Haynes to act in haste," he cautioned. "This is a regrettable turn of events, but we must not allow it to push us into actions that could cause greater remorse in the future."

Ben Knight was the only politician to express his outrage openly.

"How many more people are going to be allowed to fall victim to Yegor Durgunov?" he seethed in an interview with Dean Walsh. "First it was innocent American citizens and now the president of Russia. President Haynes should use the full authority of his office to demand the immediate release of our hostages."

"Does that include the use of the military?" Walsh asked, anticipating a tiptoe.

Ben didn't skip a beat. "If necessary? Absolutely."

☆   ☆   ☆

As Borofsky's condition improved, newshounds sniffed around for something to fill the usual lull between the conventions. Always eager for a new heroine, the media leaped upon the naming of Kate Siegel as Humanitarian of the Year by the Children's Defense Fund. *Newsweek* put her picture on the cover, heralding her as "the national spokeswoman for America's children." *Time* ran a feature on how she had impacted the legal system, demonstrating the awesome power of grassroots advocacy. Major newspapers in those states where legislation to jail child molesters for life was being considered ran laudatory pieces on her indefatigable efforts to eliminate parole for predators who targeted children. Each of the networks had interviewed her for their nightly news shows. Naturally, Kate gave Celia enough to fill half of NTN's magazine show.

The night of the dinner, Celia planted herself in the lobby of the Mayflower Hotel, stopping every notable— and there were many—for a comment. She would decide which ones to keep later, in the editing room.

Beth Haynes's was a keeper: "Kate Siegel has become the spokeswoman for the preservation of innocence."

"I'm proud that I played a role in making certain the NOMORE! legislation made it through Congress," vice-presidential candidate Georgie Hughes boasted.

Much as Celia adored Georgie, that was made-for-TV campaign rhetoric simply begging to be challenged.

"While it's true you sponsored the bill in the House, NOMORE! wasn't your triumph alone. Benjamin Knight, your likely opponent, pushed the bill in the Senate."

Georgie, too cagey to allow herself to be drawn into a debate, spun Celia's comment around so that her interview ended on a positive note. "It's a tribute to Kate Siegel that she had both sides of the aisle on her side."

Celia smiled as she wished Georgie luck in the election and concluded the segment.

Zoë cold-shouldered Celia, but Celia refused to be put off. She planted herself in Zoë's path and stuck a microphone in her face, blocking all avenues of escape.

"Zoë Vaughn, foreign policy advisor to Senator Knight and longtime friend of Kate Siegel's: How do you feel about tonight's ceremony?"

"I wish it wasn't happening," Zoë said quietly, momentarily confusing Celia. "I wish Mira Siegel was alive and home with her family."

Beneath the eye of a close-up lens, Celia went to take Zoë's hand, hoping to use this moment of remembrance to rekindle their damaged friendship, but Zoë rebuffed her, responding instead to the red light of the camera.

"As for this award," she said, speaking to the invisible audience beyond the lens, "the Children's Defense Fund picked a very worthy recipient. Kate Siegel could have mourned alone, but like many women, she transformed the pain of her personal tragedy into action against a larger tragedy. She used the system the way it was designed to be used: bringing a concern of the people to the Congress created by the people, to enact protective laws for the people."

When the red light went off, Zoë started to walk away, but Celia stopped her. She dismissed her camera crew and nudged Zoë into a corner.

"I know how angry you are, and I'm sorry," Celia pleaded. "It was news. I had to air it."

"It was an innocent photograph that you deliberately misconstrued."

"I would never deliberately hurt you."

Zoë's pale green eyes became glaciers. "Are you saying you maligned my integrity, subliminally accused me of treasonous activities, and plunged an arrow into the heart of Ben's campaign by accident?"

"There was a lot of pressure on me," Celia said, debating whether or not she should tell Zoë about Clay's threats concerning Hugo. "You have to believe me. I had no choice."

"There was a lot of pressure on you?" Zoë said, mocking Celia. "Anatoly had to be hidden away in a safe house, under guard. Thanks to you, that poor man's life is in danger."

What Zoë didn't tell Celia was that she was being plagued by telephone hang-ups and had received several anonymous threats in the mail.

"I didn't mean to . . ."

"Celia," Zoë said, forcefully breaking away, "if you don't mean it, don't do it!"

Dejectedly, Celia watched as Zoë strode across the lobby into the ballroom. She was about to follow when Quinn stopped her.

"I miss you," he said.

"Too bad I can't say the same." Anxious to get away from him and catch up to Zoë, she started toward the ballroom, but he stopped her again.

"Have you been to a doctor?"

"That's none of your business," she hissed, praying that no one overheard.

"I've made it my business." She tried to pull away. He tightened his grip. "Please. Get that lump checked."

She turned her head. He pulled her close and leaned in toward her ear. "I'll go with you. Don't be afraid."

She jerked herself free and spun on him, her eyes large and moist. "All you ever talked about was how beautiful I was and what a wonderful body I had and how much you loved my breasts!"

"I love *you,*" Quinn insisted, rattled by her reaction.

"You feasted on my body. How ravenous would your appetite be if I was disfigured? Would you love me then? Would you want me if I had chemotherapy and was throwing up and lost my hair and had to wear wigs and scarves? Would I be beautiful then? How dare you tell me not to be afraid!"

She stormed away, leaving a tornado of fear in her wake.

Quinn could do nothing but stand there, frightened for her because of what could happen. Frightened for himself because he didn't know what he would do without her.

Several feet away, a reporter from another network had corralled Rick Siegel and was asking him if he and Mack Kenton had resolved their differences. Rick said they hadn't spoken since the hearings.

"In less than a week, Congressman Kenton may be the Democratic candidate for president. Though it's widely known that you're a friend of Senator Knight, would you support the Congressman if he wins the nomination?"

This was why Rick loathed the press. The question had no purpose other than to create controversy.

"I could never support a man who would sacrifice what is right on the altar of political profit," Rick retorted, giving the reporter the sound bite he wanted, raising his voice so others would catch the same story. As other microphones poked toward his mouth, he went on. "Congressman Kenton's explanation as to why he voted no on Mira's bill was disingenuous, self-motivated, and mean-spirited. This was a rare commodity: feel-good legislation designed to protect children. It was not, by any stretch of the imagination, a political ploy on my part or my wife's. We lost a daughter. Somewhere along the line, in his quest for votes, Congressman Kenton lost his soul!"

Off to the side, unbeknownst to Rick, Kate silently applauded.

Five hundred people crowded the ornate Grand Ballroom, filling not only the main floor, but the balconies and terraces as well. Georgie, Lyle, Hunt, Olivia, and the senior Hugheses were at one table along with Emily Edwards; the General was in California at a fund-raiser. Ben, his children, Loretta, Zoë, Jed Oakes, and the Jeffersons were seated at another. Celia and Quinn were up in the press section, on separate terraces.

Georgie made certain her back was to Jed. She had passed him in the lobby and ached from wanting him. If she had to face him, she wouldn't be able to hide her feelings. And she had to. Being the V.P. nominee had plunged her into a giant goldfish bowl.

Even harder than concealing her love for Jed was disguising her loathing of Lyle. He insisted upon making a game out of their public appearances, testing her calm every chance he got. Every time a camera focused on Georgie, he leaned in close—making certain he was in the picture—and whispered something taunting.

Georgie found it exhausting pretending to the world that this was a marriage. On the advice of her new confidante, Emily Edwards, she suggested to Clay Chandler that they use Hunt and Olivia wherever and whenever it seemed plausible—the same for Roy and Wade—but that she and Lyle campaign together as little as possible. As Emily had indicated, Clay was satisfied with a sketch. Georgie didn't have to fill in any details.

In what was probably an attempt at compassion, Clay had said: "Don't worry about Lyle. You're going to be on the road so much, by November you won't even remember what your husband looks like, let alone why you don't get along."

Just then, she remembered very well. Lyle's jealousy oozed from every pore. Making it worse, she could sense Jed's eyes on her back. She could see Hunt and Olivia fending off reporters, trying to adjust to the widened glare of their mother's spotlight. She could hear her name being whispered throughout the room. She should have felt exhilarated, flush with accomplishment and admiration. Instead, she felt a rush of panic, just as she had that day on the sidewalk outside school when everyone pointed fingers at her and demanded to know: Who is Georgie Hughes?

The campaign had just begun, yet Georgie couldn't wait for it to be over.

After moving speeches by Georgie Hughes and Benjamin Knight, both of whom peppered their acclamatory comments with warm reminiscences, First Lady Beth Haynes came to the podium. The program said she was to present Kate with her award. Instead, she introduced Ethan Siegel.

Ethan strode purposefully to the center of the stage, glanced at his father, who was at the table just below the podium, kissed his mother, who was seated on the dais next to the lectern, stepped onto the box provided for him, and adjusted the microphone.

He scanned the assemblage, realized how large his audience was, and froze. Fortunately, when paralysis struck, Zoë was in his sight. She cued him by exaggerating a deep breath. He followed her direction, breathed and began.

"Since my mother is about to receive an award for her work on behalf of children, I thought you should hear from *her* child."

His speech started out light and anecdotal, seasoned with amusing memoirs.

Keeley Knight listened to his monologue with lasered fascination. Recently, Keeley had sought to understand why she was so obsessed with protecting the burnish on her mother's memory. It was a difficult journey of recovery and discovery, one cobbled with the painful stones of loss and disappointment. In Ethan, she recognized a fellow traveler.

Ethan was eight when Mira was murdered; Keeley was seven when her mother was killed. Yet while Ethan regaled his listeners with specific stories, Keeley's recollections were mostly of the scrapbook variety: flat, one-dimensional images framed by generalizations. No matter how hard she fought to keep the storybook perfect, a storm of restored memories compelled her to view Felicia without the gauzy veil that hides imperfections and distorts reality.

Ethan's talk struck a chord because not only was he acutely aware of his parents' achievements and foibles, he was accepting of both. Which was why his journey appeared far more successful than hers. Although, she told herself defensively, he had lost a sibling. She had lost the person to whom a child was supposed to cleave forever: her mother. Worse, Keeley believed she had lost Felicia long before the accident that took her life.

"There used to be two of us," Ethan was saying, turning somber as he prepared to expose the raw side of his heart. "As most of you know, I had an older sister named Mira." His young voice trembled as he tiptoed through the shadows. "I loved her very much."

Again, he sought encouragement from Rick, who was battling his own phantoms.

"Mira was born with a heart defect, but to me she was perfect. She was bright and funny and unbelievably caring. We fought like any other brother and sister and occasionally, I admit, I was jealous of all the attention she got. What made Mira so amazing was that she understood how I felt and did everything she could to make up for it. When she was sick, she'd make me sit with her so that I was in the room when Mom and Dad were doing their concerned-parent thing. Whatever I did, she'd make a big deal, as if demanding equal time for me.

"In the beginning, just after Mira was killed, I didn't know what to do or how to feel. I was horrified at what had happened to her, frightened that it could happen to me, angry about what was happening to my family. And sometimes embarrassed that, again, I felt jealous and left out. The one thing I never felt was unloved."

Ethan gave Kate a wobbly smile, then turned to his father. Rick's jaw was tight, his struggle for control evident as he signaled his son to go on.

"When Mira was taken from us, no one would have blamed my mom if she had locked herself away. Not even me. But she didn't. Instead, she went on a crusade to make sure that what happened to Mira wouldn't happen to your daughter," he said, pointing to a man in the audience, "or your son," he said to a woman in the middle, "or yours," he said, pointing to several people throughout the room.

"With the help of her friends, me and my dad, and thousands of strangers who became her friends, she turned her campaign against parole for those who commit crimes against children into the law of the land."

He held out his hand, inviting Kate to stand next to him.

"Tonight, it's my honor to present my mom with the Children's Defense Fund's Humanitarian of the Year Award. Take it from someone who knows, she deserves it. She's a really remarkable woman who's always defended a child's right to be a child. Thanks, Mom."

As Kate embraced her son, the audience clambered to its feet, most wiping tears from their eyes. Zoë was too emotional to applaud. She simply stood and watched and wept. When finally they took their seats, in the silence before Kate accepted her award, Keeley's hand found Zoë's and held it.

After Ethan and the rest of the family had retired, Rick and Kate shared a few moments alone in her suite.

"I wanted you to know how proud I am," he said. "And how grateful. You've provided Mira with a living monument that befits her memory."

Rick's tone drew Kate's attention to his eyes, in which she saw a ravenous melancholy. Guiltily, she realized that at some undocumented moment in time, she had begun to think of Mira's death as her own personal tragedy. She had erased Mira's father from the equation, as if he had never loved his daughter or searched for her or died inside when she was found or mourned her after she was gone. She had discounted his grief and his rage and his resolve, counting hers as the only emotion that mattered. Kate shivered at the depth of her selfishness.

"Did you help Ethan with his speech?" she asked.

"A little."

"I suspected as much." A maternal smile warmed her countenance. "He's quite a young man, isn't he?" Rick couldn't find the voice to respond. "He takes after his father."

Still, Rick said nothing. Quickly, Kate changed the subject.

"I was at the other end of the lobby when you took on that reporter who tweaked you about Kenton." A sly grin loped across her lips. "Boy! Were you loud!" She laughed. "Very clever."

Rick tipped an imaginary hat, wondering what had prompted this delightful thaw.

"You may have handed Ben the nomination."

"That would be great," he said, seizing the opportunity. "Especially since the second reason I moved back to New York is to manage his advertising campaign."

Kate's surprise was instantaneous and, Rick thought, positive.

"The main reason is, I'd like to try and bring our family together again."

She tensed. He leaned toward her.

"I still love you, Kate. Actually, I never stopped. I think those feelings simply got tangled up in the destructive jumble of anger and self-pity I was wallowing around in."

She tried to look away, but there was a compelling force emanating from him that demanded her attention.

"Mira was my firstborn child," he said softly. "She was my fragile little flower, the delicate princess who I always believed needed her daddy to protect her, to make sure she didn't have too much sun or too little sleep or too much activity. She was the best of me and the best of you, just as Ethan is the best of both of us. When she died, I believed my best wasn't good enough, that it was my failure that had made her vulnerable to that animal."

His lips quivered slightly.

"I did what you wanted, by the way. I found a therapist and worked through an awful lot of stuff."

"Like . . ." she prompted.

"Like being furious with you for being furious with me."

Kate smiled. "Sounds fair. What else?"

"Like being ashamed when my shrink told me that most families who experience this kind of trauma fall apart. I took it as another sign of weakness. If I had been stronger or tried harder or hurt less, we could have beaten the norm." Suddenly, his eyes crinkled. "If there's anything I detest, it's being predictable."

"Yes, I know." She returned his smile until a thought crossed her mind, one that immediately narrowed her gaze. "Is this reconciliation speech your way of salving your ego?"

"This may be hard for you to believe, but I don't have much of an ego anymore."

"How about your recent successes in Hollywood? From what Ethan tells me, you're pretty high on that."

"Having people appreciate what you do is always a good thing, but it's not the only thing. That's why I do what I can for NOMORE! That's why I'm working for Ben. That's why I've volunteered to speak to groups of parents who've lost children to violent crimes." Kate's eyes widened. "Before, I took more than I gave. Now, I take only what I need and give back all that I can. It's my way of keeping faith with Mira."

Kate felt tears begin to gather and quickly wiped them away. The award, the speeches, this: it was too much too fast. She was glad Rick was coming home, yet concerned that his presence would disturb the delicate balance that had become her life. It had been a struggle, but she had moved forward. And while he didn't sound as if he wanted to go backwards, forward was, after all, a direction, not a destination.

"It'll be nice to have you close by," was all she could say.

* * *

When Quinn knocked on Celia's door she tried to ignore him, but he continued pounding until she relented.

"What do you want?" she demanded, refusing to grant him entry.

"We need to talk."

"We've said all there is to say."

He pushed against the door just as Celia was about to slam it shut. "Yes, thank you, I'd love a nightcap," he said, moving quickly inside.

"I'm fresh out of whatever you might want, including water, and frankly, Quinn, I'm not in the mood to spar with you."

"Rough night, tonight?"

"Emotional," Celia said, reflecting mostly on Ethan's speech and Kate's response.

"The tributes to Kate were moving. You have some amazing friends."

Celia nodded, but absently. Her mind and her heart were full.

"Speaking of friends," Quinn said, "I saw you and Zoë Vaughn doing an in-your-face in the lobby."

"Let's just say that with Zoë, my Q rating's at an all-time low."

"Hard to blame her."

Celia's back stiffened. "It was a legitimate story."

Quinn shrugged. "It was intriguing and fabulous television, but be honest, babe. It was mostly circumstantial."

"Like you wouldn't have aired it," she scoffed.

"I would have, but the star of the piece isn't my best friend." He eyed Celia carefully, noting that every one of her defense mechanisms had been activated. "What were you doing? Buying a leg on a co-anchor chair?"

"That's unfair."

"Unfair?" he sniffed, suddenly angry. "You want to talk unfair? How about that stuff you spouted at me earlier tonight? That crap about me loving you for your body?"

He took Celia by the arms and held her in front of him. "That's not true, and you know it!"

"Really!" Celia huffed as she tried unsuccessfully to wriggle out of his grasp.

"Yeah. Really. You know how I feel about you, Celia. I've made that as clear as I could. So you know I'm giving it to you straight when I tell you that right now I wouldn't care if you turned into a frog! All I want is for you to go to a doctor."

"And all I want is for you to leave me alone!"

She wrenched free and demanded that he go. He stood his ground for a minute or two, but when she underscored her wishes by pushing him out the door, he obliged her. She slammed the door, double-locked it, and waited to hear him walk away. He lingered for a bit, but eventually, he left.

Celia felt horribly alone, but, she chastised herself, she should have known not to get involved with a man like Sean Quinn. She should have resisted his effortless charm. But no. She had allowed herself to be taken in by his winsome ways and the similarities to her father. She had been blinded by his stunning intellect and his silly Irish humor and the volcanic feelings he was able to arouse in her. She should have known it was nothing but sex, that he was going to use her and then hurt her, just like the others. But when they were together, it felt different. It felt perfect.

Slowly, as if a magnet were drawing it, Celia's hand found its way to her chest. She touched her breast and a tear fell.

Nothing was ever as perfect as it seemed.

☆   ☆   ☆

Three days before the start of the Democratic convention, Sean Quinn broke the story of Scottie Edwards's illegitimate child. From her hotel room in Chicago, Zoë watched the report with a muted sense of satisfaction. Everything she had given Quinn was there, and more.

In 1976, following America's withdrawal from Vietnam,

Scottie Edwards served as the president's liasion to the commanding officer in Hawaii. During that time, he carried on an affair with Trude Sargent, an army nurse. The romance produced an out-of-wedlock child, a daughter named Cleo. Though his name didn't appear on Cleo's birth certificate as the father, he had paid Trude's expenses as well as the down payment on a small house in Ewa, west of Pearl Harbor. According to FBI records, when Trude was discharged from the army, she took her daughter home to Minnesota and in 1980 sued Scottie Edwards for paternity. The suit was settled for forty thousand dollars. In 1984, Trude's new husband, Ron Wells, adopted Cleo. Scottie didn't contest; he demanded Trude sign a document barring Trude from any further contact with him.

Quinn had followed up Zoë's dossier by tracking down Cleo Wells. The young woman he found was striking, with long, thick blond hair, piercing blue eyes, high cheekbones, an aquiline nose that bore more than a passing resemblance to the man she claimed was her biological father, and an anger that could only have had its genesis in the most heinous form of rejection: that of a parent for a child.

It hadn't been difficult to find Cleo because she had filed another paternity suit against the man who would be president.

"What's the point?" Quinn asked at the start of the interview.

Cleo Wells looked remarkably assured. She wasn't intimidated by the cameras or Quinn's patented green-eyed glare of skepticism.

"Scottie Edwards is my father, a fact he's chosen to ignore my entire life."

Quinn watched for signs of uncertainty: a twiddling of the fingers, excessive blinking, a dryness of the mouth. There were none.

"Are you looking for public acknowledgment of his paternity?" Quinn's tone indicated how petty he thought that was. "Or money?"

Cleo looked at him directly. "Money," she said without flinching. "My mother is desperately ill. According to her doctors, the cancer was caused by exposure to Agent Orange during her tours in Vietnam."

"Why isn't her husband, your adoptive father, taking care of her?" Quinn knew the answer, but it was better TV coming from her.

"Ron Wells died five years ago. He owned a small printing business in St. Paul. When Mom got sick, I left school and tried to take over the business, but the recession has hit us hard. It's all I can do to keep the presses rolling and a roof over our heads, let alone keep up with the medical bills."

"Why not apply to the Veteran's Administration for government assistance?" Quinn said, impressed by her unapologetic, front and center demeanor.

"I did. Unfortunately, the government doesn't move as quickly as cancer." Her chin quivered, but only for a second. "That's why I went to my natural father for help. When he refused, I sued him for eighteen years of unpaid child support."

"A spokesman for General Edwards denies the claim that he's your father."

"Then let him take a blood test."

Quinn leaned back, placed his elbow on the arm of his chair, rested his chin in the palm of his hand, and studied Cleo Wells. If she was a charlatan, she was well rehearsed and unbelievably slick. His gut said she was the real thing.

"This same spokesman says you're looking at the General's campaign as an opportunity for a big payoff."

Cleo's jaw visibly tightened. "Scottie Edwards knows I'm his daughter, and while he has never formally acknowledged it, he was right by my mom's side when I was born. Years later, when faced with a paternity suit, he settled out of court. Why would he do that if he wasn't my father?"

"To spare his wife, Emily, and their children the embarrassment of a false claim," Quinn offered.

Cleo leaned forward, baiting the camera to move in for

a close-up. "Scottie Edwards can tell the world whatever he wants. He can say he's a devoted husband and father. He can say he and my mother were simply friends. He can say he feels terrible that the health-care system in this country makes people like me do desperate things like this."

In an almost eerie imitation of Scottie Edwards, she narrowed her blue-eyed gaze, thrust her chin forward, and dared the audience to disbelieve her.

"He can say lots of things, but the truth is: Scottie Edwards is a deadbeat dad!"

Three days after the story of Scottie Edwards's love child broke, a poll was taken. The General's numbers had dropped from 60 to 52 percent.

☆   ☆   ☆

From the podium of the Omni Coliseum in Atlanta, Bill Rutledge delivered the keynote address of the Democratic National Convention. On the floor, nearly seven thousand people listened in rapt silence to the powerful oratory of the senator from California. Those near enough to see the podium watched the tall, well-built man with the ruddy complexion and dimpled smile in person. The rest kept their eyes on the huge video screens that flanked the stage.

It was a sign of the tremendous esteem in which Rutledge was held that while he reminded the nation of its roots and called for a "renewal of America's pride in its melting pot diversity," the frenetic scouting of delegates had stopped. When he finished, they were back at it. A state held an on-the-floor caucus and Mack Kenton's people or Ben Knight's emissaries were there, cajoling, arm-twisting, bargaining, doing and saying whatever they had to in order to change minds and shift votes.

Before 1952, brokered conventions were the norm; behind-the-scenes deals and vote trading were commonplace. Since then, convention delegates didn't choose the front-runner, they confirmed his nomination. This time, however, the race between Mack Kenton and Benjamin Knight was simply too close to call.

Several blocks away from the mayhem in the Coliseum, in a hotel suite overlooking Peachtree Center, Mack Kenton had come to do some bargaining of his own. When he called that afternoon to request the audience, Jed Oakes and Sam Trout advised Ben not to meet with him alone.

"Kenton wants the nomination too badly to be trusted," Sam had said. "I don't care about his holier-than-thou persona. My *kishkas* tell me he's a bad guy."

Jed agreed. "He could be wired."

Ben acceded to their wishes only because he recalled Amalia's warning about Kenton's blathering how he would come out the victor because he had angels on his shoulder or some such thing. Ben allowed Sparks Osborn to rig up a voice-activated taping device.

Kenton arrived at precisely ten o'clock that evening. He came right to the point.

"Neither of us is going to win the nomination on the first ballot. I think you know that."

Ben shrugged. He was not conceding anything.

"Once that formality is over, I'd like you to release your delegates so they can vote for me."

It was such a cheeky request, Ben laughed outright. "And why should I do that?"

"Because I have the power." Kenton's visage remained eerily sanguine and sure.

"To do what?"

"To lead this nation back onto the road of glory and greatness." His pale gray eyes burned with conviction.

In Italy, Amalia had wondered if Kenton was unbalanced. Now Ben wondered as well.

"That's an admirable ambition, Mack, but in case you failed to notice, this is not a religious crusade. It's an election, and, as we speak, I believe I have the lion's share of the votes. Since I also believe I'd make a damn good president, I'd rather leave the decision to the delegates."

Mack shook his head. "What you believe and what you'd like is of no consequence."

Ben was growing impatient. "It's late, Kenton, and I'm not in the mood for games, so if you don't mind, say whatever it is you came to say."

Annoyance evidenced itself in a pinched expression. Mack didn't appreciate being rushed.

"You're going to do what I ask because if you don't, I'm going to take my son away from you."

"What!" Ben thought he had heard wrong.

"Ryan is not your son. He's mine."

For a moment, Ben was certain he would faint. Like a fighter who had just absorbed a horrific blow, instinct demanded that he strike back with equal force, but his body was unable to comply. Instead, he staggered to a mental corner and prayed for the ringing in his brain to stop.

"Your wife, Felicia, and I had a rather long affair. Ryan is the product of that romance."

"You're lying," Ben said, barely controlling his rage.

Kenton calmly shook his head. "I'm many things, but I'm not a liar." He reached into his pocket and withdrew several sheets of paper. "These are copies of some of the letters Felicia wrote me. I think you'll find them rather enlightening."

Ben recognized Felicia's neat, feminine penmanship immediately. Unfamiliar to him was the passion contained within these billets-doux. He and Felicia had enjoyed an active, vigorous sex life, but this was a voluptuous, almost consumptive ardor, one that blazed at a constant, heated pitch, even when physical distance separated the lovers. He knew that because it was the same passion he felt for Zoë now.

The most stunning letter was the one in which Felicia issued an ultimatum:

You tell me I'm sinful. Maybe I am, but I'm not alone
when I sin and no matter how often you worry that
our affair is profane, I know that wickedness excites you.
You crave it, even while you condemn it. You need
it, even while you deny it. You thrive on it, even though
you believe it will be your undoing. I know, because
I'm wicked too. I love secrets and hidden pleasures. I get
a kick out of sneaking around and getting away with
it. But sooner or later, my darling, everything goes stale.
Eventually, even the devil demands her due.

I've made as many sacrifices as I'm going to make.
I'm sick of hearing about your wife, your children,
your public image and your personal demons. I'm willing
to leave my family. I expect you to leave yours. If you
don't make things right for us, it's over.

While Ben read Felicia's letters and confronted her infidelity, Kenton described their relationship.

"It was wrong," he admitted with an air of surprise, as if he still could not believe he had succumbed to such base temptation, "but it was beyond our control."

"Were you going to do as she asked?" Ben seethed. "Were you going to make things right for the two of you?"

Mack responded with a piteous look. "The three of us," he insisted. "Ryan is not your son, Ben. I'm sorry, but that's the way it is."

Ben winced at such hideous blasphemy. "Funny. She doesn't mention Ryan in any of these," he said, tossing the letters onto the floor like the garbage he thought they were.

Quickly, Kenton bent down, scooped up his treasures, and returned them to the safety of his inner pocket. "She was being discreet."

Ben laughed at the ludicrousness of such a statement. "She writes about wanting to rut around your bed like some horny toad, and you call that discreet?"

"I meant that she was protecting Ryan." His eyes darted about the room, seeking a more comfortable view. "In

case someone who shouldn't know about that found the
letters."

"Someone like your wife?"

"Or you."

"Okay," Ben conceded, redirecting the conversation.
"If what you say is true, why didn't you claim Ryan before?
Felicia's been dead eight years. Where've you been?"

Kenton folded his hands into a prayerful clasp, closed
his eyes for a moment, then faced Ben.

"When Felicia told me she was pregnant, I asked the
obvious: If she was certain I was the father. She said you
and she rarely slept together." He seemed happy about
that, even now.

Ben battled to maintain an impassive expression. There
was no denying that around that time, there had been a
serious breach in his marriage. He and Felicia had begun
to lead separate lives and he had begun to suspect that his
wife had found others to fill in the blanks of her existence.
But he had not been totally absent from her bed.

"You haven't answered my question," Ben insisted.
"Why didn't you claim Ryan before now?"

"The year he was born, I was in a tough fight. My House
seat was vulnerable. Felicia didn't want to ruin my chances
of being reelected."

That was easy for Ben to accept. Felicia never would
have interfered with the courting of power; it was her
aphrodisiac. It was what had brought them together in the
first place: her belief—and her father's—that he could be
groomed for higher office, that one day he would be
Speaker of the House or Senate majority leader or even
president.

Ben cringed at his own weakness. Oliver Coburn had
dangled contacts and influence and money in front of him
and he had snapped at the bait. Ben had refused to admit
the depths of his ambition back then, but he had owned
up to it often over the years, as the cracks in his marriage
became chasms. He confessed it now. Felicia had been his

passport. He had been her conduit. It had been a marriage made in political heaven.

"How about the year after that or the one after that?" Ben asked.

Kenton squirmed uncomfortably in his seat. "It never seemed to be the right time. I was married. My kids were growing. Money was tight. I was shuttling between Washington and Iowa."

"You had a career you wanted to hang on to. And I guess claiming a child from a mistress isn't exactly a demonstration of family values, is it?" Ben mocked Kenton shamelessly. Then his eyes grew hard. "Ryan was four years old when Felicia was killed."

"I still can't believe she's gone," Kenton said, his voice deep as a dirge. "I mourn her every day."

"That's touching, but what about Ryan? Where did he fit into all this? Or didn't he? Was it simply too inconvenient for you to get around to seeing him or introducing yourself as his father?"

Kenton bristled. "Your wife was going to leave you. The son you thought was yours isn't. I can understand why you might be bitter."

"And after the accident?" Ben ignored the taunt. "Why didn't you come forward then? Where were you all those months that brave little boy spent in rehabilitiation? Why didn't you come to the hospital and visit *your* son then?"

"I was selfish and cowardly." Kenton shrugged. His behavior was a mystery to him. "Felicia was gone. I felt guilty about her and anxious about what a revelation like that would do to Maribel and my other children. And yes. I was concerned about my career."

"Why now?" Ben pressed. "Because you've found a way to use him to further your career?"

"I need to atone. I need to make things right, and the only way to do that is to bring the son home to the father."

"Ryan is not a form of penance, you self-absorbed, self-righteous prick! He's a child!" Ben's eyes flared as his temper snapped its restraints. *"My* child."

"I'm aware of how much you love him," Kenton said, with exaggerated patience. "Which is why I'm offering you a chance to keep him."

"In exchange for handing you the nomination."

"Yes."

Ben felt ill. This madman was bartering Ryan for delegates. "I wouldn't even entertain such a tawdry notion."

Kenton looked incredulous, as if he couldn't possibly understand why Ben would turn down such a generous offer. Then, for a moment or two, he appeared to be weighing something. Ben hoped whatever madness had possessed him was dissipating.

"If pressed," he said with astounding magnanimity, "I might settle for the vice-presidential nod."

"You made this bullshit story up to squeeze me, didn't you, you fucking lowlife?"

Amazingly, Kenton never flinched. "Whether I did or didn't, I wouldn't think you'd want this coming out during an election campaign."

"Are you threatening me?"

The light faded from Kenton's eyes, giving him a ghostly aspect. "I'm doing what I have to do."

"You're a sick man, Kenton, but before you leave, let's get a few things straight: you're not getting the nomination. You're not getting a slot on the ticket. And if you leak one word of this deranged fable to the press, burning in hell will seem like a vacation compared to what I'll do to you!"

For an hour after Kenton left, Ben paced, his mood desultory. He had to prepare Ryan in case Kenton went to the press, but just thinking about Ryan made his heart hurt. Ryan was his baby boy, the son he had adored from the moment of his birth, the son he had nursed back to health after the car accident, protected and played ball with and told stories to, the son he skied with and swam with and hiked with. How should he tell him that a stranger might question that connection?

And what about Keeley? How would she take this public airing of her mother's infidelity? She was Felicia's most ardent supporter.

Ben might have ruminated about this all night if Sam Trout hadn't called to find out what had transpired between the two candidates. Ben might have preferred keeping this to himself, but if Kenton planned to use Ryan as a ploy, his closest aides needed to know what they were up against.

In less than half an hour Sam, Jed, and Otis were settling in for what they assumed was an all-nighter. It didn't surprise anyone when a few minutes later, Zoë joined them.

"I needed you here," Ben said quietly when he let her in.

"I could tell." She winced at the pain she read in his eyes.

Ben wasted little time describing his contretemps. He felt that the tape did a far better job of conveying the severity of the situation than anything he could say. When it was over a cautious silence prevailed.

"That man is a few ribs shy of a barbecue," Jed said, clearly stunned by what he had heard.

Zoë had watched Ben's face throughout the playback. His distress was so raw it made her want to weep.

"This lunatic must have watched Edwards's poll numbers plummet after the love child story and decided to copycat it," Sam suggested.

"We've got the edge on the second ballot," Jed said, picking up Sam's thread. "His people know it. He has to know it. I think he dreamed up whatever he thought would let him deal for the V.P. slot."

"That's already taken," Ben said, tilting his head in Otis's direction.

"We don't have the nomination yet," Otis reminded everyone. "If he decided simply to float this as a rumor on the floor, it could hurt us."

"It's not true, so it can't fly." The veins in Sam's neck pulsed as he fought to govern his anger.

"But until we prove it's bogus," Jed said, "it can make as much of a mess as a flock of pigeons after a feeding."

"Is there a chance that it is true?" Zoë asked quietly, courageously voicing what no one else had dared.

Ben's face turned ashen. "I don't know. It could be." A thunderous silence canopied the room. "During those years, Felicia and I were apart more than we were together. And yes, she had . . . companions."

While the others began to study their fingernails or spots on the carpet, Zoë looked directly at Ben.

"A blood test would stop this dead in its tracks," she said, hoping he had that pertinent information on file.

Ben recalled that horrible night in the hospital after the accident when Ryan was rushed to the operating room and they were calling for blood. Ryan's type was B. Ben was A, making him an incompatible match. Celia was the only suitable donor. She gave, Ryan recovered, and Ben didn't think about it again. Until now.

"We'd have to run a DNA test," he said, glumly. "Which would give Kenton enough time to leak this to the press, throw the convention into complete disarray, and wreak havoc with my son's life."

"Let him." Zoë's uncompromising stance startled the men around her. She probably should have directed her comments to Ben, but it hurt too much to look at him. "Ben is Ryan's father. Ben says so. Ryan's birth certificate says so. And nothing in Felicia's letters says anything different. If Kenton wants to disclaim all that, fine! Then, it's up to him to make his case and answer the question even the dumbest reporter in the corps is going to ask: 'If you're Ryan Knight's natural dad, where've you been and why are you coming forward now?' Ben has nothing to explain. Kenton does."

"I don't want Ryan or Felicia to become fodder for the tabloids," Ben lamented.

"I understand," Zoë said, "but it's not up to you. Unless you've decided to give him your delegates or substitute him for Otis, that is."

Ben issued a sardonic laugh. Everyone knew he would never capitulate to Kenton's demands.

"You should warn Ryan," Sam said quietly.

Ben's voice was hollow and low. "It doesn't seem fair."

"He knows how much you love him," Zoë said, unable to squelch the tenderness she felt. "He knows that you would never put him through this if you could help it."

"He's a trouper," Sam said. "He'll handle it. You'll see."

"Just explain that this is simply politics at its dirtiest," Jed added. His nose crinkled as if his words carried with them a foul odor.

"I was so horribly naive," Ben said darkly. "I thought even politics had limits of decency. I never dreamed that when I threw my hat in the ring I'd be throwing my son to the lions."

When Ben arrived at Royal Oaks the next day, he found Ryan and Keeley in the pool. Loretta, Avis, and Oliver Coburn were sitting in the shade of the trellised poolhouse drinking lemonade. While the adults looked surprised to see him, his children were delighted and urged him to join them for a swim, which he did.

"Shouldn't he be at the Omni?" Oliver asked, watching his son-in-law splash about. "I know his minions are working the delegates, but still."

"Perhaps the nomination is sewn up," Avis suggested.

Loretta shook her head. Her eyes had not left Ben's face since his entrance. "Something's wrong," she said. "Terribly wrong."

After a lengthy swim, Ben cajoled Ryan and Keeley out of the water and asked them to get changed. He invited his two Secret Service agents to select swimsuits from the stack of sizes Avis kept in the cabana and cool off while everyone else joined him in the orangery.

Ever the hostess, Avis went to the kitchen to instruct her maid on what to set out as refreshments. Oliver saw to the comfort of the agents. Loretta went to her son and slipped her arm around his waist.

"Whatever it is, Ben, we'll get through it," she said, with quiet certainty.

Ben's eyes filled as he felt her hand pat his back. Suddenly he was eight years old, standing in that emergency room in South Philadelphia watching the paramedics race down the hall with his father and his brother. Loretta had said the same thing then: "Whatever it is, we'll get through it." He remembered those words, her tone of voice, how she had looked, how he had felt. He remembered every agonizing second of that long, excruciating night. He had thought he'd never experience that empty, eviscerated sense of desolation again, but he was feeling that same bleakness now.

As he put his arm around Loretta's shoulder and squeezed it reassuringly, he wondered, as he always did, how she had handled losing her husband and her son, how she had found the faith to forgive God and the strength to go on. He hoped her grit was genetic because just then, he needed it.

Avis and Oliver settled themselves on the white canvas couch that faced the gardens. In the beginning of their courtship, Ben and Felicia had spent many an evening on that couch. Again, as he had over the past several hours, he pondered the princess of this manor.

When Ben first met Felicia, she presented an exquisitely wrapped package of influence and access tied with beauty and voluptuousness. It wasn't long before Ben realized that the excitement he felt was a lusting for power masquerading as love. Also, that he could never satisfy her. Someone else always did things better; her father always had more. Ben hated feeling like less, so he worked harder, staying away from home more than he wanted in the hopes of being able to give Felicia whatever it was that she wanted. Eventually, he realized that he could never please his wife. It was then that he stopped caring.

As Ryan and Keeley walked in, Ben found himself staring,

searching for confirmation of his paternity. The first place he looked was into Ryan's eyes. They were light, slightly hazel, a blend of Felicia's brown and his blue. The hooded browline was definitely his. Ryan's upper lip was bowed. Ben's upper lip was thin, without much arch. Frantically, he searched his memory until he recalled that Felicia's lips had been full and wide and bowed. Ryan was an adolescent and shorter than Ben had been at that age. Ben looked closer, trying to gauge whether Ryan's body would fight its way out of its square and into the long and lean frame of the Knights, or stay in the stocky mode of the congressman from Iowa.

"Hey, Dad! What's up?" Ryan said, twisting his baseball cap around so the Atlanta Braves insignia on the brim faced the back. In his tee shirt, khaki shorts, and barely tied high-tops, his gangly arms and legs freshly burnished by the sun, he looked like an ad for contented youth.

For a minute, Ben considered saying nothing. Then he imagined Ryan reading this stuff in a newspaper. He seated Keeley and Ryan on a love seat and pulled a chair up opposite them.

"Did something happen at the convention?" Keeley looked nervous. "Is Kenton trying to steal the nomination from you?"

Worse than that, Ben thought.

"Actually, this is about Mack Kenton." He leaned his arms on his thighs and tented his fingers. After a deep breath that stumbled over the lump in his throat, he faced his children. "And your mother.

"Mack Kenton came to my room last night with a story about him and your mom," he said to both Keeley and Ryan. "He claims they were lovers."

Ryan's eyes boggled. Ben noticed a faint blush. Like every other young person, despite whatever he saw on TV or fantasized about in the dark, Ryan found it embarrassing to think of his parents having sex. Keeley didn't blush or flinch. Her shoulders stiffened, and her eyes remained fixed on Ben.

"He also claims that you, Ryan, are his son. Not mine." Ben's voice choked over the words.

"What?" Ryan's color suddenly drained, and, for a moment, he appeared to weave. Keeley put her arm around his waist to steady him. When he recovered, anxiety overcame him. "I'm not, right? I'm not his son, am I, Dad? I couldn't be. Right?"

"I'm your dad," Ben said, intent on assuaging Ryan's concerns. "The one and only, positively, absolutely, fully certified parent. Got it?"

Ryan nodded. His eyes leaked tears of relief.

Ben held Ryan's hand while he addressed the group.

"Kenton's threatened to give this to the newspapers if I don't release my delegates after the first ballot." His gaze wandered slowly from one to the other, assessing. "I told him I wouldn't."

"Good!" Ryan's jaw was tight. His eyes were glossy. So were Ben's.

"You say that now, but if he goes to the press, your name's going to be splashed over every newspaper and TV newscast in the country. It's not going to be pretty, Ryan. They're going to talk about your mother and me and who knows what else."

Ryan nodded as if the prospective brouhaha was okay with him, but he was clearly rattled. Ben hated himself for having created this disturbance, but his failed marriage was a fact—soon to be a public fact—and whether he liked it or not, prickly questions were floating around like pollen, making everyone squeamish and uncomfortable. Even without raising the subject of a blood test, he could tell it had entered the minds of Loretta and the Coburns.

"Is he going to talk about his affair with Mommy?" Keeley asked, strangely composed.

"He's threatened to do that."

"Doesn't he care about how that might affect his family?" Avis asked.

"Obviously not."

"I'll do whatever I can to help," Oliver offered.

Ben turned to his father-in-law. This was Oliver's way of apologizing for his daughter's behavior. The man's pain was obvious.

"Thank you, Oliver," Ben said. "We may need all the help we can get."

Loretta's expression was grim, but so fierce and determined it made Ben smile inside. *We'll get through it.*

Ben turned back to Ryan, who looked unsure and nervous, the way he had when his doctors had been unable to promise a full recovery. Then, they had effected a miracle by sticking together, Ben reminded himself. This was a minor hurdle in comparison to that.

"We're still the greatest battery of all time," Ben said, using Ryan's favorite baseball parlance. "And we're going to stay that way because we're a team—just like the Knight Sox."

Ryan smiled as Ben mentioned the Little League team he had sponsored and coached.

"It's still you on the mound, me behind the plate, Keeley in the dugout. And in the stands—the grandparents."

Again, Ryan smiled, but his mouth grew wobbly as he watched tears well in his father's eyes.

"Just remember one thing: I love you, little guy."

Ryan's smile collapsed. Ben wrapped an arm around him for support.

"Was Mom planning to leave us?"

Keeley's question stunned Ben. She was staring at him, demanding that he answer her truthfully. In a moment of intense clarity, Ben realized that she had known all about her mother's affair with Mack Kenton.

"It would appear that way," he said, hating Felicia for bequeathing him the task of telling their daughter she would have been left behind.

Without another word, Keeley rose, turned, and walked into the house. Ben chased after her. When he caught up with her, he was firm and unequivocal.

"Your mother loved you."

"Not enough to take me or Ryan with her," Keeley rebutted, daring Ben to argue her point.

"I can't speak for her, Keeley. I didn't know what she was doing, so how could I possibly know what she was thinking. The only thing I'm sure of is that she loved you and your brother. Please don't question that."

He sounded so sad, it brought Keeley up short.

"It's not that I wouldn't have wanted to stay with you, Daddy. It's just . . ."

"Please," Ben said, patting her cheek. "I know you love me. I only worry that you don't realize how much I love you." Keeley bowed her head and shuffled her feet. "You're the center of my life. You and Ryan are what make everything else worthwhile."

"What if you fell in love with someone else?" Keeley asked, her voice small and tremulous.

Ben's eyes narrowed, but his mouth curled in a gentle smile. "Should I assume you're referring to Zoë Vaughn and that your real question is if I fell in love with her, would I stop loving you?"

Keeley's features crinkled as she winced in embarrassment. "Mom did."

Ben gripped Keeley's arms and looked her squarely in the eye. "I will never stop loving you."

She nodded sheepishly. Her naked need for his profession of affection embarrassed her.

"As for Zoë," Ben continued. "I do love her. Very much. In fact, I asked her to marry me. But—she turned me down."

"Because of me, I bet."

Ben kissed her forehead and stroked her hair lovingly. "No, sweetheart, because of me."

☆   ☆   ☆

All that day and throughout the evening, during the platform debate and the various speeches, Ben's people worked the floor. While they solicited votes one at a time, Zoë and Sam caucused with leaders of the larger delegations in hospitality suites at their hotel, practicing the delicate art of honest dishonesty: Listen patiently to their concerns, promise to bring the issues to Ben's attention when he assumed office, guarantee nothing. It was a tedious process that moved at a tortoise pace, but in the end, it paid off. According to Hal Kingsley's up-to-the-instant tally, they hadn't broken the deadlock on the first ballot, but hundreds of delegates had promised that after they had fulfilled their obligations, they would switch allegiances and cast their votes for Ben.

"I need to talk to you. It's important. And it's business."

When Celia heard Quinn's voice on the house phone she almost hung up, but he sounded so intense, she grew curious. And she missed him. Even more so when she opened the door and saw him standing there in khakis, a tee shirt, and a linen blazer. He looked wonderful, his face tan and healthy, his russet hair curling slightly from the humidity. She invited him in and watched him amble to the couch with definite regret.

"I have a story to give you."

His matter-of-fact manner hit her like a splash of cold water. Though she had made it quite clear the last time that she didn't want a next time, being confronted with that reality made her sad.

"This was given to me as an exclusive, but I thought you might make better use of it."

Celia eyed him suspiciously.

"Mack Kenton claims that Ryan Knight is his biological son."

"What!" Celia was so stunned, she staggered slightly. "That's absurd!"

"I thought so, too, but hey! Who would've imagined Scottie Edwards had a Cleo Wells tucked away in his past?"

Celia shook her head in disbelief. Her face had paled. Quinn went to the bar, poured her a drink, handed it to her, and watched as she took a gulp.

"I figured you might know something that would deto-
nate this bomb before it destroys innocent people."

"Why are you bringing this to me?" Celia asked. "Why
not check it out and run with it yourself?"

Quinn's mouth tilted in a bemused smile. "Because I
figure the story Zoë handed me on Cleo Wells would have
gone to you if you hadn't sideswiped her. Because I think
Mack Kenton is a slimeball for taking this public even if
it is true. And because I figured if it isn't, you would know,
could stifle him, and, at the same time, worm your way
back into the good graces of your friends."

Celia stared at him. "That's awfully . . . generous of you."

He grinned back. "You may not think so, Ms. Porter,
but I'm a helluva nice guy!" His expression sobered. "I
also don't like the idea of a kid being dragged through
the mud for no reason other than political gain."

"That boy is my nephew," she said, her voice gritty, her
eyes narrowed with sudden purpose. "Tell me what Kenton
said."

After a long discussion, Celia had agreed that without
a credible witness, Kenton might have disregarded her and
brought the story to someone else. Quinn, who insisted
on being that witness, made the call, set up the meeting
for eleven o'clock, and accompanied Celia to Kenton's
hotel room. Kenton was not pleased to see her.

"I thought you were coming alone," he said to Quinn.

"Gee. And I thought you'd be so happy to see me." Celia
brushed by him, took a seat on the couch, and adopted a
posture that told him she had no intention of leaving.

Quinn posted himself out of Kenton's line of vision,
hugging the wall in an out-of-the-way corner, his arms
folded across his chest.

"What do you want?" Kenton couldn't hide his agitation. He stomped over to a room-service tray and made a
show of pouring coffee for himself. He took his time adding
milk and sugar and slowly carried his cup to the table

nearest his chair. He deliberately neglected to offer anything to his guests.

"I want to remind you of a few things I think you've forgotten," Celia said. He glared at her over the rim of his cup. "Like the fact that you and Ryan Knight are not related."

"Says you."

Celia might have admired his gall if she hadn't been so enraged by it.

"Said Felicia." Celia delighted in watching him cringe at the mention of his lover's name. "She told me that she had dangled Ryan's paternity in front of your ego." She leaned back, letting him wait for her punch line. "I remember her laughing about it."

"She wouldn't," he protested.

"She did," Celia insisted. "While I never understood the attraction, for a long time, Felicia thought you were pretty hot, Mack. Then your ambition got out of hand." Celia shook her head and clucked her tongue. "Felicia felt that you were neglecting her. That you were spending much too much time doing the doting-husband thing for the media and the constituents back home. So she baited another hook. She insinuated that Ryan *might* be your child. You were so blinded by your hormonal urges and the pride of paternity, you never saw through the sham."

Mack started to defend himself, thought better of it, and took shelter in his coffee.

"When my nephew," Celia said pointedly, "was brought to the hospital after the accident, his doctors put out a call for blood. Knowing of your . . . involvement, I called you. Do you remember?"

In spite of himself, Kenton nodded.

"For all I knew, Felicia had lied to me and told you the truth. Maybe you were Ryan's biological father. At that moment I didn't care about anything except getting him the blood he needed."

"And in case you've forgotten," he said snidely, "I was

more than willing to help, despite what something like that could have done to my reputation."

"True, but when I asked you said you were AB. Ryan is B, as am I. As was Felicia. Ben is A, so he couldn't donate. As an AB, neither could you."

"So? What does this rambling reminiscence prove?"

"You told me you're Rh positive," Celia continued, her voice fixed on him like a well-aimed gun. "Ryan is Rh negative. So are both of his parents." Kenton's jaw tightened. "Your paternity is possible, but it's such a long shot, it's laughable."

Her eyes grew cold and her lips formed a stiff, straight line. "Except you know what, Mack? Look around. No one is laughing."

"I didn't mean this as a joke."

"I'm sure you didn't," Celia sneered, looking at him with the same aversion as one would grant an insect. "But whatever game you were playing—it's over."

Mack refused to respond. He remained in his chair, rigid and inflexible. Quinn watched Kenton's body language carefully, alert for any change.

"I was there," Celia reminded him. "I was Felicia's confidante as well as her cousin. I know the truth. I also have a large, credible following and easy, open access to the airways."

Mack clasped his hands and slid to the front of his chair. His eyes burned with venomous desperation.

"It would take time to verify your truth," he said, still exuding a cocky confidence. "By then, I would have cinched the nomination and none of this would matter."

Celia also moved forward, drawing her face close to his. Her voice was muted, but sharp as flint.

"It matters to me, Mack, which is why I'm warning you: If you go public with this travesty, I'll tear you to shreds."

Celia and Quinn's next stop was Ben's suite. When she called and requested an audience, she winced when he hesitated. On the way up, Quinn tried to reassure her, but without success. When the door opened, her knees buckled. Ben, Zoë, Jed, Sam, and Otis Jefferson were lined up like a firing squad.

"You don't have to worry about Mack Kenton leaking that trash about Ryan," she said quickly, wanting to get her announcement out as fast as possible. "I think I've convinced him it's a bad idea."

"Kenton wanted me to break it," Quinn explained. "I went to Celia looking for her to confirm or deny his allegations. More than that, I was praying she'd have some inside angle on how to put a sock in that scumbucket's mouth. And she did." He chuckled with obvious admiration. "She was a knockout! She landed her punches better than Ali in his prime."

Celia couldn't be certain, but she thought she sensed a slight thaw in the glacier facing her. Hoping to quicken the meltdown, she focused on Zoë.

"When Quinn told me what Kenton had planned, I thought it might be helpful if someone jogged his memory."

"That was good of you." Zoë remained guarded.

"Ryan's my nephew," Celia asserted, establishing priorities. "And I owed you." Celia looked from Zoë to Ben. "I owed you both."

Ben knew what it had taken for Celia to walk into that room. She had to believe that she'd be as welcome as a snowstorm in May. Yet despite the coolness he and his team had shown her since the Anatoly Chertoff fiasco, she had gone to bat for him, without hesitation and without grandstanding. Whether Kenton backed off or not, she deserved his thanks.

Ben walked across the room and embraced her. "Debt paid," he said with a squeeze.

Once Ben had signaled the end to their hostilities, Jed, Sam, and Otis tossed questions at both Quinn and Celia, trying to assess Kenton's mood and what he might do next. While the men huddled, Celia took Zoë aside.

"You've been awfully quiet," she said. "Is it because you don't think we've heard the last of Mack Kenton? Or because you have nothing to say to me?"

"What do you want me to say?"

"It appears as if Ben's forgiven me for whatever damage I may or may not have done to his campaign," Celia said, unable to shake her defensiveness. "My joy would be complete if you would forgive me as well."

"It's different." Zoë's voice was calm, yet edged. "By silencing Mack Kenton, you corked a tragedy that would have hurt Ben and his family and for that, you should be praised.

"By airing that picture of me and Anatoly, you tossed a lighted match into a tinderbox." Her eyes narrowed slightly, the edge in her voice sharpened. "I asked you not to do it. I practically begged you. And you did it anyway. I may not be able to blame you for my current predicament, Celia, but you sure as hell made it worse."

Celia's face contorted with confusion and exasperation. "I have no idea what you're talking about. Tell me. Maybe I can help."

Zoë wished she could unburden herself, but she had been warned not to. Several weeks before, she had confided to a friend in the FBI about the ransacking of her apartment and the voiceless telephone calls and menacing notes. He had run some fingerprints through the agency's computers which confirmed Arlo Reid's presence in her apartment. He had put a tap on her phone and dusted the letters, but so far, those efforts had produced nothing.

"You can't help me, Celia," Zoë said, feeling friendless and alone. "All I ask is that you don't hurt me again."

The rest of that day was hellish. By eight o'clock that evening, between cajoling delegates and wondering whether Mack Kenton had been cowed by Celia, Zoë was exhausted. Thankfully, the Convention Committee—bowing to time restrictions placed on them by the networks—

had limited both candidates to one nominating and one seconding speech each. In need of a respite, she wended her way up to the VIP section in the mezzanine so she could listen to Kate's speech with Rick and Ethan Siegel. She found the Siegels in the front row and next to them, Nona and Paddy, festooned with buttons and ribbons, waving small American flags and grinning like children.

"What are you doing here?" she asked her parents, delighted, but befuddled.

"Ben sent us passes." Paddy's tone said he thought she knew. "For tonight and tomorrow night when he accepts the nomination." He shook his head as if it was simply too amazing to comprehend. "Can you imagine? That young man used to hang out at the pub debating politics and baseball."

"I knew it even then," Nona asserted.

While Ethan went off scouting the aisles for buttons, the Vaughns, Zoë, and Rick exchanged views on Ben's chances in the general election. Nona, never one to stifle her curiosity, decided they had plenty of time to discuss the election. She wanted to know how things were between Rick and Kate. Zoë groaned, but Rick had known Nona too long to be annoyed or embarrassed.

"We're working on getting back together."

"Isn't it something? Kate giving the nominating speech?" Nona was agog.

"She's become a national figure," Rick said, his pride obvious. "Some people are even talking about her running for office."

That spiked Zoë's attention. "How would you feel about that? I mean," she said, trying to phrase her thoughts delicately, "Kate was Supermom. You were Superstar."

It was a gentle, but pointed summation of their marriage. Rick tipped an imaginary hat to Zoë.

"Our lives are different than they were before. We've changed and so our marriage has to change. We're adapting as best we can. As for her being in Washington?" Rick shrugged. "It's not for me to decide, but if she's offered the chance, I'm behind her! She's got a crackerjack mind and a bleeding heart and if you ask me, Congress could use a few like Kate."

Zoë smiled approvingly. It was nice to know that the couple she always held up as her ideal was once again functioning as a couple.

"So things between you and Kate are good?" Nona pressed.

"Yes," Rick said, leaning over and kissing the older woman on the cheek. "Things between us are very good."

"Now that you've straightened Rick out," Paddy said to his wife, with a look of loving exasperation, "would you like to tell your daughter about our cruise?"

Nona returned his look with one of her own. Then, she explained. "We couldn't celebrate our fiftieth anniversary at the time, but since we're both feeling tiptop now, we decided to treat ourselves to an Adriatic cruise."

"When do you leave?" Zoë remembered how disappointed they had been not being able to have a party or take a trip because of Nona's hysterectomy and Paddy's prostate problems.

"We fly to Milan next Friday. Monday we drive to Venice. And on Tuesday, we board the *Michelangelo.*" Paddy glowed with excitement. "I can't wait!"

"It sounds wonderful!" Zoë hugged the two of them. They deserved two weeks of idle luxury.

Just as Kate was being introduced, Ethan raced down the aisle and hurried to his place. From underneath his seat, he pulled out a placard that read, WE LOVE YOU. RICK AND ETHAN. As Kate walked across the stage—to a standing ovation—Ethan hoisted the sign high into the air. Kate stepped up to the microphone and panned the massive crowd. When she spotted the sign, she put two fingers to her lips and held them up. Zoë saw Rick wipe away a tear.

Kate began by describing the early years of her friendship with Ben: their playful rivalry, their lively debates, their vow to share special moments in each other's lives.

She recalled going to Washington to be at his swearing-in for his first term in the House.

"I remember being unbelievably moved as Omar Thatcher, the senior senator from Pennsylvania, issued the oath of office. I also remember thinking what a good thing this was, both for Ben and the country. I knew how Benjamin Knight felt about America, about the promise that existed in this great land of ours, as well as the problems that were threatening us from within. As a citizen, I felt reassured knowing that Benjamin Knight was now part of the governing body. Because as a friend, I knew that the fire in his eyes came from his gut and the eloquent words he spoke came from his heart."

She went on to describe Ben's life of public service, listing the bills he had authored and the legislation he had brought to the floor of the House during his three terms there. She spoke of his years in the Senate the same way, as years of toil and concern and accomplishment. But it was when she shifted to his personal life that the audience went from hushed to rapt.

"Ben Knight and I have death in common," she said. "I stood alongside him when he buried his wife. He shoveled dirt into the grave of my daughter."

Zoë took Rick's hand. His other hand held on to his son. Kate's shoulders were square. Her voice was clear. But the five in Row AA of the mezzanine knew that her eyes were moist.

"We also have life in common. I watched him confront the loss of his wife, the anguish of his daughter, and the wreckage of his son's body. I sat with him as the doctors recited Ryan's dark prognosis. I heard him insist that they were wrong, that there would not be a second victim to this tragedy. Over the long months that followed, Ben was father, motivator, physical therapist, spiritual guide, and best friend to Ryan Knight. Ben willed his son to stand and to walk and to run."

The applause was tumultuous. Zoë appeared withdrawn

and morose. Those around her thought she was mourning her own loss; they didn't know about Mack Kenton's plan.

"When my daughter was killed, Ben was there for me and my husband, but particularly for my son, doing what he could to help Ethan adjust to life in the wake of a senseless murder. He talked to Ethan about the way his father, Kirk, and brother, Robbie, had been gunned down in the street. He listened to Ethan's nightmares about monsters lurking in the woods and hiding in the shadows.

"More important, by his example alone, he taught Ethan to accept what happens and move on. To find something positive, even in the evilest deeds. To chase fear from his life. To stand up for what he believes. And especially, to make things better."

She paused. The emotions in that arena were so taut, no one breathed.

"It is with love and pride and honor that I nominate Benjamin Knight as the Democratic Party's candidate for president of the United States."

The ovation was long and heartfelt, given as it was for both the nominee and the woman who set forth his name. When the crowd quieted and took their seats, Kate concluded.

"Shimon Peres once said, 'You must be elected by the parents to represent the children.' This, ladies and gentlemen, is an election that is all about children: those being held by terrorists, those being abused and defiled and murdered by sexual predators, those being preyed upon by drug peddlers, and those without proper food and shelter, education and health care.

"We as parents must elect Benjamin Knight to represent our children. We must elect him to protect our children. We must elect him to make things better for our children."

In Ben's suite, the Knight family listened to Kate's speech with television cameras aimed at them. They sat with their hands clasped, their mouths determined and firm. Ben had told them Celia's news, but cautioned them that nothing was certain. Keeley and Ryan had discussed the situation and had decided that if the story was leaked to the press, they could handle it.

"I can handle anything as long as you're still my dad," Ryan had announced with whatever bravura he could muster.

During Kate's speech, the camera frequently cut to Rick and Ethan. When Zoë was caught in the frame, Keeley flushed. She had called Zoë late that afternoon.

Keeley had struggled through an awkward preamble. When she got to the reason for her call, it came off sounding blunt and a bit presumptuous. "I think it'd be really great if you and my dad . . . uh . . . got together. He needs you."

Zoë had to smother a laugh. "I appreciate your call, Keeley, but your father and I are together—on his campaign."

"That's not what I meant." This was harder than Keeley had imagined it would be. "I mean, like he . . . well, you know. This thing with Ryan has been really rough on him."

"I do know, Keeley, but it looks as if your aunt Celia has taken care of all that. And besides," Zoë said, softening, "he has you and Ryan and Loretta and the Coburns surrounding him."

"But . . ."

"It's better this way," Zoë had said.

Keeley didn't see how. But Zoë hadn't given her the chance to ask.

The roll call of the states was moving quickly. If the nominee had been certain, lengthy speeches by delegation chairs would have been the rule. This night, knowing they would need at least one more ballot, "on behalf of the great state of . . ." orations were the exception.

As the convention secretary called out each delegation's votes, individual delegates kept count on scratch pads and pocket calculators. The television audience fared better, with a "zipper" at the bottom of the screen that provided a running tally. Just as the first ballot was drawing to a deadlocked close, the telephone in Ben's suite rang. Ben waved off his Secret Service agent and answered it himself. He had been waiting for this call.

"This is your last chance," intoned the voice on the other end.

Ben's response was as icy and calm as a Wisconsin lake in January. "Actually, Kenton, this is just the beginning. Not only won't I turn over a single delegate or breathe your name and the words *vice president* in the same sentence, but you're going to rue the day you threatened me and my family."

"I have no regrets because I have nothing to lose," Kenton said with deliberate menace. "You do."

Ben's jaw tightened, and his eyes turned hard as steel. He was a man with a temper. It was not easily aroused, but when it was, it was ferocious. Thankfully, over the years he had learned not to feed the beast whenever it growled. He had also learned that to some, silence was more devastating than rage. Deciding Kenton was one of those, he put down the phone. He would deal with Kenton later.

On the second go-round, the roll call of the states decelerated, slowing to a crawl. Delegation chairs preceded the casting of their votes with travelogues about the glories of their respective states, promoting everything from pecans to prize hogs. Now and then, a state passed, hoping to be called on when their votes would be the ones to put the nominee over the top.

Ben and his family again watched from their hotel suite, the intrusive eye of a television camera trained on them, limiting their responses. Ben's staff, watching from another suite minus the camera, were free to pace and curse and hoot whenever they wanted. Jed believed the start of the alphabet was key.

"If the first ones out of the box fall into our camp,

there'll be a lotta scrambling down the line to get on the winning bandwagon.''

Alabama and Arkansas remained split. California passed. Otherwise, the early votes were Ben's. In the staff suite, no one sat. Everyone was moving, counting, waiting. And praying.

"Florida." The convention secretary called out. "One hundred and fifty-two votes."

An elderly, longtime congressman from Broward County grabbed the microphone. "The Sunshine State, with its glorious beaches and bountiful harvest, home of the winningest teams in college and professional sports, is proud to cast all 152 votes for another winner: the next president of the United States, Benjamin Knight!''

"That's it!" Jed said, pumping his fist. "They're gonna tumble."

Zoë crossed her fingers. They had a long way to go.

Georgia, Hawaii, Idaho, Illinois, and Indiana did tumble. Iowa didn't. It cast all its votes for its native son. Kansas, Kentucky, Louisiana, and Maine put themselves in Ben's column. Massachusetts and its ninety-three votes passed, as did the other behemoth states: Michigan, New Jersey, and New York.

"They're not going to steal Pennsylvania's thunder,'' Jed said, stomping around the room in his bare feet. He considered it bad luck to wear his boots while a vote was being taken. "They're going to let Ben's home state put him over."

Soon, Zoë thought, her eyes glued to the "zipper" which showed Ben on his way to a blowout.

Maryland, Minnesota, Mississippi, Missouri, Montana, Nevada, New Hampshire, New Mexico, and North Carolina went to Ben. Nebraska split. North Dakota and Oklahoma resisted the tug of a windfall and cast their lot with Mack Kenton.

Zoë thought she would come out of her skin. Sam Trout didn't look any better. Phil Halpern, Adam Schwartz, and several other aides stood in the middle of the room and stared at the TV with clasped hands, as if they were making an offering to the Omnipotent God of Political Wisdom. Jed was perpetual nervous energy, moving too quickly to gauge what planet he was on, let alone what mood he was in.

"Ohio." The convention secretary shouted, her voice growing hoarse. "One hundred and forty-seven votes."

The head of the Ohio delegation, a white-haired, bespectacled gentleman who had retired from the Senate several years before but was still much beloved, came to the microphone, touched by the applause that greeted him.

"The Buckeye State would like to pass so that the honor of casting the deciding votes can go to its neighbor, the great state of Pennsylvania, home of my former Senate colleague, their favorite son, and our future president, Benjamin Knight!"

"Pennsylvania," the secretary shouted, trying desperately to be heard above the growing din. "One hundred and sixty-seven votes."

Loretta Knight stood in the center of her delegation. She had been appointed as an alternate specifically for this moment. In their hotel suite, Ben, his children, and his in-laws watched with misty anticipation. Ryan was on the edge of his seat. Keeley bit her lip at the sight of her grandmother, proud and tall in her bright blue dress and her golden Knight pin gleaming on her lapel. Ben smiled at his mother as if she could see him.

In the staff suite, Jed was standing on a cocktail table. Sam was leaning toward the TV as if he thought he might miss it. Zoë twirled her hair around her finger and held her breath. Everyone else stood statue-still, as if someone had yelled, "Freeze!"

"The Commonwealth of Pennsylvania," Loretta said, her voice reverberating throughout the massive convention hall, "the keystone of the original thirteen American states, the place where the Declaration of Independence was signed and the Liberty Bell rings, takes enormous pride in casting all of its 167 votes for my favorite son and theirs, the next president of the United States, Benjamin Douglas Knight!''

As she said his name, her hand lightly tapped her heart. Ben nodded. His heart was just as full.

Thunderous applause roared through the arena like a wave. Feet stomped. Hands clapped. Placards waved. And blaring from stereo speakers: Elton John's ''Philadelphia Freedom.'' The hall was rocking.

Back at the hotel, Ben's crew went wild. Jed jumped off the cocktail table, grabbed Zoë, and the two of them began dancing around the room. Sam popped the cork on a bottle of Crystal champagne that had been chilling since six o'clock and let its expensive foam spill all over his slacks. For a man who liked his jeans ironed, this was a statement of profound joy.

In Ben's suite there was a great deal of hugging and congratulations. Visitors plowed into the room and surrounded Ben, everyone vying for the First Handshake. The gropers ranged from executives of the party—with whom Ben had arranged a posthoopla confab—to senators and congressmen, pushy delegates, even pushier media types and awestruck, low-level campaign workers who suddenly realized they might have signed on with a winner.

Ben gave the requisite interviews, allowing a few of the bigger reporters to nab quotes from Oliver, Avis, Loretta, who had returned from the Omni, and the children. One of Ben's senior aides was assigned the task of riding herd and shepherding them out of the suite as soon as they had their one-liners. Jed and the rest of the crew had gathered in the hall outside Ben's suite, providing a secondary target and, therefore, a reason to exit.

In the midst of the bedlam, Ben experienced a terrifying moment. It was as if a firecracker had exploded in front of his eyes, blinding him to everything that was, forcing him to look into the glaring light of his nomination and view the future.

His life, as he had known it, was gone. This evening, it had been effectively torn from his hands and turned over to the human-shredding machine known as America's election process. There would be no more quiet Sunday dinners with his family, or football games at the stadium, or the luxury of going without a tie.

He was an honest man who had gotten on this carousel with honest intentions, a man who prided himself on his integrity and his personal rapport with his constituency. Yet suddenly, he was THE CANDIDATE: a voice that needed a filter, a body trapped inside a bubble, a property protected by Secret Service agents, spin doctors, media consultants, and campaign operatives. The utter loss of personal control made him shiver.

Across the room, through the door of his suite, he spotted Zoë speaking to Barbara Frankel from the *Boston Globe* and Karen Fox from the *New York Times*. She was waving off photographers, probably because she was wearing jeans and a tee shirt. Zoë understood protocol and image better than most; foreign policy gurus did not wear cotton tees and denim from the Gap.

As Ben watched her spin the evening's events, he was reminded of a very basic reality: No man ran alone. And no campaign was ever fueled by a single issue or a single candidate or a single vision. Elections were about people— from the highest-level advisor to the Get Out The Vote volunteer to the voter himself. Whatever their individual reasons for signing on, all those connected with his campaign had aligned their futures with his. They needed to win. And they were counting on him to deliver their victory.

☆   ☆   ☆

The next morning, banner headlines in newspapers across the country trumpeted the results of the convention. While the top bar came as no surprise to the Knight camp: KNIGHT CAPTURES TOP SLOT FOR DEMS, the lower bar did: KENTON TO BE NAMED V.P. Though it was worded differently from paper to paper, the message remained infuriatingly the same. Kenton's people had leaked this story to the press in the hopes of pressuring Ben into compliance.

What it did was make Ben very angry.

That night, Mack Kenton arrived at the Omni convinced that the first order of convention business would be to nominate him as the vice-presidential candidate. While he had expected a call from Ben—either to express his anger at the press leak, his gratitude for squashing the paternity story, to negotiate terms, or, on the positive side, to have coordinated their speeches—he understood when no call was forthcoming. Ben was a proud man. Perhaps he didn't want to appear to be capitulating.

As Mack and his entourage navigated the warren of media trailers, television control centers, and campaign booths, he asked one of his aides to run ahead and see if his family was settled in the onstage gallery reserved for guests of the nominees. He could hardly wait to see his parents, Eustus and Bess Kenton, seated behind the red, white, and blue bunting, watching as he marched to the podium to accept his party's veneration. True, it was for the second position on the ticket, but life was unpredictable. Nothing was certain. Things could happen. He simply had to be in the right place at the right time.

Before leaving their hotel room, he had instructed Maribel on how to stand when they waved to the crowd, what to say to the press, how to deal with Ben's family. He told her to wear royal blue and to dress the children accordingly. Though red was popular at political functions and came across well on television, it was the color of sin. And Felicia's favorite.

When he reached the roped-off area behind the stage, he found it ringed with security. Secret Service agents checked his credentials and those of his staff. Just as his aide reported that no one was seated in the gallery as yet, Ben, his family, and his coterie approached from the other side. They, too, went through the security check. Jed Oakes,

Sam Trout, Zoë Vaughn, and several others from the campaign wished Ben well, congratulated the family, and took off for their seats within the arena. Much to Mack's surprise, Ben's family approached him and wished him well. Even Ryan.

"Good luck, Congressman Kenton," the lad said.

Mack noticed Ryan didn't extend his hand and his smile appeared forced, but he was polite. So was Ben's mother. Keeley, however, upset Mack. She was the image of Felicia, which made it impossible for him to touch her hand without quaking. Oliver and Avis Coburn walked right by him, but he attributed that to patrician reserve. They couldn't help who they were.

Maybe Ben didn't tell them. Just as well, he thought.

While they followed a security guard onto the podium, Ben stepped toward him. Mack extended his hand. Ben didn't take it.

"I know you didn't think so at first," Mack said, conjuring as much graciousness as his ego would allow, "but this is the best way. It's going to work out well for everyone. You'll see."

Ben didn't smile. He didn't get angry. He didn't spew resentment. He didn't offer an olive branch. But he did seem to agree with Mack's assessment.

"You're right," he said flatly. "This is the best way. And yes, it'll work out just the way it should."

Mack took the seat offered him, a happy man.

The gavel came down promptly, calling the convention to order. Congressman Crispin Baird of Oklahoma was introduced and after a long-winded speech extolling the many virtues of his good friend and esteemed colleague, placed the name of Thomas Mackenzie Kenton into nomination. Mack, watching on a monitor, was delighted with the speech. Crispy was a churchgoing man and had invested his oration with an abundance of scripture. Moments before Crispy began, Mack had received word that Eustus and Bess Kenton had arrived and were seated onstage. He was certain they would have approved of Crispy's words. He hoped they were impressed with his praise.

Maribel and the children remained no-shows. Mack convinced himself they had been told to wait until after his speech, when they would join him onstage.

After a short but inspired seconding speech by the former governor of Louisiana and a respectful demonstration, Mack waited for the secretary to begin the roll call of the states. Instead, Party Chairman George Gilbert introduced General Harry Cadman.

Mack's palms grew sweaty as the thunderous applause carried backstage.

I've been betrayed. The words became a drumbeat, pounding inside his head as the popular general celebrated the life of Otis Jefferson.

Cadman spoke about Otis's years of service to his country, about what a fine soldier he had been in Vietnam, what a hero he had been during the Gulf War.

Mack seethed, knowing that Ben and his cohorts had selected a general deliberately to humiliate him. He had been a conscientious objector; both Ben and Otis had been soldiers. He had been noble; they had been savages. But to the unenlightened, to those who believed war could be justified—especially now when terrorists were harboring children—they came off as heroes. He appeared the coward.

Crispy Baird, who had come backstage to sit next to him while waiting for the process to conclude, patted his knee. Mack pushed his hand away.

"You're a Judas," he hissed.

Crispy stood, and, with genuine regret, said; "I did what I could."

Mack sat frozen to his chair, unable to do anything except stare at the monitor and listen to the roar of approval when Cadman finished. He felt light-headed. His mind wandered. Suddenly, he was back in Otho, Iowa, sitting on the hard wooden pew in his father's church, being preached to about Sanctification. He was in his mother's kitchen, listening to her sermonize about what hard work Perfection was.

"But if you prove yourself worthy, the Lord's love will more than reward your struggle."

Tonight he had intended to prove himself worthy. Tonight he was to receive his reward. He shivered as reality iced his blood. Instead of ascending to a seat of state, he was about to be brought to his knees, humbled before a national assembly, mortified in front of his parents, his wife, and his children. He was numb with defeat. He didn't see the monitor or his aides hovering over him or Buck Roswell, congressman from Houston and former baseball commissioner, stride to the podium to deliver Otis's seconding speech. All he saw was his own disgrace.

When the demonstration for Otis Jefferson began, it was as if someone had shot Mack with adrenaline. He needed to get his parents out of there before the roll call. He couldn't let Eustus sit through the public embarrassment of his son. Mack bounded to his feet and tried to do an end run around the security guards, but they weren't about to let him near the stage. Nor were they going to let him leave. He was trapped, forced to watch his descent into ignominy.

George Gilbert mounted the podium, held up his hands, and begged the audience to quiet down.

"As the party chairman and the senior senator from the great state of Michigan . . ." He paused, allowing his delegation to blow horns and wave placards. "I ask this convention to take an historic step and nominate by acclimation, Otis Jefferson as our party's candidate for vice-president of the United States. All those in favor, say 'Aye'!"

The response was earsplitting.

"All those opposed?"

To Mack Kenton, the silence was more horrifying than the noise. There was not even one lone voice to cry out for him, to say that he was worthy, to say that he deserved a reward for his efforts and his struggle.

Off to the side, Otis's family was being escorted onto the platform. At the same time, Eustus and Bess were being led down off the stage and toward the closest exit. Their backs were bent and their eyes were averted so they would not have to gaze upon him. As he watched them leave he squirmed, as if failure had infested his body and was now crawling about on his flesh. He expected to see Maribel and the children following closely behind, but after several minutes had passed and they didn't appear, he assumed they had gone out another way.

Unwilling to witness Ben's triumph, Mack left the Omni. Alone, he taxied back to his hotel and went to his room. There, on the bed, he found a note from Maribel:

> *I couldn't stand by and watch you steal a false honor from well-meaning citizens. You used a young boy to try and blackmail your way into higher office. That's despicable! And so unlike the man I once knew, it frightens me. Somewhere along the way, you forgot that the first task of a public servant is to earn the public's trust. You used to have it. You used to cherish it. Yet now, you've chosen to disrespect it.*
>
> *The public should not, cannot, and I hope will not trust you with their lives or their freedom. You have broken every one of your vows: to me, to your constituents, and to God, which is why I've taken the children and gone to Oklahoma to be with my parents. I intend to sue you for divorce and for full custody. I don't want to hear from you or see you ever again.*

Mack read the letter over several times before folding it and carefully returning it to its envelope. He tucked it in his pocket and looked around the large suite, which he had envisioned overflowing with celebration. Champagne languished in a bucket of ice. The platter of hors d'oeuvres garnished with small American flags seemed to mock him.

He grabbed the back of a chair, leaned over, and breathed deeply, hoping to fill his lungs with whatever sanity Maribel had left behind. When he exhaled, the dark vapors of self-reproach and self-loathing polluted the air. A groan that started deep inside him rumbled past his lips like a primal scream.

He collapsed in a corner of the room, hugged his knees to his chest, and cried until he was spent. The fall from grace that he had fought his whole life to prevent was complete.

THE
CAMPAIGN

☆

☆ AUGUST ☆

The Knight campaign plane departed from Hartsfield Atlanta International Airport at six o'clock in the morning, headed for Washington. The revelers had partied long after the convention officially ended, yet everyone was awake and energized. Overnight polls had them in the lead, albeit not by as much as they would have liked: 54 percent to 48 percent.

"I warned you," Otis said to Ben. "Even those who proclaim themselves color-blind get nervous at the thought of a black man so close to the power."

"According to Hal's inside polling, the other side's having trouble selling the idea of a woman a heartbeat away from The Button." Ben patted his friend's knee. "Give it time."

Actually, Ben was less worried about Otis than he was about Kenton. Once the media realized that Kenton had used them to pressure Ben, they had a field day reporting his downfall. Ben came off as strong and decisive in the telling, but Kenton was unbalanced. Fearing retaliation, Ben arranged for extra security around his home and a private guard for Ryan.

His other concern was Clay Chandler's penchant for malicious mischief. After Celia had run the story about Zoë and Anatoly Chertoff, Ben, suspicious about the motivation behind it, had paid her a visit. They had been an item once. It had been brief, but they had parted friends. Also, she was his children's aunt. He couldn't believe she would go out of her way to hurt him without good reason; a story based on circumstantial evidence seemed a stretch. After a great deal of prodding, Celia confessed that Clay had her in a box: either she gave up Ben and Zoë, or he would throw Hugo to the feds.

Since then, Ben had put a couple of investigators on the eminent Mr. Chandler. What they'd turned up thus far was a substantial slush fund fed by diverted campaign money. Through this secret reservoir, Clay paid off his paparazzi, the hecklers that had become ubiquitous at Ben's rallies, as well as the various groups which conducted his opposition research and steeply slanted, highly insulting push polls. Ben could only imagine what other dirty tricks this money supported.

Recently, he found himself wondering more and more about the distribution of those tricks and whether there had been a shift in Clay's focus. Ben had been Clay's primary target for so long, he had come to accept his position in the center of the crosshairs, but Celia's piece had torpedoed Zoë's reputation more than his. Moreover, since Italy Zoë had been uncharacteristically agitated. At first, he had attributed her anxiety to the awkwardness of their personal situation. Next, he ascribed it to preconvention stress. But then, he had heard a piece of scuttlebutt about her apartment being ransacked. He had no proof, but his gut said Clay Chandler's fingerprints were all over that break-in. Ben ordered his investigators to go deeper. He was certain that if they dug down into the swamp where Clay Chandler lived and worked, they would find a cache of weapons that could be used against him.

And use them Ben would.

* * *

Throughout the *Knight Flight*—as the campaign plane had been dubbed—Ben's staff buzzed with activity. Jed Oakes and Rick Siegel batted ideas around for the media campaign, discussed the roles Ben's family members would play, and established a special team to prep Ben before each debate and in-depth interview. Kate Siegel, who had accepted the post of field coordinator, was talking to Sam Trout about how to use her grassroots network to bolster their state organizations. She felt certain she could get quality people on the ground in each of the fifty capitals. Adam Schwartz was on the phone checking with the main office about plans for their arrival that evening. After the kickoff in Washington, the entire campaign was boarding buses and driving to Philadelphia.

At their national headquarters, "high atop downtown Manayunk, overlooking the Schuylkill River," as Jed was fond of saying whenever he was asked for their address, organizers had been working for months to arrange housing and transportation for the horde of campaign workers about to descend on the city. Thanks to the generosity of local supporters who were willing to open their homes and donate their time, they had pinned down more than enough rooms and cars and drivers.

Sarah Jenks, the campaign scheduler, and pollmeister Hal Kingsley were huddled together trying to pinpoint target states. Since the ultimate goal was to win electoral votes—and a simple majority in each state was what it took to do that—the strategy was Fifty Percent Plus One. The questions were: Where are the toughest battles? And how many persuadables do we have in those battlegrounds? States where Ben stood practically no chance, they would avoid. Those they thought he would win easily, they would visit sparingly. Those where they adjudged the battle to be tight, but possible, would become targets. Both Ben and Otis, as well as a number of carefully chosen surrogates, would make appearances and commercial airtime would be purchased; amounts would vary according to Hal's numbers. Even with federal funding, as Tom Hall, their national fundraising chairman, continually reminded them: When a race is tight, you gotta spend it right!

In the back of the plane where it was relatively quiet, Phil Halpern took notes while Dr. Buddy Brown—the highly acclaimed economist from Iowa, newly recruited campaign economics advisor and former husband of Celia Porter—laid out his checklist for Ben's domestic agenda. When Otis joined them to add his input on the needs of America's urban areas, Zoë took her turn visiting Ben in the front cabin.

She was all business. "Your acceptance speech was terrific. It hit all the major themes of the campaign, but you need to come out even stronger for the immediate return of the hostages."

"It's the kids, stupid," Ben suggested, half joking.

Zoë was totally serious. "Exactly! Complain about the length of time these innocent women and children have been held captive. In fact, I think we should erect a huge billboard outside our campaign headquarters, and maybe in a few key locations around the country, that looks like a calendar and check off the days."

Ben's eyes rolled. That was a knife in Haynes's side.

"Don't worry about how Elton will deal with it," Zoë said, intuiting his thoughts. "You have no choice but to attack his handling of the situation. I love Elton, but he's blown this one big-time.

"As for Edwards, hit him hard about his shilly-shallying. Wonder aloud why the *General* isn't calling out the troops and why he appears to be coddling a bunch of international gangsters. Accuse him of not showing any backbone, of forsaking the proud tradition of the military, of being more bluster than brass."

Ben leaned in close and whispered in her ear, "You know, you can be a real hard-ass when you want to be."

She squirmed and shook her head, as if that would chase away the shivers that rippled through her at his nearness.

"We have a job to do, Senator." Her voice was soft, but definite.

"You're right. I apologize." Ben retreated unhappily. He sulked for a minute and then regrouped. "Jed told me you're not riding the bus to Philadelphia."

"I'm staying in Washington. I have an early meeting with Caleb Lind."

Now that Ben's candidacy was official, his campaign was entitled to frequent and deep security briefings. As his foreign policy advisor, Zoë would attend regularly scheduled meetings with Caleb Lind, the president's National Security Advisor, as well as the heads of the CIA and the FBI. She would also receive constantly updated briefing books from the State Department. From this plethora of information she would formulate Ben's policies and positions on America's allies and enemies.

They talked about Durgunov, how far Ben could push him without disastrous consequences and how much he could suggest without compromising the president's rescue efforts.

"I'll check my sources about what's happening with Durgunov," Zoë said, scribbling notes to herself. "As for Elton, once we know what—if any—irons he has in the fire, we'll be able to adjust our attack."

"And once this presidential campaign is over," Ben said, fixing his eyes on hers, "we'll be able to finish the conversation we started in Italy."

Zoë rose, clearly eager to escape. Ben caught her arm. "I've never been one to take no for an answer."

"Maybe not, but it's my no, and it still stands." Her voice was firm as she gently wriggled free of his grasp.

"Until," he said with an indulgent smile, "I start my personal campaign to change your mind."

They had come to join Ben and Otis, their fellow soldiers, at the Wall. Weeks before the convention, when the two men had decided on this as the place from which they wanted to launch their journey, organizers had begun contacting veterans' groups around the country. Since no one knew how the nomination would go, plans were made, then held in abeyance. The moment Ben was nominated, however, men and women who had served in that war boarded planes and buses and headed for Maya Lin's "rift in the earth."

When Ben and Otis arrived at the Mall, the sight that greeted them was startling: hundreds of Vietnam veterans and their families stood quietly along the stone path that followed the V-shaped, highly polished black granite wall, each one wearing a small ribbon of jungle camouflage cloth. After solemnly pinning ribbons to their lapels, Ben started at one end, Otis at the other, shaking hands and sharing words with those who had come to remember what none of them could ever forget.

Fifty-eight thousand, one hundred and eighty-three casualties were memorialized in those simple, haunting panels of black. Women caressed the names of lost husbands and sons, children the names of fathers they had never seen or no longer remembered. Men rubbed their fingers against the names of fallen comrades, brothers and friends, weeping unashamedly. The walk was slow, laden as it was with mourning and regret. Even the press stood by silently, granting the reunion the respect it deserved.

Ben and Otis met up at the panel which held the names of those soldiers who had lost their lives in 1969. After finding the names they sought, they laid six flowers against the wall, one for each of the men who had died in the bowels of the An Lo Valley. Then Ben stepped off the stone path and onto the lawn; to him, the ground nearest the memorial was hallowed. Jonetta joined Otis on the grass slightly behind Ben.

"This is a difficult place to be," Ben said, his eyes slowly panning the large crowd. "It's a site that whispers the names of those who went off when their country called and never returned. It memorializes the victims of a war that proved more difficult to fight than any America had ever fought before, because for the first time in our history, we were fighting an enemy on foreign soil and each other here at home.

"Even today, Vietnam remains synonymous with division. Those who went and those who didn't. Those who were for, those who were against. Those who welcomed home its veterans, those who scorned our participation. Those who couldn't bear to face the harsh, personal reality of this memorial, those who preferred the anonymous symbolism of a more traditional remembrance," he said, pointing to the statue of three soldiers and a flagpole that had been erected nearby to placate the critics of the Wall.

"Yet Vietnam taught me a vital lesson about the need to come together, the need to set aside old hatreds and make friends with onetime enemies. My school was the jungle, my teacher a man with the nerve to confront me with my own bigotry. He made me give voice to feelings I had harbored for a lifetime, to the boiling rage that had filled my heart from the day my father and brother were gunned down in the streets of Philadelphia until that morning in Vietnam.

"Through Otis Jefferson, I realized that crimes were committed by individuals, not by ethnic groups. That wars were fought by units and battalions, not by ethnic groups. And that peace and prosperity were possible only if America viewed itself as a nation. And not a collection of ethnic groups.

"The people whose names are etched on that wall are neither black nor white. They're Americans who died in the service of their country. The soldiers and the women and the children being held by Red Rage are neither black nor white. They're American prisoners. The people who are going to determine who will lead us into the twenty-first century are neither black nor white. They're American citizens. And when they—you—consider whether you want to vote for Otis Jefferson and me, don't look at us as simply black and white, judge us for who we are—Vietnam veterans, dedicated public servants, close, personal friends, and patriotic Americans.''

"Cripes! It's a damn love-in!" Clay Chandler shouted, watching the crowds swarm around Otis and Ben at the Wall.

"And a brilliant idea," an aide mumbled, certain he was out of earshot.

"I want the entire staff in here ten minutes ago!" Clay barked, his frog eyes glued to the television. "If Ben Knight plans to conduct a campaign of symbolism, fine! It'll be my pleasure to ram the Washington Monument up his ass!"

As a dozen staffers filed into Clay's office, one young woman who had worked with Clay before warned another, "Get your combat boots on, honey. It's about to get down and dirty!"

For the next three weeks, both camps conducted visual warfare.

Scottie Edwards, holding the hands of two small children, marched down Pennsylvania Avenue at the head of a delegation of hostage families. When they reached the White House, he positioned the families against the gates—which made them look like prisoners—and demanded that President Haynes take immediate action.

Georgie and Hunt opened drug youth rehabilitation clinics in Los Angeles, Chicago, New York, and Houston and spoke of the need to reinforce America's borders, beef up Customs, and get drug dealers off the streets.

Otis visited army bases in upstate New York, North Carolina, Texas, and California. Though he was hailed as a hero, he deflected his exaltations and celebrated instead "the glory of anyone who dons the uniform of the United States."

At Ellis Island, Ben talked about the need to stop scapegoating legal immigrants and to create responsible immigration policy. He took the same message to other ports of entry: San Diego, San Francisco, Los Angeles, El Paso, and, of course, Miami. There, in Little Havana, with Fabia Guevera by his side, he praised the Cuban community for turning "exile into excellence" and urged other newcomers to follow their industrious example.

Scottie Edwards visited the floor of the New York Stock Exchange accompanied by several youngsters wrapped in red tape, to point out that American business was not the enemy; government regulation was.

Emily Edwards read stories to suburban preschoolers and then went to inner-city community centers to promote her program of teaching illiterate mothers to read so they could read to their children.

Georgie donned her Western wear and rode the grazing lands in Idaho, Wyoming, and Montana, talking to ranchers about government fees and the preservation of the land.

Otis toured the ballparks, taking city kids and suburban kids onto the field and giving them batting practice, all the while talking to them—and their parents—about teamwork.

Jonetta visited battered women's shelters to point out the need for more protection for those who've been repeatedly victimized and greater awareness on the part of the judicial system about the perils of not heeding the cries of women in trouble.

Ben traveled to Disneyland, where he exhorted the United Nations to stop living in a fairy tale and start implementing sanctions. "We have children who should be here dancing with Mickey Mouse. Instead, they're languishing in prisons run by Red Rage. That isn't right!"

And outside Knight Campaign Headquarters in Philadelphia—with replications in several other cities—a huge billboard bearing pictures of all forty-six hostages—ten nurses taken from the American Hospital in Kuwait, twenty soldiers kidnapped in Korea, fifteen children and their teacher taken in Ankara—and the number of days each of them had been in captivity. The nurses, kidnapped the previous April, had been imprisoned the longest: nearly eighteen months. The shortest confinement was a year. One soldier had been killed.

Only Molly Crookshank had come home alive.

☆ SEPTEMBER ☆

Caleb Lind's office in the West Wing had a window that looked across a driveway at the Old Executive Office Building, an ornate structure which once housed the State, War, and Navy Departments. A bird enthusiast, his walls were decorated with Audubon Society prints. One wall paid homage to birds of forests and woodlands, another to those that inhabited grasslands, a third to those that lived in marshes. Flanking the door were prints of those found on America's seacoast. In addition, he had dozens of bronze and carved wooden eagles, owls, and hawks on display, making his office feel more like an aviary than a place where world issues were addressed.

This was Zoë's third security briefing. At the previous two, Caleb had welcomed her with conspicuous eagerness. He was a man who relished his job and enjoyed the back-and-forth of those who were willing to hoist the heavy oars needed to row the ship of state through the choppy waters of international diplomacy. The Danish and coffee that had been there before were present now, but his back was to her and despite the height of his leather chair, she could see that his shoulders drooped.

"Caleb," she said softly. His secretary had announced her, but he appeared preoccupied.

When he swiveled around to greet her, his mouth was pinched, his complexion gray. He looked grim.

He invited her to have some coffee. "And try the apple Danish. I was told it's particularly good this morning." He tried to smile, but his mouth resisted the effort.

Zoë helped herself to coffee, then settled in the chair facing his desk. No amount of apple Danish could sweeten whatever news he was about to deliver.

"Durgunov has taken more prisoners." His tone was blunt, but rueful. "Early this morning, in the waters off Brindisi, a heavily armed gang of hijackers commandeered an Italian luxury cruise ship, the *Michelangelo.*"

Zoë inhaled sharply and drew her hand to her lips as if to stifle a scream.

"They took all seventy-five American passengers, including your parents."

Her insides felt hollow, full of nothing but air and water, yet at the same time, hot with rage. She had felt this way once before. Then, too, it had been because terrorists had taken her family from her. She began to shake her head.

"No," she mumbled quietly, her fingers curling into fists. "I won't allow that to happen this time."

"Are you all right?" Caleb said, coming around his desk and offering her a glass of water.

"What are we doing about this?" Her voice was steady, but there was no color in her face, and her pale green eyes were moist.

"Our agents on the ground are contacting every mole in the region to ascertain where they've been taken. President Haynes called President Borofsky, who's still recuperating in a hospital."

"What did Borofsky say?" Zoë's jaw was set. She could guess what Borofsky's answer had been.

Caleb examined his shoes. "He said he would look into it."

"Can't we squeeze him?" Zoë stalked the perimeter of

Lind's office. "Durgunov's men shot him, for goodness sake! They tried to blow him away! Why can't we convince him to throw in with us?"

Caleb wanted to help her, just as he wanted to help the other hostage families, but his first duty was to uphold the policy set forth by the president who had appointed him. A mask that had grown too familiar in the past several months slipped onto his face.

"We're doing everything we can, Zoë. Try and stay calm. I'll call you as soon as I know something more."

The expression on Zoë's face was so belligerent, Caleb took a step back.

"If all you can do is tell me to stay calm," she chided, "I'd say you're not doing nearly enough!"

She stormed out of his office and stomped down the hall. When she turned into the West Wing Reception Room, she collided with Arlo Reid. Seeing him was like setting a match to a dynamite wick.

"Where is Edwards?" she demanded, startling the usually unflappable young officer at the reception desk.

"The General is on the road," Arlo snapped, dismayed by her behavior. "Now if you'll excuse me, I have my briefing with Mr. Lind." He tried to sidestep her, but Zoë blocked his way.

"After your briefing go straight to the telephone, Arlo, and tell the General I wish to meet with him."

"He's rather busy these days. He is running for president, you know."

Zoë's voice was a low rumble. "Just tell him if he doesn't arrange to see me, he might be out of the race a lot quicker than he planned."

"That sounds like a threat, Ms. Vaughn."

"It is, Mr. Reid."

That afternoon, Zoë got a call from Celia.

"Something terrible's just come over the wire," she said.

"An unnamed gunman shot Anatoly Chertoff as he was leaving the kibbutz where he had been in hiding."

"Is he alive?" Zoë's whisper was as frantic as a scream.

"As far as we know, but the news coming from Israel is sketchy." Celia paused. Her silence was weighted with recrimination. "I feel responsible."

"You're not to blame, Celia," Zoë said, her teeth grinding with fury. "This goes way beyond you and me. And poor Anatoly."

"Still." Again, Celia paused. "Once before, I told you I wanted to help. You refused to accept my offer. This time, I'm not asking, Zoë. I'm insisting."

Zoë told her to center the story around Durgunov and his widening path of violence. She also suggested that Celia dig up some pictures of Anatoly before his accident. She claimed it would illustrate the devastation of which Durgunov was capable. Her hope was that the person with the duplicate tapes would see Anatoly, recognize him, and contact Zev Shafir's people immediately.

She had just hung up the phone when she received a hand-delivered package from Ben.

"Look what my snoops turned up," the note read. *"Not exactly family viewing, but since my private eyes have told me that someone has been putting the squeeze on you, I thought you might like to squeeze back. Use with caution."*

Zoë slid the video into her VCR, pressed Play, and within seconds, found herself fascinated, disgusted, and strangely delighted.

Two days later Zoë waited impatiently in an anteroom of Harvard's Memorial Hall while Scottie Edwards addressed a packed student audience on the continuing need for a strong military. Dressed in a hooded Harvard sweatshirt, worn jeans, and sneakers, she looked like she could walk into the Yard and get lost in the crowd—which was precisely the idea. Edwards had agreed to meet her on the condition of strict secrecy. Since this speech was already on his calendar and in Boston, where Zoë could visit her family, it seemed the most likely venue.

After Edwards had finished his oration, he, Clay Chandler, and Arlo Reid were escorted from the stage of the Spenser Theatre to a small room down the hall. When they entered, they were surprised to find that Zoë was not alone. Standing by her side was a young hulk also garbed in jeans and sweatshirt.

"I thought we were going to keep this private," Edwards said.

"This is my nephew, Officer Paul Vaughn of the Boston Police Force. He's here because he's concerned about the welfare of his grandparents. And his aunt."

Scottie stole a quick glance at Arlo, who was assessing Zoë's burly companion. Arlo was small, but being a karate black belt had always given him a heightened sense of stature. Paul Vaughn was at least six-foot-three, vastly outweighed him, and, Arlo feared, was probably quite familiar with the martial arts.

"If you don't mind, Paul will make certain no one is wearing a wire."

"I certainly do mind," Clay snorted, protectively crossing his arms across his chest.

"This is an outrage!" Scottie chimed in, drawing himself up into a state of high dudgeon.

Zoë's expression remained one of complete sangfroid. Nothing rattled men like Edwards and Chandler more than female imperturbability.

"The last thing we need is another incriminating tape floating around, wouldn't you say, General?"

Paul approached Clay first. He stood in front of him and stared until he had forced Clay's arms down. Arlo sputtered as Paul patted him down, his eyes darting nervously in Edwards's direction. Scottie, every bit the officer, stood stoically still.

When Paul confirmed that the three men were clean, Zoë removed her sweatshirt and slowly pirouetted for their perusal, displaying a skin-hugging tee shirt and jeans too tight for recording devices. Scottie and Arlo scanned her as if their eyes were equipped with radar. Clay was outright ogling.

"I was terribly dismayed to hear about your parents' capture," Scottie said as she rezipped her sweatshirt.

He looked and sounded sincere. Zoë shook off an impulse to believe him. "I thank you for your concern, but it's meaningless unless accompanied by a substantive attempt to gain their release."

"What is it you think I can do?"

"You can contact your good friend, Yegor Durgunov, tell him that you're canceling whatever arrangement you have with him and President Borofsky, and that there will be serious consequences if he doesn't free the hostages immediately."

"And if I can't . . ."

"Or won't . . ." Zoë interjected.

". . . do as you ask?"

"I'll have no choice but to turn over a certain tape to the proper authorities." Zoë prayed he didn't call her bluff by asking for details.

A vein on the side of Scottie's head visibly throbbed. Arlo made a show of looking out the window, as if reconnoitering for snipers. Clay picked up the conversation.

"Where did you get this alleged tape? And how long have you had it?"

Zoë found the reactions of all three quite telling. Arlo the implacable was clearly on edge. Scottie had withdrawn, as if he needed time to regroup before the next assault. Clay's posture and tone reeked of arrogance and dismissal; his words gave him away. Instead of feigning ignorance or denying the possibility of an incriminating tape, he was admitting that such a tape existed and that its contents were incriminating.

Zoë's gaze traveled to the General, whose demeanor had shifted from bravado to guarded. Obviously, he believed she was still able to claim a network that could provide her with such a tape. Worse, his jitters confirmed that in the meeting Anatoly had described, a Mephistophelian agreement had been reached. Whether everything was proceeding as planned or something had gone awry, she didn't know. But the sudden sheen on Scottie's forehead was not the reflection of an overhead light.

"The tape came into my possession recently from a source who will remain anonymous. But those are irrelevancies, General, compared to the 119 American lives at stake."

"If you're so almighty concerned about the fate of your fellow citizens," Clay huffed as he advanced toward Zoë, "why didn't you take the tape to Haynes or the press?"

Paul, who had been standing several feet behind Zoë, stepped forward, planting himself slightly in front of her. Clay halted, but continued to glare.

Zoë refused to look at him. She directed her response to Scottie. "You're the third wheel on this troika, and unless you've completely sold yourself out, you can void this scheme before innocent lives are ruined. I'm giving you a chance, General, to make things right."

The grit and determination that usually marked the visage of Scottie Edwards seemed to dull, making him look tired and old. He walked to the window and leaned on the sill, staring at the human traffic below. Unconsciously, he loosened his tie. He felt strangled by the tangled web of deception, but like a spider caught in its own gossamer weave, he saw no easy way out. He couldn't drop out of the race. There would be a demand for explanations he could not provide and speculation he could not counter. He couldn't afford to make the bold gesture of confession, even one that had been doctored, because it exposed him to charges of treason. He couldn't rely on Borofsky. Nor could he confront Durgunov.

The most he could do was somehow to convince Zoë that in the initial instance his motives had been in the national interest. Perhaps that his goal had been to maneuver the two Russians into a position that would ultimately favor the United States. Perhaps that he had been betrayed and could not be held responsible for the actions of a madman. Since that approximated the truth, he decided to try that approach first.

"There is no troika," he said quietly. "And I can't make things right. Durgunov is operating on his own. He's a lunatic who takes no counsel and offers no apologies."

His utter dejection told Zoë that Scottie—and Borofsky—had been pushed out of the loop and no longer held any sway over the Unholy Fool. Still, she intended to press him. She needed Edwards to find out where Paddy and Nona and the others were being held, how they were, and what might happen to them.

"If you want to spare yourself the indignity of being branded a traitor, I suggest that you find a way to undo what you've done," she said, boldly setting out terms. "If anything happens to my parents, General, you'll pay, and you'll pay dearly."

Since he had no response, Scottie Edwards exited quietly and contritely, followed by his shadow, Arlo Reid. Clay Chandler lingered. Unlike his partners, he exhibited no remorse.

"You don't threaten generals," he said to her, his lips pressed flat over his teeth. "Especially one who's about to become the next president of the United States."

"Then whom should I threaten, Clay? The architect of this fiasco?"

His eyes widened. She didn't know if he tried to camouflage his pridefulness, but if he had, it hadn't worked.

"On paper, this must have looked brilliant."

"As a matter of fact it did."

"Too bad it was based on myopic political greed rather than sound foreign policy."

"Which, I gather, despite overwhelming proof to the contrary, you consider your specialty." His tone was mocking.

"And what's your specialty, Clay?" she baited. "Campaign strategy? Dirty tricks? Interminable revenge? Sexual perversion?"

Clay flushed in spite of himself. His eyes narrowed and his fists clenched. He might have lunged for her but Paul continued to stand at his aunt's side, as impenetrable as a tank.

"What are you talking about?"

Zoë faced him with a derisive stare. Her mien was calm, but her body was taut with undeniable menace.

"I saw the most interesting video recently. It wasn't so much a movie as it was a collection of short scenes with a common theme. I don't recall all of them, but some of the titles were: A man and two women. Three men and a fist. A man, a woman, lots of leather, some whips, and the CEO of a major corporation. Two women and a senator." Her eyes narrowed to a hard green line. "I don't think Scottie's supporters on the far right would approve, but what do they know about fun?"

He grabbed for her. Paul caught his arm and twisted it. Clay winced in pain.

"You wouldn't dare."

"I'd dare to do just about anything to ensure my parents' release."

Clay stared at her, his aspect changed. The light in his eyes had disappeared, making them look vacant, as if he were peering into a vast emptiness beyond the realm of ordinary vision.

"You never liked me, did you?" he muttered, looking and sounding meek.

"Actually," Zoë said, treading lightly but firmly, "I did, way back when. But the man I liked doesn't exist anymore." She shook her head, signaling a certain regret. "Frankly, Clay, I can't stand the man you've become."

Her criticism catapulted him out of wherever he had gone, returning him to the reality of the moment. His face flamed red with umbrage.

"I want that video," he snarled.

"I'm sure you do." Zoë remained unafraid and unbowed. "Everyone wants something, Clay. But only the one who gives gets."

* * *

For several days after her encounter with Edwards and his claque, Zoë agonized. Caleb Lind, as promised, was keeping her apprised of whatever information came in. To date, all the State Department had been able to confirm was that the *Michelangelo* passengers had been loaded onto several launches which had crossed the Adriatic and docked in the small Albanian port of Sarandë. From there, it was assumed, they had been flown to another location. Zoë worried that Libya was their ultimate destination.

The entire Vaughn clan, as expected, had directed all of their anxieties at Zoë and funneled all of their fears into one phrase: "You have to do something!" She was trying.

That morning, she had spoken to Zev Shafir in Tel Aviv.

"We think we found the man with the tapes," he said. "He called after he saw a broadcast about the latest attack on Anatoly. I'm glad you had your friend show 'before' pictures. This man said he never would have recognized Anatoly without them."

"So who is *he?*"

"Brian Atshul. He's a representative of the Hong Kong Dock Company with an Australian passport and impeccable credentials."

"A dock company?"

"Actually," Zev said, "he was a clever pick as a courier. His position affords him the perfect cover. As a huckster for the docks, he comes and goes as he pleases and has access to business and government leaders throughout the world. Anatoly got to him because he's the child of Holocaust survivors. Helping us has become his personal mission."

"Why didn't he come forward sooner?"

"When Anatoly handed him the package containing the tapes, all he asked of Brian was that he hold on to them. If anything happened, Anatoly said, someone would contact him."

"He didn't know about the car bomb."

"No. He left Russia that day, went off to Mongolia, Africa, and several of the Pan-Pacific nations. He returned to Australia just recently. It was only when he saw the news that he remembered he had the tapes. He called us immediately."

"How's Anatoly doing?" Zoë asked.

"Actually, he's okay."

"Good. I wish I knew that my parents were okay." Her tone was leaden.

"Our people are looking, Zoë, the same as yours are."

"That's cold comfort, Zev."

"I know. I wish I could put an end to this nightmare."

Zoë heard so much pain and frustration and love in his voice, it made her weep. At one time, she and Zev had been related; she treasured the fact that they were still so closely connected.

"The only way I can console you," he said, begging her not to lose faith, "is to remind you of a grim truth: Durgunov has already shown us he's not embarrassed to make a display of dead bodies. If something terrible had happened, Zoë, we would know."

The doorbell startled her. It was eleven o'clock. She was at Paddy and Nona's house. Her first thought was the worst. When Ben identified himself, cautious relief elbowed her dread aside. She opened the door to find him alone, dressed in jeans, leather boots, and a shearling coat that looked vaguely familiar. Even more startling was the bright red Camaro parked in front of the house. As he walked past her into the living room, he grinned.

"Neat trick, isn't it?" he said, dropping his coat on a chair and settling in as if this were his own home. "I learned it from a very savvy lady."

"Whose car is it? And how'd you get past the Secret Service?"

"It belongs to the son of one of tonight's fund-raising

chairs. And . . . it wasn't easy. Jed says if I scuff up his boots, he's going to scuff my ass."

He chuckled, but as they chatted, he appraised her. She looked adorable in her gray sweatsuit and fuzzy slippers, but there were dark circles rimming her eyes and she looked thin.

"How about fixing me a hot chocolate? Some cookies would be nice too."

"I take it you didn't eat."

"If I eat one more piece of chicken, I'm going to cluck!"

She led the way to the kitchen. When the cocoa was ready, she poured it into two big mugs, added as many tiny marshmallows as space allowed, then joined him at the kitchen table.

"Tell me how you're doing," he said, devouring one of the cupcakes Zoë had stocked for her nieces and nephews.

"On a scale of one to ten, I'm hovering somewhere around two."

She sipped her hot chocolate, smiling when she looked at Ben and noticed a milky mustache coating his upper lip.

"This visit means a lot to me," she said, watching him lick away the telltale residue. "Thanks."

"You mean a lot to me," he said seriously. "So do Paddy and Nona. I think you know that." She nodded and her eyes pooled. "I called the president and urged him to step up his efforts. I even suggested that he try another rescue mission."

Zoë wiped her eyes with the sleeve of her sweatshirt. "What did he say?"

"Notwithstanding this latest incident, he believes he's making headway and intends to stick to his course."

"Because it's worked so well up to now." Zoë's anger hovered so close to the surface, it erupted instantly. "What's wrong with him?"

Ben shrugged. He shared her frustration. "I spoke to Harry Cadman this morning. He's ready to jump into a bomber himself."

Zoë tried to smile, but it wasn't there. Instead, she twirled her hair around her finger. Ben recognized the signal: she was debating something. He sipped his cocoa, indulged himself in another cupcake, and waited.

"There are a few things you ought to know," she said.

"I'm all ears."

It took her an hour to explain about Anatoly Chertoff, Maura Silver, Dixon Collins, the other people in her department, what Anatoly said had taken place in Moscow in 1991, Edwards's apparent entanglement with Durgunov and Borofsky, and finally, the tapes.

"Zev expects to have them very soon."

She went on to tell him about her confrontation with Scottie in Boston, then speculated about what happened.

"At that Moscow meeting, they brokered a deal that would create a candidacy for Scottie. In return for which, Scottie would use his presidency to provide them with money and an unconditional affiliation with the U.S. When you think about how Scottie has gone against type and consistently shied away from criticizing either Durgunov or Borofsky, it's the only thing that makes sense."

"It certainly explains his paranoia about you," Ben said. "If he's in bed with those two, the last thing he wants is for you to go on Dean Walsh's show and say to the world, 'I told him so.' "

"But I did," Zoë said without gloating. "It appears that just what I predicted has occurred. At some point, Durgunov's appetite turned voracious. He shoved both Borofsky and Scottie aside so he could keep the entire plate for himself. It's hard for me to conjure even a scintilla of sympathy for Scottie, but I don't think this was his game plan. To me, the General looks real worried."

"He should be." Ben's jaw pulsed. "Whether he thinks he's in or out, in my book he's in—up to his eyeballs. He'd better pray that nothing happens to any of those hostages."

"By the way, thanks for Clay's home movies. They came in handy."

"He had to be involved with all this. Underhanded and nasty has become his signature."

"Add treasonous to that list. Apparently, Clay's the one who engineered this horrible scheme in the first place."

"Figures," Ben said, dejectedly. "For most of his adult life, Clay's been on a mission to rehabilitate his reputation and prove to those who doubted and betrayed him that they were wrong. Brokering the presidency would be a hell of a coup."

"I thought his primary goal was the complete and utter ruination of Benjamin Douglas Knight."

"Look at how well it all fits," Ben said, dripping sarcasm. "I decide to run for president. He's already signed on as campaign strategist for my opponent. The coincidence must have appeared like Providence!"

"I find it scary." Zoë didn't see how he could be so accepting of another man's hatred. She wasn't as generous.

Ben stroked the back of her hand. "I can deal with Clay's malevolence because in a strange way, I understand it. He thinks I did him in. He wants to do me in."

"This is not a simple tit for tat, Ben. These are dangerous times, with lives and careers at stake and Clay is . . . well, frankly, I think he's gone around the bend."

"Wherever he's gone, he doesn't bother me. What does, is that now, you've become more than an ally of mine. You've become an enemy of his. I almost wish I hadn't sent you that video."

"By the way," Zoë said, her eyes twinkling with curiosity. "Where'd you get it?"

Ben grinned as if he was hiding a box of chocolates behind his back. "Celia. She suggested we strong-arm her ex-husband, Harris Ralston. We did, and he turned out to be a fount of information about the private life of Clayborne Chandler III."

Zoë's eyebrows arched in surprise and admiration. "Good for Celia." She laughed unexpectedly. "I always said Harris Ralston was good for nothing."

When Ben explained about Clay's bartering Hugo for

Celia's cooperation, Zoë ached for her friend, knowing the lengths she was willing to go to protect her parents.

"I owe Celia a major apology," Zoë said.

"All she wants is your understanding and your friendship."

"Granted."

They sat quietly for a time, comfortable in their silence.

"What if I went public with the tapes?" Zoë asked. "If we forced their alliance out into the open, perhaps we could force Durgunov's hand."

Ben shook his head. "Celia's piece compromised us. If we came forward with this tape now, we could be accused of knowing all this before, which you did in a way, and of withholding information vital to our national security. We'd look worse than Edwards."

Zoë wasn't giving up. "Okay. What if I went to the president with what I know about Scottie and Durgunov?" she said, laying out another possibility.

Ben considered it, trying to be optimistic about Elton Haynes, but it was difficult. He wished he had more faith in his old friend, but, he supposed, if he had, he wouldn't be running for that friend's office.

"As you told me months ago," he reminded Zoë, "unless someone can guarantee the success of another rescue mission, Elton Haynes won't risk another international humiliation. His heart's in the right place, but his head's thinking about his chapter in the history books. He doesn't want to be responsible for the deaths of any more Americans. He'll continue paying off Durgunov because as long as he pays, the hostages seem safe. Getting them out is going to be the next guy's problem."

"Then you have to be the next guy."

"I'm tryin' my best, darlin'," Ben said as he reached across the table and entwined his fingers with hers.

"What if Scottie Edwards wins?" A sudden shower of tears dampened her cheeks. "What'll happen to my parents then?"

"He's not going to win. And Paddy and Nona are going to be fine."

Zoë wept softly, keeping her hand in his. "Dixon Collins and Maura Silver and Anatoly Chertoff aren't fine," she murmured.

Ben twisted his head to the side, as if he wasn't certain he heard her correctly. "A light has dawned. Did you reject my proposal because you were afraid something might happen to me if I was associated with you?"

She shrugged. "People around me have been hurt or humiliated or worse. My parents have been kidnapped. My apartment was ransacked. I've been threated and harassed by hang-ups. Yes. At the time, it seemed like the best thing to do."

Without letting go of her hand, Ben rose from his chair, walked around the table, knelt down in front of her, and looked deep into her eyes.

"Letting me think you didn't love me was worse than anything Clay Chandler, Scottie Edwards, Arlo Reid, or the Devil himself could do to me."

Zoë sighed. "It may sound irrational, Ben, but Durgunov and his gang seem to be everywhere."

"What does that have to do with us?"

She caressed his cheek softly, but her aspect remained grim. "They have an agenda that hinges on Scottie Edwards being elected president. In case you haven't noticed, you're the fella who's getting in their way."

"And I shall continue to do so." Ben stood and leaned against the table. "I'm not going to hand the presidency over to Scottie Edwards. I'm not going to let Yegor Durgunov get away with his crimes. And I'm not going to stop loving you. So you have a choice: You can stay here and make yourself crazy worrying. Or you can get back to work so that yours truly gets to walk at the head of the inaugural parade.

"As for the love and marriage part, my proposal still stands. Since I never would deny Paddy the pleasure of walking you down the aisle or Nona the joy of hosting a wedding, I'm willing to wait until they're back. Okay with you?"

Zoë stood and laced her arms around his neck. "You're okay with me," she murmured.

He held her, and, for the moment, at least, she felt safe.

Zoë was in Washington watching the news and proof-reading a Middle East policy paper for Ben when her doorbell rang.

"If you don't mind," Clay Chandler said, oiling his way past her into the living room. "I don't want to talk in the hall."

"I'd show you around," Zoë said sarcastically, "but since you probably accompanied your stormtroopers when they went through my apartment, I doubt that's necessary."

She would have respected him more if he'd had the decency to look embarrassed. He didn't.

"We would like that tape."

"Which one? Scottie and the boys? Or you, your wife, your friends, and your toys?"

"Both," he spit through gritted teeth.

Zoë shook her head. "I don't think so."

Clay scrutinized her carefully. While he wanted both tapes, his first priority was the recording of the Moscow meeting; that was far more hazardous. One was treason; the other was pornographic, but wouldn't result in his hanging. Neither he nor Scottie was certain that Zoe actually possessed the tape, but neither one was brave enough to call her bluff. Instead, they would deal for her silence and draft a response in case she refused and went to the press.

Scottie would claim that the meeting was an attempt to mediate a compromise between the leaders of Russia's two feuding factions as a way of protecting American invest-ments. He would further contend that in light of Durgu-nov's impressive showing in his last election, Scottie had no choice but to treat him with respect.

Dealing with Zoë was far more difficult. She was a principled woman who refused to budge off her position. Scottie had badgered her about Ben's campaign; she hadn't quit. Arlo had wrecked her apartment; she hadn't been frightened off. Clay had disgraced her on international television; she hadn't taken her explanation or accusations public. Clay viewed that as an indication of her ambition. Scottie read it as another of her damnable traits: She wouldn't accuse someone without incontrovertible proof. If she had recently gotten her hands on that tape, however, she had her proof. Which was why Clay had fed Durgunov the information about Zoë's parents being on that cruise ship. They became his trump card.

Zoë's attention had wandered to the television screen. Dean Walsh was recapping the hijacking of the *Michelangelo* as a lead-in for coverage of Ben's speech the night before in Chicago. It had been a searing condemnation of Elton Haynes's handling of the situation as well as a blistering attack on Edwards's bizarre reluctance to support military action against Durgunov. As NTN replayed Ben's verbal assault, Zoë savored the displeasure that washed over Clay's face.

"He's a charismatic orator, don't you think?"

She could almost hear his teeth grinding as he looked away from the screen and fixed on her.

"I'm here to offer you a quid pro quo," he said matter-of-factly, refusing to give her the satisfaction of reacting to her gibe.

"The tape in exchange for what?"

"We'd be willing to try and contact some intermediaries who might be able to negotiage the release of your parents."

Zoë shook her head. "Willing. Try. Might be able. Did you ever hear the old saw about the tape in the hand is worth two in the bush?"

"That tape is not what it seems," he insisted.

"When I listened, it seemed to tiptoe along the borders of treason."

"You're taking it completely out of context! This was an incident of intelligence-gathering and fence-building that has taken on an entirely new aspect in light of Yegor Durgunov's dementia. You can't blame General Edwards for the acts of a psychopath!"

"I could sure as hell try," she said.

Clay flushed. "I need something to give Durgunov so he can save face. Don't you understand that?"

On the television, the scene had shifted to outside Knight Campaign Headquarters in Philadelphia. A second billboard had gone up, this one covered with photographs of the seventy-five passengers of the *Michelangelo*. Zoë's gaze froze on the two pictures at the end of the bottom row.

"I'll tell you what I understand," she said with cold simplicity. "I want my parents back safe and sound. When I get that, you'll get your tape."

☆ OCTOBER ☆

The polls fluctuated wildly. Despite numerous offers to settle, Cleo Wells refused to drop her paternity suit. Each time her name popped up in print—the tabloids were off on a feeding frenzy—or her sad face appeared on TV, Scottie's numbers sagged.

Scottie followed Clay's advice and hammered away at Ben's long-standing friendship with Elton Haynes as well as his party affiliation, implying, of course, that voting for Ben was the same as reelecting Haynes. The guilty-by-association theory worked quite well in some quarters. Whenever there was a flurry of stories about Haynes's failure to free the hostages, Ben's figures took a dive.

In mid-October, Quinn wiped Cleo Wells and the hostages off the front pages.

"We lead off this evening with some startling revelations about vice-presidential candidate, Georgie Hughes. According to information received earlier today, when Ms. Hughes was fourteen, she was raped by a man on her father, Governor Hughes's, staff. The crime was never reported. When it was discovered she was pregnant, she was flown to a hospital in Mexico, where an abortion was performed.

Upon her return, she was sent to private school in the East and the matter was dropped. Her assailant was never charged. He simply disappeared. It's been alleged that the governor paid the man to leave the country.

"I caught up with Ms. Hughes late this afternoon in New York where she was campaigning."

The scene shifted from the studio to an elegant hotel room. Georgie, sitting ramrod straight in a fussy French chair, looked pale, but composed.

"Is this true?" Quinn asked. "Were you the victim of a sexual assault?"

"Yes."

"Did Scottie Edwards know about this before selecting you as his running mate?"

"No."

"Should we assume you remained silent because you wanted to run, and your party's platform demands a constitutional amendment banning abortion?"

Georgie looked perturbed. "That's extremely simplistic, Mr. Quinn. And, I might add, naive and insensitive. I remained silent because rape is a nightmare that no woman should ever have to endure. This was a terrible chapter in my life, one I hoped I'd never have to relive."

"What do you say to your conservative supporters who oppose abortion under any circumstances?"

"I understand their position and I respect it, but for me, at fourteen years old, to bear a child that had been conceived by an act of violence was unthinkable."

Quinn started to ask another question, but Georgie stopped him.

"At the risk of offending you and others who might like to make this *the* overarching issue of the campaign, let me state here and now, that this will be my only interview on the subject.

"As for the facts: Yes. I was raped as a teenager. Yes. I had an abortion. No, my family did not buy my assailant's silence. They did not charge him because they wanted to spare me the intrusive headlines and torturous court appearances that would have followed such a charge. He left the country of his own accord. Not prosecuting my attacker was a mistake, and I regret it, but it's in the past. Now, if you don't mind, Mr. Quinn, I don't intend to speak of this again.''

But the public could talk about nothing else. The eleven o'clock news was filled with it, as were the morning papers, the morning and afternoon talk shows, and the next several TV news cycles. Georgie Hughes's abortion was the scandal *du jour*.

Georgie flew to Dallas immediately after her interview with Quinn. She stormed into her house, where she found Lyle snuggled happily in their den, enjoying a bourbon and her televised misery.

"Are you proud of yourself?" she asked, positively spilling over with fury. "Are you getting a kick out of seeing me stripped bare and humiliated coast to coast? Is it fun to watch my father being grilled by so-called investigative reporters?"

"I can't imagine what you're talking about." He twisted around so he had a full view of her. She was an apocalyptic vision of barely constrained anger, a tornado caught in that split second before its destructive winds touch down and devastate the earth.

"You!" she shouted. "You gave that story to Sean Quinn. You went back on your word! You sold me out, you lowlife bastard! That's what I'm talking about!"

Lyle spread his arms and held his hands palms up. "I'm innocent," he proclaimed. "In case you've forgotten, Sean Quinn's been sharing sheets with your good friend Celia Porter. My guess is that in an explosion of passion, she ratted you out."

Georgie shuddered with disgust. "Celia would never do that. She understands the concept of loyalty, something that's clearly beyond your reach."

"Okay," he hypothesized, as blithely as if they were playing a game of *Clue*. "Then perhaps it was your lover, Jed Oakes."

"What!"

Lyle gulped down the last of his bourbon, gaining immense satisfaction out of watching Georgie's face flush.

"It makes perfect sense," he explained. "The man's in the middle of a close presidential campaign. If he wants to further his career, he needs this victory. You and he may be great in the sack, but to a guy like Oakes, winning beats whoopee every time."

He stifled a smirk and studied her through narrowed eyes, as if he was posing a serious question.

"You can understand that, can't you? After all, isn't the Hughes family motto: A win is a win, no matter what?"

Georgie couldn't bear to breathe the same air as he did. She raced to her bedroom and locked the door, trying to keep Lyle and his smarmy accusations as far away from her as she could. But later, lying alone in bed unable to sleep, she wondered about Jed. During their first campaign, he spent a lot of time in Dallas. Someone might have known. Someone might have told him.

"So what!" she said aloud. "He wouldn't."

But he did love to win. And this race was important. And she hadn't heard from him.

Over the next several days, Georgie managed to keep to her schedule while somehow finding time to sit with Hunt and Olivia. The twins were loving and supportive and more concerned about her than they were about the ugly publicity. She found time to visit with Roy, who had come under attack not only for not prosecuting his daughter's rapist, but for possibly funding his escape. Several old enemies had dusted off their axes and ground them on every talk show that would have them: "All Roy ever worried about was reelection." "He was always throwing his money around." "It was just like him to put his career before his daughter." And then, with obvious joy, they pointed out that Roy had lost that election anyway. The consensus: It served him right.

No one came forward to confirm that Georgie's version was the truth, because no one other than Roy and Bunny knew anything about it—including Georgie's siblings.

After a long day in Denver, campaigning and avoiding the A word, Georgie retired to her suite only to find Jed waiting for her.

"Don't worry. No one saw me," he said, coming out from behind an armoire. "I'm a master of disguises."

She kicked off her shoes and sat on a chair, pointing him to one on the other side of the room. He didn't argue, but neither did he understand the chilly reception.

"How're you doing?"

"As well as can be expected, considering the fact that this morning I was condemned by the conservatives and martyred by the moderates." She smiled, but there was no happiness in the gesture. "Lyle thinks you gave the story to Quinn."

It was such a non sequitur and so absurd that it struck Jed momentarily dumb. When he recovered, he responded as evenly as he could.

"Lyle's an asshole. I didn't know the story, so I couldn't have given it to anyone. If you want to know where Quinn got it, ask him."

"I did. He won't reveal his source." She shifted in her seat. "Why didn't you call me when you heard?"

"Because I didn't know where you were or when you'd be alone, and I figured the last thing you needed was for a rumor to start about us." He stopped for a breath, then continued. "And as long as we're doing the question thing, why did you think you couldn't tell me you were raped?"

"It's an ugly tale."

"True, but it happened, and it was haunting you." He hated the sight of her hanging her head. "I would have listened, consoled you, reaffirmed my love for you, and respected your privacy." *Which was more than Lyle did.*

"I felt ashamed," Georgie said. Her voice was hollow as

an echo coming from another time. "Also, I was terrified of the exposure. I didn't want people pointing fingers at me and whispering behind my back. I didn't want to go into a courtroom and tell them what he did to me."

She stared at her lap, her fingers in constant motion. Jed pulled a footstool up to her chair and sat next to her.

"He hurt me." She inhaled sharply, as fearful as she must have been then. "And when he was finished, he threatened me."

Jed took her hands and held them. She was shaking. He went to the bar and poured her a brandy, which she accepted gratefully.

"Today, I wish we'd prosecuted him, but then, I was terrified that he'd hurt me again. I also was horrified at the idea of a scandal." She laughed. "Truth is, I'm not too crazy about it now."

"Listen," Jed said. "If you need me to help you get through this, I'm here."

Georgie leaned over and kissed him. He moved next to her on the couch and rested her head on his shoulder. For hours, they talked. She told him how hard it had been to go away to school, how ashamed she felt and how frightened she was that the other girls might find out. She told him how she had buried herself in her schoolwork, using it as a way of proving she was a good girl and as an excuse not to go out on dates. Lyle Mercer was the first man she ever had sex with, other than the rapist.

It was nearly two o'clock in the morning when Jed announced he had to leave.

"You going to be okay?" he asked.

"I'm not having fun, that's for sure."

"You just hold that gorgeous head up high and you'll make out just fine. You've got nothing to be ashamed of, Georgie. The press knows that, and they'll back off soon. You'll see."

Georgie nodded, but the gesture lacked confidence.

"I wish you were managing my campaign," she said.

Jed grinned. "Of course you do! I'm the best there is!"

Georgie laughed. "That you are."

She kissed him gently. He grabbed his jacket and reluctantly headed toward the door. As he bent down to kiss her good-bye, Jed noticed the slight downturn of her lips.

"No fair tugging at the heartstrings, little girl. No matter how sad you look, I have to go." His eyes twinkled. "I owe it to America to beat up on that dog Edwards until he barks for mercy."

"Whatever happened to all that stuff about undying love?" she said, feigning devastation.

He slid his arm around her waist and pulled her so close, she could hardly breathe. As he pressed her against him, his lips spread into a slow, sexy smile.

"This isn't about me and you and undying love," he said. "This is about politics, sugar, and for now, much as I'd prefer foolin' around with you, I'm still in bed with Benjamin Knight."

☆   ☆   ☆

The first debate was held in an auditorium on the campus at the University of Wisconsin. An NTN/*New York Times* poll had Knight/Jefferson down by seven points. Even though Scottie had admitted paternity and settled with Cleo Wells—which had boosted Ben's ratings—the story about Georgie had had the opposite effect. While the Edwards/Hughes ticket lost support from the conservative camp—provoking a sharp rise in the Undecided column—moderate Republicans who favored choice with restrictions joined with many female Democrats who publicly applauded Georgie's bravery and deplored the need for her to remain silent.

Onstage, Ben and Scottie answered questions from the three-journalist panel. The only heated moments occurred when the regional head of the Associated Press asked Scottie about his appearance at the AGA convention in Spokane.

"Was your address an endorsement of the American Gunowners Association position on the repeal of the assault weapons ban? And should your appearance at their convention be construed as support for the Patriot movement?''

Scottie's response bordered on the brusque, belying the calm expression on his face.

"My position, Ms. Zebert, has not changed since I was first asked that question several years ago." His tone implied that she was either an idiot or a noisome media pest seeking a gotcha! "While I support the right to bear arms, I don't believe in putting high-tech weaponry in the hands of the untrained."

He paused. Alana Zebert waited, uncowed. When it became clear he intended to bunt the second part of her question she repeated it.

"And the extremists known as the Patriot movement, General? Do you stand with them? Or against them?''

"Not everyone who calls himself a Patriot is an extremist, Ms. Zebert. There are many people in this country who worry about the intrusion of big government into the private corners of our lives. They worry about what our children are learning in school and what they're watching on TV. They think we pay too much in taxes and receive too little in the way of services. I don't call that extreme.

"It is true," he continued quickly, disallowing argument, "that there are groups of disgruntled citizens who call themselves Patriots who sometimes react to perceived government conspiracies with violence. They're criminals and should be prosecuted just like anyone else who breaks the law."

When it was his turn, Ben played the picador and stuck Scottie with another spear by asking about the extent of Arlo Reid's involvement with the militias. Ben's research team had discovered Arlo's name mentioned in several Patriot newsletters and magazines.

Edwards parried with an explanation that made a comeback impossible. "Colonel Reid is a decorated soldier, Senator Knight. He's often asked to speak to reservists and others who believe in the honor of military service. As a decorated veteran, I'm sure you understand the need for such role models."

In the end, neither side could claim a win.

After, while their press secretaries spun the results for the media hounds, Scottie and Ben stayed behind to shake hands with members of the audience and sign autographs. Ben was about to leave when he was accosted by Clay Chandler.

"Well, well. Senator Knight."

More out of habit than anything else, Ben extended his hand. Clay stuffed his in his pockets.

"Nice to see you, too," Ben said, his blue-eyed gaze turning stone cold.

"You think you're going to win this?"

Ben nodded confidently. "As a matter of fact, I do."

Clay shook his head and stared at Ben as if he were to be pitied. "I won't let you," he said, his voice reverberating with reproach. "I'll do whatever it takes, but I will not lose to you."

Ben was tired. His patience was thin. And Clay's blood feud was becoming stale.

"I'm not running against you, Clay, so pack up your dueling swords and go home. Better yet, get off my case and get a life!"

Clay pursed his lips and hissed like a pressure cooker as Ben walked away. Years of cumulative rage bubbled as he watched his enemy march into a crowded circle of acceptance and adulation. As they took Ben in and embraced him, Clay fumed.

It struck him that perhaps Ben didn't understand: he *was* running against Clay. This wasn't an election, it was the last round in a conflict that had begun when they were boys and Judge Clayborne Chandler had insinuated Ben into Clay's life, always holding the fatherless boy up as an example to his own son, always making Clay work harder than he could and aim higher than he should in order to be worthy of his father's praise. It had taken Clay years to rebuild his reputation after the debacle at the court, years for his father to be able to look directly at him instead of avoiding his eye, years for him to be welcome in his parents' home, among his parents' friends and his father's colleagues.

When Fate had intervened with this electoral confrontation, the notion of going head to head with Ben had infuriated Clay. But then, upon reflection, he decided that waging war in a national arena was properly titanic: What better way to settle the score than to pit two giants against each other in an epic contest of wills.

If Clay won, his past would be erased, his intellect would be validated, and his membership in the upper echelon of power brokers would be confirmed.

If Ben won, however, he would be president of the United States and Clay would once again be a loser.

As Clay turned his back on Ben and left the hall, he reaffirmed a vow he had taken a long time ago: That was simply not going to happen.

Quinn waited until he saw Celia sign off with her crew. Before she could give him the slip, he took her by the arm and led her out the door, down the steps of Bascomb Hall onto the green.

"I spoke to Hugo last week," he said as if he and Celia's father were golfing buddies. "He's very worried about you."

Celia's eyes popped. "You didn't tell him about . . ."

"The lump? No. He's concerned because I'm whipping your ass in the ratings." He grinned and waited for Celia to respond. She didn't.

"After all," he continued, "I got a lot of play on the Edwards love-child story. And my coverage of the campaign has been outstanding, if I do say so, and of course I do." He studied her out of the corner of his eye. She was not amused. "He was upset about that Chertoff guy getting popped. He was afraid you'd be hit by the fallout."

Guilt veiled Celia's eyes, but she remained withdrawn.

"He told me you ran that story under duress, that if you hadn't, there would've been repercussions. He implied the repercussions would have hurt him."

No change of expression. No confirmation or denial.

Quinn went on. "He wondered if you had given me the piece on Georgie Hughes." That got a reaction. Celia practically growled. "I told him I had another source for that one. You'll be happy to know he believed you had too much integrity to betray Georgie."

Celia sighed. Dean Walsh and Titus Mitchell weren't nearly as impressed with her adherence to principle. They had called her on the carpet and demanded to know why, considering her connections, NTN had been scooped on two major stories. They were willing to write off the love-child piece to dumb luck. Georgie's abortion was something they believed Celia had to have known about. She refused to reveal whether or not she had known, but she did tell them that even if she had, she never would have given the story to them or anyone else. They had given her a bye, but not happily.

"Are you done?" She wrapped her coat around her. It was a few days before Halloween, yet it was bitter cold in Madison.

"No. Actually, I'm not." He slipped his arm through hers and led her to a car. "Do us both a favor. Don't make a scene. Just come with me."

They drove down University Avenue, turned left onto a side street, and pulled up in front of a small run-down house typical of campus dwellings that could sleep anywhere from one to fifty.

"Why are we stopping here?" Celia said. "I'm hungry. I thought you were taking me to dinner."

"I will, but first, there's someone I want you to meet."

They rang the bell and were greeted by a pretty young woman with russet hair and green eyes.

"This is my baby sister, Megan. Meggie, this is the famous Celia Porter."

Megan led them inside a living room that was homier

and in much better taste than Celia would have expected. The furniture was used and eclectic, but fresh flowers and a lot of books had created a cozy ambience that put her immediately at ease. They munched on veggies and chip dip and chatted for a while about growing up a Quinn. They had been there half an hour or so when Celia began to suspect there was another purpose to this visit.

"Not that I'm not charmed to meet you," she said, "but your brother isn't the most trustworthy chap, and this is beginning to smell like a setup."

Megan smiled shyly. "I'm a doctor at the University Hospital, taking my residency in gynecology and obstetrics."

"I'm not having a baby." Celia glared at Megan, who remained unchastened.

"According to Sean, you have a lump on your breast that you've left unchecked. He thought that perhaps here, with me, you'd be willing to submit to an examination."

She was soft-spoken, but there was a serious edge to her voice, one that said she didn't accept irresponsibility on matters of health.

Celia surrendered. "Let's get it over with."

"I understand your fear, Celia, but the sooner we examine you, the sooner you'll have the facts."

Megan had set up in the kitchen. After a thorough physical examination, she aspirated the lump, wiped a slide, and studied the fluid under a microscope.

"I'm going to send this to a lab for confirmation, but from what I can see, it's not malignant. I believe it's a benign cyst."

Celia's relief was instantaneous. Megan wasn't offering congratulations.

"If this had been cancer, you would have died, Celia, and that would have been tragic, because you could have prevented it."

Celia looked away. She didn't want to be reprimanded.

"There are many cancers we can't cure, but if we catch

breast cancer early enough, our rate of success is excellent.''

"They diagnosed my mother's breast cancer early,'' Celia said, striking back. "She had a lumpectomy and they told her she'd be fine. Two years later, she had third-stage invasive breast cancer. They operated on her, mutilated her, poured chemicals into her body and still, she died. Don't talk to me about success.''

"Our older sister died of breast cancer,'' Quinn said, leaning against the frame of the kitchen door. "That's one of the reasons Meggie chose this specialty. So she could spare others what happened to Kathleen. And Nell.''

Celia glanced from Megan to Quinn. "Why didn't you say anything?''

"Because you had made your mother's cancer your personal tragedy and your private burden. It was a subject that was completely off-limits. Rather than upset you, I respected your wishes. But,'' he said, walking into the room and draping his arm around his sister's shoulder, obviously pleased to have an ally, "I wasn't going to let you die.''

Celia's mouth quivered as she looked up at him. She felt grateful and stupid. "It wasn't any of your business.''

"I love you, too,'' he said, swooping her into his arms and hugging her close. He could feel her tears on his neck. "Now, say 'thank you' to Meggie.''

"Thank you,'' Celia sputtered.

"And now, say 'thank you' to Quinn.''

She stepped out of his embrace, looked deep into his Irish eyes and caressed his cheek. "Thank you,'' she whispered.

Quinn's mouth curled into a slow smile. "You're welcome.''

☆   ☆   ☆

The second debate, held in Phoenix, Arizona, switched from a panel of journalists to a town meeting moderated by Dean Walsh. Each candidate was permitted an opening statement before squaring off in front of an audience of registered voters selected by lottery. After the first few questions, it seemed clear that the open forum favored Ben's more personal style. He succeeded there for the same reason he went over well on the talk shows: vox populi. People felt they could talk to Ben, that they "could call this guy" or take a microphone and ask him what he thought about things that mattered to them. Though only a handful of Americans actually got to speak to the candidates directly, they became surrogates for the voter at home. Ben played to both crowds by leaving his wooden stool, walking over to his questioner, and giving his answer face-to-face. There was nothing harsh or off-putting about him and it showed, in person and on camera.

Edwards came off looking stiff and remote. His answers were crisp and factually correct, but void of emotion. In this setting, the unruffled, dignified demeanor that usually served him so well became a liability. During a time when the fate of the hostages was becoming a national obsession, military reserve translated into indifference.

It was near the end of the debate when the momentum shifted sharply. An elderly gentleman rose and confronted General Edwards. His hands shook as he held the microphone, but his voice was firm.

"My name is Jack Persis and I live here in Phoenix. My grandson, Tom Anderson, was the soldier Red Rage killed and left on the steps of that church in Bucharest."

A horrifed gasp raced through the audience. Scottie stiffened. Ben leaned forward, unable to believe what was happening. The names of every participant selected by the lottery had been run through a computer to make certain that no one was related to the campaign staffs of either candidate, the candidates themselves, the president, or the immediate families of the hostages. Somehow, someone had missed Jack Persis.

"General Edwards," the man began, his head bobbing slightly. "You say you think Senator Knight is making things worse by threatening military retaliation. You say you think strong negotiations and leadership are the keys to solving this problem. I don't think so, sir. That Durgunov guy murdered my grandson. What I'd like to know is why you won't go after this gang of terrorists with everything we've got?''

The applause was deafening. Jack Persis seemed not to hear it. He continued to stare at Scottie waiting for a response. On television, the minute that transpired between the asking and the answering seemed like an eternity.

"I deeply regret your tragedy, Mr. Persis," Scottie said. "Your grandson was a fine soldier and a brave American. My argument with Senator Knight is that number one, he's threatening something he can't deliver. He's a candidate for president, not the commander in chief, which make his bold words nothing but empty rhetoric.

"Number two, if one decides to use military force, there are several rules that must be followed: targets must be clear and precise and the amount of force used must be overwhelming. We don't know where the hostages are. Where would you like us to drop the first bomb?''

As the words left his lips, Scottie knew he had made a colossal blunder.

"How about on Durgunov's house?" Jack Persis replied, his head shaking more visibly now. "I don't get it, General. A friend of mine heard you speak at the AGA convention. He said you thought Americans had the right to protect themselves against those who attacked our liberties. He said you applauded the idea of Americans being ready, willing, and able to fight for their flag. You've said you believe in the death penalty.

"My grandson fought for the American flag, in the United States Army, not some farm-grown militia. How come he wasn't worthy of the same protection you offered those woodsy warriors?''

Scottie started to explain his presence at the conference and correct the distortions of his speech, but Jack Persis stopped him cold.

"Why isn't the savage murder of my grandson a crime worthy of death?" he shouted.

"That's not . . ."

Dean Walsh silenced Edwards by swiftly turning to Ben for a response.

"The only way to deal with bullies," Ben declared as he walked to where the old man was standing, "is with swift and overwhelming force."

Walsh held up his hands, but he couldn't stifle the burst of applause triggered by Ben's statment.

"Your role at the AGA convention comes as a surprise, General," Walsh said, hoping the audience was as curious about Edwards's unheralded appearance in Spokane as he was. "Would you like to explain why there was a news blackout on that event?"

Before Scottie could reply, Ben, positioned alongside Jack Persis and looking at one with the audience, confronted his opponent.

"The General probably didn't want the American public to know that this was not the first time he had cozied up to extremists."

"I beg your pardon." Scottie's immediate expression of high dudgeon played well on camera, but it was overshadowed by Ben's follow-up.

"Isn't your inexplicable stand on using military force against Red Rage simply reluctance to punish an old friend?"

Scottie flushed. The camera dollied in so close the lens seemed almost to touch his reddened cheek. The audience was staring in stunned silence.

"What are you talking about?" he demanded.

"I'm talking about a private meeting several years ago that took place in Moscow between you, President Borofsky, and Yegor Durgunov."

Backstage, Sam Trout, Jed, and the rest of Ben's coterie were in shock. Zoë chewed her lip, frightened that Ben had gone too far.

In the other camp, Clay Chandler's eyes practically

bulged out of his head. He turned to Arlo Reid, seeking some kind of explanation, but the small soldier was as stunned and panicked as Clay was.

"You're on record as saying you've never met Durgunov," Dean Walsh said, jumping on the lead.

Ben remained opposite Scottie, next to Persis, aligned with the people. The General sat alone.

"I was secretary of state at the time. I had come to Moscow to meet with President Borofsky. Unbeknownst to me, he invited Mr. Durgunov to join us."

Zoë couldn't believe it. In that one statement, Edwards had painted himself a liar, destroyed Borofsky's credibility, and demolished any illusion the American public might have had about President Haynes working behind the scenes with his Russian counterpart. It was suddenly, startlingly clear that Borofsky was not a friend, and that perhaps Congress should investigate more closely whatever Haynes was doing to gain the release of the hostages.

"What did you discuss?" Walsh had stopped looking at the large clock timing these proceedings.

"Nothing that bears any relevancy to the current situation, which is why I saw no need to mention it then and no need to dwell on it now."

Walsh saw how uncomfortable Scottie was. He took it as a sign to press on.

"When this hostage crisis erupted, why didn't you offer to aid in the negotiations? After all, you have a great deal of stature in the international community. You have a presence in the region. You'd already met Mr. Durgunov. Wouldn't it have been far nobler to volunteer to assist the president than to let this horrible situation drag on?"

"There was nothing I could do," he insisted.

"Because Durgunov was a friend?" Walsh probed, looking back at Ben as a way of reminding the audience where this entire exchange had begun.

"No! Because Durgunov is a megalomaniac!"

Sam Trout turned to Jed, extended his hand, and said,

"Congratulations. We've just witnessed the defining moment of this campaign!"

Though he was watching nothing but a roll of the credits, Clay could not take his eyes off the monitor. Outside, his staff was spinning Edwards's catastrophic performance, but Clay knew no one was clever enough to talk this around.

Dean Walsh's face filled the screen. The network recap had begun. As he watched a replay of the definitive exchange, Clay's heart pounded in anger and self-recrimination. This was his fault. He had completely underestimated Zoë Vaughn. Scottie kept saying how tough she was. Clay had believed she would sit tight. Instead, she had played the tapes for Ben, who had used them masterfully.

Clay clicked off the television. He didn't have to hear the polls to know that a megaton bomb had been dropped on his hopes.

THE
AFTERMATH

☆

☆ ELECTION DAY ☆

The weather forecast for most of the nation was clear, promising a large voter turnout. In each time zone, Get Out The Vote squads were up and ready before dawn. They were mostly young, energetic, and committed to their respective candidates. For weeks, they had been tacking posters to trees and telephone poles, placing them in store windows or wherever they could find space. They had handed out palm cards, worked phone banks, offered rides to the elderly and the infirm, and gone door to door, but nothing would compare to the effort that would be put forth on this day.

Ryan had nicknamed Ben's GOTV corps the KNIGHT SOX. Their symbol—a pair of socks: one, white stars on a blue ground, the other, red and white stripes—was emblazoned on baseball caps, tee shirts, sweatshirts, pins, pens, and whatever else would take a logo. Knight/Jefferson claimed to be AMERICA'S TEAM.

Not to be outdone, Scottie's GOTV troops boasted flag-printed caps with a single gold star. Tee shirts, sweatshirts, and rain ponchos that looked like army-issue bore various rank designations, marking the wearer as an officer in the General's army. As their slogan said, they were "on a march to the White House."

* * *

In Georgetown, Scottie and Emily were out early. At their polling station, they voted, shook hands with their fellow citizens, and gave the press nothing more than the standard, "It's a great day to be an American." In their car, however, Emily expressed a different sentiment.

"If you blow this, I'll never forgive you."

Scottie turned away from her and waved to the people lining the street. "I appreciate that vote of confidence, my precious, but there's no need to worry. Arlo says he has everything under control."

In Detroit, Otis and Jonetta Jefferson took their children into the booth so they could see their father's name on the ballot. When they walked out, Raina had tears in her eyes. Her brother, Dannel, looked as if his entire face was one big grin. Otis shook hands and accepted the good wishes of those inside the polling station.

Outside, a reporter asked him if it was true that he had received a number of death threats.

"We have, but according to the FBI, which monitors these things, it hasn't been an inordinate amount. All candidates become targets of people's discontent. Fortunately, the majority of Americans express their opinions with ballots, not bullets."

"How do you account for the large number of Secret Service agents assigned to your duty, then?" the reporter pressed.

"I'm a big guy," Otis laughed, trying to deflect attention from the cadre of armed agents surrounding him and his family. "They've got me on the two-for-one plan."

He waved, gave a thumbs-up, and quickly hustled Jonetta and the children into the car. Thankfully no one had asked him whether the windows of his car were bulletproof.

They were.

* * *

In Dallas, Georgie, Hunt, Olivia, and Lyle went to the elementary school that served as their polling place. When they came out they were greeted by a claque of antiabortion protesters and the usual band of reporters. Georgie was asked what she thought their chances were.

"The numbers look good," she said brightly. "Last night, CBS had us up by four."

"If you lose," a reporter from NBC asked, "will it be because of your abortion?"

It amazed Georgie how rude and callous people became under these circumstances. He was a reporter, she was seeking public office. In his mind, that entitled him to take privileges he wouldn't think of taking otherwise.

"The rape and its subsequent abortion cost me much more than any election ever could. I would hope the voters would understand that and why I didn't list rape at the top of my résumé. But," she said, staring at the reporter as if to draw attention to his maleness, "unless you've walked in my shoes, you can't know how I feel."

Hunt and Olivia glared at the reporter, linked arms with their mother, and led her to the car where Lyle was waiting. On the way back to the house no one spoke, but the air crackled. Since the story had broken, the twins had been extremely vocal in their support. Lyle had remained mute. He wouldn't speak to the press about it, nor would he discuss the matter with the family. Though each and every Hughes had accused him of leaking the story, he insistently maintained his innocence. He thought they believed him. Until today.

The moment they walked into the house, Georgie announced that she had filed for divorce that morning.

"What about the election? What if you win?" he asked.

"I win the minute you're out of my life." She was a portrait of certitude. "And you will be. Soon."

Lyle turned to the twins, who had taken up positions behind their mother. "How do you feel about the breakup of our family?"

"You're bad news," Hunt said. "You did the deed. You called Sean Quinn and ratted Mom out."

"I did not!"

Hunt snorted in disbelief. "Grandpa Roy's had a tail on you for months. He knows every phone call you've made, every meeting you took, and every bimbo you boffed. You're a loser, Dad. Big-time."

Lyle looked from Hunt to Olivia, hoping his little girl would be there for him, but she, too, appeared filled with loathing.

"Your things are packed and waiting in the garage," Georgie said. "And don't bother showing up at the plane this afternoon. You're not coming with us to Washington."

"You'll be sorry," he threatened.

Georgie shook her head at his pitiful attempt to cow her. "I'm sorry that I married you. Sorry that I took your abuse for so long. Sorry that I felt shame about something that wasn't shameful. Sorry that I subjected my children to our unhappiness. Sorry that it took me so long to gain my independence and regain my self-esteem. But, believe me, Lyle, I am not sorry I'm divorcing you."

In Philadelphia, Ben voted accompanied by Loretta, Keeley, and Ryan. Ben had just arrived home after an all-night, last-minute campaign-a-thon during which he stopped in nine states where they staged large rallies with enthusiastic crowds. Unfortunately, he knew better than to believe the roars of multitudes organized by his own people. Just as he knew not to equate network polls with the Gospel. Two had Knight/Jefferson up, two had them down. Hal's private polls had the race dead even.

At Knight/Jefferson headquarters, the site of the most action was on the second floor, which had become known as the Dugout. Partitions had been removed and desks shifted around to create a huge space that was currently

occupied by dozens of campaign workers manning the
phones, charting returns, and watching the election coverage on television. The movable wall with the national map
was clean, awaiting the first results. State directors had
begun to call in with exit polls at about ten-fifteen in the
morning. Things looked good in the North Atlantic states.
Early polls in the South were tighter.

Upstairs on three, a group of lawyers and paralegals
held court in the Boiler Room where they monitored any
reported incidents of suspected voter fraud. In Jed's War
Room, he, Zoë and the others drank coffee, watched a
dozen televisions at the same time, had telephones
attached to each ear and tried to prevent a collective nervous breakdown.

At three o'clock it looked too close to call. By four
o'clock, the tide had turned and the numbers looked really
good. By five, they were beginning to believe it was possible.

At six o'clock, Ben called and asked if Zoë would come
over to the house. Though he said repeatedly it was nothing
to worry about, that he hadn't heard any bad news about
Paddy and Nona, he was so persistent Zoë worried anyway.

Rush hour traffic dragged out the ride from Manayunk
to Chestnut Hill. By the time Zoë walked into Ben's house,
she was as ragged as a raw nerve ending. Ben greeted her
at the door with a big smile. He had napped. She was
relieved to see he looked more rested than he had when
she had seen the pictures of him at his last stop.

"You look good," she said.

"You look delicious!"

Zoë looked at him as if he had lost it somewhere over
Ohio and followed him into the living room where a fire
blazed. Loretta, Keeley, and Ryan were dressed in their
acceptance-speech finery and staring at her.

"Have a seat," Ben said, leading her to a chintz-covered
wing chair next to the fireplace. "We have something we
want to say to you."

Zoë did as he asked, but she felt uneasy. "What's going on?"

Ryan spoke first. "Do you remember when we were at Mrs. Trilling's and we talked about my dad getting married again?"

Zoë narrowed her eyes. After their tour of Amalia's villa, she had found Ryan ruminating about how he would feel if Ben took a bride. The conversation made Zoë uncomfortable, but his need was so transparent, she couldn't walk away. "Uh-huh."

"You said he wouldn't marry anyone Keeley and I didn't like and that we'd all become friends. Do you remember that?"

"Yes."

"You even said I might grow to love her." He glanced back at Ben to see how he was doing. Ben nodded. Ryan turned back to Zoë. "Well, Dad wants to marry you, and I think it's great because I already love you."

Zoë bit her lip to keep from crying. "I love you, too," she whispered, opening her arms so she could hug him.

Keeley was less secure. "Dad says no, but I kinda feel the only reason you turned him down the first time he asked was because I wasn't exactly nice to you."

"Your father's right," Zoë said, her heart aching for this young girl. "My 'no' had nothing to do with you. And for the record, I never took anything personally, Keeley. I thought you were a loving daughter who was missing her mother and looking out for her father. I'm missing my mother right now, and I've always been a daddy's girl, so I understand."

"They're going to be all right," Keeley said, trying to comfort her.

"I hope so." Zoë signaled she was all right and that Keeley could continue.

"We brought you here tonight so we could all propose to you. Daddy's the one who matters most, but if you say yes to him," Keeley warned, "you get us."

Zoë chuckled. The thought didn't disturb her, and she said as much.

"Your turn, Grandma," Ryan directed.

Loretta simply smiled. "I've thought of Zoë as a daughter for a very long time. It would be nice if she made it official."

Zoë could barely hold back her tears. Ben grabbed a small footstool, sat down, and took her hand.

"Outside of this house there are millions of people who believe that this is the most important day of my life. It is, but only if you say yes to us and agree to be my wife, their mother, and Mom's daughter." He raised her hand to his lips and tenderly kissed her fingers. "I love you."

Zoë'e eyes were flooded, but for the first time in a long while, she saw life as it could be, not as it had been. She saw a home and family and fireplaces and cookies and warmth and love. And it felt good.

"Well," she said, dabbing at her cheeks with the handkerchief Ben had supplied, looking at this eager assembly with a sense of awe. "If you want me, you've got me. Because I love you, too." Her eyes met Keeley's. "All of you."

Everyone was allowed one glass of champagne, then Zoë and Ben left to return to Headquarters and wait out the results. Otis would join them there. The families would come later. Zoë kissed everyone good-bye, held up two hands of fingers crossed, and promised to see them after the acceptance speeches. Ben spoke to his Secret Service agents, who preceded them out the door.

"I promise you," Ben said, slipping his arm around Zoë's waist, drawing her close, and tilting his head in the direction of his security detail, "no earplugs on the honeymoon."

"Good thinking," Zoë said, still on a cloud.

As they strolled out the door and down the walk, they never noticed the leaves on an evergreen shrub across the street tremble. They never saw the man lower himself to the ground and position himself at a gun mount. They were too busy being in love to know when he put his eye to the viewfinder and caught them in his sight. The first they knew of him was the whoosh just before the grenade he fired missed its mark, slammed into the trunk of a tree, and exploded.

One Secret Service agent threw his body on top of Ben. The other one took off across the street. Zoë, who had just stepped out from behind the tree, absorbed the brunt of the explosion. She was hit with flying metal objects and thrown to the ground. Since she had been been nearest the sidewalk, her head slammed into the concrete.

She was unconscious so she never heard the blast which went off a second after the first. Unfortunately for the shooter, the launcher misfired and the grenade exploded in his face, killing him and mutilating him beyond recognition.

At eleven-thirty that night, Benjamin Knight and Otis Jefferson left the hospital to make their acceptance speeches. Zoë lay in intensive care with a fractured skull, numerous lacerations, and massive internal bleeding. Her condition was stable, but serious.

With his family standing alongside him, a somber president-elect walked to the microphone and addressed the thousands who had gathered outside Knight Headquarters and the millions watching at home.

"This has been a remarkable day of mountainous highs and cavernous lows. Today, democracy exercised its greatest freedom as Americans went to the polls and cast their votes. It's always a great moment when we feel the privilege of our freedom and the power of our system. Yet today, in what will become a gruesome footnote to history, we were reminded that violence anywhere is a threat to freedom everywhere.

"We don't know who fired that grenade, but we will. Violence is never anonymous. It always has a name, just as it always has a victim. Tonight, it is assumed that I was the intended victim. The gunman failed in that attempt, striking instead Zoë Vaughn, a woman who has dedicated her life to the service of this country. And the woman who had, only moments before, agreed to be my wife.''

A brief, unsteady smile glanced across his lips in response to the surprised murmurs and sympathetic applause from the crowd.

"It is with great humility and pride that Otis Jefferson and I accept America's decision to allow us the opportunity to lead this country. And lead we will!

"On this very emotional night," he intoned, "it would be easy to lose faith and relinquish hope. It would be easy to stay on a threadbare course and stick to the status quo. But Americans don't do that. We know what violence has wrought throughout the world. And we've fought to change that. We see what havoc it wreaks here at home. And we've fought to change that. But tonight, as we pray for the safety of our citizens held in prisons abroad, and for the recovery of one in a hospital here at home, let us pledge to fight harder. Let us pledge to reach out and pull together to find a common ground and a higher ground."

They applauded loudly and fervently. Many stood arm in arm, moved by their new president's obvious pain and his willingness to share it with them.

"My personal pledge is that while we will take the oath of office on January 20 in keeping with democracy's promise of a smooth transition of power, there will be no inaugural balls unless and until each and every hostage has been released. America cannot celebrate its freedoms while some of its citizens are held captive.

"But, my friends, America will celebrate, because the first priority of this administration is to bring our people home!"

The ovation roared through the streets, then calmed at the sound of Ben's voice.

"Zoë Vaughn's parents were on board the *Michelangelo*. We don't know where they are or how they are. What we do know is that like the rest of the hostages, they're going to be released. They're going to come home. And when they do, they're going to join the rest of America at a White House wedding!''

The thunder of the crowd drowned out Ben's mumbled prayer, ''Please, God.''

Over the next several days, when Ben wasn't at the hospital, he was speaking to the FBI. A number of people were brought in for questioning: Three illegal Russian immigrants who were picked up near the Knight Headquarters with a stash of weapons hidden in the trunk of their car. Arlo Reid, who claimed he was carrying a weapon for his own protection. Clay Chandler, whose history of animosity against Ben, along with the discovery of phone numbers traced to several men with criminal backgrounds, had cast a light of suspicion on him. And General Prescott Edwards, who was interrogated over a period of days. When Ben was called back to verify certain points, he volunteered that an important tape implicating the General would be forthcoming from the Mossad. That matter was immediately turned over to the Justice Department. It was also rumored that a congressional committee was going to hold its own hearings on the General's conduct.

As for Zoë, surgery had stopped the bleeding, and she had regained consciousness, but according to her doctors, her condition was still critical.

The FBI also considered her circumstance critical, but for very different reasons. On the same day—and at almost the same time—as the attack on Ben and Zoë, two heavily armed men had been found lurking outside Otis Jefferson's home. Their interrogation convinced the FBI that the two incidents were related. A twenty-four-hour guard was placed outside Zoë's hospital room.

Forensic experts continued to work on the body of the shooter. The extent of physical destruction had made identification almost impossible.

JANUARY 20,

☆ INAUGURATION DAY ☆

They came from as far as Hawaii and as near as Virginia. Hundreds of thousands of people flocked to Washington to line the parade route, to witness the inauguration itself or simply to be in the place where history happened. At various checkpoints leading to the west side of the Capitol building, where the ceremony would take place, those who were attending the ceremonies passed through metal detectors and showed their highly prized credentials. From there, they followed color-coded signs to the various seating areas.

In the front section where members of Congress and their guests were permitted, Georgie Hughes was greeted by appreciative applause as she and her children took their seats. Her ticket might have lost, but according to the pundits she came out a winner nonetheless. The public admired her candor and her pluck throughout a difficult campaign. The announcement that she was divorcing her husband hadn't tarnished her halo; Ben's selection of her as his secretary of Health and Human Services added to its sheen. Confirmation seemed assured.

A reporter who had managed to wheedle his way through

the crowd asked her about the rumors of a romance with Jed Oakes.

"If I'm not mistaken," the pencil said, "you two were on opposite sides of the aisle."

"I guess it's as the song says: 'I was lookin' for love in all the wrong places.'"

From all around her came a chorus of laughter and applause. The crowd loved her. More important, to her at least, was that Jed loved her, and they had made their peace.

She had flown to Philadelphia the morning after the election to be with Zoë. She and Jed had met in the hospital lounge. He expressed sympathy for her loss. She congratulated him on his win. They had shuffled their feet and stared at each other.

"You were right," she conceded. "Edwards didn't deserve the Big Job."

"I'll tell you this," Jed said, nodding his head in the direction of Zoë's room. "What's happened here should show us that everything is bullshit except being with the ones you love." He shrugged his shoulders helplessly. "And you're it for me. There's never going to be anyone else, so either you say yes, or it's a permanent room at the Heartbreak Hotel for this dude."

She laughed even now when she thought about the hangdog expression on his face and how it had turned to utter delight when she agreed to marry him.

"Thinking about Jed?" Olivia asked. Georgie nodded. "He's nuts, but he loves you, Mom."

"Yes, Olivia," Georgie said happily. "He does."

Farther back, Kate, Rick, and Ethan Siegel found their seats along with the rest of the New Jersey contingent. Rick had moved back into the house. Kate had decided to run for Congress. And Ethan was busy practicing for his bar mitzvah in March. It was going to be a very special day: not only were his parents going to renew their wedding vows, but Ethan was going to share the *bimah* with a very special friend. Amalia Trilling was studying to become an adult bat mitzvah. This was her way of making up for a part of her life that had been stolen from her.

Ethan had been delighted at Amalia's request because if this day was about anything, it was about commitment and closure. While Ethan didn't want his bar mitzvah to be overwhelmed by gloomy might-have-beens, inviting Amalia to stand alongside him as they read from the Torah seemed to Ethan the best way to honor Mira and the life that had been stolen from her. The only way to fill the void.

"Good morning, ladies and gentlemen, this is Celia Porter reporting from Washington, D.C., where in a few moments, Benjamin Knight will be sworn in as president of the United States. Early this morning, President-Elect Knight and his family went to church. They were accompanied by Mr. Knight's fiancée, Zoë Vaughn, who was appearing in public with him for the first time since her release from the hospital.

"As you know, Ms. Vaughn was injured in a vicious grenade attack outside Mr. Knight's home early in the evening of election day. Over the past several months, many names were raised as possible suspects, including that of former Congressman Mack Kenton. You may recall that following his interrogation, Mr. Kenton announced his resignation from the House. He sincerely regretted the fact that during the primary season his actions had been such that he had become a viable suspect in many people's eyes as the perpetrator of this horrible act.

"Also under investigation was Clayborne Chandler III, political strategist and most recently campaign manager for General Prescott Edwards. Although he had been cleared of any involvement in the case weeks ago, Mr. Chandler was found dead this morning in his Watergate apartment of an apparent suicide.

"Mr. Chandler had come under suspicion due to the discovery of a piece of paper listing the names and phone numbers of several known mercenaries as well as a series of scrapbooks containing newspaper articles and photographs that chronicled a twenty-year blood feud between Mr. Chandler and the president-elect."

Her announcement cued a look back on Clay's life. As she watched the file footage play on her monitor, she could barely hide her disgust when a picture of Clay as Ben's best man appeared. There he stood, one arm draped around Ben's shoulders, the other with a glass raised in honor of his best friend's wedding. The voice-over neglected to identify the other people in that picture, but Celia thought about each and every one of them, what they had meant to each other then, and where they were now.

She and Zoë had been close then. The years had tugged at their relationship until it frayed. Over the past several months, however, they had walked slowly, but surely, over the bridge that separated them.

Kate—young, single, and brimming with hope for the future—was starting over. Yet remarkably, she remained imbued with a sense of faith and trust that would have been impossible for others in her situation.

Georgie. Celia thought about her and was tempted to cheer out loud. How far Georgie Hughes had come: from the self-conscious daughter of a political dynasty to a powerful political force; from an emotionally dependent wife to an emotionally fulfilled woman; from a good friend to an even better friend.

Suddenly, she remembered what Clay had said in that toast to Ben: "Twenty years from now, we're all going to want to be with him as we are now, repeating this wonderful moment of celebration. The lucky ones will be."

Celia counted herself among the lucky ones. Because she and the others not only had survived those twenty years, but had come out winners. And because these three women were still, and would always be, a part of her life.

As the playback continued. Celia focused on Ben and Clay. One man had accomplished an incredible feat. The other had died a violent death at his own hand. To those who knew them, the two events were inexorably linked.

Celia wasn't sorry Clay was dead, but if she allowed a moment of compassion, she was sorry about the way he had lived.

Instead of moving on after his disgrace at Justice, he continuously looked back, searching for a way to extract vengeance on those who had hurt him or dismissed him or underestimated him. Most terrifying: Clay came to believe that his entire existence was predicated on Ben's demise. Rather than face Ben's win and his loss, Clay preferred to die.

As the piece cut from a shot of Judge Chandler and his wife standing alone at a grave site, to a picture of a handcuffed man being ushered into the backseat of a government car, Celia turned to her co-anchor.

"After an exhaustive investigation," Quinn said, his green eyes firmly fixed on the lens, "the FBI has announced its intention to press charges against Colonel Arlo Reid. The ex–army officer and longtime aide-de-camp to General Prescott Edwards has been accused of masterminding a coordinated attack meant to kill President-Elect Benjamin Knight as well as Vice President–Elect Otis Jefferson. Sources tell us that the incriminating list of mercenaries found in Clay Chandler's office was ultimately traced to Colonel Reid. Apparently the colonel was so convinced of the moral rightness of his murderous operation that he had gone to Mr. Chandler seeking his approval. It appears that General Edwards was unaware of Colonel Reid's plan.

"Of the twenty men from Reid's paramilitary brigade involved in the planning and execution of the attack, three are in custody. A fourth died at the scene. Those who survived face federal charges of conspiracy and the attempt to assassinate both the president- and vice president–elect."

They broke for a commercial. Quinn pulled Celia toward him and kissed her. Wild hoots and catcalls filled the studio.

"Get your own babe," Quinn shouted as he waved them off and Celia flushed. "This one's mine!"

"For how long?" one of the grips taunted.

Quinn locked his gaze on Celia's face, marveling as he did every moment he was with her, and most of those when he was not, that this exquisite creature actually loved him.

"Fifty years or so sounds good," he said to Celia. "We're getting hitched on the air and off," he said to his crew.

Shortly after the election, Quinn had pitched Celia to his network brass, and they had offered her a co-anchor slot on Quinn's weekly magazine show, a daily policital show of her own, and regular features on the nightly news. Then Quinn had offered her him. She had said yes to everything.

As the entire studio burst into honest applause, Celia rose out of her seat and allowed them a gracious bow. It felt wonderful to be wanted. Even more wonderful to be respected.

The United States Marine Band struck up "Hail to the Chief," announcing the entrance of President Elton Haynes. As he stepped out of the Capitol and strode toward the front of the podium, he waved to the massive throng, shook hands with several of the guests on the platform, and took his place by his wife's side. Beth took his hand in hers and gave it a squeeze.

Senator George Gilbert issued the oath of office to Otis Jefferson, whose voice boomed out over the crowd and into history. Jonetta proudly held the Bible for her husband as he became the vice president of the United States with his children by his side.

When it was Ben's turn, he, Loretta, Ryan, and Keeley approached the podium where the Chief Justice waited. Loretta's head was high as she offered her late husband's

Bible to her son. Ben leaned over and kissed her as he placed his left hand on it. Ryan and Keeley stood like soldiers, trying hard not to giggle or cry or do anything to spoil this unbelievable moment.

In Washington, the ceremony's high point was about to begin. In various parts of the globe, a rescue mission set up two months before in cooperation with soon-to-be former President Haynes and the Chairman of the Joint Chiefs, stood in readiness. It was a massive undertaking that relied upon the painstaking efforts of Harry Cadman, Zev Shafir, and Chuck Mallory. Pooling their knowledge and their various organizations, they formed a special task force with people from Mossad, the CIA, and Interpol to track the movements of Red Rage, pinpoint the positions of the hostages, and draw up a battle plan.

"I, Benjamin Douglas Knight, do solemnly swear . . ."

From his command post in Brussels, General Harry Cadman gave the order for Operation Shining Armor to begin.

It was eight o'clock at night in the Persian Gulf. A squadron of F-16s hovered over the emirate of Bahrain like hawks, watching for anyone who would dare interfere with the landing of its rescue troops. Four helicopters alighted on the off island of Al Muharraq and, within seconds, every guard surrounding the Red Rage camp was dead. Twenty minutes later, the nurses who had been kidnapped from the American Hospital in Kuwait were airborne.

"that I will faithfully execute the office of President of the United States . . ."

One time zone away, bomber escorts zoomed into the air space over the Rigestan Desert of Afghanistan. They had been aloft for an hour, waiting for General Cadman's signal. When it came, helicopters comfortable in desert terrain touched down and appeared to kneel like camels so their passengers could disembark. Quickly, they stilled their propellers. Special Forces hit the sand and pushed toward the Lowrah River, where the Red Rage enclave was reported to be. They came upon it slowly, but their vengeance was swift. While some troops covered the dead, others went about the glorious chore of awakening children who had not seen American faces other than their own in far too long. By tomorrow evening at this time, they would be reunited with their families.

"and will to the best of my ability . . ."

It was two o'clock Tuesday morning, and the waters of the Sea of Okhotsk were calm. The only ripples were caused by silent launches carrying navy frogmen, who came ashore at the remote Shantar Island off the coast of Siberia. It took less than fifteen minutes to subdue the sentries and secure the area. It was bitter cold and most of them had warmed themselves with too much vodka, bundled themselves into warm sleeping bags, and were barely conscious. They never heard death approaching. Nor did they awaken when the soldiers kidnapped from the Korean DMZ were roused and rushed to the coast where an American ship waited off shore to bring them home.

"preserve, protect and defend . . ."

In the Sudan, with the aid of an Israeli commando group, another Special Forces group stormed an old air base just off the Red Sea, north of Port Sudan. It took nearly half an hour to vanquish the jailers and load the seventy-five elderly prisoners onto the cargo plane brought for their escape, but once on board, the mood turned jubilant. The singing and cheering were led by none other than Paddy Vaughn.

"the Constitution of the United States."

And in Moscow, Russian soldiers arrested Yegor Durgunov and turned him over to officers of the World Court, who would transport him to The Hague where he would be tried for war crimes.

Three days later, in the East Room of the White House, Paddy Vaughn walked his youngest daughter down the aisle. Zoë was a confection in a long-sleeved, delicately bustled, turn-of-the-century gown. Fashioned of ivory crepe and falling softly from a sweetheart bodice, it hugged her figure with regal simplicity. Her hair, by contrast, danced loosely beneath an orange-blossom coronet and a puff of veil. As they proceeded along the length of the room, Zoë smiled at Amalia and Toby, the entire Vaughn clan, Hugo Porter and his future son-in-law, Sean Quinn, Sam Trout, Phil Halpern, Adam Schwartz, and all the others who had become family over the past several months.

At the altar Paddy kissed her cheek, gave her hand to Ben, took his place next to his wife, Nona, and with tear-filled eyes, watched as Zoë became the wife of the president of the United States. Ryan Knight was his father's best man. Keeley Knight was Zoë's maid of honor. Georgie Hughes, Celia Porter, and Kate Siegel were her brides-maids. Jed Oakes, Sam Trout, Rick Siegel, and Otis Jefferson served as groomsmen.

As promised, all of the hostages and their families attended the wedding ceremony. Also as promised, America was invited to join in the celebration as the nine inaugural balls became Ben and Zoë's progressive wedding reception. At each one, Ben and Zoë obliged the crowd with a dance, a kiss, and by tossing a replica of the bridal bouquet into the audience.

At their last stop, Zoë slipped into Ben's arms for their dance and looked at him quizzically.

"What's the matter?" he asked.

"Do I have to call you Mr. President all the time? A little to the left, Mr. President. Umm, yes, Mr. President."

"Can we change the subject?" Ben squirmed.

Zoë laughed. "I love it when you blush. It's so . . . ordinary citizen."

"Three times tonight," Ben said, trying to ignore her gibes, "your father has reminded me that when I came to his house and asked you to sign on to my campaign, I said if I won, you would be secretary of state."

"Good for Paddy! If that's what you said, that's what you should do."

"I'd like to deliver on my promise, really I would. Unfortunately, it's out of my hands." His voice broadcast sincerity, but his expression was ever-so-slightly smug. "You can't be secretary of state. You gave up that right when you became Mrs. Benjamin Knight. According to the Bobby Kennedy statute, members of the president's immediate family are barred from serving in the cabinet."

Zoë's gaze narrowed. "If you had told me I had an alternative back in the East Room, who knows? I might have taken curtain number two."

"Yeah, right," he groused. "How about curtain number three?"

"Which is?"

"A position that suits your extraordinary talents perfectly."

"But . . ."

"But doesn't require congressional approval. Actually, it's a position that any sane president would offer you even if you weren't his wife: National Security Advisor."

As her eyes widened with surprise and pleasure, he kissed her, oblivious to the hooting crowd.

"So, what do you say? Do you accept?"

Zoë returned his kiss and smiled, her celadon eyes twinkling.

"For the second time tonight, Mr. President. I do."

Turn the page for
A sample of Doris Mortman's newest book,
OUT OF NOWHERE,
A Kensington hardcover, available now
wherever books are sold.

☆ one ☆

New York City

Tall and slim in her navy coveralls, her shiny auburn hair neatly restrained by a backward baseball cap, Amanda Maxwell worked quickly to preserve the essential history of the crime scene. She moved inside and began the overall photographs, looking at and away from the site of the event. These would provide the investigators, as well as the attorneys for both sides, eye-level views that would identify the relative location of evidence to be collected.

Overalls and eye-level orientation shots completed, she paused and determined a primary field of view. Once established, she set down a two-foot-square sheet of photo mat board that acted as a perspective grid. Making certain that the grid lay flat on the floor, she climbed atop a small stool that was part of her equipment bag, shifted the flash on her camera upward so the light would bounce off the ceiling, then, finally, looked at the victim.

Friends never understood how she could do this. They wondered why she never got sick or fainted or cried at the inhuman aftermath of violent human behavior. She tried to explain, but they couldn't understand: a lens created distance. She was there, but removed. The body—no matter what condition it was in—was the subject, the murder scene the background, her camera an instrument for collecting evidence. Difficult as it was for civilians to comprehend, police work advanced on intellect, instinct, objectivity, and dogged insistence. Emotion had no place at a crime scene; it distorted one's vision and blurred the facts.

While her colleagues watched, she photographed the victim and her surroundings. By elevating the camera, Amanda ensured the accuracy of grid measurements used by the lab to prepare a scale map. Having completed the basics, she began the tedious work of documenting the scene and the crime, frame by frame. First, she circled the body, moving from the head clockwise to the right arm, to the feet, then to the left arm, shooting up, down, and across. Then she moved in to record the wounds.

She worked quickly and thoroughly, changing perspective, making notes. Using a selection of lenses and filters, her photographs ranged from the buttons on the stereo to the food in the refrigerator, to the gaping hole where the woman's right breast had been cut away, to the breast itself, which they found tossed in the toilet, discarded as carelessly as a dirty tissue. When she had completed her routine, the medical examiner's team chalked an outline of the body, removed it, and Amanda began the procedure all over again. By repeating the same shots with the chalk image—without the chaos that always occurred when the body was still present— she was assured of having one good negative out of two shots of the same scene.

"Hey, Max!" Pete Doyle groused impatiently. He had sketched the rest of the apartment and taken measurements. He wanted to complete that part of his job in the bedroom and adjoining bathroom but couldn't start until she finished. "Anytime this century."

Amanda remained unhurried. She finished the roll, riffled through her notes, and took a quick look around to assure herself that she hadn't missed anything.

"The only thing you haven't photographed is me," Pete said. "And I'm growing a beard, for crissakes!"

"Good! It'll cover your face." As she passed him, she playfully pinched Pete's cheek.

He grabbed the bill of her NYPD baseball cap and turned it

face front. "If you're gonna wear the cap, wear it right, dammit! You look like a Met fan!"

Amanda shook her head and looked at him pitifully. "Forget it, Pete. No amount of sweet talk is going to get me to go to bed with you."

The investigator from the ME's Office and a third detective from the CSU, who had come to replace Amanda, laughed. Pete's unabashed lusting was the joke of the CSU. Pete was approaching forty and fighting hard to maintain a self-promoted reputation as a ladies' man. Amanda was in her late twenties and had made it clear from the start that she didn't date where she worked.

"Max." Harry Benson, from CSU handed her a slip of paper with an address on it. "The lieutenant wants you to head over to the One-Seven. Cleland's over there. He's caught a multiple homicide and requested your camera on-site."

Although everyone in the CSU was qualified to photograph crime scenes, as well as collect other forms of forensic evidence, Amanda was known as the best "shooter" in the unit. It wasn't unusual for her to be called in on cases where the lead detective believed that photographs would not only help in the investigation of the crime, but also in the conviction of the perpetrator.

"Bye, guys!" she said as she packed up her equipment, slung one bulky bag over her shoulder, gripped another, and started for the door.

"See you back at the house, Max," Harry said, as he set to work bagging the victim's bloody underpants. "And don't worry, after we finish here, we'll mend Pete's broken heart with a couple of beers."

Amanda eyed Pete with a critical gaze. "Just what that body needs is a few more beers."

"Love ya, babe," Pete said, sucking in his gut as he saluted her.

Amanda laughed and blew him a kiss. "Yeh. Me too you."

Walter Clarke's office was a showcase for the anal retentive. There wasn't a speck of dust or a dulled pencil point or an errant paper clip—ever. The glass partition that separated the head of New York City's Crime Scene Unit from his detectives sparkled. His furniture always looked freshly polished. And it never moved. Even after large meetings, everything was in its designated place, as if Clarke had nailed it to the floor—which some members of his squad thought he had. He was a man who believed in the sanctity of order. "A well-ordered home breeds a well-ordered mind" was his favorite saying. Some believed it was precisely that philosophy that had greased his rise to the top and made him such a good lieutenant. Others thought it made him a pain in the neck.

As Amanda approached Clarke's office, she could see he was busy. The two precinct detectives who'd worked the case that morning were there as well as a private investigator she'd seen at several different precincts. It amused her to see someone with a stubble, a leather jacket, and an open shirt slouched in a chair in the *sanctum sanitorum*, as the lieutenant's crib was called. Usually, the instant one passed through that sanitized portal, postures automatically straightened, ties were knotted, attitudes were crisp and "at attention." Clarke spotted her and waved her inside.

"Got anything, Max?" he asked, eyeing the thick folder under her arm.

Amanda looked from the Chief to the man lounging in the chair. She didn't discuss police business in front of strangers.

"Jake Fowler," Walter said, correctly interpreting her silence. "He's a PI who was tailing the victim."

Jake Fowler curled his lip at Clarke's condescending tone. He understood that most detectives, forensic and precinct, preferred to work without outside interference and, on the whole, were not exactly fans of private investigators, but still.

"Vivian Wyland was a rich girl from North Carolina with a wild streak and a drinking problem," he said, directing his explanation exclusively to Amanda.

He had royal blue eyes that focused sharply on a target,

then fixed and held. Though his overall manner was casual, Amanda sensed it was a calculated pose, meant to disarm. He was clearly taking her measure, just as she was taking his.

"Her parents had lost touch with her and were worried that something bad might happen. Turns out they were right."

Amanda opened her folder, extracted four enlarged photographs, and laid them out in front of Walter. The detectives moved around the desk so they could view them right side up. Fowler stayed where he was. His eyes traveled between the photographs and the woman who had taken them. It was difficult to tell which fascinated him more.

Amanda pointed to a faint rectangle in the center of what she described as abdominal flesh. "Since this case presented itself as a probable rape, I took a number of body shots with a UV filter. Often, it produces images of otherwise invisible materials or wounds. This," she said, tracing the outline of the rectangle, "appears to be the imprint of a belt buckle. With a Western motif," she added pointedly.

The photograph was powerful evidence. Not only could it identify a killer, but it was certain to move a jury. The last thing this group wanted was for their suspect to read about this in the newspapers and toss the buckle.

Amanda raced up the steps of the West Side brownstone where she lived, keys already jangling in her hand. She unlocked the front door, emptied her mailbox, and jogged up three flights to her apartment. It had been a long day. She would have loved a leisurely soak, but all time would allow was a quick shower. She pulled three pairs of panty hose off the shower rod where they had been drying, turned on the water, and began stripping off her clothes as she ran into the living room to check her messages.

In her bedroom, she opened the closet, studied its contents. Which of her three Little Black Dresses would she wear this evening? she wondered. This recent flurry of fancy dinners was beginning to point out major gaps in her wardrobe. Before, her social life didn't cry out for anything *Vogue;* she got by on the same clothes she used for work: slacks, sweaters, tee shirts, and blazers. The last several months had been different. She closed her eyes, snatched one at random, brought it into the bathroom, and hung it on the back of the door to steam out any possible wrinkles.

Amanda's shower was more than a luxury; at the end of every workday, she needed to scrub off the smell that insisted upon clinging to her. Perfume didn't work. Neither did simply soaping her body. The smell crept into the hollow center of her hair shafts and deep into her sinuses. For the sinuses, she kept strong peppermints in the darkroom and munched on them most of the day. For her hair, she used a lightly scented lemon shampoo.

Fortunately, her shoulder-length hair was sleek, straight, and well cut; it didn't demand endless blow-drying. She didn't like wearing a lot of makeup and there, too, she was lucky. Her skin was clear and creamy; foundation was more of a concession to convention than a requirement. She did use a light pink blush and, at night, lined, shadowed, and mascaraed her large, cocoa brown eyes. Her favorite feature was her mouth: Her lips were full, and though she enjoyed coloring them, she only owned four lipsticks—russet, wine red, pink/brown, and light mauve. Tonight felt wine red.

She slipped into her dress—black jersey, mandarin neck, long sleeves—added a pair of black suede shoes, pearl studs, and a gold watch that still looked strange on her wrist. Despite her protests, he had insisted upon giving it to her for her birthday; she only wore it when she saw him.

Downstairs, she walked to the corner of Eighty-ninth and Columbus and hailed a cab.

"The Pierre, please. Sixtieth and Fifth."

As they pulled away from the curb, she looked to see if anyone was watching her departure. Out of the corner of her eye, she thought she saw a man beneath a restaurant awning turn and follow the progress of the car. Quickly, she found her compact, flipped open the top and watched him watching her through the mirror. It was dark, and he was hidden in the shadows. He could have been waiting for a friend. Or a cab. He could have been taking refuge from the cold. Or stalking her.

The taxi stopped in front of the Pierre. She got out, walked quickly to the entrance, through the lobby to the elevators. Alone in the car, she pressed four and twelve. She got out at four and waited a few minutes before taking another elevator down to where she could exit on the Sixtieth Street side of the hotel. She waited inside while the doorman hailed her a cab, then rushed from the building into the car, her hand shielding her face from the wind.

"Tavern on the Green." Again, she scrutinized the street. This time, no one seemed to be paying attention.

In the parking lot of the famous tourist haven, she exited the taxi and was immediately spirited into a sleek, black limousine.

"Good evening, Miss Maxwell."

"Good evening, Thompson. Where to tonight?"

La Crémaillère was a charming country restaurant situated on the border of New York and Connecticut. They had been here before, so there was no need for Amanda to identify herself. Robert, the owner, greeted her effusively and immediately escorted her to a table in the front room, near the fireplace.

The gentleman she had come to see stood and watched her progress. He was a dignified-looking man with salt-and-pepper hair and that polished, well-tended look so prevalent among the very rich. A broad smile enlivened his face as she approached. He embraced her warmly. When she was seated, he fussed to make sure she was comfortable. A waiter poured her some wine.

She took a sip, nodded her satisfaction to the waiter, and tipped her glass toward her host. "Excellent! As always."

"You're sure you like it?"

"I'm sure."

"Did you have any trouble getting here?"

"None at all." She found his nervousness endearing. It was as if he still couldn't believe she was in his life.

"You look very beautiful this evening." His hand reached across the table, found hers, and squeezed it. "And thank you for wearing the watch. I know you hate it."

She laughed. "I don't hate it. It's just . . . well, not quite my style," she said.

"And what exactly is your style?"

Amanda glanced at his expensive Italian suit, his bespoke shirt, silk tie, thick gold cuff links and perfectly buffed nails. Almost reflexively, she looked at her own hands, unmanicured and bare except for the watch. Her dress, which had put a big dent in her paycheck, probably didn't cost as much as his cologne.

"Simple, unadorned, frugal and more often than not, police issue," she said without defense.

"You're far too special a woman to be unadorned."

"It's what I'm used to. Accessories make me uncomfortable."

"You could learn to love pretty things," he said gently, trying not to push.

"Maybe, but right now, my life doesn't exactly lend itself to furs and jewels."

"That could change, you know. All you have to do is think seriously about my offer to come into the business."

"I did think about it," she said.

"Seriously?"

She pursed her lips in concern. He had leaped to the conclusion that she was going to accept. That thought obviously pleased him. "I know it's hard for you to believe," she said, sorry to disappoint him, "but I like what I do."

"I'm not asking you to give up photography. Your work is really quite spectacular. It's the . . . police stuff ." He literally squirmed.

Amanda smiled in sympathy. She couldn't blame him for finding her job so distasteful. Why would anyone encourage spending one's life in the company of dead bodies. "I haven't dismissed the idea completely, though. I've been reading the material you gave me and studying the business section of the *Times*."

"And?" he said eagerly.

"I'm interested, but," she cautioned, "not hooked."

"That just means I have to work harder at convincing you."

"Let's go slow with that, okay?" She leaned over and caressed his cheek. He held her hand there. "For now, I'd rather concentrate on us."

"Whatever you want," he said in a voice raspy with emotion.

If she needed time, he would give it to her; he was grateful to have it to give. And if, after time had passed she still felt the same way, he would accept her decision rather than doing what he usually did, which was to bulldoze over her concerns and/or personal wishes and dismiss them as irrelevant. Though he was accustomed to having people compliment him on his strengths, which he believed were many, he wasn't unaware of his faults. He knew he was arrogant, demanding, egotistical, often disrespectful and highly impatient. Also, like many men who had achieved his astonishing level of success, he believed most people's feelings and opinions were secondary to his.

But this lovely young woman wasn't most people. He was Lionel Baird. And Amanda was his daughter.

She had reentered his life six months before on a steamy Wednesday night in August. He was in the bar at the Four Seasons sipping a very cold vodka as he waited for his estranged wife, Pamela Richardson Baird. Their appointment was for six-thirty. It was nearly seven. He decided to give her until the hour, then he intended to leave. Suddenly, a young woman slid into the chair opposite him.

"I'm sorry, but I'm expecting someone," he said crisply.

"I know."

"Well, then, if you don't mind . . ."

"I'd like you to take a walk with me," she said softly.

"Who the hell are you? And what do you want?"

"I'll tell you who I am—outside."

"I don't go anywhere without my bodyguard."

She shrugged. "Fine. He can walk behind us or in front of us. He can't walk with us."

Overwhelmed by curiosity—and impressed with the fact that she wasn't at all cowed by him—Lionel paid the check, signaled for Bruno to follow them, and did what the young woman asked. With a vigilant, square-bodied Bruno trailing several paces behind, they left the restaurant, turned right and then right again, onto Park Avenue. She didn't look like a terrorist with her summery dress clinging to her shapely body and her hair blowing in the gentle evening breeze. But, he reminded himself, danger didn't always have an ugly face.

Lionel stopped and looked at her. "Who are you?" he demanded again.

"I'll let you figure that out," she said mysteriously. "But let's keep walking. I don't want to attract an audience."

As they strolled up Park Avenue, she reminisced about things only his daughter could have known, because they were moments only he and his daughter shared: the day he took her to Yankee Stadium and they almost caught a foul ball; the day he taught her to skim rocks on the lake in Central Park; the day she brought him to school in Miami for show-and-tell.

"I wanted my friends to know I really did have a father," the young woman said softly.

Slowly, Lionel turned to her. He remained wary, but she had his full attention.

"You bought me that pink camellia because you said it

matched the color of my dress. That was the day you took me to the ballet for the first time. We saw *Swan Lake.*"

Lionel grabbed her arm. He was trembling with emotion. His eyes bored into hers. "How do you know these things?"

"I know because I was there," she said quietly. "I'm your daughter, Ricki."

Lionel shook his head in disbelief. Anger flooded his eyes. "What is this? Some kind of cruel joke! My daughter's dead!"

Hearing Lionel's voice, Bruno started for them. "Tell him to stay back," she insisted.

"How dare you tell me what to do!" Lionel glared at her. His face was flushed with bluster and defiance. Inside, however, he was frightened, and not because he believed she posed a threat. It was vague and fleeting, like a needle piercing skin, but deep inside a place that had been numb for twenty years, he felt an awakening.

"I'm not going to rob you or hurt you," she said. "Now tell him to back off!"

Lionel hesitated, then held up his hand, halting the beefy man's approach.

"Thank you," she said.

"Just get on with it," he ordered.

She reached into her handbag and pulled out a small toy which she handed to Lionel. It was a tiny caboose from a set of electric trains. Lionel gasped. He had bought this for his daughter at F.A.O. Schwarz. She was about four. They had been talking about names. He had told her she was named Erica after his mother, Frederica. When she asked after whom he was named, he had answered, "the trains." When she didn't understand, he took her into the huge toy store and showed her an enormous display of electric trains, all imprinted with the name Lionel. Then he let her select whichever car she wanted. She picked the little red caboose.

"I wasn't supposed to take anything with me," the woman claiming to be his Ricki said, "but I made Mom sew this into my pillow. It's been with me all along."

* * *

In the months that followed, father and daughter met frequently. Lionel was obsessed with every facet of Amanda's life in hiding. She explained about WITSEC and how she and Cynthia eventually wound up in the Northwest, living as Beth and Amanda Maxwell. She told him their only contact with their past were letters to and from the Stantons. And she told him about the United States marshal she came to call Uncle Sam.

She wouldn't tell him Sam's last name, the names she and her mother had used or the towns they had lived in before Washington, what Cynthia was doing or where she was living now.

He inquired about Amanda's love life.

Amanda answered quite matter-of-factly: "I don't have one."

"Why not?"

"You have to trust someone before you can love them, and, as you can imagine, I'm not big on trusting."

With a humorless, ironic laugh, Lionel agreed. He had eliminated trust from his emotional repertoire twenty years ago when he watched a news report about a house in Miami bursting into flames that took the lives of a woman and a nine-year-old child he had been assured would be safe.

"Neither am I," he said. "Which is probably why I'm about to be divorced for the third time."

"Well, at least this time, you won't be alone," Amanda said, a warm smile burnishing her lips.

"Nope! I've got my Ricki back, and all's right with the world."

Instantly, the smile disappeared. In its place was stark annoyance.

"I've told you a dozen times to call me Amanda, not Ricki. I don't know whether it's an innocent mental block or some stubborn ego thing, but get over it. If you don't, you're going to get us both killed!" He started to dismiss her concerns as an overreaction, but she stopped him cold. "They're out there," she stated with unalterable conviction. "And they're still looking for us. This is not a game, Lionel. They want us dead."

Her voice was low and chilling in its intensity.

"Have you and . . . Beth ever had any reason to believe that your cover was blown?" he asked.

Amanda paused. Lionel might have taken her hesitation as a slight, but he quickly realized it was a survival mechanism. It pained him to see how automatic it was.

Lionel took her hand in his. It pained him to think of all the horrors she had endured in her young life. Worse, it wasn't over.

"They know you're alive," he said, his face paled by that realization. "Do they know where you and your mother live?"

"No," she said with an eerie calm. "If they did, we'd be dead."

"So what do we do?"

She looked at her father and wondered whether it had been cruel to reenter his life. Just then, his face was etched with fear. She wished she could press a button, exit, and return his life to whatever it had been before. But that wasn't possible.

"We do what they're doing, Lionel," she said. "We watch. And we wait."

THE LUCKY ONES
Doris Mortman

RECEIVE

$2.00 REBATE

WITH PURCHASE OF *THE LUCKY ONES*

To receive your rebate, SEND:

- This original certificate.
- The proof of purchase symbol with ISBN #.
- Original dated cash register receipt with book purchase price circled.

Mail to:
THE LUCKY ONES Rebate
P. O. Box #1120
Grand Rapids, MN 55745-1120

Please print

Name

Address

City

State   Zip

Telehone # (optional)

This certificate must accompany your request. No reproductions accepted. Void where prohibited, taxed, or restricted. Offer available to U.S. and Canadian residents only. Allow 6 weeks for mailing of your refund payable in U.S. funds. OFFER EXPIRES 11/30/98.

ZEBRA
BOOKS

PROOF-OF-PURCHASE
ISBN: 0-8217-5920-5